MALCOLM X, BLACK LIBERATION, & THE ROAD TO WORKERS POWER

Also by Jack Barnes

BOOKS & PAMPHLETS

Cuba and the Coming American Revolution (2007)
The Changing Face of U.S. Politics (2002)
Their Trotsky and Ours (2002)
The Working Class and the Transformation of Learning (2000)
Capitalism's World Disorder (1999)
For a Workers and Farmers Government in the U.S. (1985)
Malcolm X Talks to Young People (1969)

FROM THE PAGES OF 'NEW INTERNATIONAL'

Revolution, Internationalism, and Socialism:
The Last Year of Malcolm X (2008)
Capitalism's Long Hot Winter Has Begun (2005)
Our Politics Start with the World (2005)
U.S. Imperialism Has Lost the Cold War (1998)
Imperialism's March toward Fascism and War (1994)
The Revolutionary Character of the FSLN (1994)
The Opening Guns of World War III (1991)
Politics of Economics: Che Guevara and Marxist Continuity (1991)
The Coming Revolution in South Africa (1985)

COLLECTIONS AND INTRODUCTIONS

Teamster Rebellion/Dobbs (2003)
The History of American Trotskyism/Cannon (2002)
Playa Girón/Bay of Pigs/Castro, Fernández (2001)
Making History: Interviews with Four Cuban Generals (1999)
In Defense of Revolutionary Centralism (1999)
Marxism and Terrorism/Trotsky (1995)
The Eastern Airlines Strike/E. Mailhot (1991)
FBI on Trial (1988)
The Leninist Strategy of Party Building/J. Hansen (1979)
The Lesser Evil? (1977)
James P. Cannon as We Knew Him (1976)
Revolutionary Strategy in Fight against Vietnam War (1975)

Malcolm X
Black Liberation
& the Road to
Workers
Power

JACK BARNES

PATHFINDER

NEW YORK   LONDON   MONTREAL   SYDNEY

Edited by Steve Clark and Mary-Alice Waters

Copyright © 2009 by Pathfinder Press

ISBN 978-1-60488-021-2
Library of Congress Control Number 2009938178
Manufactured in the United States of America

First edition, 2009
Fourth printing, 2012

Cover design: Toni Gorton

Cover photo: Malcolm X leaving plane in London after being refused entry
to France by government there, February 9, 1965. In November 1964, on
the way back from his second trip to Africa and the Middle East that year,
Malcolm had spoken to a packed house at Paris's large Mutualité meeting
hall. He had been invited to speak there again in February at a meeting
cosponsored by organizations of African students and African Americans
living in France. (Credit: Topham/The Image Works)

Back cover: Jacob Lawrence, image from *The Migration of the Negro*,
1940–41, series of sixty works, tempera on gesso on composition board,
each 18 x 12 inches. © 2009 The Jacob and Gwendolyn Lawrence Foundation,
Seattle/Artists Rights Society (ARS), New York

Pathfinder

3 3001 00983 0307

www.pathfinderpress.com
E-mail: pathfinder@pathfinderpress.com

To

Contents

PART IV. ENDING THE DICTATORSHIP OF CAPITAL, ENDING RACISM

Photos and Illustrations

About the Author

Jack Barnes is national
secretary of the Socialist
Workers Party. He has been
a member of the party's
National Committee since
1963 and a national officer
since 1969. He is a contrib-
uting editor to *New International* magazine.

As a leader of the Young
Socialist Alliance from 1961 through early 1966, Barnes both
conducted the January 1965 interview with Malcolm X for
the *Young Socialist* magazine and then discussed its publication and ongoing projects with Malcolm. Barnes joined the
Young Socialist Alliance in December 1960, a few months
after a trip to Cuba in July and August of that year. Following
his return, he helped organize at Carleton College in Minnesota one of the largest and most active campus chapters
of the Fair Play for Cuba Committee. In 1961 he joined the
Socialist Workers Party.

As Midwest organizer of the Young Socialist Alliance,
Barnes led a successful four-year campaign to defend three
students in Bloomington, Indiana, all YSA members, indicted
in May 1963 for "assembling" to advocate the overthrow of
the State of Indiana by force and violence. Their "crime" had
been organizing and attending a campus meeting at which
a national YSA leader who was Black had spoken on the

fight for Black freedom, including the right to self-defense against racist violence. In 1965 Barnes was elected national chairman of the Young Socialist Alliance and at the same time became director of the SWP and YSA's work in the United States and internationally to advance the growing movement against the Vietnam War.

Since the mid-1970s Jack Barnes has led the effort in the Socialist Workers Party, and with others worldwide, to build communist parties the large majority of whose members and leaders are industrial workers and trade unionists actively engaged in broad political work that advances along the road to workers power and an end to the dictatorship of capital. This political course toward forging parties proletarian both in program and composition is recorded in numerous articles and collections of Barnes's speeches and writings, some of which are listed at the front of the book.

About the Editors

Steve Clark, a member of the Socialist Workers Party National Committee since 1977, is editorial director of Pathfinder Press and managing editor of *New International* magazine. He is the editor of *Malcolm X Talks to Young People* and other collections of speeches and writings by Malcolm X.

Active from the mid-1960s to the early 1970s in the fight to halt the U.S. war in Vietnam, Clark joined the Young Socialist Alliance in 1970 and Socialist Workers Party in 1971. He was editor of the *Young Socialist* magazine (1974–75) and YSA national secretary (1975). He edited the *Militant* newsweekly (1977–80) and the socialist news magazine *Intercontinental Press* (1981–84).

In July 1980 Clark interviewed Maurice Bishop, central leader of the workers and farmers government in the Caribbean island of Grenada, for the *Militant* and is editor of *Maurice Bishop Speaks: The Grenada Revolution and Its Overthrow, 1979–83* and author of "The Second Assassination of Maurice Bishop" in *New International*. Among Clark's other articles in *New International* are "Farming, Science, and the Working Classes" and "The Politics of Economics: Che Guevara and Marxist Continuity," co-authored with Jack Barnes.

✳

Mary-Alice Waters, a member of the Socialist Workers Party National Committee since 1967, is president of Pathfinder Press and editor of *New International* magazine. Won to revolutionary working-class politics under the impact of the rising mass struggle for Black liberation in the early 1960s and the advancing socialist revolution in Cuba, Waters joined the Young Socialist Alliance in 1962 and Socialist Workers Party in 1964. She has helped lead the SWP's work in the fight for women's liberation in the United States and internationally.

Waters was editor of the *Young Socialist* (1966–67) and YSA national secretary and chairperson (1967–68). She covered the 1968 student-labor uprising in France for the *Militant* and edited the working-class newsweekly from 1969 through the early 1970s. She was editor of *Intercontinental Press* magazine (1979–81).

The editor of a series of more than twenty books on the Cuban Revolution, Waters has spoken widely in the United States and elsewhere on that revolution and its lessons for working people and youth the world over. She is an author, editor, and contributor to numerous books and pamphlets, including *Is Socialist Revolution in the U.S. Possible?*; *Capitalism and the Transformation of Africa*; *Cosmetics, Fashions, and the Exploitation of Women*; *Rosa Luxemburg Speaks*; and *The Changing Face of U.S. Politics*. She has written many articles for *New International* magazine.

Introduction

BY JACK BARNES

This is a book about the dictatorship of capital and the road to the dictatorship of the proletariat.

A book about the last century and a half of class struggle in the United States—from the Civil War and Radical Reconstruction to today—and the unimpeachable evidence it offers that workers who are Black will comprise a disproportionately weighty part of the ranks and leadership of the mass social movement that will make a proletarian revolution.

It is a book about why this revolutionary conquest of state power by a politically class-conscious and organized vanguard of the working class—millions strong—is necessary. About why that new state power provides working people the mightiest weapon possible to wage the ongoing battle to end Black oppression and every form of exploitation and human degradation inherited from millennia of class-divided society. And how participation in that struggle itself changes them to the point they are politically capable of carrying that battle through to the end.

This is a book about the last year of Malcolm X's life. About how he became the face and the authentic voice of the forces of the coming American revolution.

✳

"Dictatorship of capital? Dictatorship of the proletariat? What do these terms have to do with our world today?" That's the refrain working people in the United States and most of the rest of the world hear over and over again in schools and daily papers, and from TV and radio "commentators." Above all, we hear it voiced by every middle-class political current—"socialist," "green," or whatever—claiming to speak and act in the interests of the oppressed and exploited.

Above the din, the answer remains: It's *not* "our" world. And which class will rule is the question that ultimately matters for toilers everywhere—now more than ever.

The depression and social crisis that have deepened and spread worldwide over the last year have torn yet another veil from the face of capitalism, from the consequences of bourgeois rule for working people. The fact that the ruling families of the United States and other capitalist countries *dictate*, and will continue to dictate, the use of whatever degree of state power is necessary to defend and advance their own class interests is increasingly evident. As is the fact that they do so, and will continue to do so, regardless of the toll on many hundreds of millions the world over, the vast majority of humanity.

Since early 2008, banks and financial institutions such as Fannie Mae, Freddie Mac, Merrill Lynch, AIG, Citigroup, General Electric, General Motors (yes, GE and GM!), and scores of others have been deemed "too big to fail" by the ruling-class families and their government. Literally trillions of dollars in federal outlays and "guarantees" have been marshaled—conjured from their printing presses outright, in fact—in order to save these bastions of finance capital, or more accurately, to save their major *bondholders*, which is another way of describing the U.S. ruling class. They are determined to ensure that *their* enormous accumulation of interest-bearing wealth, produced by working people over centuries, remains secure.

Top partners and executives of Goldman Sachs, Citigroup, JPMorgan Chase, and other Wall Street houses are cycled back and forth to policy-making posts at the Treasury Department, Federal Reserve, and other government and quasi-government agencies (with a university stint sometimes wedged in between), like cards dealt by a mechanic at a poker table. The faces "managing" the financial crisis under the recent Republican White House resurface in the current Democratic administration, with or without new hats, and often with résumés stretching back to previous presidencies under both capitalist parties.

Those *not* "too big to fail" under the rule of capital are obvious as well. They include the rapidly expanding millions of workers being thrown out of jobs due to plant shutdowns, "cost-cutting" layoffs, "furloughs," "no-match" letters, deportations, and farm foreclosures. They include shuttered mom-and-pop stores from the largest cities to the smallest towns. They include employed working people whose wages, which already buy less than they did forty years ago, have fallen even more sharply the last twelve months. They include those, insured and uninsured, forced into bankruptcy by catastrophic medical expenses. They include those evicted from houses as a result of mounting bank foreclosures, as well as millions more forced from apartments on which they are no longer able to pay rent. These "new homeless," as they're called in the bourgeois media, are hidden from view, as they more and more often find themselves and their families packed together with others in a single residence.

"We serve and protect"—that promise is displayed on squad cars across the United States from which cops harass and brutalize workers day in and day out, disproportionately singling out African Americans, Latinos, and immigrants as targets. For working people, those words will always be a contemptible lie. But for the ruling class and privileged middle layers, they are a truthful summary of the function of the U.S. state apparatus—the armed forces; the multitude of local, state, federal, and military cop and spy agencies; the courts, bail-bond sharks, and probation and parole officers; the over-stuffed jails and prisons, with their evermore frequent, dehumanizing lockdowns and gang-controlled life, organized by those who run the "penal system" and overseen by thuggish prison guards (a true microcosm of bourgeois social relations). The U.S. state is the largest repressive apparatus in world history, with the highest—and increasing—incarceration rate of any country on earth.

These institutions of class rule, of bourgeois "law and order," *do* brutally serve and protect the property, profits, and assumed prerogatives of the U.S. capitalist class—from the streets, factories, fields, mines, border crossings, and prisons across the United States, to Afghanistan, Pakistan, Iraq, and beyond.

Working people can and will wrest concessions from the ruling class in the course of sharpening struggles against the crisis-fueled assaults on our jobs, living conditions, and elementary human dignity, on our political liberties and right to unionize, and against the march toward increased military spending and bloodier wars abroad. But these concessions cannot alter the laws underlying the operations of the capitalist system itself or forestall its further devastation of our lives and livelihoods. They cannot end the dictatorship of capital.

Only the conquest, and exercise, of state power by the working class and expropriation of finance capital can lay the foundations for a world based not on exploitation, violence, racial discrimination, class-based pecking orders, and dog-eat-dog competition, but on solidarity among working people that encourages the creativity and recognition of the worth of every individual, regardless of sex, national origin, or skin color.

A socialist world.

❋

Over the past half century, two developments above all have transformed revolutionary prospects for working people in the United States. They have had a deep impact on the capacity and effectiveness, the proletarian character, of the

Socialist Workers Party and Young Socialist Alliance.

One is the conquest of power in 1959 by the workers and farmers of Cuba. That triumph not only opened the road to socialist revolution in the Americas. It marked a renewal in action of the proletarian internationalist course first pointed to by Karl Marx and Frederick Engels more than a century earlier and then carried out in life by workers and peasants in Russia in 1917 under the leadership of V.I. Lenin and the Bolshevik Party.

The other is the post–World War II rise of the popular struggle for Black liberation in the United States, from which Malcolm X, its outstanding single leader, emerged. Even in the early 1960s, while Malcolm was still the best-known spokesman for the Nation of Islam, leaders of the Socialist Workers Party recognized in his words and deeds an uncompromising leader of unusual caliber. The Nation itself was a bourgeois-nationalist, religious organization, as it remains today. As Malcolm pointed out after his public break from the Nation in March 1964, it "didn't take part in politics" and its hierarchy, led by Elijah Muhammad, was "motivated mainly by protecting its own self-interests."

But Malcolm's voice was increasingly that of a revolutionary leader of the working class. And during the last year of his life, the political clarity of his words advanced with blinding speed.

In January 1965, less than a year after his split from the Nation, Malcolm told a television interviewer, "I believe that there will ultimately be a clash between the oppressed and those that do the oppressing. I believe that there will be a clash between those who want freedom, justice, and equality for everyone and those who want to continue the systems of exploitation.

"I believe that there will be that kind of clash," Malcolm said, "but I don't think that it will be based upon the color of the skin, as Elijah Muhammad had taught it."

Speaking on behalf of the Young Socialist Alliance to a March 1965 New York City memorial meeting a few weeks after Malcolm's assassination, I pointed out how relentlessly Malcolm had pressed beyond his origins in the Nation of Islam to emerge in world politics as the outstanding "leader of the struggle for Black liberation" in the United States. "To his people he first and foremost belongs." At the same time, to young people of all backgrounds attracted to the working class and proletarian politics, in this country and around the world, Malcolm X had become "the face and the authentic voice of the forces of the coming American revolution. He spoke the truth to our generation of revolutionists. . . . Malcolm challenged American capitalism from right inside. He was living proof for our generation of revolutionists that it can and will happen here."

Almost half a century later, I have nothing to change in that assessment, and I can still recognize the young socialist who made it. But I am aware that no one would ever recognize *this* Malcolm X, the living Malcolm we knew—the Malcolm who kept fighting and growing to the last day of his life—if their knowledge of his political course came solely from *The Autobiography of Malcolm X* prepared by journalist Alex Haley, or from the 1992 movie *Malcolm X* directed by Spike Lee. Together those are the main sources of "information" about Malcolm today, having been read or viewed, in multiple languages, by literally tens of millions the world over. Both, however, freeze Malcolm's *political* trajectory in April 1964 when he made the hajj to Mecca, only a month after his public break with the Nation of Islam. Everything after that pilgrimage gets short shrift in both autobiography and film. But Malcolm's experiences and the political conclusions he drew didn't stop there. In fact, he had barely begun.

This misrepresentation of Malcolm X is also what readers discover in *Dreams from My Father: A Story of Race and Inheritance*, the 1995 memoir by Barack Obama, today the

had no internal discussion and decision-making structure that enabled a leadership to determine a political course. The Nation functioned on the basis of "revelation" and decree. No fight to clarify political perspectives was possible. As a result, Malcolm—whose standing in the Nation had been second only to Elijah Muhammad, and in the true regard he enjoyed among its members second to none—brought few with him from the organization when the split came. While those who joined Malcolm were disciplined cadres, it was not yet a *political* discipline. It was a discipline still grounded in individual moral qualities, not in *political* convictions and habits forged, tempered, and internalized over time in the course of mass work and class-struggle action.

The task confronting Malcolm X during the final months of his life was to build a political cadre. He was starting from scratch. It would take time. And as Malcolm knew from the outset, *time* was something that forces in and around the Nation, as well as federal and local police agencies, here and abroad, were determined to deny him.

＊

Malcolm put great store in meeting and collaborating with other revolutionaries, at home as well as around the world. He held in high esteem fighters who at great sacrifice had done battle to overturn colonial regimes across Africa and Asia. He was particularly drawn to the revolutionary leadership of the secular government of Algeria, many of whom, as Malcolm pointed out, were "white," and few of whom continued to practice the Islamic faith. Led by Ahmed Ben Bella, Algeria's workers and peasants government, unlike other newly independent nations in Africa and the Middle East, was organizing working people to challenge not only the power and prerogatives of their former French colonizers, but of Algeria's homegrown landlords and capitalists as well.

Malcolm was increasingly influenced by the international-ist example of the Cuban Revolution, too. He had expressed solidarity with and admiration of that revolution and its leadership since its opening years, demonstratively welcom-ing Fidel Castro and Ernesto Che Guevara to Harlem. "The Cuban Revolution—that's a revolution. They overturned the system," Malcolm told an overwhelmingly Black audi-ence in Detroit in November 1963, in his last major talk as a Nation of Islam leader. But in 1964 and early 1965—as Malcolm saw more clearly the need to advance the "global rebellion of the oppressed against the oppressor, the exploited against the exploiter"—his political attraction to the Cuban Revolution grew.

In January 1965, when Malcolm addressed a public meet-ing hosted by the Socialist Workers Party and Young So-cialist Alliance in New York City, he opened his remarks by saying, "It's the third time I've had the opportunity to be a guest of the Militant Labor Forum. I always feel that it is an honor and every time that they open the door for me to do so, I will be right here." Malcolm was a man of his word. He meant "every time."

Malcolm relished *doing* things together with fellow revo-lutionaries. Once there had been enough time and experi-ence for mutual confidence to develop, Malcolm was eager to exchange hard-won lessons about *how* to do more. He wanted to share information with other revolutionaries about "contacts," as he called them—individuals, especially young people, whom each of us had gotten to know in the course of political work here in the United States, in Africa, or elsewhere.

At the same time, Malcolm was neither naïve nor un-knowledgeable about the sharply conflicting political courses of different organizations in the working-class movement calling themselves Marxists or communists, including, in the early and mid-1960s, the Communist Party USA, the

Progressive Labor Party, and the Socialist Workers Party. In New York in particular, it was impossible to function in the Black movement at the time without knowing members and supporters of these parties. The Communist Party USA alone had had thousands of African American members in Harlem as recently as the thirties and early forties.

Malcolm knew full well that the CPUSA and its sister organizations throughout the international Stalinist movement despised his uncompromising opposition to the political course of leaders of civil rights organizations who sought *to reform* "the system of exploitation" in the United States and worldwide, rather than—as Malcolm, with increasing clarity, aimed to do—organize a revolutionary movement *to overturn* it.

Malcolm opposed *both* imperialist political parties in the United States. His refusal to call for a vote for incumbent Democrat Lyndon Johnson against Republican Barry Goldwater in the 1964 presidential election—a position he held in common with the Socialist Workers Party and virtually no other organization in the workers movement in the United States—was particularly galling to Communist Party leaders. For some three decades, support to the Democratic Party and its candidates had been the lodestar of the CP's class-collaborationist course in U.S. politics.

A few weeks after the November 1964 elections, Malcolm told participants in a rally in Paris, France, that "the shrewd capitalists, the shrewd imperialists" in the United States "had the whole world—including people who call themselves Marxists—hoping that Johnson would beat Goldwater. . . . Those who claim to be enemies of the system were on their hands and knees waiting for Johnson to get elected—because he is supposed to be a man of peace," Malcolm said. "And *at that moment* he had troops invading the Congo and South Vietnam!"

A few months later, in early February 1965, authorities

at the Paris airport barred Malcolm from reentering France to participate in another gathering he had been invited to speak to there. Later that month, at a meeting of the Organization of Afro-American Unity in Harlem, Malcolm explained that even before the French government had denied him entry, the Communist Party there had made sure that the largest trade union federation in France not only refused to rent its meeting hall to organizers of the Paris event for Malcolm, but also "exercised its influence to prevent them from getting" another location they had attempted to secure.

*

"What the Bolshevik Revolution Taught Us," the third section of this book, includes the transcripts of discussions in 1933 and 1939 on the Black liberation struggle in the United States with Bolshevik leader Leon Trotsky. Those discussions appear here under the title, "The National Question and the Road to the Proletarian Dictatorship in the United States"— an accurate summary of their content, as opposed to "Leon Trotsky on Black Nationalism and Self-Determination," the title of the book in which the transcripts have been available since 1967.

In those discussions, Trotsky urged the Socialist Workers Party leadership to turn the party toward deeper and broader involvement in the struggle for Black freedom along the line of march of the revolutionary fight for power in the United States. The party "cannot postpone this extremely important question any longer," Trotsky had written to SWP leader James P. Cannon in 1939 during Trotsky's several days of discussions with party members.

Unless the SWP meets this political challenge, Trotsky said during those discussions, "our party cannot develop— it will degenerate. . . . It is a question of the vitality of the party. . . . It is a question of whether the party is to be transformed into a sect or if it is capable of finding its way to the most oppressed part of the working class."

This book is a commitment and a weapon in continuing to rise to that challenge today and tomorrow.

✽

Malcolm X, Black Liberation, and the Road to Workers Power could never have come into being without the leadership collaboration over nearly half a century of proletarian cadres of the Socialist Workers Party who are Black.

The book is a product of the disciplined efforts of these and other SWP cadres, including the generations who have been leading the work since the mid-1970s to build a party that is working class in composition as well as program and action. Who have been in the front ranks standing off racist thugs assaulting school buses, demonstrations, and picket lines. Who carry out communist political activity in the industrial working class and unions. Who join in strikes, union organizing drives, and shop-floor skirmishes small and large. Who have organized inside the imperialist armed forces against racism and denial of their rights as citizen soldiers. Who take to the streets with others to protest cop brutality, to demand legalization for immigrant workers, to say no to the death penalty, and to champion the right of women to choose abortion. Who have participated in and campaigned to build the National Black Independent Political Party and other organizations seeking to advance Black rights along proletarian lines. Who work to educate about and mobilize opposition to the imperialist policies of the U.S. government and its never-ending march toward widening militarization and spreading wars.

What readers will find in these pages is the fruit of decades of political activity by communist workers and youth campaigning with the *Militant* newsweekly and other publications on street corners, at plant gates, to students, on strike picket lines, and at social protest actions and meetings. By proletarian cadres who have organized and participated in communist leadership schools, helping to educate themselves and others about the lessons of more than 150 years of revolutionary struggle by working people. By those who have run as Socialist Workers Party candidates for posts from local office to president of the United States, and have done so in opposition to nominees—whatever their skin color—of the Democratic, Republican, and other bourgeois and petty-bourgeois parties.

By cadres who have never tired of getting in the face of race-baiters, red-baiters, and outright bigots and demagogues of every stripe who have sought to deny that workers, farmers, and young people who are Black—and *proud* to be Black—can and will become communists along the same road and on the same political basis as anyone else.

Working together with these comrades—through many crises and conjunctures, including the global capitalist panic still in its early stages today—has taught me much of what readers will discover in these pages. Putting these lessons down on paper is one of my obligations, and my name appears as author. But I could not have come to these conclusions in any other way than as part of a tested and disciplined proletarian cadre, including these men and women of African origin, who, in their lives and activity, remain true to their revolutionary convictions to this day.

It is to them that *Malcolm X, Black Liberation, and the Road to Workers Power* is dedicated.

NEW YORK CITY
OCTOBER 4, 2009

PART I

The Political Legacy
of Malcolm X

He Spoke the Truth
to Our Generation
of Revolutionists:
In Tribute to Malcolm X

by Jack Barnes
March 5, 1965

On February 21, 1965, Malcolm X was assassinated as he took the podium at the Audubon Ballroom in Harlem. He was to be the featured speaker at a rally of the Organization of Afro-American Unity. Two weeks later, on March 5, a memorial meeting for Malcolm was organized by the leadership of the Socialist Workers Party and Young Socialist Alliance. The event was hosted by the Militant Labor Forum. More than 200 people packed the forum hall at 116 University Place, just off Union Square in Lower Manhattan.

The following are major excerpts from the talk presented at that meeting by Jack Barnes, national chairman of the Young Socialist Alliance at the time. Clifton DeBerry, the 1964 Socialist Workers Party candidate for president, chaired the meeting. Also speaking were Malcolm's secretary and close collaborator James Shabazz; Farrell Dobbs, national secretary of the SWP; and Robert DesVerney, a writer for the *Militant.*

I would like to speak tonight not only on behalf of the members of the Young Socialist Alliance, but also the young rev-

"What often made youth who listened to Malcolm X start down the road to becoming proletarian revolutionists? First and foremost, he spoke the truth—unadorned, unvarnished, and uncompromising," said Jack Barnes, national chairman of the Young Socialist Alliance, at March 5, 1965, memorial meeting for Malcolm X in New York City (above). Some 200 people attended the event, organized by the Socialist Workers Party and YSA.

olutionists in our movement around the world who would want to speak at a memorial for Malcolm X but who cannot be here. This is especially true of those in Africa, the Middle East, France, and England, who recently had a chance to meet, see, and hear Malcolm.

Malcolm was the leader of the struggle for Black liberation. He was, as stated at his funeral by Ossie Davis, our Black shining prince, the manhood of the Harlems of the world. To his people he first and foremost belongs.

But he was also the teacher, inspirer, and leader of a much smaller group, the revolutionary socialist youth in America. He was to us the face and the authentic voice of the forces of the coming American revolution. He spoke the truth to our generation of revolutionists.

What attracted revolutionary youth worldwide to Malcolm X? More important, what often made youth who listened to him—including youth who are not Black—start down the road to becoming revolutionists? I think there were two things above all. First, he spoke the simple truth—unadorned, unvarnished, and uncompromising. Second was the evolution and content of Malcolm's political thought.

Malcolm saw the depth of the hypocrisy and falsehood that cover the real social relations that make up American society. To him the key was not so much the lies that the ruling class and its spokesmen propagated, but the lies and the falsehoods about his people—their past and their potentialities—which they accepted.

Malcolm's message to the ghetto, his agitation against racism, was a special kind. What he had to say and what he did stemmed from a study of the history of Afro-Americans. He explained that in order for Black Americans to know what to do, to discover who they really are—to know how to go about winning freedom—they had to first answer three questions: Where did you come from? How did you get here? Who is responsible for your condition?

Malcolm's truth was so explosive because it stemmed from a careful study of how the Afro-American was enslaved. He publicized the facts that have been suppressed from standard history books and kept out of the schools. While in the Black Muslims and after he left, Malcolm taught that the process by which the Africans were made into slaves was one of dehumanizing them. Through barbarous cruelty, comparable to the worst Nazi concentration camps, they were taught to fear the white man. They were systematically stripped of their language, culture, history, names, religion, of all connections with their homes in Africa—of their identity. They were named *Negro,* signifying this lack of identity and this denial of their African origin.

Especially after their "emancipation," the Christianity they were taught was the Christianity of meekness and submission and of their reward in heaven. They were taught that Africa was a jungle where people lived in mud huts, and that the white man had done them a great favor in bringing them to America.

Malcolm asked the Black American: Who taught you to hate yourself? Does *he* hate himself? Who taught you to be a pacifist? Was *he* a pacifist? Who said Black people cannot defend themselves? Does *he* defend himself? Who taught you not to go too far and too fast in your fight for freedom? Did *he* stand to lose something by the speed of your victory? Who taught you to vote for the fox in order to escape from the wolf? What does the fox give you in return?

All these questions, and so many more, needed no answers. All the questions were directed to those who had nothing to lose and no stake in the system as it exists now.

Malcolm's political thought was the other important factor in the development of those who were taught by him. First, he believed in and explained the need for Afro-American unity in action. He felt it was necessary to base your alliances on that unity, and reject unconditionally any degrading or compromising alliances. It is only upon the basis of this unity, and the dignity and self-respect that goes along with it, that the battle for freedom can be waged. Those who would bypass this step would condemn Black Americans to be a tail to the kite of other, more conservative forces.

"We cannot think of uniting with others until after we have first united among ourselves. We cannot think of being acceptable to others until we have first proven acceptable to ourselves. One can't unite bananas with scattered leaves."[1] Malcolm knew that Afro-Americans had had enough of this kind of unity—with the liberals, the Communist Party, and the Socialist Party.

Secondly, he spoke of self-defense, and the real source of violence. He continually pointed out that the source of violence was the oppressor, not the oppressed. He continually pointed to the use of violence by the oppressor. Out of one side of its mouth the government and press preach pacifism to the American Negro, while out of the other side comes the cold announcement that they will destroy as many North Vietnamese as they wish. Malcolm never tired of pointing out the hypocrisy of this form of pacifism, its ineffectuality, and its degrading and belittling character.

Malcolm told us ten months ago, at the first Militant Labor Forum at which he spoke, that "if George Washington didn't get independence for this country nonviolently, and if Patrick Henry didn't come up with a nonviolent statement, and you taught me to look upon them as patriots and heroes, then it's time for you to realize that I have studied your books well. . . . No white person would go about fighting for freedom in the same manner that he has helped me and you to fight for our freedom. No, none of them would. When it

---

1. "A Declaration of Independence" (March 12, 1964), in *Malcolm X Speaks* (Pathfinder, 1965, 1989), p. 34, [2009 printing].

comes to Black freedom, then the white man freedom-rides and sits in, he's nonviolent, he sings 'We Shall Overcome,' and all that stuff. But when the property of the white man is threatened, or the freedom of the white man is threatened, he's not nonviolent."[2]

Thirdly, unlike any other Black leader, and unlike any other mass leader in my lifetime, he continually exposed the real role of the Democratic Party, and pointed out what a mistake it was to believe the federal government of this country would free Afro-Americans. He said, "The Democrats get Negro support, yet the Negroes get nothing in return. The Negroes put the Democrats first, yet the Democrats put the Negroes last. And the alibi that the Democrats use—they blame the Dixiecrats. A Dixiecrat is nothing but a Democrat in disguise. . . . Because Dixie in reality means all that territory south of the Canadian border."[3]

Rather than simply direct his fire at the puppets, Malcolm X always sought to expose those who were *really* responsible for maintaining the racism of this society. When New York Police Commissioner [Michael] Murphy attacked him and others as "irresponsible," Malcolm responded that Murphy was only doing his job. Mayor [Robert] Wagner, Murphy's boss, was the one responsible for the charge, he said.

Malcolm never tired of explaining and demonstrating that it was the federal government currently headed by President [Lyndon] Johnson, a Democrat, that was responsible for maintaining racism in the North and South. In doing this, he showed the continuity between the inhuman treatment

---

2. "Speech on Black Revolution" (April 8, 1964), in *Two Speeches by Malcolm X* (Pathfinder, 1965, 1987, 1990), p. 12 [2008 printing], and the question period from that speech in Malcolm X, *By Any Means Necessary* (Pathfinder, 1970, 1992), pp. 45–46 [2008 printing].

3. *Two Speeches by Malcolm X*, p. 21.

of Negroes and the responsibility for the condition of Black people borne by those who run this society today. As one of his comrades, Brother Benjamin [Karim], pointed out at a recent meeting of the Organization of Afro-American Unity, the North is responsible for the racism in the South, because "they won the Civil War."

It was in talking about the Democratic Party that another aspect of Malcolm came clearly to the fore. This was his ability to translate the complex and important ideas which he developed and absorbed into the language of those he knew would change the world. The ability to speak clearly to the oppressed has been a unique genius of all great revolutionary leaders in history.

The *Militant* reported that Malcolm, at his press conference in Harlem following his return from Africa eight months ago, spoke of President Johnson as being hypocritical. He pointed out that LBJ's closest friend in the Senate, Richard Russell, was leading the fight against the civil rights bill. Malcolm was challenged by a reporter who doubted that Johnson's friendship with Russell proved anything. Malcolm looked at him with his usual smile and said, off the cuff, "If you tell me you're against robbing banks and your best friend is Jesse James, I have grounds to doubt your sincerity."[4]

The final point in his political development that was so important for the education of those young people who followed him, looked to him, or in many ways were educated by him, was his revolutionary internationalism.

Malcolm gave at least three reasons for his internationalist outlook. First was the common identity of the power structure which practiced racism in this country and which practiced imperialism abroad. "This system is not only rul-

---

4. "Malcolm X Back from Africa—Urges Black United Front," in the June 1, 1964, issue of the *Militant*.

ing us in America—it's ruling the world," he said.[5]

Second, only through Afro-Americans realizing that they were part of a great majority of nonwhites in the world who were fighting for and winning freedom would they have the courage to fight the battle for freedom with whatever means necessary.

Malcolm said that "among the so-called Negroes in this country, as a rule the civil rights groups, those who believe in civil rights, they spend most of their time trying to prove they are Americans. Their thinking is usually domestic, confined to the boundaries of America, and they always look upon themselves as a minority. When they look upon themselves upon the American stage, the American stage is a white stage. So a Black man standing on that stage in America automatically is in the minority. He is the under-dog, and in his struggle he always uses an approach that is a begging, hat-in-hand, compromising approach." But, he said: We don't beg, we don't thank you for giving us what you should have given us a hundred years ago.[6]

Last was the fact that in the final analysis freedom could only be won in one place when it was won everywhere. In Africa, he said, "Our problem is your problem. . . . Your problems will never be fully solved until and unless ours are solved. You will never be fully respected until and un-less we are also respected. You will never be recognized as free human beings until and unless we are also recognized and treated as human beings."[7]

---

5. "At a Meeting in Paris" (November 23, 1964), in *By Any Means Necessary*, p. 146 [2008 printing].

6. *Two Speeches by Malcolm X*, p. 16.

7. *Malcolm X Speaks*, p. 91. From a memorandum submitted by Mal-colm X to the July 17–21, 1964, meeting of the Organization of African Unity in Cairo, Egypt.

Though Malcolm X came from the American ghetto, spoke for the American ghetto, and directed his message to the American ghetto first of all, he became a figure of world importance, and developed his ideas in relation to the great events of world history in his time.

If Malcolm X is to be compared with any international figure, the most striking parallel is with Fidel Castro. Both of them belong to the generation that was shaped ideologically under the twin circumstances of World War II and the monstrous betrayals and defaults of Stalinized Communist parties. These men found their way independently to the revolutionary struggle, bypassing both Social Democracy and Stalinism.

Each started from the struggle of his own oppressed and exploited people for liberation. Each embraced the nationalism of his people as necessary to mobilize them to struggle for their freedom. Each stressed the importance of the solidarity of the oppressed all over the world in their struggle against a common oppressor.

Fidel did not start out as a thoroughgoing Marxist or as a revolutionary socialist. Like Malcolm, he was determined to pursue the national liberation of his people by "whatever means necessary" and without any compromises with those with any stake in the status quo.

Fidel Castro's dedication to political independence and to economic development for Cuba led him to opposition to capitalism. So, also, Malcolm's uncompromising stand against racism brought him to identify with the revolutions of the colonial people who were turning against capitalism, and finally to conclude that the elimination of capitalism in this country was necessary for freedom. Just as Fidel Castro discovered that there can be no political independence and economic development in a colonial country without breaking from capitalism, so Malcolm had come to the conclusion that capitalism and racism were so entangled in the United

States that you had to uproot the system in order to eliminate racism.

Malcolm's Black nationalism was aimed at preparing Black people to struggle for their freedom. "The greatest mistake of the movement," he said in an interview in the February 25 *Village Voice*, "has been trying to organize a sleeping people around specific goals. You have to wake the people up first, then you'll get action."

"Wake them up to their exploitation?" the interviewer asked. "No, to their humanity, to their own worth, and to their heritage," he answered.[8]

Everything he said to Black people was designed to raise their confidence, to organize them independently of those who oppressed them, to teach them who was responsible for their condition and who their allies were. He explained that they were part of the great majority—the nonwhites and the oppressed of the world. He taught that freedom could be won only by fighting for it; it has never been given to anyone. He explained that it could be won only by making a real revolution that uproots and changes the entire society.

Thus it is not surprising that many who considered themselves socialists, radicals, and even Marxists could not recognize and identify with Malcolm's revolutionary character. They could not recognize the revolutionary content of this great leader clothed in the forms, language, and dark colors of the American proletarian ghetto.

Even with all his uniqueness and greatness as an individual, he could not have reached this understanding unless the conditions in this country were such that it was possible. Even though no one can fill his shoes, the fact that he did what he did, developed as the revolutionary leader he was,

---

8. "We Have to Learn How to Think" (interview with Marlene Nadle for the *Village Voice*), in Malcolm X, *February 1965: The Final Speeches* (Pathfinder, 1992), pp. 250–51 [2008 printing].

is the proof of more Malcolms to come.

He was a proof as Fidel is a proof. Fidel stood up ninety miles away from the most powerful imperialism in the world and thumbed his nose and showed us, "See, it can be done. They can't go on controlling the world forever."

Malcolm went even further than Fidel, because Malcolm challenged American capitalism from right inside. He was the living proof for our generation of revolutionists that it can and will happen here.

Our job, the job of the YSA, is to teach the revolutionary youth of this country to tell the difference between the nationalism of the oppressed and the nationalism of the oppressor, to teach them to differentiate the forces of liberation from the forces of the exploiters; to teach them to hear the voices of the revolution regardless of the tones they take; to teach them to differentiate between the self-defense of the victim and violence of the aggressor; to teach them to refuse to give an inch to white liberalism and to reach out to Malcolm's heirs, the vanguard of the ghetto, as brothers and comrades.

YOUNG SOCIALIST

MARCH-APRIL 1965   25¢

Interview with Malcolm X

Free Speech Fight at Berkeley

Indiana Students Again Face Jail

Cover of March–April 1965 issue of *Young Socialist* magazine
carrying January 18, 1965, interview Malcolm X gave to leaders of
the Young Socialist Alliance. **"The press has purposely and
skillfully projected me in the image of a racist, a race
supremacist, and an extremist,"** Malcolm told the **YSA**
leaders. **"I'm not a racist. I'm against every form of
racism and segregation, every form of discrimination."**

'Young Socialist' Interview

by Malcolm X
January 18, 1965

In January 1965 Malcolm X was interviewed for the *Young Socialist* magazine by Jack Barnes, national chairman of the Young Socialist Alliance, and Barry Sheppard, a staff writer for the *Militant* newspaper. At a meeting with Barnes a few days later, Malcolm reviewed and approved the text, which was published in the March-April 1965 issue of the *Young Socialist* magazine.

YOUNG SOCIALIST: What image of you has been projected by the press?

MALCOLM X: Well, the press has purposely and skillfully projected me in the image of a racist, a race supremacist, and an extremist.

YOUNG SOCIALIST: What's wrong with this image? What do you really stand for?

MALCOLM X: First, I'm not a racist. I'm against every form of racism and segregation, every form of discrimination. I believe in human beings, and that all human beings should be respected as such, regardless of their color.

YOUNG SOCIALIST: Why did you break with the Black Muslims?

MALCOLM X: I didn't break, there was a split. The split came about primarily because they put me out, and they put me out because of my uncompromising approach to problems I thought should be solved and the movement could solve.

I felt the movement was dragging its feet in many areas. It didn't involve itself in the civil or civic or political struggles our people were confronted by. All it did was stress the importance of moral reformation—don't drink, don't smoke, don't permit fornication and adultery. When I found that the hierarchy itself wasn't practicing what it preached, it was clear that this part of its program was bankrupt.

So the only way it could function and be meaningful in the community was to take part in the political and economic facets of the Negro struggle. And the organization wouldn't do that because the stand it would have to take would have been too militant, uncompromising, and activist, and the hierarchy had gotten conservative. It was motivated mainly by protecting its own self-interests.

I might also point out that although the Black Muslim movement professed to be a religious group, the religion they had adopted—Islam—didn't recognize them. So religiously it was in a vacuum. And it didn't take part in politics, so it was not a political group. When you have an organization that's neither political nor religious and doesn't take part in the civil rights struggle, what can it call itself? It's in a vacuum. So all of these factors led to my splitting from the organization.

YOUNG SOCIALIST: What are the aims of your new organization?

MALCOLM X: There are two organizations. There's the Muslim Mosque, Inc., which is religious. Its aim is to create an atmosphere and facilities in which people who are interested in Islam can get a better understanding of Islam. The aim of the other organization, the Organization of Afro-American Unity, is to use whatever means necessary to bring about a society in which the twenty-two million Afro-Americans are recognized and respected as human beings.

YOUNG SOCIALIST: How do you define Black nationalism, with which you have been identified?

MALCOLM X: I used to define Black nationalism as the idea that the Black man should control the economy of his community, the politics of his community, and so forth.

But when I was in Africa in May, in Ghana, I was speaking with the Algerian ambassador, who is extremely militant and is a revolutionary in the true sense of the word (and has his credentials as such for having carried on a successful revolution against oppression in his country[9]). When I told him that my political, social, and economic philosophy was Black nationalism, he asked me very frankly: Well, where did that leave him? Because he was white. He was an African, but he was Algerian, and to all appearances, he was a white man. And he said if I define my objective as the victory of Black nationalism, where does that leave him? Where does that leave revolutionaries in Morocco, Egypt, Iraq, Mauritania? So he showed me where I was alienating people who were true revolutionaries dedicated to overturning the system of exploitation that exists on this earth by any means necessary.

So I had to do a lot of thinking and reappraising of my definition of Black nationalism. Can we sum up the solution

---

9. In 1962 Algeria won its independence from France following an eight-year war of liberation. At the time Malcolm is describing, a popular revolutionary government in Algeria led by Ahmed Ben Bella was organizing urban and rural working people to make increasing encroachments against capitalist social relations. That workers and peasants government was overthrown in a coup led by Houari Boumedienne in June 1965.

to the problems confronting our people as Black nationalism? And if you notice, I haven't been using the expression for several months. But I still would be hard pressed to give a specific definition of the overall philosophy which I think is necessary for the liberation of the Black people in this country.

YOUNG SOCIALIST: Is it true, as is often said, that you favor violence?

MALCOLM X: I don't favor violence. If we could bring about recognition and respect of our people by peaceful means, well and good. Everybody would like to reach his objectives peacefully. But I'm also a realist. The only people in this country who are asked to be nonviolent are Black people. I've never heard anybody go to the Ku Klux Klan and teach them nonviolence, or to the [John] Birch Society and other right-wing elements. Nonviolence is only preached to Black Americans, and I don't go along with anyone who wants to teach our people nonviolence until someone at the same time is teaching our enemy to be nonviolent. I believe we should protect ourselves by any means necessary when we are attacked by racists.

YOUNG SOCIALIST: What do you think is responsible for race prejudice in the U.S.?

MALCOLM X: Ignorance and greed. And a skillfully designed program of miseducation that goes right along with the American system of exploitation and oppression.

If the entire American population were properly educated—by properly educated, I mean given a true picture of the history and contributions of the Black man—I think many whites would be less racist in their feelings. They would have more respect for the Black man as a human being. Knowing what the Black man's contributions to science and civilization have been in the past, the white man's feelings of superiority would be at least partially negated. Also, the feeling of inferiority that the Black man has would be replaced by a balanced knowledge of himself. He'd feel more like a human being. He'd function more like a human being, in a society of human beings.

So it takes education to eliminate it. And just because you have colleges and universities doesn't mean you have education. The colleges and universities in the American educational system are skillfully used to miseducate.

YOUNG SOCIALIST: What were the highlights of your trip to Africa?

MALCOLM X: I visited Egypt, Arabia, Kuwait, Lebanon, Sudan, Ethiopia, Kenya, Tanganyika and Zanzibar (now Tanzania), Nigeria, Ghana, Liberia, Guinea, and Algeria. During that trip I had audiences with President Nasser of Egypt, President Nyerere of Tanzania, President Jomo Kenyatta (who was then prime minister) of Kenya, Prime Minister Milton Obote of Uganda, President Azikiwe of Nigeria, President Nkrumah of Ghana, and President Sékou Touré of Guinea. I think the highlights were the audiences I had with those persons because it gave me a chance to sample their thinking. I was impressed by their analysis of the problem, and many of the suggestions they gave went a long way toward broadening my own outlook.

YOUNG SOCIALIST: How much influence does revolutionary Africa have on the thinking of Black people in this country?

MALCOLM X: All the influence in the world. You can't separate the militancy that's displayed on the African continent from the militancy that's displayed right here among American Blacks. The positive image that is developing of Africans is also developing in the minds of Black Americans, and consequently they develop a more positive image of themselves. Then they take more positive steps—actions.

So you can't separate the African revolution from the mood of the Black man in America. Neither could the colonization of Africa be separated from the menial position that the Black man in this country was satisfied to stay in for so long. Since Africa has gotten its independence through revolution, you'll notice the stepped-up cry against discrimination that has appeared in the Black community.

YOUNG SOCIALIST: How do you view the role of the U.S. in the Congo?[10]

MALCOLM X: As criminal. Probably there is no better example of criminal activity against an oppressed people than the role the U.S. has been playing in the Congo, through her ties with Tshombe and the mercenaries. You can't overlook the fact that Tshombe gets his money from the U.S. The money he uses to hire these mercenaries—these paid killers imported from South Africa—comes from the United States. The pilots that fly these planes have been trained by the U.S. The bombs themselves that are blowing apart the bodies of women and children come from the U.S. So I can only view the role of the United States in the Congo as a criminal role. And I think the seeds she is sowing in the Congo she will

---

10. The Congo declared its independence from Belgium June 30, 1960. The prime minister of the newly independent government was Patrice Lumumba, who had led the liberation struggle there. Washington and Brussels moved swiftly to prepare Lumumba's overthrow, organizing attacks by Belgian troops, units of mercenaries, and forces of the imperialist-backed secessionist regime of Moise Tshombe in Congo's southern, mineral-rich Katanga province. In face of this onslaught, Lumumba took the fatal step of requesting military help from the United Nations. In late 1960 Congolese army officer Joseph Mobutu, at the instigation of Washington and Brussels, deposed Lumumba and placed him under arrest. As Swedish troops wearing the blue berets of UN "peacekeepers" looked on, Mobutu handed Lumumba over to Tshombe's forces, who murdered the Congolese leader in January 1961.

In 1964 Tshombe was installed as Congolese prime minister. Forces that looked to Lumumba, based in the country's eastern provinces, rebelled. Mercenaries and Belgian troops aided Tshombe in crushing the uprising. Washington organized a force of U.S. planes flown by U.S. pilots to carry out bombing and strafing missions. Thousands of civilians were killed in putting down the revolt.

have to harvest. The chickens that she has turned loose over there have got to come home to roost.

YOUNG SOCIALIST: What about the U.S. role in South Vietnam?

MALCOLM X: The same thing. It shows the real ignorance of those who control the American power structure. If France, with all types of heavy arms, as deeply entrenched as she was in what then was called Indochina, couldn't stay there,[11] I don't see how anybody in their right mind can think the U.S. can get in there—it's impossible. So it shows her ignorance, her blindness, her lack of foresight and hindsight. Her complete defeat in South Vietnam is only a matter of time.

YOUNG SOCIALIST: How do you view the activity of white and Black students who went to the South last summer and attempted to register Black people to vote?

MALCOLM X: The attempt was good—I should say the objective to register Black people in the South was good because the only real power a poor man in this country has is the power of the ballot. But I don't believe sending them in and telling them to be nonviolent was intelligent. I go along with the effort toward registration, but I think they should be permitted to use whatever means at their disposal to defend themselves from the attacks of the Klan, the White Citizens' Council, and other groups.

---

11. From 1946 to 1954 the French government waged a war against liberation forces in Vietnam, which was then part of the French colonial empire. With France unable to defeat the independence movement, the war ended in a partition of the country. The liberation forces took power in North Vietnam and, under the workers and peasants government established there, the toilers went on to expropriate the landlords and capitalists. The French occupiers withdrew, and a U.S.-supported neocolonial regime was established in the south. Facing a renewal of the liberation struggle in South Vietnam, by the early 1960s Washington had sent thousands of troops, initially called "advisers." By 1968 there were 540,000 U.S. combat troops in Vietnam.

YOUNG SOCIALIST: What do you think of the murder of the three civil rights workers and what's happened to their killers? [12]

MALCOLM X: It shows that the society we live in is not actually what it tries to represent itself as to the rest of the world. This was murder and the federal government is helpless because the case involves Negroes. Even the whites involved, were involved in helping Negroes. And concerning anything in this society involved in helping Negroes, the federal government shows an inability to function. But it can function in South Vietnam, in the Congo, in Berlin,[13] and in other places where it has no business. But it can't function in Mississippi.

YOUNG SOCIALIST: In a recent speech you mentioned that you met John Lewis of SNCC in Africa. Do you feel that the younger and more militant leaders in the South are broadening their views on the whole general struggle?

---

12. In June 1964 three civil rights workers—two white, one Black—were murdered by the Ku Klux Klan in Philadelphia, Mississippi. The bodies of Michael Schwerner, Andrew Goodman, and James E. Chaney were not found until August 4. The state of Mississippi never handed down murder indictments for the killings.

In late 1964 the U.S. Justice Department indicted nineteen men on federal conspiracy charges in connection with the killings, but charges were dropped two years later. In 1967 twenty-one men were arrested by the FBI, again on conspiracy charges under federal civil rights laws. Seven were convicted and sentenced to prison terms ranging from three to ten years, with none serving more than six.

In 2005 Edgar Ray Killen, an organizer of the Klan attack who had not been convicted in the 1967 trial, was tried on Mississippi state manslaughter charges. Killen, eighty at the time, was convicted and sentenced to sixty years in prison.

13. During the 1960s, the United States maintained a garrison of more than five thousand troops in Berlin. In October 1961 U.S. and Soviet tanks had faced each other in a standoff across the newly built Berlin Wall in the heart of the partitioned and occupied city.

MALCOLM X: Sure. When I was in the Black Muslim movement I spoke on many white campuses and Black campuses. I knew back in 1961 and '62 that the younger generation was much different from the older, and that many students were more sincere in their analysis of the problem and their desire to see the problem solved. In foreign countries the students have helped bring about revolution—it was the students who brought about the revolution in the Sudan, who swept Syngman Rhee out of office in Korea, swept Menderes out in Turkey.[14] The students didn't think in terms of the odds against them, and they couldn't be bought out.

In America students have been noted for involving themselves in panty raids, goldfish swallowing, seeing how many can get in a telephone booth—not for their revolutionary political ideas or their desire to change unjust conditions. But some students are becoming more like their brothers around the world. However, the students have been deceived somewhat in what's known as the civil rights struggle (which was never designed to solve the problem). The students were maneuvered in the direction of thinking the problem was already analyzed, so they didn't try to analyze it for themselves.

In my thinking, if the students in this country forgot the analysis that has been presented to them, and they went into a huddle and began to research this problem of racism for themselves, independent of politicians and independent of all the foundations (which are a part of the power structure), and did it themselves, then some of their findings would be shocking, but they would see that they would never be able

---

14. In 1960 student-initiated demonstrations in South Korea and Turkey led to the ouster of South Korean president Syngman Rhee and Turkish premier Adnan Menderes. Sudanese ruler General Ibrahim Abboud resigned in November 1964 following a month of student demonstrations.

to bring about a solution to racism in their country as long as they're relying on the government to do it.

The federal government itself is just as racist as the government in Mississippi, and is more guilty of perpetuating the racist system. At the federal level they are more shrewd, more skillful at doing it, just like the FBI is more skillful than the state police and the state police are more skillful than the local police.

The same with politicians. The politician at the federal level is usually more skilled than the politician at the local level, and when he wants to practice racism, he's more skilled in the practice of it than those who practice it at the local level.

YOUNG SOCIALIST: What is your opinion of the Democratic Party?

MALCOLM X: The Democratic Party is responsible for the racism that exists in this country, along with the Republican Party. The leading racists in this country are Democrats. Goldwater isn't the leading racist—he's a racist but not the leading racist.[15] The racists who have influence in Washington, D.C., are Democrats. If you check, whenever any kind of legislation is suggested to mitigate the injustices that Negroes suffer in this country, you will find that the people who line up against it are members of Lyndon B. Johnson's party. The Dixiecrats are Democrats. The Dixiecrats are only a subdivision of the Democratic Party, and the same man over the Democrats is over the Dixiecrats.[16]

YOUNG SOCIALIST: What contribution can youth, especially students, who are disgusted with racism in this society, make to the Black struggle for freedom?

---

15. In the 1964 presidential election, the Republican candidate Barry Goldwater was defeated by Democratic incumbent Lyndon B. Johnson.

16. The "Dixiecrats" were the openly segregationist wing of the Democratic Party dominant at the time in most of the U.S. South.

MALCOLM X: Whites who are sincere don't accomplish anything by joining Negro organizations and making them integrated. Whites who are sincere should organize among themselves and figure out some strategy to break down the prejudice that exists in white communities. This is where they can function more intelligently and more effectively, in the white community itself, and this has never been done.

YOUNG SOCIALIST: What part in the world revolution are youth playing, and what lessons may this have for American youth?

MALCOLM X: If you've studied the captives being caught by the American soldiers in South Vietnam, you'll find that these guerrillas are young people. Some of them are just children and some haven't yet reached their teens. Most are teenagers. It is the teenagers abroad, all over the world, who are actually involving themselves in the struggle to eliminate oppression and exploitation. In the Congo, the refugees point out that many of the Congolese revolutionaries are children. In fact, when they shoot captive revolutionaries, they shoot all the way down to seven years old—that's been reported in the press. Because the revolutionaries are children, young people. In these countries the young people are the ones who most quickly identify with the struggle and the necessity to eliminate the evil conditions that exist. And here in this country, it has been my own observation that when you get into a conversation on racism and discrimination and segregation, you will find young people are more incensed over it—they feel more filled with an urge to eliminate it.

I think young people here can find a powerful example in the young *simbas* [lions] in the Congo and the young fighters in South Vietnam.

Another point: as the dark-skinned nations of this earth become independent, as they develop and become stronger, that means that time is on the side of the American Negro. At this point the American Negro is still hospitable and friendly and forgiving. But if he is continually tricked and deceived and so on, and if there is still no solution to his problems, he will become completely disillusioned, disenchanted, and disassociate himself from the interest of America and its society. Many have done that already.

YOUNG SOCIALIST: What is your opinion of the worldwide struggle now going on between capitalism and socialism?

MALCOLM X: It is impossible for capitalism to survive, primarily because the system of capitalism needs some blood to suck. Capitalism used to be like an eagle, but now it's more like a vulture. It used to be strong enough to go and suck anybody's blood whether they were strong or not. But now it has become more cowardly, like the vulture, and it can only suck the blood of the helpless. As the nations of the world free themselves, then capitalism has less victims, less to suck, and it becomes weaker and weaker. It's only a matter of time in my opinion before it will collapse completely.

YOUNG SOCIALIST: What is the outlook for the Negro struggle in 1965?

MALCOLM X: Bloody. It was bloody in 1963, it was bloody in 1964, and all of the causes that created this bloodshed still remain. The March on Washington was designed to serve as a vent or valve for the frustration that produced this explosive atmosphere.[17] In 1964 they used the civil rights bill as

---

17. The August 28, 1963, March on Washington drew more than 250,000 people for a rally at the Lincoln Memorial. The march called for passage of civil rights legislation then pending in Congress. Malcolm X opposed the political perspectives of the leadership of the march, but he participated in the action. That evening, speaking with a *Militant* reporter covering the demonstration in D.C., Malcolm, at the time still the leading spokesman for the Nation of Islam, said that while march leaders were "talking about a 'civil rights revolution,'" the truth is that revolution is not a halfway process. "You are either free or not free." (The *Militant*, September 16, 1963.)

a valve.[18] What can they use in 1965? There is no trick that the politicians can use to contain the explosiveness that exists right here in Harlem.

And look at New York Police Commissioner Murphy. He's coming out in headlines trying to make it a crime now to even predict that there's going to be trouble.[19] This shows the caliber of American thinking. There's going to be an explosion, but don't talk about it. All the ingredients that produce explosions exist, but don't talk about it, he says. That's like saying 700 million Chinese don't exist. This is the same approach. The American has become so guilt-ridden and filled with fear that instead of facing the reality of any situation, he pretends the situation doesn't exist. You know, in this country it's almost a crime to say there's a place called China—unless you mean that little island called Formosa.[20] By the same token, it's almost a crime to say that people in Harlem are going to explode because the social dynamite that existed last year is still here.[21]

----

18. The Civil Rights Act of 1964, signed into law by President Johnson, barred discrimination in voting, public facilities, schools, and employment.

19. On January 10, 1965, New York Police Commissioner Michael J. Murphy sharply condemned Black leaders such as Malcolm X who had pointed to growing frustration among Blacks and predicted outbreaks of resistance. Such statements, Murphy implied, were causing the trouble.

20. Until the early 1970s, the U.S. government refused diplomatic recognition to the People's Republic of China, maintaining that the capitalist government of Taiwan (Formosa) represented China.

21. In what the government and big business press called a "riot," the anger of Blacks in Harlem and the Brooklyn neighborhood of Bedford-Stuyvesant had exploded into the streets for five days in July 1964 in the aftermath of the cop killing of a fifteen-year-old Black youth, James Powell. The uprising was sparked by the actions of New York police. The cops had broken up a demonstration demanding the arrest

So I think 1965 will be most explosive—more explosive than it was in '64 and '63. There's nothing they can do to contain it. The Negro leaders have lost their control over the people. So that when the people begin to explode—and their explosion is justified, not unjustified—the Negro leaders can't contain it.

---

of the officer who had killed Powell. They arrested protest organizers and then staged a cop riot, beating and arresting Harlem residents and killing one.

Malcolm X: Revolutionary Leader of the Working Class

by Jack Barnes
March 28, 1987

Between late February and early April 1987, Jack Barnes spoke to more than 700 people on "Malcolm X, His Life and Its Meaning for Today" in five cities across the United States (Atlanta, Georgia; Pittsburgh, Pennsylvania; Los Angeles, California; Chicago, Illinois; and New York City). At the time, as Barnes mentions in the talk printed here, he was assisting Pathfinder Press with the preparation of *Malcolm X: The Last Speeches.* For the first time in more than fifteen years, previously unpublished speeches by Malcolm were soon to be available.

The following is Barnes's presentation at the March 28 meeting in Atlanta, expanded and edited for publication, as well as excerpts from the discussion period. The audience of 125 included many—trade unionists, students, and others—who two months earlier had participated in a march of over 30,000 in Forsyth County, Georgia, to protest segregation and Ku Klux Klan violence against Black rights demonstrators. Also in attendance were organizers of a Chattanooga, Tennessee, fight against police brutality; David Ndaba, a representative of the

African National Congress of South Africa; students from the Atlanta University Center, Emory University, and Georgia State; a dozen members of the Nation of Islam; activists from the Atlanta Committee on Latin America; and a Haitian community leader from Miami, Florida.

The face of Malcolm X is seen worldwide today. It can be found everywhere. I saw a portrait of Malcolm on a wall in Nicaragua when I was there last November celebrating the twenty-fifth anniversary of the founding of the Sandinista National Liberation Front. You see his picture on murals all over North America (including Canada, both the French- and English-speaking parts). Watching news coverage of antiapartheid actions by South African gold miners, you'll see T-shirts with Malcolm's image imprinted on them. I went to a play about Malcolm in Pittsburgh in February, and the opera *X: The Life and Times of Malcolm X* opened to packed houses at the New York City Opera last year. If you took part a few months ago in demonstrations in New York's Howard Beach neighborhood against the lynching of twenty-three-year-old Michael Griffith by a racist gang, you would have been marching alongside many people carrying placards with photos of Malcolm. Each February, around the anniversary of his assassination in February 1965, there are articles, meetings, film showings, and other events about his life and example.

But those of us who continue learning from Malcolm's political example, and organize to keep it alive in word and deed, have a responsibility to recognize that with each passing anniversary, we are one year further away from Malcolm's *living presence* in politics and the class struggle. Malcolm's message, like that of other martyrs of the working classes, and of all great revolutionary leaders, becomes blurred. Different people give it a different political meaning, a different class content. Many try to tame it, to make it compatible with this or that illusory scheme to reform capitalism, to make imperialism "more peaceful," to support one or another bourgeois politician in the Democratic or Republican parties. But Malcolm never ceased denouncing such notions. With Malcolm no longer among us to speak and act for himself, and with the direct impact of his political activity receding further into the past, those who wish to distort his revolutionary course have an easier time. Malcolm's message seems to dissolve into an image, a simple commodity for sale.

As that happens, what gets lost—sometimes intentionally—is the modern revolutionary leader whose concrete political legacy is needed more than ever each time working people begin fighting. The idea, often unspoken, begins to be spread that while Malcolm was a "prophet" in his times, what he *said* and what he *did* have become less "relevant" today. Not that Malcolm wasn't a great leader, the purveyors of such notions will say. Not that his traits as an individual don't remain praiseworthy. But he was operating "way back" in the 1960s, under different social and political conditions. So the political conclusions Malcolm began drawing, especially during the last few months of his life, have little relevance to today's world. Time marches on.

No matter how veiled or prettified, that's a fairly common view of Malcolm's significance more than two decades after his assassination.

Others narrow in on the fact that Malcolm was a wonderful speaker. But that, too, ends up being a way to devalue the significance of Malcolm's political legacy, to diminish the strategic course he had thought out and was organizing to implement. Because what Malcolm spoke about were *political* ideas with *practical* implications, carefully reasoned ideas based on decades of experience in struggle by the oppressed and exploited not only in the United States but in revolutions the world over.

"**Malcolm *was* an effective speaker,**" **says Barnes. "He was the opposite of a demagogue. He spoke like he was having a conversation with you—an insistent conversation, but a conversation. He appealed to the mind, to the determination, and to the selflessness of those he was addressing, not to your preconceptions, emotions, or prejudices. He tried to wake you up to the facts, to the truth, including about yourself.**" Above, Malcolm speaking at Harlem rally, June 23, 1963, one of a series of regular open-air Saturday meetings. Left, some of those listening.

Malcolm *was* an effective speaker. To be in the same room with him, to hear him from a podium, had a powerful impact. He worked at speaking clearly, because he knew it was important to explain ideas. He knew it was not easy to dissect and clarify oppressive social relations that are papered over and obfuscated by the rulers. But Malcolm was never a "show-off" speaker. He had a quiet but powerful voice. He didn't fashion himself a revolutionary "preacher." He spoke the "King's English," not street talk. He didn't lace his words with rhymes, alliteration, or political doggerel, in order to get around difficulties or deflect attention from inconsistencies.

Malcolm spoke like he was having a conversation with you—an insistent conversation, but a conversation. He was the opposite of a demagogue. He appealed to the mind, to the determination, and to the selflessness of those he was addressing, not to your preconceptions, emotions, or prejudices. He tried to wake you up to the facts, to the truth, including about yourself. In that, he was like other outstanding revolutionary leaders—from Karl Marx, V.I. Lenin, and Leon Trotsky, to Patrice Lumumba, Che Guevara, Maurice Bishop, and Fidel Castro.

Above all, however, what Malcolm said must be available *in writing*. Because that political record needs to be read, reread, thought about, and studied. It needs to be accessible, so it can be checked against various latter-day "memories" or "interpretations." That's why it's important that so many of his speeches and interviews, especially from late 1963 to his death in February 1965, are in print in hundreds of pages of books and pamphlets. Pathfinder Press, which publishes several of these collections, has announced plans to release in coming months another book by Malcolm, containing previously unpublished speeches.[22]

---

22. *Malcolm X: The Last Speeches* was published by Pathfinder in mid-1989.

Coming out of our discussion tonight, I hope many of us will go back and read Malcolm's last speeches and interviews, perhaps some of us for the first time. Because while it's great to listen to tapes of Malcolm's talks, *reading* and *studying* what he had to say is part of the irreplaceable work of absorbing and preparing *to act* on the lessons of revolutionary struggle from past centuries.

Malcolm was not the wild, violent hatemonger that millions have been taught he was by the bourgeois media, both during his lifetime and since. Those of you old enough to have been politically active during the late 1950s or in the 1960s can recall how Malcolm was portrayed by the daily newspapers, by magazines like the *Saturday Evening Post*, and by national television networks. Their aim was to get people to stop listening to him, and, eventually, that false image helped set him up to be killed. But their caricature of Malcolm was false and misleading when he was a leader of the Nation of Islam, and even more so—were it possible—after his break with the Nation in early 1964.

There's an additional distortion that some since Malcolm's death have used to blunt the impact of his revolutionary political message. They imply that during the final months of Malcolm's life, he was converging with other prominent figures who made significant contributions to the fight for Black rights, including some who even gave their lives in the course of that struggle, but who acted on the conviction that U.S. capitalist society, its government, and its twin political parties could be pressured into advancing the interests of the oppressed. The main example, of course, is the "Malcolm-Martin" theme we hear so much about these days—from sentimental popular songs to drawings and wall hangings, from the mass media to academic research, writings by former revolutionaries, and so on.

Malcolm certainly was ready to show respect and appreciation to anyone who devoted their life to the fight against racism and for Black equality. He was ready for united action to advance common demands on the powers-that-be in the fight for Black liberation, colonial freedom, and other goals. But Malcolm was also always ready to expose and rebut not only the lies but the political dead ends offered by these same individuals. He punctured the pretensions of misleaders whose overall outlook, strategy, or tactics politically disarmed the oppressed, taught us to rely on the promises and "good will" of any section of the exploiters and their political parties, and left us defenseless in face of racist terror, police violence, or other imperialist horrors. Concretely, it's simply false that Malcolm during his last year was converging politically with Martin Luther King—with King's bourgeois pacifism, his social-democratic ideas, his commitment to the reformability of capitalism, his support for the imperialist Democratic Party and various of its politicians.

Malcolm's legacy and socialist revolution in the U.S.

The reason we need to learn about Malcolm, the reason we need to read and discuss what he said, is not simply in order to do justice to a great revolutionist. We need to understand and absorb Malcolm's political legacy because it's a powerful political tool we must have to help make a socialist revolution in the United States. It aids us in gathering and unifying the forces among working people and youth who will forge a working-class party able to lead such a revolution. It is needed by anyone, here or anywhere else on earth, who wants to be part of an international revolutionary movement of the kind Malcolm was so determined to help build—a movement to rid humanity of all forms of oppression and exploitation.

You're living in "a time of revolution," Malcolm told a young audience at the Oxford Union, the student debating society at that British university, in December 1964. That was Malcolm's message. Revolution, he said, was the ques-

POST

THE SATURDAY EVENING POST JANUARY 26•1963 20c

POST

We sailed
The Columbus Way
Dwight D.
Eisenhower!

No children for me! *A biography exclude of* / **Black Muslims** *Black Muslims*

Malcolm X, Muslim strong man, shows his power over an audience
with a demand for money to finance transportation to rallies.

Black Merchants of Hate

*Fanatic and well disciplined, Negro "Muslims" threaten to turn
resentment against racial discrimination into open rebellion.*

by ALFRED BALK and ALEX HALEY

One pleasant spring evening a few years ago in New York's swarming Negro ghetto, Harlem, a policeman broke up an argument in an old, time-honored way: He clubbed one of the participants over the head and hauled him to the station. There the man was cursed, insulted and beaten until his face and body were bloody.

and a tall, light-skinned Negro, Malcolm X, the sect's local leader. "That crowd's ready to explode," one police official told him. "Will you use your influence against violence?"

"Guarantee that our brother will get medical treatment," Malcolm said tersely. "Pledge that the men who beat him will be punished."

Who are the Black Muslims? Are they, as one columnist described them, "the Mau Mau of the American Negro world," and therefore a dangerous threat to our society? Or has the menace of this group been exaggerated?

We were assigned by *The Saturday Evening Post* as a biracial team to find out. For this report we interviewed

strators and th
deride students
attempt to int
"Why should a
self to try an
university?" or

Another maj
Negroes away
they call "a wh

**"The daily newspapers, magazines like the *Saturday Evening Post*,
and national television networks portrayed Malcolm as a wild,
violent hatemonger," says Barnes. "Their aim was to get people
to stop listening to him, and, eventually, that false image helped
set him up to be killed. But their caricature of Malcolm was false
and misleading when he was a leader of the Nation of Islam, and
even more so—were it possible—after his break with the Nation
in early 1964."**

Above, *Saturday Evening Post* (January 26, 1963) featured article, "Black
Merchants of Hate." Caption to photo of Malcolm reads: "Malcolm X, Muslim
strong man, shows his power over an audience with a demand for money. . . ."

tion of questions confronting "the young generation of whites, Blacks, browns, whatever else there is. . . . I for one will join in with anyone, I don't care what color you are, as long as you want to change this miserable condition that exists on this earth."[23]

If we don't read what Malcolm said—the conclusions he drew from experiences he worked through at an accelerating pace in the closing year of his life—then, as we engage in battles today and tomorrow, all of us will be weaker as thinking, political people. Not less energetic, not less inspired (we will suffer that, also)—but *less political.*

U.S. imperialism's victory in World War II laid the basis for a quarter-century-long capitalist expansion that reached its apex in the late 1960s. Together with the effects of the U.S. rulers' postwar witch-hunt, this stabilization of world capitalism reinforced the bureaucratization of the labor officialdom that had been consolidated during the war and its aftermath. It accelerated the political retreat and weakening of the union movement in the United States.

As part of their overall class-collaborationist and pro-imperialist course, top officials of the AFL-CIO and its affiliates refused to mobilize the weight and power of the unions as part of the massive proletarian movement for Black rights. This movement exploded into nationwide consciousness with the Montgomery, Alabama, bus boycott of 1955–56 and picked up momentum over the following decade. Not only did the officialdom's default undermine efforts to organize the "right-to-work" South and reverse the steady weakening of the union movement nationwide. Above all, it made it more difficult for workers and youth to recognize social and political questions such as the fight for Black rights, for

23. "Any Means Necessary to Bring About Freedom" (Oxford University, December 3, 1964), in *Malcolm X Talks to Young People* (Pathfinder, 2002), p. 35 [2008 printing].

women's equality, and against imperialist war as *class questions* in which the labor movement has a life-or-death stake and must join in unconditionally.

"Fighters in these battles were forced to detour around the union movement because of the roadblock thrown up by the labor bureaucracy," the Socialist Workers Party explained in 1979. "They had to organize against the opposition of the labor officialdom, which not only defended the domestic and foreign policies of the imperialists but denounced and slandered uncompromising leaders of struggles against their policies. To millions of radicalized young activists, including industrial workers, the class-struggle strategy of transforming the labor movement into a fighting instrument mobilizing the working class in battle against exploitation and oppression seemed utopian. The fundamental class conflict underlying all politics was successfully camouflaged."[24]

Since the mid-1970s, however, the stability of the global capitalist order has begun to be shaken by the accumulating social and political consequences of declining profit rates and intensifying competition for markets among the employers in the United States, other imperialist countries, and the most industrially advanced nations in the colonial world. To gain an edge on their rivals, the bosses in one industry after another, and in one country after another, have launched an offensive against the take-home pay, social wage, and job conditions of working people. In face of these blows, the working class and unions have been pushed toward the center stage of politics, where they will remain until decisive battles not only have been joined but are resolved in favor of one or the other of the contending classes.

At the same time, the conquests of the hard-fought battles

---

24. "Building a Revolutionary Party of Socialist Workers" in Jack Barnes, *The Changing Face of U.S. Politics* (Pathfinder, 1981, 1994, 2004), p. 239 [2008 printing].

for Black liberation, as well as the spur they gave to struggles for women's rights, have had a deepgoing political impact on the consciousness of the working class in the United States. These gains have narrowed—not eliminated—long-standing divisions among workers promoted by the capitalist rulers and have laid the basis to put the unions on a firmer footing to engage in coming fights.

Before World War II three-quarters of African Americans lived in the states of the old Confederacy, the majority of them in rural areas. That changed rapidly during the first half of the 1940s as a result of labor shortages in the war industries. Blacks moved off farms and out of small towns and migrated to cities in the North and West, as well as in the South. Refusing to bow to patriotic pressures to subordinate their struggle for equality to the capitalists' war effort, they organized protests to fight their way into jobs in war production and other industries from which they had long been barred—struggles socialist workers championed, took part in, and covered widely in the *Militant*.[25] By the mid-1960s more than half the Black population lived in the North, three-quarters in cities.

In a talk Malcolm gave in February 1965, just a few days before he was killed, he described the impact of this rapid urbanization and proletarianization on the city of Lansing, Michigan, where he spent much of his youth:

> Up until the time of the war, you couldn't get inside of a plant. I lived in Lansing, where Oldsmobile's factory

25. For a detailed account of struggles during World War II by Blacks and others against the racist color bar in U.S. industries, the armed forces, and society as a whole—taken from the pages of the socialist newsweekly, the *Militant*—see *Fighting Racism in World War II* (Pathfinder, 1980). These struggles helped lay the basis for the rise of the mass Black rights movement in the subsequent two decades.

was and Reo's [a now-defunct auto company]. There were about three [Blacks] in the whole plant and each one of them had a broom. They had education. They had gone to school. I think one had gone to college. But he was a "broomologist."

Prior to World War II there were a lot of "broomologists" among the relatively small number of factory workers who were Black. Only in the steel mills, packinghouses, and coal mines were there substantial numbers of Blacks in the industrial work force at that time.

Malcolm continued:

When times got tough and there was a manpower shortage, then they let us in the factory. Not through any effort of our own. [Malcolm was wrong about that.] Not through any sudden moral awakening on their part. [He was dead right about that.] They needed us. They needed manpower. Any kind of manpower. And when they got desperate and in need, they opened up the factory door and let us in. . . . Then we began to learn how to run machines.[26]

In 1933 the exiled Bolshevik leader Leon Trotsky made the accurate observation that on the whole in the United States at that time, no "common actions took place involving white and black workers." There was no "class fraternization" between them, he said.[27] What had been true since the defeat of Radical

---

26. "Not Just an American Problem, but a World Problem" (February 16, 1965), in *Malcolm X: The Last Speeches* (Pathfinder, 1989), pp. 145–73 [2008 printing]. Also in Malcolm X, *February 1965: The Final Speeches*, pp. 147–76.

27. Trotsky's remarks, from the transcript of a discussion with U.S. communist leader Arne Swabeck, appear elsewhere in this book (see pp. 239–56).

Reconstruction, however, had slowly begun to change after World War I, first with the extension of struggles by share-croppers and tenant farmers across the South, and then with the rise of the mass social movement centered on the struggle to build industrial unions. Workers who were Black and workers who were white fought shoulder to shoulder in battles that established the unions making up the newly formed Congress of Industrial Organizations (CIO). The biggest changes came in the wake of World War II, however, especially under the powerful social and political impact of the Black rights struggles from the mid-1950s through the early 1970s. Common actions and class fraternization among workers regardless of skin color became more and more frequent in the course of strikes, organizing drives, and other battles.

The years following Malcolm's assassination were also marked by revolutionary victories in the world. In 1975 Vietnamese liberation fighters defeated U.S. imperialism after a long and bloody war, reunifying their country. The Portuguese colonial empire, the last in Africa, was brought down in the mid-1970s, and Cuba's twelve-year record of internationalist solidarity with the Angolan people in face of ongoing aggression by South African forces—backed by Washington—is today weakening the foundations of the apartheid regime as well. Workers and farmers governments were brought to power by popular revolutions in Grenada and Nicaragua in 1979, and we've learned rich political lessons by participating as partisans in those revolutions. The socialist revolution in Cuba is today deepening its proletarian internationalist course through what they call the Rectification Process.[28]

---

28. See "Cuba's Rectification Process: Two Speeches by Fidel Castro" in *New International* no. 6; "Che's Proletarian Legacy and Cuba's Rectification Process" by Mary-Alice Waters in *New International* no. 8; and "U.S. Imperialism Has Lost the Cold War" by Jack Barnes in *New International* no. 11, pp. 240–48 [2006 printing].

For all these reasons and more, all of us are better equipped today to understand and act on the political conclusions Malcolm X was drawing at the end of his life. And that includes the many here tonight who never had the opportunity to see Malcolm, to meet with him, or to hear him speak.

Malcolm's early life

I can't recount the story of Malcolm's life this evening, of course. That would be impossible, and it's not the aim of this gathering. The broad outlines are known by many of you who've read the *Autobiography*—something I'd recommend to anyone who hasn't done so.[29] But a few points about his early life are important to appreciating his later political development.

Malcolm was born in 1925 in the Midwest, in Omaha, Nebraska. His mother, Louise Little, was born in Grenada. Her father was white. That's where Malcolm got his complexion, the color of his hair, and his nickname "Red."

Malcolm's father, Earl Little, was a Baptist minister, and, as Malcolm explained in the *Autobiography*, "a dedicated organizer" for Marcus Garvey's Universal Negro Improvement Association.[30] Earl Little was a Black man who refused to simply accept the conditions Black people were told was their place. Just before Malcolm was born, the Ku Klux Klan in Omaha sent mounted night riders with torches to surround the family's home and shatter every window with their rifle butts.

---

29. *The Autobiography of Malcolm X*, with the assistance of Alex Haley. First published in 1965, shortly after Malcolm's death, it is available in a number of editions.

30. The Universal Negro Improvement Association, led by Marcus Garvey, attracted support from hundreds of thousands in the United States and the Caribbean in the 1920s. Its proposed solution to racist oppression was that Blacks organize to go back to Africa to help liberate the continent from colonial rule and, in the process, to settle there.

When Malcolm was almost four years old, Earl and Louise Little and their children moved to Lansing, Michigan, where Earl continued to preach the gospel and spread Garvey's message. There Malcolm's father aroused the ire of a white-supremacist group called the Black Legion by refusing to live in the part of town where Black people were supposed to keep to themselves. So the Black Legionnaires burned the Littles' house to the ground. A couple of years later, in 1931, when Malcolm was six years old, his father was found nearly dead, run over by a streetcar with his head bashed in; he died hours later. Malcolm says in the *Autobiography* that Blacks in Lansing were convinced Earl Little had been beaten by Black Legionnaires and left on the tracks to be killed.

That experience had a lifelong impact on Malcolm.

A second experience marked young Malcolm very, very deeply. That was watching his mother eventually succumb to the unbearable pressures of trying to survive these racist horrors and support a large family, scraping by on a small pension, welfare, and "working, when she could find any kind of job." When Malcolm was in his early teens, she went into a state hospital, where she spent the next quarter of a century. Louise Little was never the same person again.

By the time Malcolm had finished eighth grade, his experience in life—like that of many young people who are Black, or who are from working-class families—gave him little reason to continue in school. He headed down the only road that seemed open to him to use his talents, his ability, his intelligence. After moving to Boston to live with his sister in 1941, he soon became deeply involved in the life of the streets. He became a hustler, a thief, a pimp. "Every instinct of the ghetto jungle streets, every hustling fox and criminal wolf instinct in me" more and more dominated Malcolm's days and nights, as he put it in the *Autobiography*.

Malcolm also learned the deadly facts of life about the

streets. Had he continued down that road, he said, he would have ended up either "a dead criminal in a grave" or "a flint-hard, bitter . . . convict in some penitentiary, or insane asylum. Or, at best, I would have been an old, fading Detroit Red, hustling, stealing enough for food and narcotics, and myself being stalked as prey by cruelly ambitious younger hustlers such as Detroit Red had been."[31]

The inevitable happened. Malcolm, a buddy of his nicknamed Shorty, and two female accomplices were grabbed by the cops for several burglaries in the Boston area. The average burglary sentence for somebody with no previous record in Massachusetts was about two years at the time, Malcolm explained in the *Autobiography*. But when the judge announced the sentences on each of three counts, Malcolm was given eight-to-ten years to run concurrently; his buddy got the same; and the women one-to-five years. According to Malcolm, Shorty nearly collapsed when the judge read the sentences, since he didn't know what the word "concurrently" meant.

Those sentences were Malcolm's fourth big lesson. The first two lessons were what he had learned about the reality of racism in capitalist America from what happened to his father and mother. The third was the inescapable self-destruction, the loss of any sense of self-worth, that comes out of the life of the streets—as opposed to engagement in social and political activity, as opposed to living in history. The fourth was: Know your place! Because the reason Malcolm and Shorty got such stiff sentences was that their two accomplices, their girlfriends, were white. The price they were going to pay for that transgression was made unmistakably clear by the judge.

So Malcolm spent 1946 to 1952 in the joint. Later, when

---

31. *The Autobiography of Malcolm X*, chapter 15: "Icarus."

he spoke about those years publicly, he loved to comment: "Don't be shocked when I say that I was in prison. You're still in prison. That's what America means: prison."[32]

Awakened to our worth

But an important thing happened to Malcolm while he was serving time. He met a fellow inmate who encouraged him to take advantage of the prison library and correspondence courses. "When I finished the eighth grade back in Mason, Michigan," he recalled, "that was the last time I'd thought of studying anything that didn't have some hustle purpose. And the streets had erased everything I'd ever learned in school; I didn't know a verb from a house." So he signed up for correspondence lessons in English grammar and began to read a little bit.

Boston's Charlestown State Prison, Malcolm said, was a hellish place that "had been built in 1805—in Napoleon's day—and was even styled after the Bastille." The "toilet was a covered pail," and from Malcolm's cot his outstretched hands and feet could touch both walls of the stinking cell. Through the efforts of his sister Ella, Malcolm was transferred to the Norfolk Prison Colony in late 1948. The new prison's library "was one of its outstanding features," he said. Unlike Charlestown, where inmates had to pick available titles from a mimeographed list, "At Norfolk, we could actually go into the library, with permission—walk up and down the shelves, pick books. There were hundreds of old volumes."

Malcolm described how he worked his way through the dictionary, literally copying it down on tablets, page by page, word by word. At first he read aimlessly, he said, "until I learned to read selectively, with a purpose." For the rest of his time in prison, "in every free moment I had, if I was not reading

---

32. "Message to the Grass Roots" (Detroit, November 10, 1963), in *Malcolm X Speaks*, p. 20.

in the library, I was reading in my bunk. You couldn't have gotten me out of books with a wedge." After "lights out" at ten o'clock, Malcolm would sit on the floor, catching the glow through the slit in his cell door to read by, then jumping back on the bunk as guards made their hourly rounds.

Malcolm read widely: Will Durant's *Story of Civilization*, H.G. Wells's *Outline of History*, W.E.B. Du Bois's *Souls of Black Folk*, Gregor Mendel's *Findings in Genetics*, Carter G. Woodson's *Negro History*; books on slavery by Frederick Law Olmstead, Fanny Kemble, and Harriet Beecher Stowe; works by Homer, Shakespeare, as well as Spinoza, Kant, and others "of the old philosophers, Occidental and Oriental," as he put it.

Mastering the discipline to read, to study, *to work* at thinking about what he was reading—all this changed Malcolm profoundly. This "homemade education," as he called it, "awoke inside me some long dormant craving to be mentally alive." It contributed to making Malcolm X among the most truly educated, capable revolutionary politicians of our times.

It is from these experiences that Malcolm learned, both for himself and his relations with others, the irreplaceable importance of coming to recognize and believe in your own value as a human being. During one of the last interviews before his death in 1965, a journalist asked him: Is your aim to awaken Blacks in the United States "to their exploitation"? "No," Malcolm replied, "to their humanity, to their own worth."[33] His goal was to convince the oppressed and exploited of our *worth*, to wake us up to our worth.

The Nation of Islam

While Malcolm was in prison, several family members introduced him to the Nation of Islam. Neither politics nor

---

33. "We Have to Learn How to Think," in *February 1965: The Final Speeches*, pp. 250–51.

religion, as we usually think of them, accounted for Malcolm's conversion. Instead, he was attracted to what he perceived as the self-discipline, focus, and sense of self-respect that members of the Nation instilled in one another. Recalling his efforts in prison to emulate that discipline—together with the impact of his studies—Malcolm said in the *Autobiography* that it was "as though someone else I knew of had lived by hustling and crime. . . . I would be startled to catch myself thinking in a remote way of my earlier self as another person."

In August 1952, after almost seven years behind bars, Malcolm was released on parole. At twenty-seven years of age, he was still a young man. Initially returning to Michigan, he worked for several months in a furniture store and then on assembly lines at a truck factory and at a Ford Motor Company plant. Beginning mid-1953 he spent the next eleven years of his life as an active, full-time leader of the Nation of Islam, moving from Detroit to Boston to Philadelphia and then, in June 1954, to New York City. By the end of that decade he had become the Nation's most nationally prominent and capable spokesperson, as well as the founder and editor of its newspaper, *Muhammad Speaks*. In the eyes of tens of millions—as a result of his speeches across the country, his appearance on TV talk shows, and above all his unmistakable energy, militancy, courage, and integrity—he had become the image of the Nation of Islam.

By the early 1960s, however, Malcolm was increasingly bumping up against the limits of the bourgeois nationalism of the Nation of Islam. The Nation's leadership sought to carve out a place for itself within the U.S. capitalist system. Malcolm, to the contrary, was being politically drawn more and more toward the rising struggles for Black freedom in the United States and revolutionary battles by the oppressed and exploited the world over. As he addressed audiences in Harlem and in Black communities across the United States, as well as on college campuses, Malcolm spoke out intransigently against U.S. imperialist policies at home and abroad. He condemned anti-Black racism, discrimination, and night-riding violence, as well as world capitalism's profit-driven plunder and oppression of Africa, Asia, and Latin America.

Malcolm's course led to gradually sharpening clashes with Elijah Muhammad and the rest of the leadership of the Nation. In face of these mounting conflicts, Muhammad gagged Malcolm in late 1963, using as a pretext Malcolm's public reply to a question about the assassination of President John F. Kennedy. Referring to the racist bigotry and violence that pervaded social relations in the United States, Malcolm had simply observed that Kennedy's death was a case of "the chickens coming home to roost."

Recognizing that Elijah Muhammad fully intended to silence him permanently, in March 1964 Malcolm announced that he had left the Nation of Islam. The break marked an important step in what would become an accelerating political evolution over the next eleven months. Malcolm refrained at first from publicly criticizing the Nation, even stating initially that he still accepted Muhammad's "analysis" and "solution" to the problem of Black oppression. "I did not leave of my own free will," Malcolm told reporters at the press conference he had called. "But now that it has happened, I intend to make the most of it. Now that I have more independence of action, I intend to use a more flexible approach toward working with others to get a solution to this problem."[34]

As Malcolm gained more experience in doing just that—"working with others," both in this country and around the world—his revolutionary outlook deepened and he spoke out more and more openly about what led him to break with the Nation of Islam.

---

34. "A Declaration of Independence," in *Malcolm X Speaks*, p. 32.

"My former statements were prefaced by 'the Honorable Elijah Muhammad teaches thus and so.' They weren't my statements, they were his statements, and I was repeating them," Malcolm told interviewer in December 1964, referring to time when he was spokesman for Nation of Islam. But now, Malcolm said, "the parrot has jumped out of the cage."

Malcolm at Harlem bookstore after March 12, 1964, news conference announcing he had left the Nation of Islam.

His scope kept widening, as Malcolm often put it.

Two days before his assassination in February 1965, according to photographer and writer Gordon Parks, Malcolm told Parks: "I did many things as a Muslim that I'm sorry for now. I was a zombie then. . . . I was hypnotized, pointed in a certain direction and told to march."[35]

Malcolm had blocked out of his mind questioning things he knew were not true, that he didn't want to confront. He hadn't looked square in the face at realities that were convincing him more and more that the Nation of Islam offered no way forward. During the period he had been a spokesperson for the Nation, as he told radio talk-show host Bernice Bass in December 1964, "my former statements were prefaced by 'the Honorable Elijah Muhammad teaches thus and so.' They weren't my statements, they were his statements, and I was repeating them."

But now, Malcolm added, "the parrot has jumped out of the cage."[36]

The final fifty weeks

After March 1964 Malcolm began speaking and acting on his own, as a political leader. This is the Malcolm X whose speeches, interviews, and statements you've read in Pathfinder books. Whose thoughts and ideas many of you know to one degree or another. But this block of time—a grand total of fifty weeks, as it turned out, not even a full year— was precious for Malcolm. He had fifty weeks to organize, to go through new experiences, to reflect on those experiences and draw lessons, to collaborate with other revolution-

---

35. "One Big Force Under One Banner" (interview with Gordon Parks, February 19, 1965), in *February 1965: The Final Speeches*, p. 241.

36. "Our People Identify with Africa" (interview with Bernice Bass, December 27, 1964), in *Malcolm X: The Last Speeches*, p. 99.

ists here and abroad, to discuss and work out his views, to improve and correct them, to face up to contradictions and begin resolving them. In short, to take the path that made Malcolm X who he was. To discover his worth.

Malcolm spent more than half that time abroad—nearly twenty-six weeks in Africa and the Middle East, and an additional two weeks plus in Britain and France. Those trips had a tremendous political impact on him.

So it was over the course of only twenty-two weeks in the United States that Malcolm began building two separate organizations—first the Muslim Mosque, Inc., and then, in June 1964, the Organization of Afro-American Unity (OAAU). It was during those weeks that he gave the big majority of speeches and interviews explaining his rapidly evolving revolutionary outlook to broader and broader audiences.

Many of the views Malcolm advocated and explained at the end of his life were quite different from those he had still held to one degree or another in March 1964. He had gone through not primarily an evolution, but overlapping *revolutions*, so to speak.

Malcolm X emerged on American soil as the most representative revolutionary leader with a mass hearing in the latter half of the twentieth century. He converged politically with other revolutionists the world over, including proletarian revolutionists, communists, here in the United States. He was going in the direction the world revolution was going, *against* colonialism and capitalism, and *with* those who were pushing revolutionary struggle forward. Many individuals, in many countries, who aspire to lead revolutions on their home turf are still catching up with Malcolm on many fronts.

Malcolm's course during these final months is sometimes described as a new form of Pan-Africanism, and Malcolm himself used that term a few times. But "Pan-Africanism" captures neither the scope nor the revolutionary political character of Malcolm's internationalism and anti-imperialism. Malcolm, of course, recognized the shared aspects of the oppression facing those of African origin—and of their resistance to that oppression. Because of the combined legacy of colonialism and chattel slavery, Blacks shared many such elements whether they lived and toiled in Africa itself, in the Caribbean and Latin America, in Europe, or what Malcolm, echoing Elijah Muhammad's marvelous term, called "this wilderness of North America."

"Many of us fool ourselves into thinking of Afro-Americans as those only who are here in the United States," Malcolm said in one of his last talks, just five days before he was assassinated. "But the Afro-American is that large number of people in the Western Hemisphere, from the southernmost tip of South America to the northernmost tip of North America, all of whom have a common heritage and have a common origin when you go back to the history of these people. . . . [And when Africans] migrate to England, they pose a problem for the English. And when they migrate to France, they pose a problem for the French."[37]

At the same time, Malcolm increasingly identified with, championed, and explained revolutionary struggles the world over—from the Chinese Revolution, to the Cuban Revolution, to battles for national liberation wherever they were being fought, and by people of whatever hue of skin color.

At this meeting tonight, however, I want to try to make the case that is perhaps the most important of all, not just for revolutionists in this country but those around the world. I want to make the case that *Malcolm X was a revolutionary leader of the working class in the United States.*

That may sound strange, for a number of reasons. It may sound strange because of the small degree of support Mal-

---

37. "Not Just an American Problem, but a World Problem," in *February 1965: The Final Speeches,* pp. 149–50.

colm had among workers who were Caucasian, at least those he knew of. It may sound strange because of the weakened state of the labor movement and procapitalist positions of the union officialdom that I described earlier, views that were diametrically opposed to Malcolm's. It may sound strange, if for no other reason than that Malcolm himself never directly addressed this question.

But the fact remains that the social and political transformations that will be wrought by a popular revolution in the United States—a revolution that will be led by the vanguard of the working class, or else go down to a bloody defeat— are decisive for the oppressed and exploited the world over. Among other things, the conquest of power by the working class and its allies—the establishment of the dictatorship of the proletariat—is the necessary step that can open the road for Blacks, and for all supporters of Black rights, to successfully fight to end racist oppression of every kind once and for all.

In the leadership of revolutionary working-class struggles in this country, workers who are Black will occupy a vanguard place and weight disproportionate to their numbers in the U.S. population. That's what all modern history teaches us. That fact is testified to by the record of powerful social and political struggles in the United States: from battles during the closing years of the Civil War itself; to Radical Reconstruction and the efforts to prevent the imposition of peonage among the freed slaves; to the struggles that built farmers movements and the industrial unions in the 1920s and 1930s; to the mass proletarian movement that toppled Jim Crow segregation, fueled the rise of greater political self-confidence and nationalist consciousness among Blacks in the 1960s, and inspired what became the mass movement against the imperialist war in Vietnam.

Malcolm X was a legitimate political heir to all these struggles.

But who are *Malcolm's* heirs?

Following his assassination, some who looked to Malcolm were disappointed because the political organization he founded and led, the OAAU, died with him. Given the enemies they faced, none of the relatively few OAAU cadres Malcolm had brought over from the Nation of Islam were able to step forward to carry on the fight and shoulder the leadership to continue Malcolm's revolutionary political course. That's a fact.

But the heirs of Malcolm X *will* come forward—all over the world, including right here in the United States—as revolutionary struggles advance, as the exploited and oppressed organize to resist the devastating consequences of capitalist crises and imperialist domination and wars. More leaders like Malcolm *will* come forward, including in the labor movement. And they will need to know who Malcolm was, what Malcolm stood for, what he fought for and dedicated his life to.

Emancipation of women

To demonstrate the breadth and revolutionary significance of Malcolm's political evolution, it's useful to look at a couple of questions on which many might assume his views changed little—women's emancipation and religion.

Some might think it's "unfair" to begin with the question of women's rights, women's position in social and political life, their place in revolutionary struggles and the leadership of those struggles. After all, Malcolm was assassinated prior to the rise of the women's liberation movement at the end of the 1960s. The modern communist movement has a long and proud record in support of the emancipation of women— from its founding manifesto drafted by Marx and Engels and published in 1848, to the Communist International in Lenin's time, to today.[38] But prior to the women's movement,

---

38. For a discussion of that record, see *Feminism and the Marxist Movement* by Mary-Alice Waters (Pathfinder, 1972).

none of us saw things the way we see them now.

Maybe it's also unfair because of Malcolm's religious background and the second-class status of women in all the modern monotheisms—whether they trace themselves back to Abraham, Paul the Evangelist, or Muhammad. As Malcolm himself explained in his *Autobiography*, Islam—including the Nation of Islam, whose spokesperson he had been until late 1963—has "very strict laws and teachings about women, the core of them being that the true nature of a man is to be strong, and a woman's true nature is to be weak, and while a man must at all times respect his woman, at the same time he needs to understand that he must control her if he expects to get her respect."[39] (Such attitudes extend considerably beyond Islam, as we well know.)

But we should follow Malcolm's standard: in politics, stating the truth is never "unfair." And Malcolm can withstand the test.

When Malcolm left the Nation, he didn't initially have much to say about the rights or social position of women. But in the *Autobiography*—the draft of which had been completed, with the help of journalist Alex Haley, only shortly before the assassination—Malcolm tells a story that sheds light on the speed and degree of his later evolution on this question. (In reading the *Autobiography*, we should always keep two things in mind. First, that the interviews were begun while Malcolm was still in the Nation, with Elijah Muhammad's approval. And second, that Malcolm was denied the opportunity to review and edit the final draft, or bring it in line with his views at that time. According to Haley, the assassination coincided with the days he and Malcolm had tentatively set aside for that review.)

Toward the end of the *Autobiography*, Malcolm is de-

---

39. *The Autobiography of Malcolm X*, chapter 13: "Minister Malcolm X."

scribing his visit to Beirut, Lebanon, on the last day of April 1964. Going out for a walk, he says,

immediately my attention was struck by the manner-
isms and attire of the Lebanese women. In the Holy Land
[Saudi Arabia] there had been the very modest, very
feminine Arabian women—and there was this sudden
contrast of the half-French, half-Arab Lebanese women
who projected in their dress and street manners more
liberty, more boldness. I saw clearly the obvious European
influence upon the Lebanese culture. It showed me how
any country's moral strength, or its moral weakness, is
quickly measurable by the street attire and attitude of
its women—especially its young women. Wherever the
spiritual values have been submerged, if not destroyed,
by an emphasis upon the material things, invariably,
the women reflect it. Witness the women, both young
and old, in America—where scarcely any moral values
are left.[40]

So that's how Malcolm still approached the question of women's social position a month or so after his break with the Nation. The emphasis remained on religious standards of modesty and sexual morality.

At roughly this same time, Malcolm was still an unequivo-cal opponent of what he called "intermarriage." In the *Au-tobiography*, once again, Malcolm writes: "I'm right *with* the Southern white man who believes that you can't have so-called 'integration,' at least not for long, without inter-marriage increasing. And what good is this for anyone? Let's again face reality. In a world as color-hostile as this, man or woman, black or white, what do they want with a mate

---

40. *The Autobiography of Malcolm X,* chapter 18: "El Hajj Malik El-Shabazz."

of the other race?"[41] And when Malcolm was interviewed by writer A.B. Spellman the same week he announced his departure from the Nation, Malcolm had this to say about the stance of the new organization he had launched, Muslim Mosque, Inc.: "[W]e do oppose intermarriage. We are as much against intermarriage as we are against all of the other injustices that our people have encountered."[42] He still considered intermarriage "an injustice." He equated it with the rape and involuntary concubinage that women of African origin were subjected to under slavery, colonial domination, and more recent conditions of exploitation and racist oppression.

By the end of Malcolm's second trip to Africa and the Middle East in 1964, between early July and late November,[43] however, his views had undergone a striking change—one that paralleled the evolution of how he thought and acted on other social and political questions. At a news conference during a stopover in Paris following that trip, Malcolm said that one of the things he had noticed during his travels was that

> in every country you go to, usually the degree of progress can never be separated from the woman. If you're in a country that's progressive, the woman is progressive. If you're in a country that reflects the consciousness toward the importance of education, it's because the woman is

---

41. *The Autobiography of Malcolm X*, chapter 15: "Icarus."

42. "An Interview by A.B. Spellman" (March 19, 1964), in *By Any Means Necessary*, p. 31.

43. Malcolm's two trips to Africa and the Middle East in 1964 were his second and third visits to those regions. In 1959, as a leader of the Nation of Islam, he had traveled to Egypt, Saudi Arabia, Iran, Syria, and Ghana.

aware of the importance of education.

But in every backward country you'll find the women are backward, and in every country where education is not stressed it's because the women don't have education. So one of the things I became thoroughly convinced of in my recent travels is the importance of giving freedom to the women, giving her education, and giving her the incentive to get out there and put the same spirit and understanding in her children. And I am frankly proud of the contributions that our women have made in the struggle for freedom and I'm one person who's for giving them all the leeway possible because they've made a greater contribution than many of us men.[44]

Malcolm took these views a step further a month later during the December 27 radio interview with Bernice Bass I mentioned earlier. "One thing I noticed in both the Middle East and Africa," Malcolm said, "in every country that was progressive, the women were progressive. In every country that was underdeveloped and backward, it was to the same degree that the women were undeveloped, or underdeveloped, and backward. . . . [I]t's noticeable that in these types of societies where they put the woman in a closet and discourage her from getting a sufficient education and don't give her the incentive by allowing her maximum participation in whatever area of the society where she's qualified, they kill her incentive."[45]

This is a very advanced level of political understanding: that you can measure the degree of progress and develop-

---

44. Excerpt from interview in Paris (November 1964), in *By Any Means Necessary*, pp. 214–15.

45. "Our People Identify with Africa," in *Malcolm X: The Last Speeches*, p. 94.

ment of a society by the place of women in its social, economic, and political life.[46] Unlike Malcolm's remarks just a few months earlier about women in Beirut, where female "modesty" and religious "morality" had been his starting point, now Malcolm was using *political* criteria. He overcame simple prejudice—which is what Malcolm's earlier views reflected, whether expressed by him or by anyone else—and began replacing them with facts about the social position of women. He began talking about what women can and do accomplish to advance human progress, to advance revolutionary change, if barriers erected against them begin to be torn down.

Malcolm also changed his mind on interracial marriage. Appearing on a television talk show in Toronto, in mid-January 1965, Malcolm was asked by the host, Pierre Berton, whether he still held his earlier views on this question. Malcolm replied: "I believe in recognizing every human being as a human being—neither white, black, brown, or red; and when you are dealing with humanity as a family there's no question of integration or intermarriage. It's just one human being marrying another human being, or one human being living around and with another human being."

What needs to be attacked, Malcolm told Berton, is the racist society that produces attitudes "hostile toward inte-

---

46. In 1844, in one of the early works along the road that led him a few years later to become a founding leader of the modern communist workers movement, Karl Marx saluted an observation by utopian socialist Charles Fourier. Fourier had said, "The change in a historical epoch can always be determined by women's progress towards freedom." (*The Holy Family* in Marx and Engels, *Collected Works*, vol. 4, p. 196). In the 1880 booklet *Socialism: Utopian and Scientific*, Marx's lifelong political collaborator, Frederick Engels, again paid tribute to Fourier for being "the first to declare that in any given society the degree of woman's emancipation is the natural measure of the general emancipation." (Pathfinder, 1972, 1989, 2008, p. 55.)

gration and toward intermarriage and toward these other strides toward oneness" of human beings, not "the reaction that develops among the people who are the victims of that negative society."[47]

In assessing the evolution of Malcolm's attitude toward women's rights—including the place he had come to recognize women would occupy in coming revolutionary struggles in the United States and worldwide—we should also note the shattering impact on Malcolm of his discovery that Elijah Muhammad was sexually abusing young female members of the Nation of Islam. According to Malcolm, this was the single fact, more than any particular political conflict per se, that marked a turning point in his relationship with the Nation. It deeply shook Malcolm's confidence in the religious, political, and moral integrity of Elijah Muhammad and of the Nation of Islam itself.[48]

Political differences alone are often not enough initially to convince tested leaders to break with a movement or organization in which they've invested their efforts, their energies, their convictions for many years. Malcolm had had growing doubts about the Nation's political course since at least the summer of 1962, when Elijah Muhammad put the kibosh on a campaign Malcolm was leading to protest a deadly cop assault against several Nation members in Los

---

47. Excerpt from interview by Pierre Berton (January 19, 1965), in *Malcolm X Speaks*, p. 218.

48. In April 1963 Malcolm found out, directly from Elijah Muhammad himself, that Muhammad had engaged in sexual relations with a number of young women working as staff members at the Nation of Islam headquarters in Chicago. Several had become pregnant. Abusing his authority in the Nation, Muhammad subjected these young women to degrading internal trials for "fornication" and suspended them from membership. Two of the young women filed paternity suits against Muhammad in Los Angeles in 1964, but court papers were never served and the legal action was dropped.

Angeles.[49] But as Malcolm himself acknowledged, he kept trying to close his eyes to those conflicts, anticipating that prospects for altering this course could improve over time. It took something more deeply wrong—deeply corrupting to the very foundations of the movement he thought he stood for—to precipitate the break.

When another Young Socialist Alliance leader and I interviewed Malcolm for the *Young Socialist* magazine in January 1965, he told us: "I felt the movement was dragging its feet in many areas. It didn't involve itself in the civil or civic or political struggles our people were confronted by. All it did was stress the importance of moral reformation—don't drink, don't smoke, don't permit fornication and adultery. When I found that the hierarchy itself wasn't practicing what it preached, it was clear that this part of its program was bankrupt."[50]

---

49. In April 1962 Los Angeles cops shot seven unarmed members of the Nation of Islam. One of the Muslims was killed and another crippled for life. The cops then arrested sixteen Nation members on trumped-up charges of "criminal assault against the police." Sent by Elijah Muhammad to Los Angeles to organize a response to this assault, Malcolm launched a broad-based protest campaign in southern California that reached far beyond the Nation. "Whether you are white or black, this is your fight too," said literature on the defense effort. "Today, it is our temple," Malcolm said at a protest rally in Los Angeles, "but tomorrow it will be your churches, your lodges, and your synagogues." As preparations were under way that summer to step up defense efforts nationwide, however, Elijah Muhammad called a halt to the public campaign, limiting further activity to the courts. Looking back on this experience in a talk to young Mississippi civil rights activists on New Year's Day 1965, Malcolm said: "That's what split the Muslim movement. . . . Some of our brothers got hurt, and nothing was done about it. Those of us who wanted to do something about it were kept from doing something about it." ("See for Yourself, Listen for Yourself, Think for Yourself: A Discussion with Young Civil Rights Fighters from Mississippi," in *Malcolm X Talks to Young People*, p. 105.)

50. See the previous item in this book, p. 46.

Finally, Malcolm deepened his understanding of the importance of combating the oppression of women as he watched them help lead the fight for Black rights in this country. When Fannie Lou Hamer came to New York in December 1964 to win support for the freedom struggle in Mississippi, Malcolm spoke alongside her at a rally in Harlem and gave her a platform that night at the meeting of the OAAU.[51] Malcolm also admired and worked with Gloria Richardson, who had refused to call off demonstrations in Cambridge, Maryland, in face of white-supremacist thugs and the National Guard—as well as public rebukes by conservative Black leaders—and who publicly solidarized with Malcolm's call for the right of self-defense against racist terror.

I mentioned earlier Malcolm's insistence that the aim of the movement he was working to build was to awaken Blacks "to their humanity, to their own worth." During the final months of his life, Malcolm also deepened his understanding that the fight to liberate *half of humanity* from their oppression, and to assert in action *their* political worth,

---

51. Fannie Lou Hamer was a longtime fighter for Black rights in Mississippi and the central leader of the fight to oust the state's segregationist delegation from the August 1964 Democratic Party convention. Her accounts of racist brutality in Mississippi drew nationwide attention during that convention. When the effort to oust the cracker delegation was rejected, the Mississippi Freedom Democratic Party announced its own candidates for the November election and then called on Congress to refuse to seat those who were elected on the Jim Crow ticket. Malcolm's speech at the December 20, 1964, Harlem rally for Hamer is published in *Malcolm X Speaks* under the title, "With Mrs. Fannie Lou Hamer." His talk at the OAAU meeting where Hamer spoke that evening is published in the same book under the title, "At the Audubon."

The "head of the Cracker Party" resides in the White House, not in Mississippi, Malcolm told the Harlem rally. "It's controlled right up here from the North. . . . [T]hese Northern crackers smile in your face and show you their teeth and they stick the knife in your back when you turn around." (*Malcolm X Speaks*, p. 127.)

sharply increased the potential forces of revolution in this country and around the world.

Keep religion in the closet

What about the evolution of Malcolm's views on religion and revolutionary politics?

First, in order to minimize misunderstanding about the political points we need to clarify, let me emphasize that I'm not calling into question Malcolm's assertions up till the final days of his life that he remained a Muslim.

We're looking at something else. What did Malcolm think about the place of religion in building a modern revolutionary movement, a revolutionary organization? Once again, there's no single answer that holds good for the entire final fifty weeks of Malcolm's life. But the position he had arrived at prior to his assassination is clear.

To begin with, when Malcolm made public his break from the Nation in March 1964, the only organizational step he announced was the establishment of a religious organization. "I am going to organize and head a new mosque in New York City, known as the Muslim Mosque, Inc.," he told the press. "This gives us a religious base, and the spiritual force necessary to rid our people of the vices that destroy the moral fiber of our community."[52]

A few days later Malcolm told an interviewer that during his time in the Nation of Islam, "Many obstacles were placed in my path, not by the Honorable Elijah Muhammad, but by others who were around him, and since I believe that his analysis of the race problem is the best one and his solution is the only one, I felt that I could best circumvent these obstacles and expedite his program by remaining out of the Nation of Islam and establishing a Muslim group that is an

---

52. "A Declaration of Independence," in *Malcolm X Speaks*, p. 33.

action group designed to eliminate the same ills that the teachings of the Honorable Elijah Muhammad have made so manifest in this country."[53]

Only a few weeks later, however, Malcolm's emphasis was already shifting. As opportunities expanded for Malcolm to collaborate with others, he began stressing that being a Muslim was not a precondition to common political action in combating the oppression of Blacks. There was no religious litmus test.

He made that point clear, for example, during a talk he presented to an April 3 gathering in Cleveland, sponsored by the local chapter of the Congress of Racial Equality (CORE), on "The Negro Revolt—What Comes Next?" The meeting was held in a Methodist Church. In closing his talk, which Malcolm titled "The Ballot or the Bullet," he said he wanted to add "a few things concerning the Muslim Mosque, Inc., which we established recently in New York City. It's true we're Muslims and our religion is Islam," Malcolm said, "but we don't mix our religion with our politics and our economics and our social and civil activities—not any more. We keep our religion in our mosque. After our religious services are over, then as Muslims we become involved in political action, economic action and social and civic action. We become involved with anybody, anywhere, any time and in any manner that's designed to eliminate the evils, the political, economic and social evils that are afflicting the people of our community."[54]

Less than a week later, when Malcolm spoke to the Militant Labor Forum in New York City for the first of three times, he made the same point. Malcolm said he was still a Muslim, "That just happens to be my personal religion.

---

53. "Interview by A.B. Spellman," in *By Any Means Necessary*, p. 26.

54. "The Ballot or the Bullet" (Cleveland, April 3, 1964), in *Malcolm X Speaks*, p. 51.

But in the capacity in which I am functioning today, I have no intention of mixing my religion with the problems of 22 million Black people in this country."[55]

And a few days after that, speaking to the Group on Advanced Leadership in Detroit, Malcolm said: "This afternoon, it's not our intention to talk religion. We're going to forget religion. If we bring up religion, we'll be in an argument. And the best way to keep away from arguments and differences, as I said earlier, is to put your religion at home, in the closet, keep it between you and your God." With several Christian pastors in the audience, Malcolm couldn't help himself, adding: "Because if it hasn't done anything more for you than it has, you need to forget it anyway."[56]

Almost each speech during those initial weeks after his break from the Nation seemed to mark another step. But it was only upon Malcolm's return from his first of two trips to Africa and the Middle East that year that he set out to build a political organization open to all African Americans, regardless of religion or other beliefs. In late June 1964 he called together a public meeting in Harlem to establish the Organization of Afro-American Unity (OAAU). "Up until now," Malcolm said, "these meetings have been sponsored and paid for by the Muslim Mosque, Inc. Beginning next Sunday, they will be sponsored and paid for by the Organization of Afro-American Unity."[57]

---

55. "Speech on 'Black Revolution'" (Militant Labor Forum, New York, April 8, 1964), in *Two Speeches by Malcolm X*, p. 7.

56. Excerpt from talk at meeting of Group on Advanced Leadership (April 12, 1964), in *By Any Means Necessary*, p. 215. The Group on Advanced Leadership was a Black nationalist organization in Detroit, founded in November 1961. Its most prominent leaders were Rev. Albert Cleage, Milton Henry, and Richard Henry.

57. "OAAU Founding Rally" (June 28, 1964), in *By Any Means Necessary*, p. 93.

So Malcolm's first step, in March 1964, had been to act decisively on his deeply held conviction that those—such as Elijah Muhammad—whose individual conduct flew in the face of their stated beliefs were not qualified to serve as a guide to either religion or to politics.

By June, however, Malcolm had taken another step: that religion itself cannot be a guide to effective modern political action. That religion and religious organizations need to be separated from political organization, so people can work together to build a revolutionary political organization—a form of practical activity that transcends religious beliefs or affiliations. "Because whether he was a Methodist or a Baptist or an atheist or an agnostic, [Blacks] caught the same hell,"[58] as Malcolm told a meeting at the Corn Hill Methodist Church in Rochester, New York, just five days before he was assassinated.

Meeting with a group of Mississippi youth visiting Harlem on New Year's Day 1965, Malcolm explained that he and others who had left the Nation of Islam had recognized "that there was a problem confronting our people in this country that had nothing to do with religion and went above and beyond religion. A religious organization couldn't attack that problem according to the magnitude of the problem, the complexity of the problem itself. So those in that group, after analyzing the problem, saw the need, or the necessity, of forming another group that had nothing to do with religion whatsoever. And that group is what's named and is today known as the Organization of Afro-American Unity."[59]

This was a crucial advance. Because while Malcolm to

---

58. "Not Just an American Problem, but a World Problem," in *February 1965: The Final Speeches*, p. 169.

59. "See for Yourself, Listen for Yourself, Think for Yourself," in *Malcolm X Talks to Young People*, p. 83.

our knowledge remained a Muslim, and thus committed to a revealed religion whose tenets are not testable, he also came to the conviction that such revelations are not, and cannot be, valid criteria for revolutionary politics. The criteria, goals, and methods of political activity must be open to objective discussion, debate, and testing in common by all those who come together in the fight, regardless of other views, beliefs, or affiliations of any kind, and he explicitly included nonbelievers. That's the only basis on which more and more people can be drawn into the struggle and discover—through practical political activity, in the course of battles—the most effective ways to combat and eliminate racism, oppression, and capitalist exploitation.

As I noted earlier, Malcolm didn't imitate the rhetoric of a preacher when he spoke. He never tried to get anybody to accept what he said on the basis of authority. He encouraged the Mississippi youth to learn how to "see for yourself and listen for yourself and think for yourself. Then you can come to an intelligent decision for yourself."[60] He always tried to increase the political confidence of those he was speaking to.

"I put it to you just as plain as I know how to put it," Malcolm told the young civil rights activists from Mississippi. "There's no interpretation necessary."[61]

There's no interpretation necessary.

That's a very important sentence. Malcolm was a straight shooter. He spoke clearly. Nobody had to "divine" what he was saying. His words could be misused. But they could not be misinterpreted due to ambiguity, let alone "irony" with its accompanying whiff of cynicism.

Malcolm had no dreams to offer. "I don't see any American

---

60. "See for Yourself," *Malcolm X Talks to Young People*, p. 78.

61. "See for Yourself," *Malcolm X Talks to Young People*, p. 113.

dream," he said in April 1964. "I see an American nightmare."[62] He sought to explain the source of that waking nightmare, which he increasingly recognized as the capitalist system of oppression and exploitation here and around the world. And he began organizing to open a discussion on a way forward to fight our way out of that nightmare.

Nor did Malcolm try to develop a "liberation theology," Islamic or otherwise. Because he concluded, based on years of firsthand experience, that such an effort could only narrow, weaken, and disorient a revolutionary movement. While there is no evidence that Malcolm had become an atheist during the last year of his political activity, he had become *a-theistic* in carrying out revolutionary politics and all civil, secular activity. He kept his religion—however it may have been evolving—"in the closet," as he put it.

I think we appreciate Malcolm's contribution in this regard more fully today than we did at the time. Speaking for myself, I was convinced—and I still am—that Malcolm would sooner or later have put religion behind him. But that's a different question, of course, and one that can never be settled. What's decisive is Malcolm's evolution, in word and deed, to advancing common political activity by revolutionists.

Black nationalism

What about Black nationalism? Malcolm's evolution here is easier to understand today than it was twenty-two years ago, because of what has been conquered in the U.S. working class since that time. Today we have a working class in this country that is different in significant ways from the one Malcolm knew. It is more reflective of the gains of the Black struggle of the 1950s and 1960s, both in composition and social and political attitudes. It is more international in

---

62. "The Ballot or the Bullet," in *Malcolm X Speaks*, p. 38.

makeup, bringing in experiences of struggles in other countries, a working class in which broader layers have been affected and inspired by advances of the world revolution.

When Malcolm began his final fifty weeks outside—and then beyond—the Nation, he considered himself a Black nationalist. That's unambiguous. Speaking of the launching of the Muslim Mosque, Inc., Malcolm said, "Our political philosophy will be black nationalism. Our economic and social philosophy will be black nationalism. Our cultural emphasis will be black nationalism."[63]

At the time, Malcolm was even still occasionally speaking of separation as the eventual goal. "We still believe in the Honorable Elijah Muhammad's solution as complete separation," he told interviewer A.B. Spellman a few days after announcing he had left the Nation. "The 22 million so-called Negroes should be separated completely from America and should be permitted to go back home to our African homeland. . . ."

Malcolm called that "a long-range program," one he admittedly had no idea how to achieve. Later in that very same interview, in fact, he told Spellman that, "A better word to use than separation is independence. This word separation is misused. . . . When you're independent of someone you can separate from them. If you can't separate from them it means you're not independent of them."[64]

So already, within days of leaving the Nation, Malcolm, in practice, was asserting the *right* of the oppressed Black nationality to determine their destiny independent of the dictates of their oppressors, up to and including separation, if that proved necessary. He was not presenting a plan to trans-

---

63. "A Declaration of Independence," in *Malcolm X Speaks*, p. 33.

64. "Interview by A.B. Spellman," in *By Any Means Necessary*, pp. 28, 31–32.

port Blacks to Africa, or to carve out a separate nation-state from territory in the U.S. South. The "political, economic, and social philosophy of black nationalism instills within [the Black man] the racial dignity and the incentive and the confidence that he needs to stand on his own feet and take a stand for himself," Malcolm told Spellman.

The "short-range program," Malcolm said, "is that we must eat while we're still here, we must have a place to sleep, we must have clothes to wear, we must have better jobs, we must have better education. . . . We must be in complete control of the politics of the so-called Negro community. . . ."[65]

That's what Malcolm meant by Black nationalism. That's where he stood at the time of his open break from the Nation.

By the last months of Malcolm's life, however, he had come to a different conclusion. During the January 19, 1965, Toronto television interview mentioned earlier, Pierre Berton asked Malcolm whether he still advocated a Black state in North America. "No," Malcolm replied, "I believe in a society in which people can live like human beings on the basis of equality."[66]

Malcolm had explained the reasons for his changing views on Black nationalism more fully the day before flying up to Toronto, during an interview for the *Young Socialist* magazine on January 18, 1965. "How do you define Black nationalism, with which you have been identified?" I asked Malcolm. And I didn't know beforehand what his answer was likely to be.

Malcolm said that when he had been in Ghana during the first of his trips to Africa in 1964, he had met with the Algerian ambassador there, "who is extremely militant and

65. "Interview by A.B. Spellman," in *By Any Means Necessary*, p. 28.

66. Excerpt from interview by Pierre Berton, in *Malcolm X Speaks*, pp. 218–19.

is a revolutionary in the true sense of the word (and has his credentials as such for having carried on a successful revolution against oppression in his country)." When they started talking about Black nationalism, Malcolm said, the ambassador responded, "Well, where did that leave him? Because he was white. He was an African, but he was Algerian, and to all appearances, he was a white man. And he said if I define my objective as the victory of Black nationalism, where does that leave him? Where does that leave revolutionaries in Morocco, Egypt, Iraq, Mauritania? So he showed me where I was alienating people who were true revolutionaries dedicated to overturning the system of exploitation that exists on this earth by any means necessary."

And that was the goal Malcolm now believed had to be fought for and achieved: "overturning the system of exploitation that exists on this earth by any means necessary." So, he told us, "I had to do a lot of thinking and reappraising of my definition of Black nationalism. Can we sum up the solution to the problems confronting our people as Black nationalism? And if you notice, I haven't been using the expression for several months."

You can find Malcolm's reply in *Malcolm X Talks to Young People*, which we brought out as a Young Socialist pamphlet in 1965 and have kept producing and distributing ever since.[67] It's on the sales table in the back of the room.

Malcolm made a similar point the very next day in the Toronto TV interview with Pierre Berton that I've referred

---

67. The pamphlet *Malcolm X Talks to Young People* (which has never gone out of print in almost half a century) has subsequently been expanded into a short book of the same name. The paragraphs from the 1965 *Young Socialist* interview quoted above appear on pages 47–48 of this book. A more extensive assessment of the shift in Malcolm's views on Black nationalism can be found in the article "Black Liberation and the Dictatorship of the Proletariat" in Part IV.

to before. Malcolm said he was convinced the world was heading toward "a political showdown, or even a showdown between the economic systems that exist on this earth." And due to the colonial powers' attitude "of superiority toward the darker-skinned people," he said, the divisions in the world often do "almost boil down along racial lines." But then Malcolm went on:

> I believe that there will ultimately be a clash between the oppressed and those that do the oppressing. I believe that there will be a clash between those who want freedom, justice, and equality for everyone and those who want to continue the systems of exploitation. I believe that there will be that kind of clash, but I don't think that it will be based upon the color of the skin, as Elijah Muhammad had taught it.[68]

Malcolm had also started thinking more and talking more about the ways that racism and national oppression are embedded in the very workings of the capitalist system. Speaking at a Militant Labor Forum in May 1964, right after returning from his first trip to Africa and the Middle East that year, Malcolm pointed to the example set by the Chinese and Cuban revolutions, where the capitalists and landlords had been expropriated. In contrast, he said, "The system in this country cannot produce freedom for an Afro-American. It is impossible for this system, this economic system, this political system, this social system, this system, period."

Malcolm returned to this point in the question period, when he was asked what political and social system he advocated. "I don't know," he replied. "But I'm flexible." And

---

68. Excerpt from interview by Pierre Berton, in *Malcolm X Speaks*, p. 238.

he repeated: "You can't have capitalism without racism."[69]

Malcolm didn't just say this because he was speaking to an audience he knew in its majority were socialists. He said similar things to his own organization, the OAAU. "You can't operate a capitalistic system unless you are vulturistic," he told an OAAU rally in Harlem in December 1964, after returning from his second trip to Africa that year. "You have to have someone else's blood to suck to be a capitalist. You show me a capitalist, I'll show you a bloodsucker."[70]

And in his last public talk, on February 18, three days prior to his assassination, Malcolm told an audience of 1,500 at Barnard College in New York City that "it is incorrect to classify the revolt of the Negro as simply a racial conflict of Black against white, or as a purely American problem." Rather, Malcolm said, "we are today seeing a global rebellion of the oppressed against the oppressor, the exploited against the exploiter."[71] That's the revolution that must be won.

This evolution is important, because Malcolm took Black nationalism dead seriously. He recognized that Blacks in the United States—descendants, in their great majority, of Black Africans kidnapped and brought in bondage to be sold into chattel slavery in the New World—had been forged as a nationality over the century following the Civil War, emancipation, and then the rise and defeat of Radical Reconstruction. In struggling against that oppression, Blacks had a right to national self-determination—all the way from their own forms of political organization, to control

---

69. "The Harlem 'Hate Gang' Scare" (Militant Labor Forum, New York, May 29, 1964), in *Malcolm X Speaks*, p. 84.

70. "At the Audubon" (New York, December 20, 1964), in *Malcolm X Speaks*, p. 139.

71. "A Global Rebellion of the Oppressed against the Oppressor" (February 18, 1965), in *February 1965: The Final Speeches*, pp. 183–85.

over schools and other institutions in their own neighborhoods, up to the establishment of an independent state on
the soil of this country, if they became convinced conditions
had reached the point that separation offered the only way
forward—*We've had enough!*

Malcolm, however, had come to understand that there's
a very important difference between recognizing the *right*
to a separate state—anyone who doesn't can't help but be an
apologist for American imperialism and its racist underpin-
nings—and *advocating* that course or *acting* on it. Because
if in order to open the road to ending Black oppression, it is
necessary to make a revolution to overturn the most powerful capitalist state on earth—as Malcolm was becoming
convinced it was—then first you have to think seriously
about the social forces and alliances necessary to accomplish
such a historic task.

Malcolm's decision to stop referring to his political course
as Black nationalism had nothing to do with a retreat from
encouraging Blacks to take pride in their own heritage and
history of struggle—to recognize their own worth as human beings, as the equals of all other human beings. It had
nothing to do with denying the historical culpability of the
ruling landowners and capitalists in the United States—
who were overwhelmingly Caucasian and largely remain so
today—for chattel slavery, national oppression, and exploitation. It had nothing to do with stepping back from intransigently combating the anti-Black racism that is promoted
by the propertied rulers and permeates all social classes
and institutions in this country, including the labor movement. Changing his views on any of that would have been
unthinkable for Malcolm. It *was* unthinkable.

But what *was* new, what Malcolm *did* change—and he
did so openly and frankly—was his recognition that to
eliminate racism in the United States and worldwide, you
must overthrow the international social system that, in

order to survive and expand, produces and reproduces that exploitation and oppression every minute of every day of every year. Malcolm came to understand that *this task* could not be accomplished without a movement reaching well beyond the United States and well beyond peoples of African origin—without a struggle involving all those with nothing to lose but their chains, all those organizing for revolutionary change, whatever their skin color or national origin.

A world perspective

The evolution of the class struggle over the past quarter century continues to confirm this internationalist revolutionary perspective, which members of the Socialist Workers Party and Young Socialist Alliance shared with Malcolm. It continues to confirm that Malcolm's political ideas and example were not simply valuable for their time, but offer a guide for revolutionists today and tomorrow. That's ultimately the only test by which anyone can judge revolutionary leadership—a *political* test. It is the measure of Malcolm's true stature as an international proletarian leader.

Malcolm's revolutionary convictions have been validated in many ways, but let's start with one in our own hemisphere. Let's start with the Grenada Revolution of March 13, 1979.[72] That's when the workers and farmers of that small Caribbean island, under the leadership of the Maurice Bishop–led New Jewel Movement, overturned the U.S.-

---

72. For an account of the accomplishments of the Grenada Revolution—and its overthrow in October 1983 by a Stalinist faction led by Bernard Coard, opening the way to an invasion by Washington a week later—see "The Second Assassination of Maurice Bishop" by Steve Clark in *New International* no. 6 and *Maurice Bishop Speaks: The Grenada Revolution and Its Overthrow, 1979–83* (Pathfinder, 1983).

backed dictatorship of Eric Gairy. They brought to power a workers and farmers government that organized and led them in throwing off the boot of U.S. and British imperialist domination and beginning to transform the social relations that for so long had perpetuated capitalist exploitation and oppression. In short, Grenada's toilers were led to begin discovering their own worth, and were *organized to act* on that knowledge.

Maurice Bishop was part of the generation of revolutionists, both biologically and politically, that came right after Malcolm. As I noted earlier, Malcolm has many heirs and will have millions more, including right here in the United States and other imperialist countries. But it's useful to point to one who helped lead workers and farmers to power— because the revolutionary class struggle for political power was the direction in which Malcolm was heading during the last year of his life, and the single most important goal around which Malcolm and other committed revolutionaries converged.

Maurice Bishop came to politics under the impact of the "Black Power" movement in the Caribbean, which was itself deeply influenced by Malcolm and the Black struggle in the United States. Bishop, as a young man in college in the United Kingdom, had read and studied Malcolm. (A prime example of Malcolm's notion that if you print the truth, it gets around.)

Two years before the Grenada Revolution, in a 1977 interview with the Cuban weekly *Bohemia*, Bishop said that the political impetus in founding the New Jewel Movement had come from "the ideas of 'Black Power' that developed in the United States and the freedom struggle of the African people in such places as Angola, Mozambique, and Guinea-Bissau." And he added that it was the Cuban Revolution that led the NJM "to develop along Marxist lines," and to recognize, "on the practical level of day-to-day political struggle, the relevance of socialism as the only solution to our problems."[73]

It was through emulating the revolutionary march to state power in Cuba that Maurice Bishop became the working-class leader, the communist leader that he was. And in the process, he too—as Malcolm had, years earlier—came to grips with the limitations of nationalism as a guide to revolutionary political action. Bishop indicated his views in an interview he gave a little more than a year after the New Jewel Movement took power in Grenada—a July 1980 interview conducted by leaders of our movement and run in full in the *Militant* in September 1980. Bishop reminded our readers that due to a common history of slavery, "There is a very close sense of cultural identity, which the people of Grenada automatically feel for American Blacks and which we have no doubt is reciprocated by the American Black community." Revolutionists in Grenada, Bishop said, "feel a particularly close affinity to American Blacks and other oppressed minorities, to the working-class movement in America." And he concluded the interview— "without intending to be disrespectful," he said—by calling on working people in the United States, whatever their skin color, to "get together and wage a consistent fight against the real enemy. Don't spend time fighting each other. . . ."[74]

Does the fact that the Grenada revolution was betrayed by a petty-bourgeois Stalinist clique around Bernard Coard— serving up the island nation to U.S. imperialism "on a silver platter," in Fidel Castro's words—diminish in any way the significance of Bishop's example? The answer is no. We helped working people in this country, in Grenada, across

---

73. Maurice Bishop, "The Struggle for Democracy and against Imperialism in Grenada," in *Maurice Bishop Speaks*, pp. 81–90 [2009 printing].

74. Bishop, "The Class Struggle in Grenada, the Caribbean, and the USA," in *Maurice Bishop Speaks*, pp. 209–11. The interview was run in the September 5, 1980, issue of the *Militant*.

the Caribbean, and around the world to draw the lessons from that counterrevolutionary coup.[75]

Cuba's revolutionary example

What about the Cuban Revolution? Some of us know of the welcome Malcolm gave to Cuban prime minister Fidel Castro when Fidel came to New York in September 1960 to speak for the first time before the United Nations General Assembly. After numerous mid-Manhattan hotels often used by UN delegations either refused accommodations to the Cuban delegation, or sought to impose a degrading and costly "damage deposit" on them, Castro and his comrades moved uptown to Harlem and registered at the Hotel Theresa.

Malcolm X had helped arrange the move and organized a defense guard for the delegation at the Theresa. Thousands of Harlem residents and supporters of revolutionary Cuba from around New York gathered outside the hotel for days to celebrate this act of solidarity by a visiting head of state. "Premier Castro has come out against lynching, which is more than [U.S.] President Eisenhower has done," Malcolm told the New York press after meeting with the Cuban leader in his room. "Castro has also taken a more open stand for civil rights for Black Cubans."[76]

Malcolm's welcome to the Cuban delegation in 1960 was genuine, but he was then still a prominent minister of the

---

75. In addition to "The Second Assassination of Maurice Bishop" in *New International* no. 6, see also the November 14, 1983, speech by Fidel Castro and related statements by the Cuban government in *Maurice Bishop Speaks*.

76. An account of the meeting between Malcolm X and Fidel Castro, based on press reports at the time, can be found in "Fidel Castro's Arrival in Harlem," in Fidel Castro and Ernesto Che Guevara, *To Speak the Truth: Why Washington's 'Cold War' against Cuba Doesn't End* (Pathfinder, 1992), pp. 209–14 [2007 printing].

Nation of Islam and would not have made this very public move without Elijah Muhammad's agreement. The Nation had a stance of support for national liberation struggles in the colonial world and gave generally positive coverage in its press to the revolution in Cuba.

Over the next few years, however, as Malcolm increasingly strained against the Nation's rejection of militant political action, he was drawn more and more openly to the example of Cuba's ongoing *revolutionary* course. "The Cuban Revolution—that's a revolution," he told an audience predominantly of African Americans in November 1963, the month during which he was later silenced by Elijah Muhammad. "They overturned the system. Revolution is in Asia, revolution is in Africa, and the white man is screaming because he sees revolution in Latin America. How do you think he'll react to you when you learn what a real revolution is?"[77]

Malcolm's attraction to revolutionary Cuba continued to grow following his break with the Nation. In his speeches and interviews, he often pointed to the Cuban Revolution, along with those in China and Algeria, as an example of what needed to be done in the United States.

In December 1964, when Cuban leader Ernesto Che Guevara came to New York to address the UN, Malcolm invited him to come to the Audubon Ballroom to speak to a meeting of the OAAU. Che initially accepted the invitation but later concluded, as he wrote in a message that Malcolm read to the audience, that security "conditions are not good for [my participation in] this meeting." And Che added: "Receive the warm salutations of the Cuban people and especially those of Fidel, who remembers enthusiastically his visit to Harlem a few years ago. United we will win."

"I love a revolutionary," Malcolm told the audience at the

---

77. "Message to the Grassroots," in *Malcolm X Speaks*, p. 21.

Audubon that night, as he prepared to read Che's note. "And one of the most revolutionary men in this country right now was going to come out here . . . but he thought better of it." Malcolm cautioned participants never to let anyone choose their friends for them. "I don't," Malcolm said. "And you shouldn't. . . . You and I should practice the habit of weighing people and weighing situations and weighing groups and weighing governments for ourselves."

Then Malcolm read the message from Che, which was met with enthusiastic applause by the crowd. Malcolm said he was glad to hear the clapping "because it lets the man know that he's just not in a position today to tell us who we should applaud for and who we shouldn't applaud for."[78]

Congo, Angola, and Cuba's internationalism

Che had spoken before the United Nations two days earlier. In that speech he had championed one of the anti-imperialist struggles Malcolm felt very deeply about: the liberation struggle in the Congo. In June 1960, after nearly a century of incredibly bloody and exploitative Belgian rule, the Congolese people had won their independence and established a government led by Prime Minister Patrice Lumumba, the central leader of the freedom struggle.

Washington and Brussels immediately organized to destroy the Lumumba government and replace it with a regime they were confident would protect imperialism's vast copper and other mineral holdings. Under United Nations cover, they engineered a coup against Lumumba in September 1960 and his brutal murder in January 1961. Over the next few years the U.S. and Belgian governments aided the new Congolese regime in combating anti-imperialist rebel forces organized by Lumumba supporters. From August

---

78. "At the Audubon" (New York, December 13, 1964), in *Malcolm X Speaks*, pp. 118–19.

1964 planes requisitioned by the CIA, sometimes refueling at a British base off the coast of Africa, bombed what they called "rebel-held villages" and ferried Belgian troops and mercenaries into the country, resulting in the massacre of thousands of Congolese people. Most of the all-white mercenaries were recruited from South Africa and the British colonial settler state of Rhodesia (now Zimbabwe), with an admixture from the United States, various countries in Europe, and some counterrevolutionary Cuban exiles.

Those murderous attacks reached a crescendo in November 1964, just prior to Che's speech at the UN. Che pointed out to the General Assembly—and above all, from that podium, to the working people of the world—that Washington and other imperialist powers had "used the name of the United Nations to commit the murder of Lumumba" and of thousands of Congolese villagers. "All free men of the world must be prepared to avenge the crime of the Congo," he said.[79]

Che and the entire Cuban leadership intended *to act* on that call. It wasn't a bluff—they *never* bluff. In fact, Che left straight from New York in mid-December for a three-month tour of Africa, during which he met with leaders of the Lumumba forces, of governments on the continent who supported the Congolese anti-imperialist rebels, and of national liberation movements in Angola and other countries then still under the boot of Portuguese colonial rule.

Che's first stop was Algeria, where he discussed the Congolese and other fronts of the international revolutionary struggle with Ahmed Ben Bella, president of the workers and farmers government that had come to power in 1962 through a revolutionary war that defeated the French colonial power. Che visited Congo Brazzaville as well—which had also re-

---

79. Ernesto Che Guevara, "Cuba's Example Shows that the Peoples of the World Can Liberate Themselves" (December 11, 1964), in *To Speak the Truth*, pp. 134–36.

cently won its independence from France, and bordered the former Belgian colony—as well as Tanzania, Guinea-Conakry, Ghana, and several other African countries.

By mid-1965 the imperialist press was chattering about Che's "disappearance," spreading their standard lie (and wish) that there had been a split in the revolutionary leadership in Cuba and that Che had been jailed or even executed. Alas, their hope was not to be realized. In fact, between April and December 1965 Che was in the Congo, leading a column of Cuban internationalist volunteers who helped arm and train the pro-Lumumba forces. After a brief return to Cuba for additional training and preparations, Che in late 1966 left for Bolivia, where he was killed in combat the following October fighting alongside Bolivian, Cuban, and other Latin American combatants to overthrow the U.S.-backed dictatorship there.

Given what Malcolm had come to know and politically admire about Fidel Castro, Che Guevara, and the Cuban Revolution, none of this would have come as a surprise to him if he had lived to see it. Nor would Malcolm have been surprised that a decade later Cuba—in response to an appeal by the newly independent Angolan government—sent 36,000 internationalist volunteers beginning in November 1975 to assist the Angolans in turning back an invasion by South Africa's apartheid regime. Pretoria was aiming to reverse the hard-fought independence Angola had won from Portugal. The internationalist combatants made the 7,000-mile trip from Cuba to Angola in rickety passenger planes—turboprops that had been retired from air fleets worldwide and were no longer even made by their British manufacturer—as well as on Cuba's only two oceangoing passenger ships and converted cargo vessels.

Only by looking at what has happened in South Africa in recent years—from the more-than-10,000-strong Soweto uprising in 1976, to the ensuing spread and deepening of the African National Congress–led struggle to bring down that racist horror—can we fully appreciate what Cuba's combat volunteers have accomplished, fighting alongside the Angolans and Namibians, by pushing back the army of apartheid. The South African regime, with Washington's encouragement, continues to this day to launch invasions into the country and to arm pro-imperialist Angolan groups such as UNITA. But what a blow would have been dealt to working people throughout Africa and the world if Pretoria's army had overrun Angola just days before it was to celebrate its freedom from Portugal in 1975!

The Cuban government has pledged that those volunteers will remain as long as the Angolan people ask for and need them—until the final and definitive defeat of South Africa's invading forces. What a day that will be in South Africa too! Then Cuba's internationalist combatants will happily return home.[80]

---

80. In late 1987, just a few months after this speech was given, what turned out to be the final major battle of the more-than-decade-long war began taking shape in southern Angola, around the hamlet of Cuito Cuanavale. By the end of March 1988, the combined force of Angolan troops, Cuban volunteers, and fighters from the South-West African People's Organisation of Namibia (SWAPO) had decisively defeated the South African invaders.

Under the impact of the victory at Cuito Cuanavale, the white supremacist regime withdrew its forces from Angola and entered talks with the Cuban and Angolan governments that ended with Pretoria having to recognize the independence of its colony, Namibia. Between the initial battles in late 1975 and the departure of the final Cuban troops in May 1991, 375,000 internationalist volunteers had served in Angola and 2,000 had been killed.

By early 1990, less than two years after Cuito Cuanavale, rising struggles by working people in South Africa forced Pretoria to lift the ban on the African National Congress and release ANC leader Nelson Mandela after almost twenty-eight years of imprisonment. The apartheid regime crumbled in face of rising mass protests over the next few years, and in 1994 Mandela was elected president in the first elections ever conducted there on the basis of universal suffrage.

It's worth noting that Nelson Mandela, Oliver Tambo, and other ANC leaders, similar in some ways to Malcolm's development, went through struggles that led them to shift away from Black nationalism as their political axis. During the 1940s, as leaders of the ANC Youth League, Mandela and others had initially raised the banner of what they called "African nationalism" as a means of pressing militant action on the conservatized leadership of the ANC at that time. But they were transformed politically by their own experiences in the early and mid-1950s mobilizing thousands of Africans, so-called Coloreds, Indians, and whites alike against the "pass laws"—the degrading internal passports all black Africans were compelled to carry with them at all times—as well as other targets of the ANC-led Defiance Campaign.

Drawing on the conquests of those battles, the ANC threw open first its ranks, and later its leading bodies, to all those who had proved themselves in struggle against the racist apartheid system. It was drawing on those hard-fought lessons that the ANC declared in its 1955 Freedom Charter "that South Africa belongs to all who live in it, black and white" and that only a state organized on that basis "can secure to all their birthright without distinction of colour, race, sex, or belief."

In July 1991 Mandela visited Cuba and spoke along with Fidel Castro to tens of thousands of Cubans and international guests. "The Cuban internationalists have made a contribution to African independence, freedom, and justice, unparalleled for its principled and selfless character," Mandela said. ". . . Cuito Cuanavale was a milestone in the history of the struggle for southern African liberation! Cuito Cuanavale has been a turning point in the struggle to free the continent and our country from the scourge of apartheid!" Mandela's speech can be found in *How Far We Slaves Have Come! South Africa and Cuba in Today's World* (Pathfinder, 1991), pp. 17–28 [2006 printing]; and is excerpted in *Our History Is Still Being Written: The Story of Three Chinese-Cuban Generals in the Cuban Revolution* (Pathfinder, 2005), pp. 179–82.

The African National Congress "is not a communist organization, and it does not strive to become one," we wrote in the magazine *New International* nearly two years ago. But it is only through "the revolutionary struggle that is being led by the ANC [that] a growing South African communist vanguard will be forged and tested." Where else could proletarian leadership in South Africa come from?[81]

'Renewal or death'

The volunteer mission in Angola is having a political impact inside Cuba, as well. That could be seen last year at the Third Congress of the Communist Party of Cuba, where Fidel Castro—in his speech to delegates introducing the newly elected Central Committee—explained that the party had underestimated the legacy of anti-black racism in Cuba, and then outlined further political steps to advance the fight to get rid of the vestiges of racial prejudice and inequality.

Fidel pointed out that blacks in Cuba—those who had been "taken from Africa and enslaved to perform work whites didn't dare do in this torrid, tropical climate"[82]—had supported the revolution, *overwhelmingly*. The abolition of slavery in Cuba in the latter half of the nineteenth century had been completely intertwined with the struggle against Spanish colonial rule, with blacks serving at all levels in the Cuban Liberation Army (right up to General Antonio Maceo). Nonetheless, under the nominally independent, U.S.-dominated "pseudo republic," as it was popularly known in Cuba, blacks had continued to be targets of discrimina-

81. Jack Barnes, "The Coming Revolution in South Africa," in *New International* no. 5, p. 63 [2009 printing].

82. Fidel Castro, "Renewal or Death," in *New International* no. 6, p. 395 [2007 printing].

tion, and sometimes outright terror, "because of the color of their skin."[83]

In stark contrast, the new revolutionary government, starting in January 1959, actively combated racist discrimination. It did so not only through decrees and legislation, but above all through speedy and vigorous enforcement by militias in any store, on any beach, at any social event, at any job interview, or anywhere else blacks or mestizos were denied equal treatment or access. Any and all distinctions based on race were "erased in our constitution and rightly so," Fidel said.[84]

That the government and party in Cuba sought to be color blind in how they functioned, however, was not enough by itself to overcome the historic legacy of chattel slavery and racist discrimination, Fidel said. That's what experience over more than a quarter century in revolutionary Cuba had shown. "We can't leave it to chance to correct historical injustices," Fidel told the congress delegates. "To really establish total equality takes more than simply declaring it in law. It has to be promoted in the mass organizations, in the youth organization, in the party. . . . [W]e can't leave the promotion of women, blacks, and mestizos to chance. It has to be the work of the party; we have to straighten out what history has twisted."[85]

And world capitalism, for centuries, has twisted everything in its path, including racial differences.

The revolutionary government and party had never asked anyone about their race "and rightly so," Fidel said. And he pointed to several prominent party leaders who, despite outward appearances, had a black or Chinese grandparent.

---

83. Fidel Castro, "Renewal or Death," p. 397.

84. Fidel Castro, "Renewal or Death," p. 401.

85. Fidel Castro, "Renewal or Death," pp. 397–98.

"Why go around asking such questions? In the past it was to discriminate, today it's for the opposite reason—so we ask."[86]

"At issue here is simply the color of skin," Fidel said. In Cuba, he added, "we are all the product of a mixture of races." Ask the imperialists "if this mixture has been easy to dissolve, divide, or crush. They haven't been able to do it." And for exactly that reason, Fidel said, the new Central Committee elected by the congress included—in addition to more workers, "and not just workers who have become leaders but workers from the factory floor"—"a strong injection of women, a strong injection of blacks and of mestizos."[87]

This political advance for the revolution in Cuba is a by-product, at least in part, of the impact of the internationalist operation in Angola. It's an affirmation of what Malcolm was fighting for, and of his confidence in the Cuban Revolution and its leadership. And it's a verification—for communist workers in the United States and other imperialist countries—of our strategic commitment to affirmative action not as a question of moral witness or sacrifice, but in order *to unite* the working class as a whole to fight more effectively against our common exploiters and oppressors, the capitalist class.

Continuity of communism

Like these relatively recent examples, the development and legacy of Malcolm X during the last year of his life are woven into the strands of proletarian political continuity opened, in our century, by the victory of the Bolshevik-led October 1917 revolution in Russia and by the first four congresses of the Communist International under the leader-

---

86. Fidel Castro, "Renewal or Death," pp. 401–2.

87. Fidel Castro, "Renewal or Death," pp. 390–91.

ship of V.I. Lenin. Reporting in 1920 to the opening session of the Second Congress of the Comintern, as it was called, Lenin celebrated the unprecedented composition of the gathering, saying it truly "merits the title of a world congress." At this congress, he said, "we see taking place a union between revolutionary proletarians of the capitalist, advanced countries, and the revolutionary masses of those countries where there is no or hardly any proletariat."

"World imperialism shall fall," Lenin added, "when the revolutionary onslaught of the exploited and oppressed workers in each country, overcoming resistance from petty-bourgeois elements and the influence of the small upper crust of labor aristocrats, merges with the revolutionary onslaught of hundreds of millions of people who have hitherto stood beyond the pale of history and have been regarded merely as the objects of history."[88]

The political reverberations of the Bolshevik revolution unleashed national liberation struggles over the subsequent half century through which the toilers transformed themselves into the *subjects of history* throughout growing portions of the colonial world. They are demonstrating that the leadership of the revolutionary workers movement is not and will not be overwhelmingly European or North American, but will reflect the composition of working people the world over.

During the past half century, the working class and industrial proletariat have grown explosively in many countries of the semicolonial world. Moreover, as we're seeing in Burkina Faso today,[89] leaders of exceptional political caliber can and

---

88. *Workers of the World and Oppressed Peoples, Unite!* (Pathfinder, 1991), vol. 1, p. 144 [2004 printing]. Also in V.I. Lenin, *Collected Works*, vol. 31, p. 232.

89. In 1983 the peasants and workers of Burkina Faso (formerly a French colony called Upper Volta), under the leadership of Thomas Sankara,

do emerge from countries, as Lenin said, "where there is no or hardly any proletariat"—and toilers from these countries still number in the hundreds of millions.

Malcolm X—speaking and acting from within the earth's strongest and wealthiest imperialist power, and from an oppressed nationality heavily working class in composition—was representative of this internationalization of proletarian leadership. It is not artificial to speak of Malcolm in the same breath as of V.I. Lenin, of Leon Trotsky, of Fidel Castro and Che Guevara, of Maurice Bishop, of Thomas Sankara, of leaders of the communist movement in the United States such as James P. Cannon and Farrell Dobbs. To do so registers something real. Not because we *want* it to, but because that's what the course of the world class struggle has *shown*. Other revolutionary leaders, from Nicaragua to South Africa, are being put to the same test—and many more will be, all over the world.

Malcolm correctly insisted that the struggle for Black freedom in the United States is part of an international struggle, a struggle for human rights not just civil rights. He refused to look at America through American eyes, or to look at the world through American eyes. He took his stand from within the oppressed and exploited in the battle for liberation the world over. That was his starting point. And that's the beginning of wisdom for any revolutionary today.

Malcolm rejected any notion that the oppressed could rely on some common humanity shared with the oppressors, or with a "well-meaning" section of the oppressors. There is no latent supply of love in the "soul" of all human beings,

---

established a popular revolutionary government and began to combat the causes of hunger, illiteracy, and economic backwardness. That government was overthrown in October 1987, and Sankara was murdered. See *Thomas Sankara Speaks: The Burkina Faso Revolution (1983–87)* (Pathfinder, 1988, 2007).

regardless of class, that can be tapped if they're shamed or pressured—or lobbied or voted for. There is no abstract, classless "humanity"; there is only human solidarity conquered in struggle as a social product of class solidarity, of solidarity in political action among the exploited and oppressed worldwide. The job of revolutionists is not to act "responsibly," which in class-divided society can only mean "responsibly" toward the rulers, or at least the bourgeois liberals and bourgeois socialists among them. What revolutionists are responsible for is to advance along the line of march toward power of the toilers, who compose the great majority of humanity.

Don't "run around . . . trying to make friends with somebody who's depriving you of your rights," Malcolm urged the Mississippi youth I mentioned earlier. "They're not your friends. No, they're your enemies. Treat them like that and fight them, and you'll get your freedom."[90]

That's why Malcolm was an intransigent opponent of the Democratic and Republican parties, an opponent of the two-party system (with its occasional third-party eruptions to blow off steam) that has tied working people to capitalist politics since well before the rise of U.S. imperialism at the close of the nineteenth century. During Malcolm's final year, the 1964 U.S. elections were in full swing, with the incumbent president, Democrat Lyndon Baines Johnson, being challenged by Republican Barry Goldwater. With the exception of the Socialist Workers Party—and Malcolm X—virtually every political current in U.S. politics claiming to speak and act on behalf of working people and the oppressed were going all out to defeat Goldwater. This was necessary to advance the fight for "peace" in Vietnam, they claimed. Some even warned of the triumph of "fascism" if Goldwa-

---

90. "See for Yourself," in *Malcolm X Talks to Young People*, p. 108.

ter were elected. The Communist Party USA was leading the pack. Of course, as we now know, the "peace candidate" Johnson, who was elected in November, went on to escalate the Vietnam War, raising U.S. troop levels *more than thirty-fold* from some 16,000 to 537,000 by the end of his term in January 1969 and initiating a murderous and sustained campaign of bombing and chemical warfare.

In July 1964, while in Africa, Malcolm learned that following a civil rights "summit meeting" in New York City, Martin Luther King and leaders of other organizations had called for a halt to demonstrations for Black freedom until after the November elections. In a statement reported in the *New York Daily News* and elsewhere, Malcolm commented that they had "sold themselves out and become campaign managers in the Negro community for Lyndon B. Johnson."[91] Exactly.

Commenting a few months later on Johnson's re-election, Malcolm told a November 1964 meeting in Paris on his return trip from Africa that the U.S. capitalists "knew that the only way people would run toward the fox would be if you showed them a wolf. . . . [They] had the whole world—including people who call themselves Marxists" (a reference to the CPUSA) "—hoping that Johnson would beat Goldwater." Malcolm continued: "Those who claim to be enemies of the system were on their hands and knees waiting for Johnson to get elected—because he is supposed to be a man of peace. And *at that moment* he had troops invading the Congo and South Vietnam!"[92]

And in early 1965, when the Johnson administration began floating trial balloons about appointing a Black to his cabi-

91. *New York Daily News*, July 31, 1964.

92. Answer to question at Paris meeting (November 23, 1964), in *Malcolm X Speaks*, p. 223.

net, Malcolm told the audience at a Militant Labor Forum in New York City, "Yes they have a new gimmick every year. They're going to take one of their boys, black boys, and put him in the cabinet, so he can walk around Washington with a cigar—fire on one end and fool on the other."[93]

A 'Malcolm-Martin' convergence?

As I noted at the opening of this talk, it is simply untrue to talk about a political convergence between Malcolm X and Martin Luther King. King was a courageous individual who helped lead powerful mobilizations for Black rights, from the time of the Montgomery bus boycott in 1955 right up until his assassination in 1968.

(By the way, the *central* organizer of the bus boycott was not Martin Luther King but a savvy trade union militant named E.D. Nixon, a longtime leader of the Brotherhood of Sleeping Car Porters and of the NAACP in Montgomery. Nixon *did* believe in being prepared for self-defense and acted prudently on his beliefs; young workers and veterans were at the center of his efforts. In 1965 the organizers of a tenth anniversary event in Montgomery did not even invite Nixon to participate and speak. In December of that year, however, the Militant Labor Forum in New York organized a dinner and program to honor him and Arlette Nixon, his wife. The event was addressed by E.D. Nixon and by party leaders Farrell Dobbs, Fred Halstead, and Clifton DeBerry. Oh, if Malcolm had still been alive to take part, what a meeting! But that's another story.)

Martin Luther King's individual courage is not the question. We're talking about two clashing *class* outlooks, two

---

93. "Prospects for Freedom in 1965" (Militant Labor Forum, New York, January 7, 1965), in *Malcolm X Speaks*, pp. 170–71. The following year Johnson did appoint the first African American cabinet member, Robert Weaver, as secretary of housing and urban development.

irreconcilable political courses.

One of the pieces of "evidence" displayed time and again to support the "Malcolm-Martin" myth is a photograph of the two of them together, smiling, after running into each other by happenstance at the United States Capitol building in Washington, D.C., in March 1964—just two weeks after Malcolm announced his break with the Nation of Islam. But there was no political content whatsoever to that chance meeting. As King himself later said in an interview with Alex Haley, "I met Malcolm X once in Washington, but circumstances didn't enable me to talk with him for more than a minute." And King went on in that same January 1965 interview to condemn what he called Malcolm's "fiery, demagogic oratory," charging that "in his litany of articulating the despair of the Negro without offering any positive, creative alternative, I feel that Malcolm has done himself and our people a great disservice."[94]

That was Martin Luther King's political assessment of the person who was arguably America's greatest single mass revolutionary leader of the middle of the twentieth century.

The actual political relations between Malcolm X and Martin Luther King were demonstrated a few months after their unplanned encounter, when King traveled to St. Augustine, Florida, in June 1964. King went there to support activists who had been repeatedly beaten by the Ku Klux Klan and arrested by cops for organizing lunch counter sit-ins and other civil rights protests. The Democratic administration of Lyndon Johnson had contemptuously spurned King's call for federal troops to protect the demonstrators and enforce their rights.

On behalf of the newly launched Organization of Afro-American Unity, Malcolm sent a telegram to King at the time

---

94. Interview with Martin Luther King, *Playboy*, January 1965.

Above, Martin Luther King and Malcolm X met only once, for a few brief moments, in halls of U.S. Capitol, where both were observing Dixiecrat filibuster of the Civil Rights Act, March 26, 1964.

"Malcolm respected and appreciated anyone who devoted their life to the fight against racism and for Black equality," says Barnes. "He was ready for united action to advance common demands. But it's simply false that Malcolm during his last year was converging politically with Martin Luther King—with King's bourgeois pacifism, his social-democratic ideas, his commitment to the reformability of capitalism, his support for the imperialist Democratic Party and various of its politicians."

saying, "If the federal Government will not send troops to your aid, just say the word and we will immediately dispatch some of our brothers there to organize self-defense units among our people and the Ku Klux Klan will then receive a taste of its own medicine. The day of turning the other cheek to those brute beasts is over."[95]

King flatly rejected Malcolm's offer, calling it a "grave error" and "an immoral approach."

Nor did that political chasm narrow over subsequent months. In early February 1965, Malcolm spoke to a group of three hundred young people at a local church in Selma, Alabama. Since the beginning of 1965, King's organization, the Southern Christian Leadership Conference (SCLC), had been leading voting rights demonstrations in and around Selma, in the course of which protesters had been subjected to cop brutality and some 3,400 had been arrested. After Malcolm had addressed a meeting of several thousand on February 3 at nearby Tuskegee Institute in Alabama, students there insisted that he go with them to Selma the next day, and Malcolm agreed. King was being held in jail in Selma at the time.

When he spoke to the young people in Selma, Malcolm again condemned the Johnson administration for its refusal to deploy federal troops to protect Blacks fighting for their rights. Malcolm said he was "100 percent for the effort being put forth by the Black folks here" and believed "they have an absolute right to use whatever means are necessary to gain the vote." But he added that he didn't believe in practicing nonviolence in face of violence by organized racist forces. He concluded: "I pray that you will grow intellectually, so that you can understand the problems of the world and where you fit into, in that world picture"—once

95. A photocopy of Malcolm's actual telegram can be found online at www.brothermalcolm.net/mxwords/letters/telegramtomartin.gif.

again the internationalist starting point, "broadening your scope," that Malcolm was always working to promote. And then he continued:

"And I pray that all the fear that has ever been in your heart will be taken out, and when you look at that man, if you know he's nothing but a coward, you won't fear him. If he wasn't a coward, he wouldn't gang up on you. . . . They put on a sheet so you won't know who they are—that's a coward. No! The time will come when that sheet will be ripped off. If the federal government doesn't take it off, we'll take it off."[96]

What Malcolm had to say about the struggles in St. Augustine, Selma, and elsewhere reminds me of Che Guevara's answer, during his visit to New York in December 1964, in reply to a question about how he saw the Black rights struggle in the United States. "It seems that racial violence is rampant in some U.S. states," Che replied. "In face of that, different responses are possible. You can crouch a little more to see if the blow hurts less. You can protest vigorously and then receive more blows. Or you can answer blow for blow. But that's easy to say; it's very difficult to do. And you must prepare in order to do that."[97]

The young people in Selma met Malcolm's talk with uproarious applause. But that wasn't the response of SCLC leaders. Malcolm described *their* reaction in a speech to a February 15 meeting of the OAAU at the Audubon Ballroom

---

96. Portions of Malcolm's speech in Selma that have been transcribed from surviving tapes can be found in "The House Negro and the Field Negro" (February 4, 1965), in *February 1965: The Final Speeches*, pp. 26–28.

97. From the transcript of a December 16, 1964, discussion with U.S. supporters of the Cuban Revolution broadcast on New York radio station WBAI. Cited by Mary-Alice Waters in *Che Guevara and the Imperialist Reality* (Pathfinder, 1998), pp. 20–21 [2007 printing].

in Harlem, less than a week before he was gunned down in that same hall.

"King's man didn't want me to talk to [the youth]," Malcolm said. Malcolm was referring in particular to the current Democratic Party mayor of this very city, Andrew Young—a former U.S. congressman from here, and also U.S. ambassador to the United Nations during the Carter administration. In Selma that day, Young had schemed unsuccessfully with Coretta Scott King to stop Malcolm from being given a microphone.

"They told me they didn't mind me coming in and all of that," Malcolm told the OAAU meeting—but they didn't want him to talk, because "they knew what I was going to say." The young people, both from Selma and from Tuskegee, however, "insisted that I be heard. . . . This is the only way I got a chance to talk to them."[98]

You don't have to take Malcolm's word for it. King, who was in jail when Malcolm was in Selma, said, shortly after the assassination: "I couldn't block his coming, but my philosophy was so antithetical to the philosophy of Malcolm X—so diametrically opposed, that I would never have invited Malcolm X to come to Selma when we were in the midst of a nonviolent demonstration, and this says nothing about the personal respect I had for him. I disagreed with his philosophy and his methods."[99]

And in a column for the Harlem-based weekly *Amsterdam News*, written a few weeks after Malcolm's assassination, King wrote that when his wife Coretta had spoken with Malcolm in Selma, Malcolm had "expressed an interest in working more

98. "There's a Worldwide Revolution Going On" (New York, February 15, 1965), in *February 1965: The Final Speeches*, p. 142.

99. King's testimony in *Williams v. Wallace*, a class-action lawsuit filed against then Alabama governor George Wallace during the Selma protests.

I want to make the case that Malcolm X was a revolutionary leader of the working class in the United States.

JACK BARNES, MARCH 1987

Malcolm X speaks to 300 determined youth, February 4, 1965, in Selma, Alabama, where voting rights militants faced brutal cop attacks and racist violence. At young protesters' insistence, Martin Luther King's associates grudgingly let Malcolm speak. "Broaden your scope," he encouraged the youth. Seek to "understand the problems of the world and where you fit into" it. Pointing to cowardice of racists, as shown by sheets they often wore, Malcolm told youth: "The time will come when that sheet will be ripped off. If the federal government doesn't take it off, we'll take it off."

The struggle for Black freedom in the United States is part of an international struggle, Malcolm insisted, a struggle for human rights, not just civil rights. His starting point was from within the oppressed and exploited the world over.

JACK BARNES, MARCH 1987

"The Afro-American," said Malcolm X, "is that large number of people from the southernmost tip of South America to the northernmost tip of North America with a common heritage and common origin." **Top,** some 10,000 march to Caroni, Trinidad, in March 1970 calling for united action by those of African and Indian descent. Action was part of mass "Black Power" mobilizations across Caribbean.

"There is no better example of criminal activity against an oppressed people than the U.S. role in the Congo," said Malcolm X in 1965. **Above,** while supposedly under protection of UN "peacekeepers" in late 1960, independence leader and former prime minister Patrice Lumumba (right) was arrested and murdered by U.S.-backed Congolese forces.

"The United States' complete defeat in Vietnam is only a matter of time," said Malcolm X in 1965, as the massive U.S. troop escalation was just beginning. **Facing page,** antiaircraft unit defends Vietnam from murderous U.S. bombing raids.

You're living in "a time of revolution," Malcolm told young people in the United Kingdom in December 1964.

Facing page, top, independence fighters, called the Mau Mau by Kenya's British imperialist rulers, launched struggle in early 1950s that eventually drove out the colonial power. **Above,** working people in Zagreb greet Yugoslav partisan troops liberating city from German occupation, May 1945. Workers and peasants went on to topple capitalist rule in Yugoslavia. **Facing page, bottom,** farmers in China burn deeds of former landlords during 1951 land reform that followed revolutionary victory ousting capitalist regime of Chiang Kai-shek.

"I think 1965 will be more explosive than '64 and '63," said Malcolm X in January of that year. "The social dynamite is still here. There's no way they can contain it." **Right,** National Guard deployed to Watts area of Los Angeles, August 1965, as Black community rebelled against racist indignities and cop brutality.

> **"The Nation of Islam leadership put me out because of my uncompromising approach to problems that should and could be solved. I felt the movement was dragging its feet. It didn't involve itself in the civil or political struggles our people confronted."**
>
> MALCOLM X, JANUARY 1965

Above, Malcolm interviewed at Brooklyn, N.Y., construction site, where he joined July 1963 action called by CORE and Urban League to protest hiring discrimination. "Wherever Muslims got involved in action, anywhere in the country," Malcolm said in February 1965, "it was action I was involved in, because I believed in action."

Facing page, top, Malcolm X speaks at July 1962 rally in New York City called by hospital workers union Local 1199 to back union recognition fight. **Middle,** Malcolm in Los Angeles courthouse displays picture of Ronald Stokes, killed by police. In response to murderous 1962 cop assault on Nation members there, Malcolm organized an effective protest campaign until recalled by Elijah Muhammad. **Bottom,** Malcolm addresses Harlem meeting to support student boycott of segregated city school system, March 15, 1964.

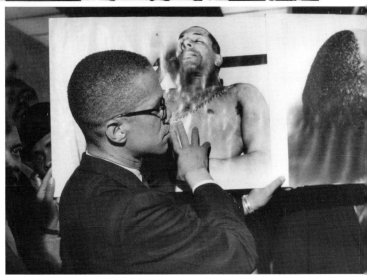

"In Ghana I spoke with the Algerian ambassador, a revolutionary in the true sense of the word. When I said my philosophy was Black nationalism, he asked me frankly, where did that leave him? Because to all appearances he was a white man. He showed me I was alienating people who were genuine revolutionaries. So I had a lot of reappraising to do. I haven't been using the term 'Black nationalism' for several months."

MALCOLM X, JANUARY 1965

"I believe there will be a clash between those who want freedom, justice, and equality and those who want to continue the systems of exploitation," Malcolm said in January 1965. "But I don't think it will be based upon the color of the skin, as Elijah Muhammad teaches." **Above,** Malcolm on stage with the Nation of Islam leader in Harlem, August 1961.

Facing page, top, some of 3,000 delegates to June 1955 Congress of the People, Kliptown, South Africa, which adopted Freedom Charter of the African National Congress, proclaiming, "South Africa belongs to all who live in it, black and white." "Similar in some ways to Malcolm's development," Barnes says, Nelson Mandela and other young ANC leaders went through struggles that led them to shift away from Black nationalism as political axis.

THERE SHALL BE **WORK** AND **SECURITY**

ALL SHALL ENJOY EQUAL **HUMAN RIGHTS**

ESTERN NATIVE TOWNSHIP

AFRICA MAYIBUYE

After being forced out of the Nation of Islam in early 1964, Malcolm X came to reject its opposition to intermarriage. "I believe in recognizing every human being as a human being—neither white, black, brown, nor red," Malcolm said in January 1965. "When you are dealing with humanity as a family, there's no question of integration or intermarriage. It's just one human being marrying another human being." It was not until 1967 that the U.S. Supreme Court at last declared state laws barring interracial marriage unconstitutional, following struggle by Mildred and Richard Loving **(above)** to overturn their conviction in Virginia.

> **"One of the things I became thoroughly convinced of in my recent travels is the importance of freedom for women."**
>
> MALCOLM X, NOVEMBER 1964

"I am frankly proud of the contributions our women have made in the struggle for freedom." **Above, Gloria Richardson** led 1962–64 campaign of Black community in Cambridge, Maryland, refusing to call off protests despite National Guard's year-long occupation of city or to urge nonviolence in face of white-supremacist thugs. **Facing page, top right, Fannie Lou Hamer,** former sharecropper, led fight to oust Mississippi's segregationist delegation from August 1964 Democratic Party convention. Malcolm X collaborated with both Richardson and Hamer.

"One thing I noticed in the Middle East and Africa, in every country that was progressive, the women were progressive. In every country that was underdeveloped and backward, women were kept back to the same degree." **Facing page, bottom,** women in literacy class held in cow barn in central Morocco, 2004, where 90 percent of women still can't read or write. Under proimperialist monarchy, adult female illiteracy is some 60 percent for country as a whole. **Facing page, top left,** women soldiers march in Burkina Faso, West Africa, August 1985, two years after popular revolutionary government led by Thomas Sankara took power.

I've never heard anybody teach nonviolence to the Ku Klux Klan. And I don't go along with anyone teaching our people nonviolence until someone is also teaching that to our enemy. We should protect ourselves by any means necessary when we are attacked by racists."

MALCOLM X, JANUARY 1965

Left, preparing to register to vote in Lowndes County, Alabama, 1966. In area where no Black had been able to vote for at least sixty years, Lowndes County Freedom Organization ran a campaign independent of Democratic Party and organized to defend its candidates and supporters. **Above,** Freedom Ride bus firebombed by racists near Anniston, Alabama, May 1961. Riders were demanding federal government action to desegregate public interstate transportation.

CAROLINA EDITION	**Journal and Guide**	ASIAN FLU-- "What To Do" Helpful Advice from an Expert Page 20

VOL LVII No. 41   NORFOLK, VIRGINIA, SATURDAY, OCTOBER 12, 1957   20 PAGES   PRICE 15 CENTS

CITIZENS FIRE BACK AT KLAN

Ku Kluxers Use Guns At Monroe, NC

Shots Exchanged Near Residence Of NAACP Head

Special to Journal and Guide
MONROE, N. C. — It has been reported here that a group of Ku Klux Klansmen, some of them robed and masked, swapped gunfire with a group of colored citizens near the home of the president of the local NAACP branch late Friday night.

Police officials say that as shots were fired, but Union county NAACP Vice-President Robert F. Williams said Klansmen — in a caravan

fired on a group of some 50 to 60 colored citizens near the home of the NAACP president, A. F. Perry.

    • • •

MR. WILLIAMS also said that when someone in the colored gathering returned the fire, police officers came over to disarm them.

Police Chief A. A. Mauney has a different version of the affair, however. He says that several police cars were in the caravan of "about 80 cars" that "disbanded" when a train cut across its path. The chief said that he had instructed his men to get in front of the caravan and if any violations occurred to stop the procession.

    • • •

EVEN THOUGH North Carolina law forbids the wearing of masks in public gatherings, Chief Mauney said that he had had reports that some of the Klansmen were hooded.

Police officers in cars in the caravan said that they did hear "what sounded like a carbine near the doctor's house" even though they deny that there was gunfire.

Top, at January 1966 rally, Charles Sims, a leader of Deacons for Defense in Bogalusa, Louisiana, warns Klan that days when Blacks won't defend themselves are over. Deacons, many of them army veterans, organized to guard their communities against racist attacks.

Above, one of self-defense units organized by U.S. army veterans who beat back Ku Klux Klan terror in Monroe, North Carolina, 1957. *Journal and Guide* is Virginia-area weekly whose readership is overwhelmingly Black.

"Young people most quickly identify with the struggle and the necessity to eliminate the evil conditions that exist."

MALCOLM X, JANUARY 1965

"I think young people can find a powerful example in the young *simbas* [lions] in the Congo and young fighters in South Vietnam," Malcolm told young socialists. **Facing page, left,** Vietnamese youth from Chi Lang village "volunteer in anti-U.S. war of national salvation," banner says.

Above right, Malcolm X talking with students at Tuskegee University, February 1965. They insisted Malcolm come with them and speak at meeting in Selma, Alabama, the next day.

Above, center, in April 1967 400,000 march in New York against Vietnam War, demanding "Bring the GIs home now!" Sign at right says: "Black men should fight white racism, not Vietnamese freedom fighters."

Below left, Andrew Goodman, James Chaney, Michael Schwerner, civil rights workers murdered by Ku Klux Klan in Philadelphia, Mississippi, June 1964. The state of Mississippi never handed down murder charges.

"The Cuban Revolution—that's a revolution. They overturned the system."

MALCOLM X, NOVEMBER 1963

"Cuba's commitment to the systematic eradication of racism is unparalleled," Nelson Mandela told tens of thousands in Matanzas, Cuba, on July 26, 1991, where he spoke together with Cuban president Fidel Castro. "But the most important lesson you have for us is that no matter what the odds, no matter the difficulties, there can be no surrender! It is freedom or death!"

"For the Cuban people, internationalism is not merely a word but something we have seen practiced to the benefit of large sections of humankind," Mandela told the Matanzas rally. "It is unparalleled in African history to have another people rise to the defense of one of us." **Right,** Cuban troops in Angola, 1981, helping defeat invading South African apartheid forces.

Washington's efforts to overthrow Cuba's revolutionary government began in reaction to May 1959 land reform and intensified as Cuban working people took other measures in their interests, such as expropriation of U.S.-owned oil refineries. **Above,** Havana bus drivers, training with wood substitutes for rifles, mobilize in response to strafing of Havana by U.S.-backed counterrevolutionaries in October 1959 and call for arms to defend revolution. **Below,** Cubans at mass rally at close of First Latin American Youth Congress vote to approve expropriation of major U.S.-owned industries, August 1960.

"Don't run around trying to make friends with somebody who's depriving you of your rights," Malcolm urged young civil rights fighters from Mississippi. **"They're not your friends, they're your enemies. Treat them like that, fight them, and you'll get your freedom."**

MALCOLM X, JANUARY 1965

Above, at July 1964 New York City "summit," Martin Luther King and leaders of other civil rights groups called a halt to protests for Black freedom until after November elections. "They have sold themselves out and become campaign managers in the Negro community for Lyndon B. Johnson," Malcolm X responded. Here, participants in summit meeting (from left): Bayard Rustin, Jack Greenberg, Whitney Young, James Farmer, Roy Wilkins, King, John Lewis, A. Philip Randolph, Courtland Cox.

Above, right, "They have a new gimmick every year," Malcolm X told a Militant Labor Forum in January 1965. "They're going to take one of their black boys and put him in the cabinet, so he can walk around Washington with a cigar—fire on one end and fool on the other." Here Robert Weaver, the first Black appointed to a cabinet post—secretary of housing and urban development—receives pen from President Lyndon Johnson at September 1965 signing of bill creating the department.

"They had the whole world, including people who call themselves Marxists [a reference to the U.S. Communist Party among others] on their hands and knees hoping Johnson would be elected—because he is supposed to be a man of peace," Malcolm told Paris press conference in November 1964. "And at that moment he had troops invading the Congo and South Vietnam!" Malcolm X and the Socialist Workers Party were the only voices in the working class refusing to back Johnson over Goldwater as a "lesser evil."

THE MILITANT
Published in the Interests of the Working People
Vol. 28 - No. 25   Monday, June 22, 1964   Price 10c

Socialist Nominee Blasts Johnson for Not Stopping St. Augustine Klansmen

Clifton DeBerry

1964 SWP presidential candidate Clifton DeBerry, **inset right,** demands federal government defend civil rights fighters in St. Augustine, Florida, against cop and Ku Klux Klan violence.

Malcolm spoke the truth to our generation of revolutionists. He was the face and authentic voice of the coming American revolution.

JACK BARNES, FEBRUARY 1965

The Fort Jackson 8, on South Carolina army base in 1968, were among thousands of active-duty soldiers radicalized by struggles for Black rights and against Vietnam War. Trumped-up charges landed several in the brig in wake of open-air gatherings where they listened to tapes of Malcolm X, talked about the war, and organized petition to post commandant requesting permission to hold meeting on base "at which all those concerned can freely discuss the legal and moral questions related to the war in Vietnam and civil rights of American citizens both within and outside the armed forces." In course of activities, GIs United Against the War was founded and spread to other bases. Fort Jackson 8 defense won broad national and world support and all charges were eventually dropped.

From left: Andrew Pulley, José Rudder (partly hidden), Delmar Thomas, Edilberto Chaparro, Tommie Woodfin, Dominick Duddie, Joe Cole, Curtis Mays. Cole was member of Socialist Workers Party before being drafted. Pulley joined Young Socialist Alliance and SWP after discharge and was party's 1972 candidate for vice president of United States.

closely with the non-violent movement, but he was not yet able to renounce violence and overcome the bitterness which life had invested in him. . . . Like the murder of Lumumba, the murder of Malcolm X deprives the world of a potentially great leader. I could not agree with either of these men. . . ."[100]

So, no, there was not a "Malcolm-Martin" convergence during that last year. To the contrary, the divergence widened, as there was a clarification of Martin Luther King's conviction that capitalism and its injustices could be reformed. Meanwhile, Malcolm never stopped advancing in his commitment to the need for the oppressed and working people of all skin colors, continents, and countries to join together in revolutionary struggle against the capitalist world order responsible for racism, rightist violence, the oppression of women, economic exploitation, and war.

A movement of political equals

Finally, Malcolm was committed politically to reaching out to young people. Without doing so, he understood, it was impossible to build a revolutionary movement. That was a lesson of every modern revolution.

"Our accent will be upon youth," Malcolm said in one of the first interviews he gave after breaking with the Nation of Islam. The youth, he said, "have less of a stake in this corrupt system and therefore can look at it more objectively, whereas the adults usually have a stake in this corrupt system and they lose their ability to look at it objectively because of their stake in it."[101]

Malcolm was pointing to something the communist movement has long recognized, even if he used different language:

---

100. "Nightmare of Violence," in the March 13, 1965, issue of the *Amsterdam News*.

101. "Interview by A.B. Spellman," in *By Any Means Necessary*, p. 28.

that there is a material basis for the place of young people in revolutionary struggles. Youth are in a state of flux, with an entire lifetime ahead of them. For a relatively brief time, they are less tied down with families, financial pressures, mortgages, illnesses, disappointments, and other conservatizing encumbrances. They tend to respond more quickly and more easily to social and political ills all around them. As Lenin pointed out, even the class position of young people is not completely settled. Plus, on average, young people are stronger, more limber, more energetic, more fit for combat.

That's why, even while Malcolm was still in the Nation, he always sought out young audiences to speak to: on campuses, or to gatherings of young political militants. It's one of the reasons he responded so readily to our request that he do an interview for the *Young Socialist* magazine in early 1965. I went back to Malcolm's office a few days later with the transcribed interview ready for him to edit and approve for publication. I told him I would be going to Algeria in a few months as part of a Young Socialist Alliance delegation to an international youth festival there. He responded immediately and enthusiastically. Malcolm was eager to put us in touch with young revolutionists he had met—he also called them "contacts"—during his trips to Africa and the Middle East and to make sure, among other things, that they got copies of the *Young Socialist* featuring the interview with him.

We had asked Malcolm during the interview, "What part in the world revolution are youth playing, and what lessons may this have for American youth?" I hadn't anticipated the first point he made. He started off by talking about the captives being taken by U.S. soldiers during the Vietnam War. The majority of them are young people, he pointed out—"most are teenagers," but "some haven't yet reached their teens." Something similar was true in the Congo, he added. That's why, when the imperialist troops "shoot captive revolutionaries," they often "shoot all the way down to seven years old."

In Vietnam, the Congo, and other countries on the frontlines of struggle, Malcolm said, "the young people are the ones who most quickly identify with the struggle and the necessity to eliminate the evil conditions that exist. And here in this country, it has been my own observation that when you get into a conversation on racism and discrimination and segregation, you will find young people are more incensed over it—they feel more filled with an urge to eliminate it."[102]

But Malcolm also saw "youth" as a practical, political question—not just biological, not just a matter of a person's number of years on earth.

"Old people don't bring about a change," Malcolm had said at the OAAU's homecoming rally for him in late November 1964, after returning from the second Africa trip. That's a lesson he had confirmed everywhere he traveled. But Malcolm was quick to make his point more precise: "I'm not saying this against anybody that's old—because if you're ready for some action you're not old. I don't care how old you are. But if you're not ready for some action, I don't care how young you are, you're old. . . . [A]ny time you begin to sit on the fence, and your toes start shaking because you're afraid too much action is going down, then you're too old; you need to get on out of the way. Some of us get too old while we're still in our teens."[103]

Malcolm's words remind me of nothing so much as Jim Cannon's call on the leadership and ranks of the Socialist

---

102. "Interview with the *Young Socialist*" (January 18, 1965), p. 55 in this book.

103. "The Homecoming Rally of the OAAU" (New York, November 29, 1964), in *By Any Means Necessary*, pp. 173–74.

Workers Party in October 1941 to begin carrying out a bolder policy in our trade union work. This was right on the eve of Washington's entry into World War II and only weeks before he and seventeen other leaders of the SWP and of the Teamsters organizing drive in the Midwest were sentenced, railroaded to prison for their opposition to U.S. imperialist aims in that war. "I don't know of anything more disgraceful for a young revolutionist than to get settled down and get so encumbered in a place that he cannot move," Jim said. "It would be a damn good thing for him if he had a fire to blow away some property encumbrance and make him footloose and revolutionary again."[104]

That's true for revolutionists of any age.

That's the spirit and the political example of Malcolm X for workers and youth in the United States and the world over.

From the Discussion Period

QUESTION: You mentioned that a new book of Malcolm's speeches will be coming out relatively soon, based on some tapes that haven't previously been transcribed [*Malcolm X: The Last Speeches*]. Is there anything new in there that we didn't know before about Malcolm or his views, or that wasn't widely known? Also, what about Malcolm's wife, Betty Shabazz? What's happened to her since Malcolm's assassination?

BARNES: Let me take the questions in reverse order.

What about Betty Shabazz? I'm not acquainted with her personally, but I'll tell you what I know. After Malcolm's death, she raised their six daughters, and then she went back

---

104. "It Is Time for a Bolder Policy in the Unions" (October 11, 1941), in James P. Cannon, *The Socialist Workers Party in World War II* (Pathfinder, 1975), p. 207 [2002 printing].

to school. Today she has an administrative position at Medgar Evers College in Brooklyn. Right from the beginning, from shortly after Malcolm's assassination in 1965, she has helped facilitate efforts by Pathfinder Press to make sure that Malcolm's speeches and interviews get into print and stay in print.

Betty Shabazz recently wrote a brief article for *Essence* magazine, in which she talked a little bit about what Malcolm was like as a person, including musical preferences, much of which was new to me. Malcolm "loved all kinds of music," she said. "Max Roach and Abbey Lincoln Aminata Moseka were his favorites, but he also listened to symphonies. We went to Duke Ellington concerts, and it was Malcolm who took me to my first two operas: *La Traviata* and *La Bohème.*"

I was struck by that in particular, since I have weaknesses in the same directions musically. Malcolm's love for jazz is well known, of course ("*You* can't dance to it. . . ."). But I hadn't realized he liked opera, especially Romantic nineteenth-century operas. The two Betty Shabazz mentions, by Verdi and Puccini, are so unlike the political Malcolm—soap operas in plot, about unrequited love, centered on characters whose morals and values and place in society were not his. Of course, similar things are true of the musical and artistic responses of most of us, in different ways. Anyway, after reading her account, I had fun trying to imagine Malcolm—who worked very hard, under nerve-racking conditions—trying to steal a few hours of relaxation, of uplift, listening to *Don Carlo*, slumped in a seat at the Metropolitan Opera trying not to be recognized for a little while.

Is there anything new?

Now, on the first part of the question. Is there anything new about Malcolm or his views in the forthcoming book? No, there's not much new, if by that you mean things that are politically surprising or unanticipated by those already acquainted with Malcolm's speeches and political evolution. Once outstanding revolutionary leaders reach a certain stage in their political lives—whether it's Lenin, or Che, or Malcolm X—it's very unlikely that anything is going to be found that substantively alters our understanding of what they stood for and fought for.

A number of years ago, in 1980, for example, a large number of Leon Trotsky's unpublished papers were opened to the public for the first time at Harvard's Houghton Library. Pathfinder Press, the main publisher of Trotsky's writings, sent a team up to review the files, and there was certainly valuable material—letters, articles, and other items that add to the richness of Trotsky's explanation of communism's political legacy. But nothing "new" in the sense I just explained. How could there be? Trotsky wrote and spoke throughout his adult life on the biggest questions of world politics. He was personally involved at the very center of them. He wrote about the impact and reflection of those events within the communist movement and among various individuals and currents. Dozens of collections and thousands of pages of his writings are in print. How could we be surprised?

Similarly with Malcolm. The unpublished speeches contain wonderful material—I've discussed some of it here tonight. But Malcolm never raised something he considered important only once and then never came back to it. He didn't say different things to ingratiate himself with different listeners. He spoke to the same questions and used the same examples from the events of the day.

You don't have to rely on me to corroborate that. Malcolm's speeches and interviews, to many different audiences, are available for all to read. When he came "downtown" three times in 1964 and early 1965 to speak at the Militant Labor Forum, for instance, he saluted the *Militant* newspaper for telling the truth, including about him and the movement he was trying to build. But Malcolm said the same thing to a meeting of the OAAU at the Audubon Ballroom in Harlem in January 1965: "None of the newspapers ever talk about our meetings; they don't help us publicize it in any way, shape, or form, other than the *Militant*—the *Militant* does."[105] And he kept a stack of the most recent issue of the *Militant* on sale outside his office in the Hotel Theresa—it cost a dime back then.

So there's not some "unknown" Malcolm you're going to discover in the new speeches.

That being said, there is one thing that we've known about since the final weeks of Malcolm's life but that has never before been detailed in print in Malcolm's own words. That is his account of Elijah Muhammad's secret dealings in the early 1960s with leaders of the racist and ultrarightist Ku Klux Klan, American Nazi Party, and National States Rights Party. Malcolm told the story in a speech at the Audubon Ballroom on February 15, a talk that will be published for the first time in the new book.

The previous day Malcolm's home in Queens had been firebombed in the middle of the night. Someone had tossed the explosives into several windows, including into the room where three of his daughters were sleeping. Substantial damage was done to the house, but fortunately neither Malcolm, Betty, nor any of the girls were injured.

Nation of Islam leaders quickly spread the rumor that Malcolm had organized the bombing himself as a publicity stunt. "When the Klan bombs your church, they say you did it," Malcolm told participants in the OAAU meeting. "When they bomb the synagogue, they say the Jews bombed their own synagogue. This is the Klan tactic," he said. And

---

105. "Speech at Audubon Ballroom" (January 24, 1965), in *Malcolm X on Afro-American History* (Pathfinder, 1967, 1970, 1990), p. 50 [2009 printing].

Malcolm added that he was going to "tell you why the Black Muslim movement is now adopting the same tactics against Black people."[106]

In February, for the first time in several months, Malcolm began speaking publicly about what he had known all along to be the truth: that leaders of the Nation of Islam not only wanted to see him dead but were actively pursuing that goal. And Malcolm knew that the U.S. government and New York City cops were very much aware of that fact and were inclined, without much persuasion, to look the other way.

"Why do they want to bomb my house?" Malcolm asked the audience. "Why don't they bomb the Klan? I'm going to tell you why."

And then Malcolm recounted the Nation leadership's relations with the Klan. He said that in December 1960 he had been sent by Elijah Muhammad to Atlanta, Georgia— to this very city where we're meeting tonight—to negotiate face to face with top leaders of the Ku Klux Klan. "I'm ashamed to say it, but I'm going to tell you the truth," Malcolm said. "I sat at the table myself with the heads of the Ku Klux Klan."

Elijah Muhammad, Malcolm explained, was soliciting help from Klan leaders to obtain a county-sized tract of land in either Georgia or South Carolina, "so that his program of separation would sound more feasible to Negroes and therefore lessen the pressure that the integrationists were putting upon the white man. I sat there. I negotiated it. I listened to their offers. And I was the one who went back to Chicago and told Elijah Muhammad what they had offered. . . .

"From that day onward," Malcolm said, "the Klan never interfered with the Black Muslim movement in the South."

---

106. "There's a Worldwide Revolution Going On," in *Malcolm X: The Last Speeches*, p. 108. Also in *February 1965: The Final Speeches*, p. 109.

In fact, Malcolm confirmed accounts in the big business press about Nation of Islam leaders attending Klan rallies. Malcolm said that Elijah Muhammad regularly corresponded with George Lincoln Rockwell, head of the American Nazi Party, and that Rockwell had attended a Nation of Islam rally at Muhammad's invitation. Malcolm added that Nation leaders also maintained good relations with J.B. Stoner, chairman of the white supremacist National States Rights Party.[107]

Over the few days following that meeting, Malcolm briefly mentioned Elijah Muhammad's ties to rightists in several published or broadcast interviews, and they've been referred to in later writings about him. But Malcolm's own detailed account has never before been in print. So that makes our knowledge more concrete.

QUESTION: I am a member of the Nation of Islam. I wanted to say something about your statement that Malcolm X used the word "abuse" about the treatment of young women by the Honorable Elijah Muhammad. I'm a woman, and I've always been treated respectfully in the Nation of Islam. I've never been abused or heard of abuse. How could he have said this, with the evidence of all the men and women—including Malcolm X himself—who've been picked up by the Nation of Islam and transformed from pimps, prostitutes, and drug addicts into independent, intelligent, and productive people? You described it yourself in your talk. We're taught in my religion that when you train a man you've trained one individual, but when you train a woman, you train a whole nation. So I don't understand how anybody can say the Honorable Elijah Muhammad abused women.

BARNES: The word "abuse" was mine. I can't swear Mal-

---

107. "There's a Worldwide Revolution Going On," in *Malcolm X: The Last Speeches*, pp. 118–19, 130. This speech and other material on the Nation of Islam's relations with the Ku Klux Klan and kindred ultra-rightists can also be found in *February 1965: The Final Speeches*.

Speaking to Harlem rally in February 1965, almost a year after his public break with Nation of Islam, Malcolm recalled that in 1961 Elijah Muhammad had invited American Nazi Party leader George Lincoln Rockwell to attend a Nation rally in Washington, D.C. At that very time, Rockwell's Nazis were driving a "Hate Bus" across South to rally support for Klan attacks on "Freedom Riders" mobilizing to desegregate interstate transportation. (Rockwell is seated, center, at Nation meeting and standing, right, by "Hate Bus," Seven Corners, Virginia.)

At same Harlem rally, Malcolm told his supporters: "I'm ashamed to say it, but I'm going to tell you the truth." He disclosed that in 1960 he'd been sent by Elijah Muhammad to negotiate with Ku Klux Klan leaders in Georgia to ask for help in obtaining large tract of land in South so Nation's "program of separation would sound more feasible to Negroes."

colm used it. But that *is* the content Malcolm gave to Elijah Muhammad's conduct, as anyone knows who has read what Malcolm had to say about the treatment of these women. I don't challenge what you say about the impact the Nation has had on many individuals, helping them turn around their lives. I've never read anything that leads me to believe Malcolm changed his mind about this either. Getting involved for the first time in an organization or a cause—be it religious, civic, or political—can and sometimes does have a transformative effect on the life of an individual. It depends on the person.

Political, not individual solutions
But Malcolm came to recognize that those individual transformations are not nearly enough to change the wretched economic, social, and political conditions confronting Blacks and all working people here and around the world.

First, Malcolm insisted that the leaders of *any* organization had to be true to its principles in their own lives and behavior, or else the organization's moral core would rot and corrupt everything it touched. This is why Malcolm was so shaken by his discovery, from Elijah Muhammad's own mouth, of the hypocritical conduct of the Nation's top leader.

Second, and most important, Malcolm recognized that the oppressed and exploited had to organize and struggle for *revolutionary political solutions,* and that this is an international fight. It didn't matter where you were born. It didn't matter what the color of your skin is. It didn't matter what language you speak. It didn't matter what religious beliefs you do or do not hold. The oppressed need to join together in a revolutionary political struggle "to change this miserable condition that exists on this earth," as he put it.

How do human beings become ground down in the first place? It's not because we're born that way. It's not genetic. It's not the inevitable product of skin pigmentation. Malcolm was not a Calvinist Christian: he didn't think some people are born in a state of grace, while others aren't.

People get driven down, we are degraded, by the workings of an exploitative social system—a system whose capitalist rulers rely on racist, antiwoman, and other forms of discrimination and oppression—that denies us the possibility of developing and using our abilities. That denies us our dignity, our sense of worth as creative, productive members of society. So people get ground down, are often overtaken by rage. Denied outlets for the use of our intelligence, we find ways of relying on cleverness instead, just in order to get by.

In the *Autobiography* Malcolm says that Elijah Muhammad "virtually raised me from the dead. Everything I was that was creditable, he had made me."[108] From Malcolm's own experience in the Nation, however, he came to understand that once you've been raised from the dead—it's not a bad metaphor, a form of it happens to many of us along the road to becoming revolutionists—but once you've cleaned yourself up, once you've begun to recognize your worth, you still wake up in the morning and realize there's not one less hungry person in the world. You still wake up knowing that not a single one of the economic and social roots of oppression have been changed—here in the United States, in Africa, in the Caribbean, in Latin America, in Europe, in Asia, or anywhere else.

That takes revolutionary political action, and an organization not afraid of combat and dedicated to that goal.

History doesn't repeat itself

QUESTION: You've described Malcolm X's political evolution as a revolutionary, as a leader of the working class. In the

---

108. *The Autobiography of Malcolm X*, chapter 16: "Out."

course of trying to find ways to fight effectively against the oppressors and for Black rights, he developed new and different political insights and better methods. Do you think that same kind of evolution can happen over and over again?

BARNES: I don't think deepgoing social and political struggles simply repeat themselves, much less the development of world-class proletarian political leadership.

Struggles advance, often in the face of enormous difficulties, and then they get shoved back. In face of new experiences and assaults by the exploiters, working people move forward once again, we make conquests, and we organize to defend and build on those conquests. Under certain circumstances, leaders and leaderships of outstanding political caliber emerge.

That happened in Germany in the late 1840s. It happened in Russia in the opening decades of this century. It happened during the Minneapolis and Midwest Teamsters battles of the 1930s. It happened in Cuba in the late 1940s and 1950s. You can think of other examples. There is a substantial element of chance, of historical accident involved. But when and where it does happen, those leaderships leave a political legacy that becomes part of the political patrimony of the working class and its allies worldwide, of whatever race, color, and background.

In addition to African American leadership of popular struggles throughout the South during Radical Reconstruction, including battles involving toilers who were white,[109] there were significant examples from the late nineteenth century and well into the twentieth of joint struggles across the color line, especially among debt-ridden farmers and union coal

---

109. For a discussion of the accomplishments and bloody defeat of Radical Reconstruction, including suggestions for further reading, see two other articles in this book: "Radical Reconstruction" in Part II and "Black Liberation and the Dictatorship of the Proletariat" in Part IV.

miners. Workers who were Black took part in the working-class-led social movement of the 1930s that built the industrial unions, especially in the mines, steel mills, and textile and tobacco factories. Those battles, in turn, laid the basis for ongoing struggles for Black rights throughout World War II—including the resistance to being "broomologists," as Malcolm said.

Initial experiences in factory work, learning new job skills, and in union struggles—learning new skills there too!—increased confidence among layers of Blacks. So did experiences in the armed forces, including in segregated units. All that was the leavening that made possible the rise of the proletarian-led struggle for Black rights following World War II and expanding into the 1950s and 1960s. That struggle, moreover, was part of an advancing wave of revolutionary victories against imperialist domination and capitalist exploitation that swept from Asia and Africa through the Middle East, the Caribbean, and Latin America.

The social and political consciousness and attitudes of tens of millions of working people in this country—Blacks, whites, Mexicanos, Puerto Ricans, Salvadorans, Guatemalans, and many others—were transformed. The combativity demonstrated in those fights encouraged young people and others to build the movement against the Vietnam War in the 1960s, as well as to launch a new stage in the fight for women's emancipation.

All these battles have left us with a different world today, and with a different working class—one that's larger, substantially immigrant, with a much weightier component that is Black. For that very reason, however, we're not going to see *a simple repeat* of any of these struggles. We'll build on what we've conquered: on our unions, on our victories over important aspects of racist and antiwoman bigotry and discrimination. Those triumphs, however, raise the stakes in labor's battle against capital, in the revolutionary working-class struggle for political power. The necessity of class-conscious proletarian leadership becomes even greater—a leadership in which the social and political weight of workers who are Black, who are Latino, who are female will be greater than ever before.

Working people don't have to give up anything we've earned in struggle. But we can add to it. We must add to it. In that sense—even with the grave weakening of the labor movement as a result of the class-collaborationist, pro-imperialist course of the union officialdom—the working class is stronger than at any time in history, both in this country and worldwide.

That doesn't mean we're anywhere close to revolutionary class battles in the United States today. It doesn't mean there won't be setbacks and defeats along the road to a victorious socialist revolution. But it does increase our odds of winning, *if* we succeed in building a strong-enough working-class leadership, tempered in class battles and schooled in the strategic and programmatic lessons from battles by those who came before us.

It all depends on *what we do*. I recently attended a luncheon in New York for African National Congress leader Oliver Tambo. "We have already won in South Africa. The apartheid regime will be overthrown," Tambo said. "That's been determined by history. But how many thousands and tens of thousands will have to give their lives in that process will be determined by what we do there, and by what you do here."

It's that double lesson that strikes me as the most important one.

A power struggle in the Nation?

QUESTION: It's wrong, it seems to me, to talk about Malcolm X's development as a human being, and about his ideology as a leader, without attributing this to the Most

Honorable Elijah Muhammad. It was from those teachings that Malcolm—while he was still in prison—first learned about Islam and began to think as he did. Before he turned to those teachings, Malcolm loved only himself, he didn't think in terms of loving Black people.

So I want to ask you a question. Don't you think Malcolm X was just engaged in a power struggle with the Most Honorable Elijah Muhammad?

BARNES: I agree that it's impossible to talk about Malcolm's development as a human being without taking account of the influence of Elijah Muhammad. Malcolm said that before encountering the Nation, he not only had no respect for Black people, he had no respect for *any* people—and, above all, he had no respect for *himself.* That's a fact.

But that's not the only fact. Malcolm talked about being "raised from the dead" in the very same section of the *Autobiography* where he describes the devastating impact on him of what he had learned about Elijah Muhammad's sexual conduct with several young women in the Nation in Chicago. That shattering experience helped Malcolm face up to reality. It made him face that he had been moving in a different direction from Elijah Muhammad politically for some time. I've already pointed to numerous examples, and there are many more. Malcolm came to see that these were not tactical differences. His course was the opposite of that of Elijah Muhammad. They were on different *class* trajectories.

There's no evidence of any kind that Malcolm X launched a power struggle against Elijah Muhammad. Elijah Muhammad had *all* the power in the Nation of Islam; Malcolm had *none.* That's how the Nation of Islam was structured—and Malcolm never sought to challenge that. Yes, Elijah Muhammad grew envious and resentful of Malcolm. He increasingly feared Malcolm's ability to reach out to and attract young Blacks.

But Malcolm's attraction was a political attraction. Malcolm wasn't a prophet. He wasn't a demagogue. He didn't have *charisma*—I looked up that word in a dictionary; it's not a compliment, it's not something you want to have said about you.

The divergence wasn't over power; it was over *what to do*. It wasn't just about treating women with respect, but about the full involvement of women in the social and political struggle for liberation. The divergence was about whether it's ever defensible, under any conditions, to sit down and make deals with the Ku Klux Klan. About whether or not to organize a mass campaign in the streets—against the cops, and against the government—when African Americans are gunned down by the cops, as members of the Nation had been in Los Angeles. About whether whites are "a race of devils," or whether revolutionists judge every human being on the basis of what they *do*, not the color of their skin.

When he was instructed by Elijah Muhammad to sit down with the Klan, Malcolm may have rationalized the meeting as "just a tactic" along the road to Black liberation. But Malcolm came to understand that not all tactics are acceptable for revolutionists. "Tactics" that demobilize, demoralize, mislead, and miseducate working people—tactics that lower our confidence in our capacity to make revolutionary change, that imbue worship of "leaders," that undermine our sense of worth—those tactics are *never* acceptable.

When FBI Director J. Edgar Hoover publicly slandered Martin Luther King in 1964 as the "most notorious liar" in America, it was not a clever "tactic" for King to issue a statement saying that Hoover had "apparently faltered under the awesome burden, complexities and responsibilities of his office." It was not a clever "tactic" for King to say he had "nothing but sympathy for this man who has served his country so well." Much less was it acceptable for the best-known leader of a major Black rights organization to then organize a meeting with the director of U.S. imperialism's top police agency and later report to the press that the conversation had been "very friendly, very amicable." King announced that he and J. Edgar Hoover—yes, J. Edgar Hoover!—had reached "new levels of understanding."[110]

That was a disorienting miseducation for all those who looked to King because of the demonstrations for civil rights he had helped organize and lead. It was a kick in the gut to their confidence, to their self-respect, to their combativity. Above all, it undermined their political understanding of the fact that the U.S. capitalist government and its cops are *enemies* of the oppressed—but, that, of course, was not the opinion of Martin Luther King. It *was* the conclusion that Malcolm had come to, however. Malcolm believed a revolution was needed to overturn that government, its repressive bodies—the cops, the courts, the armed forces—and the capitalist class those institutions served and defended.

During the last months of his life, Malcolm no longer agreed, as we were discussing with the other sister, that religion can be an answer to all questions, a complete way of life, including a means to combating oppression and exploitation. Your religion, or lack of religion, is your own business, Malcolm said. But your political life as a revolutionist—your commitment to overthrowing the system that drives human beings to the point where they have to be "raised from the dead"—is something else again. Malcolm threw in his lot with all those who looked forward above all to revolutionary action. That is the road to the transformation not of this or that individual, but of millions and hundreds of millions as we engage in revolutionary political activity and then begin

---

110. King's telegram to Hoover and his statement to the press following the meeting with Hoover can be found in David J. Garrow, *Bearing the Cross: Martin Luther King, Jr., and the Southern Christian Leadership Conference* (New York: William Morrow, 1986).

reconstructing society on new foundations.

Malcolm came to see that the Nation of Islam was not practicing authentic Islam. But that wasn't the source of his growing frustration with Elijah Muhammad and with the Nation's course. It was the barriers the Nation erected to its members getting involved in the fight for Black rights, in carrying out politics, in collaborating with other revolutionists, in the United States and around the world. It was the yawning gap between the Nation leadership's words and deeds. Malcolm more and more looked to revolutionary leaders such as Patrice Lumumba in the Congo, Ahmed Ben Bella in Algeria, Fidel Castro and Che Guevara in Cuba as examples of how to live your life—not to Elijah Muhammad.

The assassination

QUESTION: Some people say that the top leadership of the Nation of Islam organized the assassination of Malcolm X. The prosecution said it was the three men they arrested, all of them current or former Muslims, and that the motive was Malcolm's break from the Nation. All three were convicted and given long sentences. Others say it was the federal government and the New York cops. I'd like to hear your opinion.

BARNES: Much is still not known and may never be known about Malcolm's assassination. Both the government and those in and around the leadership of the Nation of Islam are determined to keep it that way.

Having said that, the best starting point may be a couple of things we discussed earlier this evening. The U.S. and Belgian governments wanted to get rid of Lumumba in the Congo. As it turned out, they didn't have to do so directly. Instead, under the UN flag, they sent imperialist troops into the country and stood aside as rightist Congolese forces did the deed. Washington wanted to get rid of Maurice Bishop and destroy the workers and farmers government in Grenada. Once again, they were saved the trouble by a Stalinist clique in the New Jewel Movement led by Bernard Coard, who organized a counterrevolutionary coup and murdered Bishop and many other Grenadan revolutionists and working people. Then the U.S. government sent its troops and occupied the island in the face of virtually no resistance from a devastated and demoralized population.

In my opinion, something along those lines was clearly involved in the brutal assassination of Malcolm X too.

I've said there's a lot we don't know. What do we know?

We know that Talmadge Hayer was wounded by one of Malcolm's guards at the Audubon Ballroom and arrested there, and that two other men—Norman 3X Butler and Thomas 15X Johnson, both well-known members of the Nation of Islam—were subsequently picked up and indicted. We know that Hayer confessed during the trial and insisted he had not been a member of the Nation at the time. We know that Hayer testified that neither Butler nor Johnson was involved in any way. Hayer's testimony was corroborated by close associates of Malcolm on the scene at the Audubon, who said they hadn't seen either Butler or Johnson in the room and would never have admitted two such notorious thugs from the Nation's paramilitary "Fruit of Islam" if they had been spotted. We know the prosecution pressed its case nonetheless, and all three were convicted and given sentences of twenty years to life. Butler was released on parole a couple of years ago; Johnson was paroled just a few weeks ago; and Hayer is still in.[111]

We also know that ten years ago, in late 1977 and early 1978, Hayer again filed affidavits with the court not only reaffirming that Butler and Johnson had nothing to do with

---

111. Butler had been paroled in 1985. Johnson was paroled in February 1987. Hayer has been out of prison on a work-release program since 1988, although he has repeatedly been denied parole.

the murder of Malcolm, but naming four members of the Nation's mosque in Newark, New Jersey, as his associates in the assassination. Once again the government refused to reopen the case or give a new trial to Butler and Johnson.

And we know that the prosecution never put Gene Roberts—one of Malcolm's bodyguards at the Audubon that afternoon—on the witness stand during the trial, and that five years later it was revealed he had been a New York City undercover cop.

It's not an either-or question. A great deal has come to light since the 1970s about the spying, harassment, and infiltration carried out by federal, state, and local police agencies against the unions, socialist and communist organizations, and groups and individuals fighting for Black rights, against the Vietnam War, and in opposition to government policies. We know how cop agencies at every level helped foment murderous factional vendettas within the Black Panthers and between the Panthers and rival organizations—government disruption efforts made much easier by the toxic brew of Maoism and petty-bourgeois nationalism that marked the politics and methods of these groups during the sixties and early seventies.

Much of the information about cop operations such as those was revealed in the course of the thirteen-year-long political fight by the Socialist Workers Party and Young Socialist Alliance against spying and harassment by the FBI and other government agencies and officials. That fight, organized around a lawsuit against these cop agencies, ended in a federal court ruling in our favor last year. A real victory![112]

Yes, there's good reason to believe that individuals in or

---

112. See *FBI on Trial: The Victory in the Socialist Workers Party Suit against Government Spying* edited by Margaret Jayko (1988), and *Cointelpro: The FBI's Secret War on Political Freedom* by Nelson Blackstock (1975, 1988), both published by Pathfinder.

around the Nation were directly involved in the assassination of Malcolm X, and that Nation leaders encouraged or helped organize such plans. At the same time, the U.S. capitalist rulers and their government and police agencies hated and feared Malcolm and his political example, and we know from history the brutal means they use to defend their class interests here and around the world. Sometimes that can best be done simply by being "slow" in "reacting."

Based on what we do know, the two "explanations" seem complementary to me, not mutually exclusive.

A convergence with other revolutionists

QUESTION: Malcolm X is often presented as someone who counterposed Black nationalism to the civil rights movement. But the gains of that mass social movement put the entire working class in this country in a better position to fight. Was there a political evolution by Malcolm X on this question, too?

BARNES: Malcolm's hands were tied so long as he remained in the Nation. Every time he took an initiative toward action in the streets, as he did not only in Los Angeles but several times in New York as well, he would be called to order by Elijah Muhammad. That's why, as he told us during the *Young Socialist* interview, he became politically disgusted that the Nation "didn't take part in politics," it didn't "take part in the civil rights struggle."[113]

During the discussion period in mid-February at the last OAAU meeting where Malcolm spoke, a questioner asked him, "Don't you think the organization should have some direct demonstrations, for instance, on discrimination in housing?" Malcolm replied: "I'm for anything you're for as long as it's going to get some results. . . . As long as it's in-

---

113. "Interview with the *Young Socialist*," p. 46 in this book.

telligent, as long as it's disciplined, as long as it's aimed in the right direction, I'm for it."[114]

But Malcolm always insisted on several things.

First, Blacks had the right and the responsibility to defend themselves against assaults by racists and the cops.

Second, there could be no reliance on the oppressors and their political parties—no moratoriums on protests to help get some Democrat or Republican or anyone else elected.

Third, picket lines, demonstrations, and other protest actions were *part* of a broader strategy along the road to building a revolutionary organization, toward making a revolution that would overthrow the social and political system responsible for racism and oppression.

And fourth, that what many people called a civil rights movement in the United States was in fact just one front— even if a very important one—of a worldwide struggle for human rights, of a worldwide revolution.

We've already discussed Malcolm's initiative in response to racist assaults on Black rights demonstrators in St. Augustine, Florida, and his trip to Selma, Alabama. We've talked about the discussions he organized in Harlem with young civil rights activists who had come up to New York from McComb, Mississippi. We've talked about his support for the efforts of Mississippi civil rights leader Fannie Lou Hamer, as well as those of Gloria Richardson and others in Cambridge, Maryland. Malcolm backed efforts by Black rights fighters and their supporters in Michigan to run candidates independent of the Democratic and Republican parties on the Freedom Now Party ticket. He gave encouragement to Clifton DeBerry, who ran for president in 1964 on the Socialist Workers Party ticket and was the first Black ever to contest for that office.

---

114. "There's a Worldwide Revolution Going On," in *February 1965: The Final Speeches*, p. 139.

Malcolm was always eager to be in the trenches alongside anyone who was fighting in an effective way that could take even one step toward victory over racism, oppression, and exploitation.

At the same time, Malcolm had to make the decisions that leaders and cadres of any small revolutionary organization must make. He had to decide how to use the time and scarce resources of his movement, a movement that was still just emerging when he was cut down. Given the influence of both the Nation of Islam and class-collaborationist misleaders of major civil rights organizations, Malcolm correctly placed great importance on the place of propaganda, of explaining the truth about the roots of Black oppression and the necessity of revolutionary organization and change.

Malcolm weighed all these considerations carefully during the twenty-two weeks he had to organize and carry out activity in the United States. He knew that without an organization of cadres who knew what they were fighting for, how and why they were doing so, and how to be disciplined, simple "activism" wouldn't advance the goal. But he also knew that without active engagement in the central struggles of the day, such a cadre could never be forged and tested in action.

Freed from the constraints of the Nation of Islam, Malcolm was turning toward the broader movement for Black rights and toward struggles to stop imperialist wars against the peoples of the semicolonial world. He saw the need to work and fight alongside those engaged in struggles, whether or not he agreed with the politics and strategy of their current leaders.

But Malcolm was *not* converging with the leadership of the civil rights movement in those years. In fact, his revolutionary political course during the months following his break from the Nation led him to accelerate his *political divergence* from those who acted on the pretense that the capitalist order could be reformed and improved. The millions of working people and youth who were being misled along that course could be fought for and won politically over time—that was Malcolm's conviction and his goal.

As for the vast majority of those who were *doing* the misleading, they would not be won over. They had to be taken on and defeated politically. There wasn't a millimeter of convergence with such forces.

Malcolm converged politically with other revolutionists, *worldwide*. That's why what Malcolm said, and what he did, remains so important today—and will continue to be until workers and the oppressed in this country and around the world have accomplished the goals he fought and lived for.

PART II

The Vanguard Record of Blacks in Struggles by Workers and Farmers

Radical Reconstruction: Its Conquests and the Consequences of Its Defeat

by Jack Barnes
August 1984

The vanguard place of workers who are Black in leading broad, proletarian-based social and political battles in the United States is amply confirmed in the history of the class struggle. The record goes back to the closing years of the U.S. Civil War, and especially to the postwar battle for Radical Reconstruction in which Blacks provided leadership in substantial parts of the South both to freed slaves and to exploited farmers and antislavery workers who were white. It has continued through battles by urban and rural working people, both Black and white, ever since.

The following assessment of the conquests of Radical Reconstruction and the heavy blow dealt to all toilers in the United States by its defeat is taken from an article by Jack Barnes on "The Fight for a Workers and Farmers Government in the United States," reviewing lessons learned by the communist movement through a century and a half of efforts worldwide to build an alliance of workers and rural toilers essential to a successful fight for state power.

The international working-class movement knows something about the devastating effects on toilers of forced dispossession from the land. That is how the modern hereditary proletariat was born—through the wholesale ruin of rural producers over several centuries. The rising capitalist class had to take away the lands and commons from masses of small farmers and rural producers and deprive them of their tools. It had to deprive them of any means of supporting themselves except by selling their labor power to a capitalist.[1]

In the United States, the formation of a hereditary proletariat took a different form from that in Europe and many other parts of the world. Throughout most of the eighteenth and nineteenth centuries, the working class in this country was created in large part through immigration—often of peasant families driven off their land in Europe. Many immigrants became small farmers. As a result, the growth of the U.S. working class throughout the nineteenth century went hand in hand with an expansion of the farming population. This was true despite the fact that many small farmers were already being expelled from the land in the eastern United States, with some heading westward to homestead and others into the cities in search of work.

Only since the beginning of the twentieth century, especially since the 1920s, has the growth of the U.S. working class through the ruin of small farmers resulted in a decline in the number of independent commodity producers on the land.

Following the revolutionary abolition of slavery, the creation of the Black proletariat was also integrally linked to the land question. In this case, however, proletarianization did not primarily involve the dispossession of Black farm-

---

1. One of the best descriptions of this process is in Karl Marx, *Capital*, vol. 1, chapter 27, "The Expropriation of the Agricultural Population from the Land."

ers (although that *has* been the fate of millions of farming families that are Black over the past one hundred years).

Instead, freed slaves in their great majority were *denied land*. In the initial two years following the Civil War, most ex-slaves were impressed into contract labor gangs on plantations under the notorious Black Codes adopted by most state governments of the vanquished Confederate slavocracy. This reactionary legislation was implemented with no effective opposition from Republican Andrew Johnson, who had become president following the assassination of Abraham Lincoln in April 1865. Blacks organized in the South to resist this effort by the planters to restore virtual slave labor conditions. They won the support of small sectors of the northern labor movement, as well as that of a layer of industrial capitalists and their representatives in Congress who were alarmed at efforts by the former slave owners to reassert their political influence.

As a result of this postwar struggle, by 1867 Radical Reconstruction regimes had been set up throughout the South, with the mandate of the U.S. Congress, backed up by the power of the Union Army. These new governments repealed the Black Codes and adopted legislation barring some of the most onerous provisions of the labor contracts that had been imposed on Black agricultural laborers.

The proletarianized ex-slaves, however, wanted more than better contracts and labor-law reform. They waged a struggle for land—for a radical agrarian reform that would break up the old plantations of the former slave owners and divide the land for use not only by the freed slaves but also by other small rural producers. They fought for the tools, livestock, cheap credit, and other things they would need to make a go of it as free farmers. "Forty acres and a mule" became their battle cry, one that echoed around the world and down through the years.

Exploited farmers and other toilers in the South who were

white also fought for land, for tools, for better conditions. Many initially joined in struggle with freed Black slaves. Small farmers and propertyless rural working people made up the big majority of the population in all these states. In five states Blacks were a majority.

In South Carolina, in particular, for a number of years following 1867 the exploited producers, led by Blacks, took big strides toward establishing a popular revolutionary government that, with Union troops in the background but clearly visible, advanced the class interests of the freed slaves, small farmers, and other working people. Throughout most of Radical Reconstruction the legislature there was majority Black, and the state government's social base among the freed slaves and other working people was organized through Union League chapters in many communities and an extensive popular militia.

The Second American Revolution did not come to an end in 1865 with the Union triumph over the slaveholders. No, it continued for more than a decade, through the rise of Radical Reconstruction. By 1870 the fight to get the Thirteenth, Fourteenth, and Fifteenth amendments to the Constitution adopted had been won, and Blacks and other toilers had begun breathing life into these hard-won rights to emancipation, citizenship, and suffrage.[2]

We should remember that African Americans were not granted the right to vote in the United States *for almost five years* following the Confederate Army's surrender at

---

2. The Thirteenth Amendment, ratified in 1865, abolished slavery and involuntary servitude in the United States. The Fourteenth Amendment, ratified in 1868, guaranteed U.S. citizenship to the freed slaves. The Fifteenth Amendment, ratified in 1870, guaranteed African Americans the right to vote. Since the end of World War II, the "due process" and "equal protection" clauses of the Fourteenth Amendment have been used as the basis for legislation and rulings won by working people protecting the civil rights of Blacks, immigrants, and women.

Appomattox Court House in April 1865. Voting qualifications remained the prerogative of each state government until February 1870, when the Fifteenth Amendment was ratified, stating, "The right of citizens of the United States to vote shall not be denied or abridged by the United States or by any State on account of race, color, or previous condition of servitude."

In April 1865, in his last speech, Lincoln for the first time had publicly proposed very limited suffrage for Blacks, saying: "I would myself prefer that [the right to vote] were now conferred on the very intelligent, and on those who serve our cause as soldiers." John Wilkes Booth, who was in the audience for that speech and murdered Lincoln only a few days later, wrote that even this suggestion had confirmed him in his determination to carry out the assassination.

Two years after that, with the adoption by Congress of the Reconstruction Act of March 1867, suffrage for Black males was made a precondition for readmission to the Union of the former Confederate states. But the readmission of the southern states turned out not to be a guarantee of male suffrage for Blacks.

Between 1863 and 1870, when the Fifteenth Amendment was adopted, proposals to enfranchise Blacks were defeated in more than fifteen northern states and territories! Outside the South only Iowa and Minnesota had adopted universal male suffrage. In fact, when the Fifteenth Amendment was submitted to the states for ratification in early 1869, it was initially rejected by the legislatures in New York, New Jersey, Ohio, California, and Delaware, among others.

The U.S. ruling class, its schools, and bourgeois historians hide or distort what happened during Radical Reconstruction. But this revolutionary experience of the producing classes is a story that needs to be told by a proletarian party in the United States, as an example of what many of our predecessors fought for a century ago—a forerunner of the kind of fighting workers and farmers alliance we are struggling for today. This story will find a ready audience among fighters in the factories and on the farms.

The most advanced of these Radical Reconstruction regimes, such as those in South Carolina and Mississippi, adopted immediate and democratic demands in the interests of working people. This progressive social legislation included the barring of racial discrimination; universal suffrage for males regardless of race; property taxes that fell heaviest on plantation owners and the moneyed classes; the first free public schools in the South (including desegregated and tuition-free university education in South Carolina); public hospitals and medical care for the poor; public-relief systems; the elimination of whipping and other cruel and inhuman punishments; and expanded grounds on which a woman could obtain a divorce.

Working farmers and artisans who were white faced the same exploiters as the freed slaves. Many of them had opposed secession from the Union, hated the privileged slavocracy that ruled the Confederacy, and supported emancipation. During the Civil War, Marx and Engels closely followed reports in the southern press of resistance by farmers and small-town and city working people against conscription and taxation. Substantial numbers of these toilers welcomed the measures carried out during Radical Reconstruction and joined in defending them.

None of the Reconstruction governments, however, had both the will and the power to enforce an expropriation of the big plantation owners that could have made possible a radical land reform, since the appointed Union Army commanders in each state held effective veto power over legislation and its enforcement. While some of these officers were more radical than others, none were willing to countenance a broadside attack on the landholdings of the southern property owners.

Even in South Carolina, where legislation to meet the land

"In South Carolina, the Radical Reconstruction regime throughout most of this period had a majority Black legislature," says Barnes, **"and its social base among freed slaves and other working people was organized through Union League chapters and an extensive popular militia in many communities."** Above, members of South Carolina legislature, 1868. Fifty were African American, thirteen white.

Center row singles out president of legislature and lt. governor Lemuel Boozer and speaker of legislature Franklin J. Moses—both white Republicans and natives of South Carolina. Moses is identified as the person "who raised the Confederate Flag on Fort Sumter" at opening of Civil War. Words beside Boozer's photo say, "40 acres and a mule"—the popular call for land for freed slaves and other rural poor.

"The revolutionary experience of the producing classes during Radical Reconstruction is a story that needs to be told by a proletarian party in the United States," says Barnes. **"It is an example of what many of our predecessors fought for a century ago—a forerunner of the kind of fighting workers and farmers alliance we are struggling for today."** Above, inset, Mississippi state House of Representatives and Senate, 1874–75. Enlargement shows some Republican House members (on right side), several Democrats in House (bottom left), and a few Senators (top left). As federal troops pulled back and White League terror mounted, number of African Americans in Mississippi legislature fell from 64 of 153 members in 1873 (42%) to 21 in 1876 (14%)—and soon afterwards, none for most of next century.

hunger of the freed slaves went the furthest, it never went beyond a homestead law allotting relatively meager funds *to purchase* land for distribution, together with property tax laws that did result in some big landholdings being forfeited to the state government by defaulting planters.

By and large, however, most freed slaves did not get any land, and were instead forced into sharecropping, tenant farming, and wage labor in the fields and towns. Often they worked under conditions of virtual debt peonage for large plantation owners. Of the white farmers and the few Black farmers who did have their own small acreage, many fell deeper and deeper into debt bondage. They often lost their land and ended up in the same situation as the majority of freed slaves and poorest whites.

The aspirations of the liberated and proletarianized Blacks, and their allies among southern white working people, were blocked by the growing power of the U.S. capitalist class, which during those same postwar years was landing significant blows against the working class and young labor movement. The final defeat of Radical Reconstruction required a bloody counterrevolution. The deal between the Democratic and Republican parties to withdraw Union troops from the South in 1877 accelerated a reign of terror by the Ku Klux Klan, the Knights of the White Camelia, and other racist gangs beholden to the interests of the exploiters.[3]

Farrell Dobbs explained this culminating chapter of the defeat of Radical Reconstruction in the first volume of *Revolutionary Continuity: Marxist Leadership in the U.S.*

---

3. In the 1876 presidential election, the Democratic Party candidate Samuel Tilden won more than 51 percent of the popular vote, but neither Tilden nor the Republican Rutherford Hayes tallied the required 185 electoral votes to become president. A deal worked out by a commission of Democratic and Republican members of the U.S. Congress handed the White House to Hayes in return for a pledge to withdraw all Union troops from the South, a promise Hayes rapidly fulfilled.

Farrell wrote:

> By 1877, Radical Reconstruction had gone down to
> bloody defeat and not only Afro-Americans but the en-
> tire working class had suffered what remains the worst
> setback in its history. The defeat was engineered by the
> dominant sectors of industrial and rising banking capital,
> a class that was incapable of carrying through a radical
> land reform in the old Confederacy and rightly feared
> the rise of a united working class in which Black and
> white artisans and industrial workers would come to-
> gether as a powerful oppositional force, allied with free
> working farmers.
>
> The rural poor and working class were forcibly di-
> vided along color lines in the years following 1877. The
> value of labor power was driven down and class solidar-
> ity crippled. Jim Crow, the system of extensive segrega-
> tion, was legalized. Racism spread at an accelerated pace
> throughout the entire United States.[4]

This defeat was suffered not only because the freed slaves,
who aspired to get land in order to become working farmers,
were betrayed by the bourgeoisie and both capitalist political
parties. It also occurred because the U.S. working class and
its organizations were as yet still too weak and politically
inexperienced to provide a labor leadership for the kind of
class-struggle social movement that could have made possible a massive expropriation and redistribution of land to
the freed slaves.

The defeat of Radical Reconstruction was devastating for
prospects to build a fighting alliance of workers and farm-

---

4. Farrell Dobbs, *Revolutionary Continuity: Marxist Leadership in
the U.S., The Early Years (1848–1917)* (Pathfinder, 1980), pp. 69–70
[2009 printing].

ers, Black and white, in this country. Any united action by the oppressed and exploited more and more also had to confront the development of U.S. imperialism during the final decades of the nineteenth century. The robber barons of rising finance capital encouraged racist poison as part of their ideological justification for imposing U.S. domination on the black-, brown-, and "yellow"-skinned peoples of Puerto Rico, Cuba, the Philippines, and Hawaii.[5]

The blows that defeated Radical Reconstruction were felt in the 1880s and 1890s in the financial crises and depression-like conditions that led to a groundswell of protest among farmers across the southern and middle-western United States. This emerging farmers' movement, known as the populist movement, took some significant initial steps to involve Black farmers and organizations such as the Colored Farmers' Alliance. These efforts were ultimately aborted, however, by the hand-in-hand expansion of Jim Crow at home and Uncle Sam abroad. Few populist leaders were able to stand up to these ruling-class pressures, and by the mid-1890s many had joined in the capitalist-orchestrated chorus of racism and jingoism.

The U.S. working-class movement at that time was as yet incapable of developing a political leadership that could present an anticapitalist and anti-imperialist program and strategy to the ranks of labor, to exploited farmers, and to landless Black proletarians.[6]

---

5. In 1898, at the dawn of the imperialist epoch, Puerto Rico, Cuba, and the Philippines, former colonies of Spain, were seized by Washington as victor's booty in what the U.S. rulers called the Spanish-American War. That same year, U.S. imperialism militarily seized, and later annexed, the then-independent country of Hawaii.

6. Farrell Dobbs discussed the objective factors underlying these political limitations of the U.S. labor movement at the close of the nineteenth century in *Revolutionary Continuity: Marxist Leadership in the U.S.,*

In 1877 Marx had anticipated that the powerful nation-wide strikes sparked by railroad workers in the United States that year, even if not successful,[7] might produce new clarity among the exploited about the deadly consequences of being tied politically to the bosses and landlords. It could create conditions in which a vanguard of the U.S. working class could provide leadership to exploited farmers and to the freed slaves. "This first eruption against the oligarchy of associated capital which has arisen since the Civil War will of course be put down," Marx wrote to Engels, "but it could quite well form the starting point for the establishment of a serious labour party in the United States."

Marx continued that the decision of newly elected Republican president Rutherford Hayes to withdraw Union troops defending Reconstruction governments in the South "will turn the Negroes into allies of the workers, and the large expropriations of land (especially fertile land) in favour of railway, mining, etc., companies will convert the peasants of the West, who are already very disenchanted, into allies of the workers."[8]

But this was not to be. The economic and political reserves

The Early Years. See in particular the chapters "Indigenous Origins" and "Gains and Setbacks," as well as the related articles and letters by Marx and Engels, written at the time, in the appendix to the book.

7. A strike initially by rail workers in Martinsburg, West Virginia, in July 1877 spread over the next few weeks to fourteen states. Some hundred thousand workers in rail and other industries engaged in what became the first nationwide strike in U.S. history. By the beginning of August these workers' battles had been crushed by the combined force of company thugs, city and state cops, and above all U.S. troops deployed by Republican president Rutherford Hayes.

8. Letter from Karl Marx to Frederick Engels, July 25, 1877, in Marx and Engels, *Collected Works* [hereafter *MECW*], vol. 45, p. 251. See also the forthcoming *The Second American Revolution: Marx and Engels on the U.S. Civil War* (Pathfinder, 2010).

of the rising U.S. industrial bourgeoisie were far from exhausted, and thus the class-collaborationist illusions among working people still had deep taproots. The class-struggle leadership of the working class and its revolutionary core were still too small in numbers and inexperienced in class combat. Over the next half century the United States would become the world's mightiest imperialist power, and the U.S. labor officialdom would become Uncle Sam's handmaiden.

Moreover, the defeat of Radical Reconstruction dealt a devastating blow to Blacks and other U.S. working people. The U.S. working class became more deeply divided by the national oppression of Blacks that was institutionalized in the South on new foundations in the bloody aftermath of 1877. U.S. labor's first giant step toward the formation of major industrial unions did not come for another six decades, and the formation of a labor party, anticipated by Marx 108 years ago, remains an unfulfilled task of our class to this day.

Nonetheless, Marx could not have been more correct about the alliance of social forces that would have to be at the center of a successful revolution in the United States—the working class, toilers who are Black, and exploited farmers.

Jim Crow, the Confederate Battle Flag, and the Fight for Land

by Jack Barnes
June 2001

Farmers who are Black face the same onerous conditions as other exploited producers on the land in the United States. In order to make ends meet, many of them, like other small farmers, must also work a job for wages. They are caught in a scissors between, on the one hand, the fluctuating prices they pay for seed, fertilizer, fuel, and other inputs they have to buy long before harvesting and selling their crops, and, on the other hand, the prices they eventually receive for the products of their labor. They are debt slaves to giant agribusiness suppliers and middlemen, and above all to the banks and other lenders.

Whether working farmers rent acreage, or are shackled to a mortgage and other payments on loans secured by land, buildings, and equipment, more and more of them since the end of World War II have faced foreclosure and been driven off the soil. According to government figures, the number of farm operators in the United States has dropped by nearly two-thirds since 1940. Meanwhile, farmland has declined by only 13 percent over that same period and agricultural output has increased more than two and a half times.

In addition to the burdens confronting all exploited farmers, those who are Black also face racist discrimination by banks, agricultural monopolies, and federal farm agencies in securing loans. Since the mid-twentieth century, the decline in the numbers of farm operators who are African American has been substantially greater than the overall drop, falling by more than 90 percent. Over the past several decades, Black farmers have not only joined other farmers in tractorcades and protest actions of all kinds. They have also mobilized to demand redress and compensation for the consequences of such historic discrimination.

The following is excerpted from a talk by Jack Barnes to a 2001 socialist conference in Oberlin, Ohio, organized by the Socialist Workers Party and Young Socialists.

Communist workers must take seriously the *history* of current struggles by farmers who are Black. We need to recognize their place in an ongoing continuity reaching back to the U.S. Civil War and Radical Reconstruction—the Second American Revolution—and the decades of reaction that followed in the countryside, towns, and cities across the South.

Many of these farmers are fighting to continue cultivating land that their kin have farmed for generations.[9] For a

---

9. In 1999 a federal judge approved a settlement of a class-action lawsuit, *Pigford v. Glickman,* against racist discrimination in government-funded loans and other services for farmers who are Black. Washington agreed to give each farmer who could provide evidence of discrimination between 1981 and 1996 a $50,000 tax-exempt payment, debt forgiveness, and preferential treatment on future loan applications. Although farmers' organizations leading the fight rejected the settlement as inadequate, the judge handed down the consent decree and appointed a monitor to review farmers' claims. As of 2008, according to the monitor's office, of the 22,500 farmers who filed for compensation, around 14,000 had been approved by a court-appointed arbitrator. Since the filing period

Black family in the U.S. South to have held onto land for that long means that previous generations fought and survived the lynch-mob terror of organized white-supremacist night riders that continued, and often accelerated, in the wake of the defeat of post–Civil War Radical Reconstruction. This came closer to fascist violence on a broad scale, and over an extended period, than anything else ever seen in this country.

In the decade following the defeat of the slavocracy in 1865, the rising northern industrial bourgeoisie—now re-knitting links with powerful landholding, commercial, and emerging manufacturing interests across the South—settled once and for all that it had no intention of meeting the aspirations of freed slaves for the radical land reform captured by the popular demand for "forty acres and a mule." Doing so, first of all, would have deprived these exploiters of a cheap supply of jobless laborers. What's more, the bourgeoisie correctly feared that an alliance of free farmers, Black and white, together with the growing manufacturing and machinofacturing working class in the cities, could pose a strong challenge to intensifying exploitation in town and country, North and South.

In 1877 the U.S. rulers withdrew federal troops from the states of the old Confederacy. These troops had been the armed force of last resort standing between the freed Black toilers, on the one hand, and gangs of well-armed reaction-

---

was so short and most farmers who are Black did not learn of the settlement in time to file, some 65,000 claims have been denied on grounds that farmers failed to meet the October 1999 filing deadline. In 2008 legislation was introduced into the U.S. Congress to reopen the claims process. In mid-2009, following further protests by Black farmers, the Obama administration announced that it would propose a $1.25 billion fund to "close the chapter" on the settlement—a cap well below the estimated $2 to $3 billion that would be necessary to make the payments to farmers ordered under the consent decree.

ary vigilantes, on the other. Throughout the closing decades of the nineteenth century and well into the twentieth, successive generations of organizations such as the Knights of the White Camelia, the White League, the Ku Klux Klan, the White Citizens' Councils, and many others—named, unnamed, or renamed—carried out an unrelenting reign of terror against the Black population in the South.

This systematic violence helped the capitalists drive toilers who were Black into virtual peonage as sharecroppers and tenant farmers, and made it possible for Jim Crow segregation to be imposed and codified into state law in one southern state after another. These gangs were also organized to break the spirit of any class-conscious worker or farmer anywhere in the South who wasn't Black—"nigger lovers"—and to prevent them from linking arms with toilers who were Black in common struggles for land, for public education, for cheap credit and railway rates, for labor union rights, or anything else in the interests of the oppressed and exploited. Anti-Catholic, anti-Chinese, and anti-Semitic prejudice and discrimination reached new heights.

Some of you may have already seen the exhibit of lynching photographs at the New York Historical Society that has been in Manhattan this year and will travel to other cities. If not, I recommend it.[10] Many of the photos are actual postcards of these outrages, produced by the organizers of the lynch mobs and widely distributed to popularize and legitimatize lynching as a "family activity." (Yes, a family activity. The lynchers and their "neighbors" brought their kids to a "community gathering" so they could watch "the nigger" twist in the wind, and then enjoy a picnic.) The

---

10. A reference to the exhibit, "Without Sanctuary: Photographs and Postcards of Lynching in America." Also see James Allen et al, *Without Sanctuary: Lynching Photography in America* (Santa Fe, New Mexico: Twin Palms, 2000).

aim of this officially sanctioned terror was to try to limit resistance by Blacks throughout the South. The photos are a powerful reminder of the history we've been discussing here, and the accompanying text and related displays point out that the decision to steal land from Black farmers often precipitated the lynchings.

As we work alongside farmers who are fighting to stay on the land, we should know this history—*our* history. The land isn't just a way to make a living. Nor is it just a symbol. The current resistance is often a link in battles that go back more than a century and a quarter. Together with fights by workers and the labor movement, these hard-fought battles by generations of farmers helped hold off some of the most reactionary consequences of the defeat of Radical Reconstruction that would have set back, much further than they did, the struggles of working people in the United States. And they helped make possible a new wave of struggle decades later, North and South, that by the end of the 1960s had brought the Jim Crow system crashing down.

The battles for Black freedom in rural counties, small towns, and cities across the South, and extending to the North, helped in turn to transform the possibilities for workers and farmers alike throughout this country, and throughout other parts of the world under assault by Washington. The conquests of this mass proletarian-based movement laid a foundation, among other things, for a common struggle with common demands by working farmers in the United States today, as part of a fighting worker-farmer alliance resisting the profit-driven course of the capitalist class. It attracted, politicized, and gave courage to several generations of youth who would provide the energy for struggles against the Vietnam War, against discrimination in all government employment and the armed forces, for the defense and extension of civil liberties and civil rights, for women's emancipation, and for an accompanying broad political radicalization.

**The Second American Revolution
did not come to an end in 1865.
It continued for more than a decade,
through the rise of Radical Reconstruction.**

JACK BARNES, 1985

The results of history remain alive for us, unresolved contradictions that never completely go away so long as the class questions posed by giant social and political conflicts remain unsettled and have yet to become a weapon in the hands of militants today. The full consequences of the defeat of Radical Reconstruction will only be uprooted following the victory of a proletarian revolution in this country. That's why struggles over state governments displaying the Confederate battle flag, or over statues or holidays in tribute to political or military leaders of the slaveholders' rebellion, continue to have weight in the class struggle many decades—indeed almost a century and a half—after it was routed in a bloody civil war.[11]

These fights today in South Carolina, Mississippi, and elsewhere are not about Blacks and supporters of civil rights being mean to somebody in the South whose great granddaddy was a Confederate soldier who "fought bravely" and was "a good man." Let's stipulate that. Many Confederate

---

11. The biggest of these fights was in South Carolina. On January 17, 2000, some fifty thousand people marched in Columbia, South Carolina, to demand the Confederate battle flag be taken down from the state capitol. The flag had been raised over the building in 1962 by the all-white state legislature as an act of defiant support to Jim Crow segregation and encouragement to those carrying out violent assaults on demonstrations for Black rights. Among the organizers of the Columbia march were members of International Longshoremen's Association Local 1422 in Charleston. Three days later ILA pickets at the docks protesting the use of scab labor by a shipper were assaulted by six hundred cops in riot gear. Several unionists were injured, eight arrested, and five indicted on felony charges of instigating a riot. In November 2001, in face of a growing defense campaign involving thousands of workers around the country, prosecutors dropped the frame-up felony charges and replaced them with misdemeanors, to which the workers pled no contest and were fined $100 each.

In July 2000, by vote of the state legislature, the Confederate banner was taken down and moved to a flagpole on capitol grounds next to a monument to fallen Confederate soldiers.

The U.S. rulers try to hide the history of Radical Reconstruction, just as they try to hide the history of labor battles. The truth explodes every racist and anti-working-class notion about what Blacks can accomplish, about the potential of fighting alliances between toilers who are Black and white, and much more.

JACK BARNES, 2006

"By 1870 the fight to get the 13th, 14th, and 15th amendments to the Constitution adopted had been won. Blacks and other toilers had begun breathing life into these hard-won rights to emancipation, citizenship, and suffrage," Barnes says. To exercise the right to vote during Reconstruction, African Americans often needed disciplined organization and self-defense. **Above,** recently enfranchised Blacks in Lincoln County, Georgia, rifles in hand, ford a creek on their way to the polls.

The Second American Revolution
did not come to an end in 1865.
It continued for more than a decade,
through the rise of Radical Reconstruction.

JACK BARNES, 1985

Below, January 1, 1863, the First South Carolina Volunteers, a Union Army Black combat regiment, listen to reading of Emancipation Proclamation, which freed all slaves in Confederate states and welcomed their enlistment. During Civil War some 200,000 Blacks served in Union Army as enlisted men and noncoms (officers were white); another 300,000 served among the army's laborers, spies, and servants. **Inset,** soldiers in U.S. Colored Artillery practice gun drills. Black Union soldiers were paid less and often given inferior weapons and medical care. **Bottom left,** victory parade of Union Army troops in Washington, D.C., May 1865, a month after surrender of Confederate forces. **Below,** Union troops under the command of Gen. William Sherman in Georgia. The "March to the Sea" from May to December 1864 effectively cut the Confederacy in half and dealt it a mortal blow.

After 1867, the exploited producers, led by formerly enslaved Blacks and backed by Union troops, took strides toward establishing popular democratic governments that advanced the class interests of the freedmen, small farmers, and other working people.

JACK BARNES, 1985

Reconstruction governments implemented laws barring race discrimination, establishing free public schools, taxes on large landholders, universal male suffrage, expanded rights for women, and public relief. Militias organized defense against counterrevolutionary assaults. Social conquests were popular among toilers of all skin colors.

This page, above, Blacks confronting counterrevolutionary mob, as symbolically represented in July 1868 *Harper's Weekly*. Person at center depicts official of Freedmen's Bureau, established in 1865 and initially headed by a Union Army general. **Opposite page, top,** both women and men participated in election campaign meetings in Reconstruction South, like this 1868 gathering. **Middle,** public schools, like this one in Vicksburg, Mississippi, were open to Blacks of all ages and both sexes. **Bottom,** May 19, 1870. Six-mile-long march in Baltimore, Maryland, celebrates passage of 15th Amendment to the U.S. Constitution, guaranteeing Black men right to vote. Only Iowa and Minnesota in the North had adopted universal male suffrage; similar measures had been defeated in more than fifteen northern states and territories.

> **"By 1877 Radical Reconstruction, betrayed by the northern bourgeoisie, had gone down to bloody defeat and not only Afro-Americans but the entire working class had suffered what remains the worst setback in our history."**
>
> FARRELL DOBBS, 1980

Above, counterrevolutionary White League army parades triumphantly in Lafayette Square, New Orleans, January 1877, as federal troops abandon Louisiana's elected Reconstruction government. For nearly a century following this defeat, Jim Crow "legal" segregation in South, the bulwark of de facto race segregation across U.S., divided rural poor and working class along color lines.

In final decades of 19th century, united action by oppressed and exploited had to confront growing hegemony of U.S. finance capital. Rulers annexed Hawaii and in 1898, in first war of imperialist epoch, deployed troops against Spain for control of Cuba, Puerto Rico, the Philippines, and Guam. **Facing page, top,** U.S. invasion force in Puerto Rico, which remains a U.S. colony to this day.

Former slaves waged a struggle for land. "Forty acres and a mule" became their battle cry. The northern industrial bourgeoisie and top Union Army command opposed broadside attack on landholdings of southern property owners. Blacks were forced into sharecropping, tenant farming, and wage labor in fields and towns. **Below,** cotton picking on Southern plantation in mid-1870s. Many former slaves worked for big plantation owners under conditions of virtual debt peonage.

"The capitalist ruling class, incapable of carrying through a radical land reform in the old Confederacy, rightly feared the rise of a united working class in which Black and white artisans and industrial workers would come together, allied with free working farmers."

FARRELL DOBBS, 1980

Workers in Baltimore, Maryland, battle state troops, July 20, 1877, as struggle by rail workers became first nationwide strike in U.S. history. "This first eruption since the Civil War against the associated oligarchy of capital," wrote Karl Marx, was a harbinger of the class forces—the working class, toilers who are Black, and exploited farmers—that would have to be at the center of any successful revolution in the United States.

soldiers did fight bravely and were good men; in their big majority they were the sons of workers and farmers, like most soldiers in any modern army, especially those in the infantry. What does that have to do with the murderous political meaning, both then and now, of the battle flag of the Confederate army, an army vanquished and crushed for all time 136 years ago?

When displayed today, that flag is an emblem of, and encouragement to, reactionary forces who are determined to preserve as much as they can of the consequences of a bloody counterrevolution that shaped the trajectory of the U.S. class struggle in the twentieth century. It is a rallying point for forces who are *acting* on that determination. It is a symbol of the fight by deadly enemies of labor to turn back the gains of the civil rights movement and to divide and weaken the working class in this country. It is the flag of cowards on the highways, assaulting the dignity of Blacks day in and day out with stickers and medallions on their rearview mirrors, windows, and bumpers. It is the banner under which, only a few years ago, brutal and bloody assaults against Blacks were launched. And, most important, it remains a banner under which such assaults—against African Americans, immigrants, Jews, abortion clinics, gays, and other targets of reaction—often *are* and *will be* launched until the capitalist roots of that Dixie rag are ripped out of the ground by the toilers of this country and replaced by the dictatorship of the proletariat.

Class-conscious workers and farmers always strive to function in the present as a part of ongoing history. We don't approach the present as simply a *moment*. We don't approach social phenomena and political activity like a collection of snapshots to look at, one by one by one. To do so would mean bowing to the pragmatism instilled in the consciousness of working people by the very operations and history of the capitalist system in the United States, a pragmatism that guides the functioning of the bourgeoisie itself. The last thing workers and farmers are supposed to do in this country is to think in historic—contradictory and complex—terms, let alone act on this understanding. All the history we're supposed to know and believe in can be boiled down to this: "America is the land of opportunity. If you work hard and stay out of trouble, you can get ahead, become your own boss, and maybe get a business and hire some workers yourself some day." That's it.

We are often involved in battles that go back generations—whether it's a struggle by Black farmers, or a fight by coal miners or uranium miners to defend hard-won union rights and government-funded medical benefits, or decades-long battles around textile mills or packing plants. Whenever we do find ourselves in the midst of such battles, we should take special pleasure in these experiences and draw from them everything we can.

Among other reasons, knowledge of that living history can be a source of proletarian humility—as well as a reminder of our responsibility. Because it helps workers, including ourselves, to understand that individual actions don't count for much unless they are part of a sustained, disciplined, and collective effort over time. Unless they are part of a historic timeline of class combat we are fully conscious of. It reminds us that irresponsibility or indiscipline results in a needless respilling of blood already shed.

Robert F. Williams, the Cuban Revolution, and Self-Defense against Racist Violence

by Jack Barnes
October 1996, March 2001

In June 1964 Malcolm X offered to dispatch members of the Organization of Afro-American Unity (OAAU) to St. Augustine, Florida, to help organize defense guards for civil rights protesters there. Demonstrators engaged in lunch-counter sit-ins and other actions to demand desegregation of public facilities were repeatedly being beaten by Ku Klux Klan thugs and jailed by local cops. "If the federal government will not send troops to your aid," Malcolm wrote to King in a telegram cited earlier, "just say the word and we will immediately dispatch some of our brothers [former members of the Nation's Fruit of Islam, trained by Malcolm in New York] to organize self-defense units among our people." King indignantly rejected the offer.

A quarter century earlier, in March 1938, Bolshevik leader Leon Trotsky, forced into exile in Mexico, had offered similar counsel—in this case to more receptive ears—to a visiting leadership delegation from the Socialist Workers Party. At the time, gunmen, scabs, city cops, and other goons mobilized by the incipient fascist mayor of Jersey City, New Jersey, Democrat Frank Hague, were carrying out a reign of terror against unionists and other militants in Hudson County. In face of these rightist attacks, Trotsky urged communists to tell workers there: "If the federal power cannot control the mayor, then we, the workers, must organize for our protection a workers' militia and fight for our rights."

In August 1938, a few months after that discussion with Trotsky, and as a direct result of it, SWP cadres who for almost five years had been part of the leadership of Teamster Local 544 in Minneapolis, Minnesota, helped organize a 600-strong Union Defense Guard to meet growing threats by fascist forces there. A fascist cadre called the Silver Shirts had been invited into Hennepin and Ramsey counties, financed by the employers, to assault militants and bust up the increasingly powerful union movement, which had become the organizing center of labor battles across the entire upper Midwest—as far west as Seattle, and south into Oklahoma and Texas. In the wake of disciplined mobilizations by the union defense units, the fascist goons left town and called off their organizing efforts.

Trained and tempered in this spirit, in the 1960s the Socialist Workers Party and Young Socialist Alliance helped spread the truth about and joined in defense efforts on behalf of Black rights fighters who organized to guard their communities and their protest actions against the Klan, the White Citizens' Council, and other racist outfits. Most prominent among these militants were the Deacons for Defense and Justice in Louisiana and Mississippi, and the NAACP chapter in Monroe, North Carolina, led by Robert F. Williams.

Ed Shaw, a member of the Socialist Workers Party and Clifton DeBerry's vice-presidential running mate on the party's 1964 ticket, had first gotten to know Robert F. Williams in the early 1950s when they were working the night shift together in the Curtiss-Wright aircraft engine plant in Woodbridge, New Jersey. Williams had just returned from the Korean War, where he had served in the Marines. During World War II Shaw had been a seaman in the merchant marine, including on the perilous "Murmansk Run" convoys transporting U.S. "Lend Lease" war matériel to Arctic ports in the Soviet Union. These two young workers hit it off fast.

A few years later Williams moved back to Monroe, North Carolina, where he had been born, and soon became head of the NAACP chapter there. Under his leadership, the chapter recruited hundreds of members as it conducted an uncompromising fight against Jim Crow discrimination. This included organizing Blacks to defend themselves, armed when necessary, from violent attacks by the Ku Klux Klan and other racist forces.

A defender of the Cuban Revolution, Williams was also a founder and spokesperson of the Fair Play for Cuba Committee in 1960.

Below is a 1996 message sent by Jack Barnes to the Robert Williams Tribute Committee, which was organizing a meeting to celebrate Williams's life. The meeting, which took place in Detroit on November 1 of that year, had originally been planned to honor Williams while he was still alive. Williams died on October 15, however. Barnes's letter was written prior to Williams's death.

The Socialist Workers Party welcomes this opportunity to greet and pay tribute to Robert F. Williams. His integrity and courage as a leader of the struggle against racism, exploitation, and oppression set an important example for a generation becoming active in politics in the late 1950s and early 1960s. The struggles he helped initiate and lead to desegregate public facilities in the Jim Crow South, and to organize self-defense of the Black community against Ku Klux Klan night riders, made Monroe, North Carolina, in those years an emblem of resistance to bigotry and social injustice, not just in the United States but around the world.

In 1958–59 Robert F. Williams came to the defense of

two Monroe schoolboys—one seven years old, the other nine, both of them Black—who were arrested and railroaded to jail on charges of "assaulting and molesting a white female." Their "crime"? That one of the boys had been kissed by a seven-year-old white girl in the presence of the other boy (the latter was convicted as an "accomplice"). Williams and other militants in Monroe launched the Committee to Combat Racial Injustice, in which, alongside many others across the country, members of the Socialist Workers Party and Young Socialist Alliance participated. Many of its supporters later formed the Committee to Aid the Monroe Defendants in 1961, when Williams himself was framed up on kidnapping charges and driven into exile for eight years.[12]

I met Robert Williams in early 1961, when Black rights supporters and members of the Fair Play for Cuba Committee at Minnesota's Carleton College organized a meeting at which he was a featured speaker,[13] along with Ed Shaw, a Midwest leader of the Fair Play for Cuba Committee who was also a leader of the Detroit branch of the SWP at that

---

12. In August 1961, in the midst of mobilizations by white racist mobs in Monroe and efforts by the Black community to defend itself, a car carrying a white couple took a wrong turn and wound up in the heart of Monroe's Black community. To ensure the couple's safety following threats by a few individuals to do them harm, Williams took them to his house for several hours until it was safe for them to leave. For this he was framed on kidnapping charges and became the object of an FBI manhunt. Williams and his family were able to elude the net, and he eventually made his way to Cuba, where he received political asylum. In 1965 Williams moved to China, where he stayed until his return to the United States in 1969.

13. Williams was one of the eight African Americans among the thirty signers of an April 1960 full-page ad in the *New York Times* launching the Fair Play for Cuba Committee. Others included television journalist Richard Gibson and novelists James Baldwin, Frank London Brown, John O. Killens, and Julian Mayfield.

time.[14] Williams was on a nationwide speaking tour in defense of the Cuban Revolution and in support of the sharpening mass struggle for Black rights. The meeting had an enormous political impact on all of us. I recall being struck during the discussion period by how each of the speakers appeared equally comfortable in fielding questions about either the socialist revolution unfolding in Cuba or the battles for Black rights under way in this country, or both.

Working people and youth today need to learn and relearn this history, so we can emulate these examples. Doing so will better prepare all of us to resist probes against our democratic rights, as the bipartisan rulers press to take back social gains won by labor and civil rights struggles earlier in this century. In the course of such battles, as Malcolm X said, young fighters will recognize and assert their self-worth and transform themselves as they work to transform society. These militants are and will be the best tribute to those like Robert F. Williams in whose footsteps they tread.

Once again, on behalf of the Socialist Workers Party I send greetings to Robert Williams, Mabel Williams, and other participants in the Detroit meeting your committee is organizing.

In solidarity and in fond salute,
Jack Barnes
National Secretary
Socialist Workers Party

---

14. Shaw and Williams had stayed in contact since the early 1950s. While working at the aircraft plant in Woodbridge, New Jersey, Williams became a regular reader of the *Militant*. The April 13, 1953, issue contains a poem on the fight against Jim Crow that Williams had sent to the paper.

One of the first acts of the Cuban Revolution in early 1959 was to ban racial discrimination in employment and public facilities, putting an end to Jim Crow practices that had been imposed in Cuba with the U.S. occupation of the island in 1898. Other measures stamping the revolution's working-class trajectory included a radical land reform that ended the system of vast landed estates and gave deeds to over 100,000 landless peasants, as well as a literacy drive that taught close to a million people to read and write, wiping out illiteracy in a single year. In the second half of 1960 the major imperialist and Cuban-owned capitalist enterprises were expropriated by massive mobilizations of working people across the island, registering the end of the dictatorship of capital and the establishment of the dictatorship of the proletariat in Cuba, the opening of the socialist revolution in the Americas.

Jack Barnes was in Cuba during those days of revolutionary upheaval. He was there on a college grant to study the ongoing land reform. While doing so he participated in a number of other activities, including the First Latin American Youth Congress in Havana in July 1960. Like thousands of youth around the world, over the previous months he had been drawn to the new Cuban government's revolutionary course. And during the summer months in Cuba, he became determined to bring back firsthand knowledge about the revolution to share with others in the United States.

When Barnes returned to school in Minnesota that fall, he helped form a campus chapter of the Fair Play for Cuba Committee, which among other activities organized the meeting for Robert F. Williams referred to in the tribute above.

The excerpt below, describing this period, is from *Cuba and the Coming American Revolution* by Jack Barnes, published in 2001.

As Cuban workers and farmers pressed forward their social-ist revolution and U.S. aggression mounted in reaction to their gains, the lessons transformed the way we looked at the battle for Black rights in the United States as well. The mass proletarian struggle to bring down the Jim Crow system of statutory segregation throughout the South, with its various forms of discrimination extending throughout the country, was marching toward bloody victories at the same time that the Cuban Revolution was advancing. We could see in practice that there were powerful social forces within the United States capable of carrying out a revolutionary social transformation like the working people of Cuba were bringing into being.

The core of the activists defending the Cuban Revolution were young people who had cut their political eyeteeth as part of the civil rights battles, supporting the Woolworth lunch counter sit-ins[15] and joining or supporting marches and other protests in Alabama, Georgia, Mississippi, and elsewhere in the South.

The many faces of reaction, some in Ku Klux Klan hoods, others with sheriff's uniforms and FBI jackets protecting them; the lynchings and murders on isolated country roads; the dogs and water cannons unleashed on protesters—all were burned in our consciousness as part of the lessons we were learning about the violence and brutality of the U.S. ruling class and the lengths to which it will go to defend its property and prerogatives.

And we were learning lessons, too, from the self-defense

---

15. On February 1, 1960, four Black college students led an organized protest at a whites-only lunch counter at a Woolworth's department store in Greensboro, North Carolina, sitting down and asking for service. Their request was refused and they remained seated until closing time. Within days, similar sit-ins spread to other southern cities, and support picket lines took place outside Woolworth's stores across the United States. Thousands were soon involved in such protests, which eventually won desegregation of lunch counters at Woolworth's and at other places throughout the South.

organized by Black veterans in Monroe, North Carolina, and elsewhere in the South. Immediately following the U.S. defeat at the Bay of Pigs, during a debate in one of the six committees of the United Nations General Assembly, Cuban foreign minister Raúl Roa read a message that former Monroe NAACP president Robert F. Williams had asked him to convey to the U.S. government.

"Now that the United States has proclaimed military support for people willing to rebel against oppression," Williams wrote, "oppressed Negroes in the South urgently request tanks, artillery, bombs, money, use of American air fields and white mercenaries to crush racist tyrants who have betrayed the American Revolution and Civil War."

We rapidly came to see that the legal and extralegal violence directed against those fighting for their rights and dignity as human beings here in the United States was one and the same as the mounting overt and covert aggression against the people of Cuba. We took part in the struggle for Black rights as part of the *world* class struggle. It became totally intertwined for us with the stakes in defending the Cuban Revolution.

This was exemplified above all by the convergence of the Cuban Revolution and Malcolm X, whose voice of uncompromising revolutionary struggle—by any means necessary— was then increasingly making itself heard. Malcolm welcomed Fidel Castro to the Hotel Theresa in Harlem during the Cuban delegation's trip to the United Nations in 1960. Malcolm invited Che Guevara to address a meeting of the Organization of Afro-American Unity during Che's trip to New York in 1964.[16]

---

16. Both Fidel Castro's 1960 meeting with Malcolm X and Malcolm's invitation to Guevara in 1964 are described in Part I of this book in "Malcolm X: Revolutionary Leader of the Working Class," pp. 109–11.

For us, these and other expressions of the growing mutual respect and solidarity that marked relations between Malcolm X and the Cuban leadership were further confirmation of our own developing world view.

The Cosmopolitan 'Meritocracy' and the Changing Class Structure of the Black Nationality

by Jack Barnes
November 2008 and April 2009

This chapter is based on reports presented by Jack Barnes to an April 11–13, 2009, Socialist Workers Party leadership conference in New York and a November 22, 2008, talk by Barnes to a public meeting of some 375 participants held in Newark, New Jersey, sponsored by the SWP and Young Socialists.

The tongue-in-cheek anointment of William Jefferson Clinton as "the first Black president" of the United States during a Congressional Black Caucus awards dinner in September 2001 was more than simply a post-cocktails laugh line. It registered the consolidation of a bourgeoisified social layer of African Americans, a by-product of the increasing class stratification of the Black population and an inevitable capitalist perversion of victories won by the Black rights movement of the 1950s and 1960s. This process was reinforced by the credit-fueled capitalist "prosperity" and "good times" that began unraveling only in the latter half of the opening decade of the twenty-first century.

Within the Black nationality there had been a significant growth of middle-class and professional layers, even a bourgeois layer—to a degree unthinkable to people of all classes and races in the United States no more than a quarter century earlier. Well before his term in the White House began in 1993, Clinton had recognized the significance of this development for the stability of capitalist rule in the United States, and in particular its importance for the Democratic Party at the local, state, and federal levels. Clinton appointed many more Blacks to his administration than did any of the forty-one presidents before him, or, so far, the two after him. He named nine African Americans to cabinet-level positions and nine as assistants to the president, not to mention thousands of appointments to other posts throughout the federal bureaucracy.

The Black Caucus members were honoring Clinton for his contribution to the career advancement of their own social peers, not for promoting the economic and social advancement of the toiling majority of African Americans or of workers and farmers as a whole in the United States.

It's important for the working-class movement to understand the scope and pace of the expansion of this layer of the Black population in recent decades, as well as its limits.

The proportion of Blacks in the United States with annual family incomes between $50,000 and $100,000 (in constant 2006 dollars) has jumped from 12 percent in 1967 to 23 percent in 2006. Some one in ten Black families today—9.1 percent—have annual incomes of more than $100,000 (again in 2006 dollars), compared to under 2 percent only forty years ago.

As recently as 1988 there had never been a single chief executive officer (CEO) of a major U.S. corporation or corporate division who was Black—*not one*. Today there are more than twenty. And not of small companies "the average American" has never heard of. Over the last half decade, businesses known the world over that have had CEOs who are Black include American Express, Merrill Lynch, Time Warner, Sears, Fannie Mae, Duke Energy, Dun & Bradstreet, Symantec, Aetna, Oracle, Xerox, and Avis. The most recent addition, the new chief executive at Xerox, is both female and Black.

This is the tip of a new *social layer* of the African American population, a layer (as opposed to a large handful of individuals) that has existed for only a generation or two at most. It is different from the small middle class among African Americans throughout most of the twentieth century: school teachers; preachers at large churches; owners of funeral parlors, auto dealerships, and other small businesses catering to Blacks; and a handful of lawyers, accountants, and doctors practicing almost exclusively in Black neighborhoods and serving Black-owned businesses.

One indication of the newness of this middle class within the African American nationality is the lag between the growth in its members' median annual *income*—which expanded quite rapidly, once certain racist barriers had been battered down by the Black rights movement—and their median *wealth*, which takes a lot more time to accumulate and to pass along tax free through inheritance and family trusts and foundations. The median annual income of Blacks is now 62 percent of that of whites, up from 56 percent in the 1960s. For Blacks who are married, median family income is now 80 percent of that of comparable families both of whose adults are white. But the median net worth of Black families (not just those who are married)—that is, their accumulated wealth—remains less than 20 percent that of whites. And a much higher percentage of the wealth held by Blacks is accounted for by a house, not by stocks, bonds, and other capital. In that sense, Blacks, relative to whites, remain "house rich and cash poor," as the old expression goes.

But that, too, has been changing. In fact, based on government figures, a little more than 10 percent of those categorized as "nonwhite or Hispanic" directly own stocks today (that is, not just indirectly—and for most, insecurely—through limited participation rights in a pension fund, medical plan, etc.), up nearly 60 percent from a quarter century ago. The respective figure for those categorized as "non-Hispanic whites" is 24.7—that is, roughly two and a half times the percentage of "nonwhite or Hispanic" stock owners.

A few hundred thousand African Americans, roughly 0.4 percent of Black households, hold bonds. In this case, the respective figure for non-Hispanic whites is 3.8 percent—that is, nearly ten times the percentage of African American bondholders. (For the tiny handful of propertied ruling families, bonds—government, agency, and corporate—are the single biggest storehouse of the "permanent" wealth they obtain from their share in the total surplus value squeezed from exploiting the social labor of workers, farmers, and other toiling producers around the world.)

This well-off social layer of the African American population also has substantially more weight than ever before among Democratic Party officeholders and functionaries. Forty-three members of the U.S. House of Representatives today are Black—10 percent—up from only four members, or less than 1 percent, in 1963. The number of state legislators who are African American has tripled since 1970, and nearly a third were elected in districts with predominantly white populations. Today Blacks are mayors of some 50 of the 600 U.S. cities with populations of 50,000 or more, while prior to 1967 there had not been a single African American mayor of a major city for almost a hundred years—since the bloody crushing of Radical Reconstruction.

In fact, this social layer of the Black population has become the third leg of the "coalition" that turns out the vote for the imperialists who run the Democratic Party—the other two being the trade union officialdom and the patronage-based political machines of major U.S. cities. The political representatives of this layer have replaced the "Dixiecrats," the Democratic Party functionaries of the former Confederate states, who prior to the defeat of Jim Crow segregation in the 1960s had for decades formed the institutional bulwark of that racist system and guaranteed the Democrats' viability as a national party.

Barack Obama and the 'meritocracy'

This growth of the Black middle classes and newly enlarged Black bourgeoisie, which rose on the crest of the debt-driven capitalist expansion of the 1980s and 1990s, is a shift that is already largely behind us. Politically it culminated during the Clinton administration of 1993 to 2000.

Despite what is often said in the capitalist media and elsewhere, the election of Barack Obama as president registers not the existence of this social layer among African Americans but something different in the evolution of class relations in the United States. It's not "a Black thing." The new administration owes its ascension to the explosive growth over the past few decades of a new stratum of bourgeois-minded professionals and middle-class individuals—*of all colors and hues*—in cities, suburbs, and university towns across the country.

From the beginning of his years in Arkansas state politics in the mid-1970s, Clinton had opportunistically recognized what the by-products of the conquests of the Black rights struggle opened for Democratic Party politicians such as himself. From the outset he actively *worked* to ensure himself and his party a broader and broader "Black vote." Clinton's relationship with the Congressional Black Caucus and bourgeois misleaders of civil rights, labor, and women's organizations was to some degree symbiotic, but he certainly needed these "brothers and sisters" as much, if not more, than they needed him.

The Obama phenomenon came later and is quite different. Not only did Obama not need to exert substantial effort during his election campaign to win the Black vote, there is virtually nothing he could realistically have done *to lose it*. The same is true, even if to a slightly lesser degree, among Latinos, and even among student youth, including a sizable majority of students who are white. As a result, the new president's relationship with the Black Caucus and civil rights and other misleaderships is decidedly not symbiotic; *they* need *him*, not vice versa. (The broader Democratic Party congressional "leadership" is another and more difficult problem for the new administration.)

This expanding layer of the comfortable middle classes, whose place in bourgeois society *is* registered by the 2008 presidential election results, is composed of the handsomely remunerated staffs of so-called nonprofit foundations, charities, "community organizations," and "nongovernmental organizations" (NGOs)—in the United States and worldwide; of well-placed professors and top university administrative personnel; of attorneys, lobbyists, and others. The lives and livelihoods of these growing foundation- and university-centered strata in capitalist society—who, along with bankers and businessmen, cycle back and forth into and out of government positions—are themselves largely unconnected to the production, reproduction, or circulation of social wealth. Their existence is more and more alien to the conditions of life of working people or other producers of *any* racial or national background.

This reality was reflected in the presidential election results in November. Obama, of course, largely locked up the so-called Black vote. That isn't what pushed him so decisively over the top in the race against Republican John McCain, however. Among the most striking changes from previous elections is that Obama won 52 percent of the votes from those with annual incomes of more than $200,000, whereas

Democrat John Kerry had won 35 percent of this layer only four years earlier.

And for the first time in many decades, the Democratic presidential candidate in 2008 won more than 50% of the votes in the nation's largely white suburbs, compared to the 41% and 47% share taken by Clinton in 1992 and 1996. What's more, while the Republicans still dominated many suburbs populated by more established "old wealth"—places such as New Canaan and Darien, Connecticut; Saddle River and Englewood Cliffs, New Jersey; or Sunfish Lake and North Oaks, Minnesota—he tallied substantial margins in towns with larger congregations of high-income professionals, the parasitic users of wealth—places such as Westport (65%), West Hartford (70%), and Greenwich (54%), Connecticut; Montclair (84%), Tenafly (64%), and Ridgewood (56%), New Jersey; Edina (56%), Minnesota; and numerous others. More than 65% of voters in Scarsdale, one of New York City's most exclusive suburbs, voted for Obama, and Westchester County—the second wealthiest county in the state, and twelfth richest in the United States—went for Obama by a 63% margin (up from 58% for Kerry in 2004 and 56% for Clinton in 1996).

The aspiring social layer the new president is part of is *bourgeois* in its class interests, its values, and its world outlook. But it is not a section of the capitalist class in becoming. It is not "entrepreneurial." It is not composed of the owners, top managers, or large debt holders of rapidly expanding new businesses—factories, farms, technology companies, or financial or commercial enterprises. The long, debt-fueled capitalist "boom" of the past three decades was marked by the stagnation of investment in capacity-expanding plant and equipment, and by an accompanying slowness in the drawing of production labor into the creation of social wealth. This stagnation of capital accumulation, together with the expansion of the middle-class layer we're discussing, are in fact two sides of the same coin. Its members enjoy high incomes, but very few can or will pass down sizable capital through family trusts to coming generations.

Instead, this is a self-designated "enlightened meritocracy," determined to con the world into accepting the myth that the economic and social advancement of its members is just reward for their individual intelligence, education, and "service." Its members truly believe that their "brightness," their "quickness," their "contributions to public life," their "service," their "sacrifices" (they humbly point out they could be making a lot more in business or banking) give them the right to make decisions, to administer society on behalf of the bourgeoisie—on behalf of what they claim to be the interests of "the people." In exchange they get bigger and better homes, obscenely expensive K-through-16-plus education for their bloodline, high-end consumer "necessities," plus the equivalent of a "law enforcement discount" on all major financial transactions. (The killing the Obamas made in acquiring their Hyde Park manse and grounds in Chicago, generously subsidized by a big-time Daley machine fund-raiser, is but one example typical of these milieus.) And believe it or not, these bourgeois wannabes see all this as social sophistication, not the conspicuous consumption of schlock.

While the existence and expansion of these strata are largely divorced from the production process, they are very much bound up with the production and reproduction of *capitalist social relations*. They have a *parasitic* existence. To maintain their high incomes and living standards, they are dependent on skimming off a portion of surplus value— "rents"—produced by working people and appropriated by the bourgeoisie. Yet the big majority of them contribute nothing to the creation of that value, even in wasteful or socially harmful ways.

Instead, many of them pursue careers—in the universities,

the media, "think tanks," and elsewhere—that generate ideological rationalizations for class exploitation and inequality (as they strive to "reform" it, of course). Others, whether as highly paid supervisory personnel, staffers, or attorneys, administer the rulers' efforts through foundations, "advocacy groups," NGOs, charities, and other "nonprofit" institutions, here and around the world, to postpone and buffer the explosive social and political responses by working people to our worsening living and job conditions.[17]

This is a social layer that is insecure in its class position. It lacks the confidence exhibited by the bourgeoisie, even by the nouveau riche bourgeoisie. The propertied rulers—comprising only hundreds of families, not thousands—*are* a confident class (except during prerevolutionary crises or times of a rapidly accelerating breakdown of the capitalist order). Not only do they own, control, and hold the debt in perpetuity on the commanding heights of industry, banking, land, and trade. They also dominate the state and all aspects of social and political life, and finance the production of culture and the arts, including its "cutting edges."

The meritocracy, to the contrary, is *not* confident. Dependent on cadging from the capitalists a portion of the wealth created by the exploited producers, these privileged aspirants to bourgeois affluence—a lifestyle they are convinced "society" *owes* them—nonetheless fear at some point being pushed back toward the conditions of the working classes. On the one hand, due to their very size as a stratum of society—*it's millions, if not tens of millions* in the United States today—they recognize that the rulers find them useful to bolster illusions in the supposedly limitless "careers

---

17. The trade union officialdom, despite their petty-bourgeois lifestyles and bourgeois outlook, is not really a part of this layer. They are still too connected, just by the character of their dues base and function in capitalist society, to the grit and grime of working.—JB.

open to talent" under capitalism. At the same time, and despite their shameless self-promotion, many of them also sense that since they serve no *essential* economic or political functions in the production and reproduction of surplus value, they live at the forbearance of the bourgeoisie. In the end, large numbers of them are expendable, especially at times of deepening social crisis.

The capitalist rulers are *utterly pragmatic* in their policies, but they *do* have class policies. They do what they deem necessary to defend their profits, their property and its accompanying prerogatives, and above all their class dictatorship. They *use* that dictatorship—they *use* their state power: their cops, their courts, their armed forces, their currency, and their border controls.

In contrast, this "meritocratic" middle layer has no class policy course of its own. To the degree they commit themselves to a course of action—often camouflaged as caring, feeling, thoughtful, and above all very intelligent—such policies are in fact derivative of the needs and demands of their bourgeois patrons. Despite the Obama *campaign's* mantra of "change," for example, the Obama *administration* is relying on exactly the same top Wall Street bankers and financiers as its predecessors, in fact, the very same moneyed interests—even the same individuals—who have been the architects of today's accelerating capitalist economic and financial crisis. And more than any other administration in the history of U.S. imperialism, its foreign, military, and "domestic security" policies are stamped by near total deference to the top echelons of the professional officer corps of the U.S. armed forces.

This is the social layer from which Barack Obama emerged. Not from the majority proletarian Black nationality. Not from the producing, entrepreneurial small-business milieu, the petty bourgeoisie. And not from the bourgeoisie. It is with the class interests and world outlook of this increasingly multinational "meritocracy" that Obama identifies.

The main public "persona" they affect is one of measured empathy, a veneer behind which lies social hypocrisy. They too "feel our pain" but lecture us—scold us—more than Clinton ever tried to get away with. The main pretension is the clarity of their thought and skill at winning over their listeners ("Let me be clear. . . .").

They resent their vulnerability in face of the actual holders of capital. It rankles and instills in them a thinly veiled cynicism toward traditional bourgeois values such as patriotism, thrift, faith, and family (that is, values *promoted* by the bourgeoisie as essential mainstays of social order, not necessarily common currency among the propertied classes themselves). And since, as Marx and Engels explained more than 150 years ago, "The ideas of the ruling class are in every epoch the ruling ideas,"[18] such cynicism also puts this elect of "intelligence" and advantage at odds with the values and standards held by broad sections of the working class in the United States as well.

Like others in his social milieu—Caucasian, Black, Latino, or otherwise—Obama thinks of himself as a cosmopolitan in the way the dictionary defines the word: *"having wide international sophistication, worldly."* Sharply different from straightforward bourgeois nationalism (usually called "patriotism").

After several primary victories in early 2008, Michelle Obama said that "for the first time in my adult life I am proud of my country." Barack Obama himself initially decided not to sport an American flag lapel pin (a decision he later reversed as the contest with Hillary Clinton became nail-bitingly tight in Pennsylvania). And when the Democratic candidate spoke to a 200,000-strong crowd in Berlin

---

18. Karl Marx and Frederick Engels, "The German Ideology," in *MECW*, vol. 5, p. 59.

last July, he announced he was "a proud citizen of the United States and a fellow citizen of the world." The Republican right raised a hue and cry over each of these incidents, and—given what has long been deemed acceptable from the standpoint of their class—they had reason for complaint.

The new president, of course, is now showing in Iraq, Afghanistan, Pakistan, North Korea, and elsewhere that his administration will unleash U.S. imperialism's massive economic power and death-dealing military might to "defend" the national borders, currency, and broader interests of this country's ruling class. That's true. But Barack Obama and many others in the meritocracy, of whatever skin color, do *not* consider themselves, first and foremost, Americans.

That doesn't mean that those in this layer are internationalists, even bourgeois internationalists, much less proletarian internationalists. But the cosmopolitans *do* identify with their privileged social peers around the world. They *do* have a social identification with these layers; they share a mission. They *do* care what professors, NGO staffers, attorneys, and other "brights"[19] in Paris, Berlin, Rome, and London think about them. They *do* rely on such support as a counterweight to the ruling families at home who ultimately tell them what they will and will not do.

---

19. In articles published in 2003 in the *New York Times* and in *Wired* and *Free Inquiry* magazines, Daniel Dennett and Richard Dawkins—university professors of philosophy and evolutionary biology respectively, and both authors of quite profitable best-sellers among the recent crop of "atheist" books—proclaimed themselves the pioneers of a global "constituency" of "any individual whose worldview is free of supernatural or mystical forces and entities." ("We" all know who that is, *and isn't*, don't "we"?) In his original *New York Times* op-ed column, Dennett disingenuously protested: "Don't confuse the noun with the adjective: 'I'm a bright' is not a boast but a proud avowal of an inquisitive world view." So "proud" that when you register online to "self-identify as a Bright," Dennett's web site promises you confidentiality.—JB

Above all, they are mortified to be identified with working people in the United States—white, Black, or Latino; native- or foreign-born. Their attitudes toward those who produce society's wealth—the foundation of all culture—extend from saccharine condescension to occasional and unscripted open contempt, as they lecture us on our manners and mores. Above all, they fear someday being ruled by those they worry could become the "great mob": the toiling and producing majority. The new president, in fact, aims to protect the meritocracy the world over from those perceived in his petty-bourgeois circles as ignorant, bad-tempered, flag-waving, gun-hugging, family-centered, religious—in fact, stupid—"populists."

It's a class question

What I've called the "meritocracy," for lack of a better term, is in large part what Richard J. Herrnstein and Charles Murray were describing in the mid-1990s in their book *The Bell Curve*.[20] As implied by the book's subtitle, *Intelligence and Class Structure in American Life*, they were attempting to provide a "scientific" rationalization for the rapidly rising income and class privileges of this particular middle-class social stratum in the United States—a stratum they euphemistically, although not modestly, dubbed "the cognitive elite."

The authors wrote that while ideological differences, at least in words, would continue to distinguish "liberals" from "conservatives," and the "intellectuals" from the "the afflu-

---

20. Richard J. Herrnstein and Charles Murray, *The Bell Curve: Intelligence and Class Structure in American Life* (New York: Free Press, 1994). For a discussion of the book at the time of its publication, see "The Bell Curve: The Scandal of Class Privilege" in Jack Barnes, *Capitalism's World Disorder: Working-Class Politics at the Millennium* (Pathfinder, 1999), pp. 181–93 [2008 printing].

ent" ("the affluent" being their lingo for the capitalist class
and its top managers and professionals), these "old lines"
had in reality begun "to blur" on the most fundamental
class questions.

"[T]here are theoretical interests and practical interests,"
wrote the authors of The Bell Curve. "The Stanford professor's best-selling book may be a diatribe against the puni-
tive criminal justice system, but that doesn't mean that he
doesn't vote with his feet to move to a safe neighborhood.
Or his book may be a withering attack on outdated family norms, but that doesn't mean that he isn't acting like
an old-fashioned father in looking after the interests of his
children—and if that means sending his children to a lily-
white private school so that they get a good education, so be
it. Meanwhile, the man with the chain of shoe stores may
be politically to the right of the Stanford professor, but he is
looking for the same safe neighborhood and the same good
schools for his children. . . . He and the professor may not
be so far apart at all on how they want to live their own
personal lives and how government might serve those joint
and important interests."

What we can add—something Herrnstein and Murray already knew—is that neither the private school nor the "safe
neighborhood" any longer need to be "lily white." In fact,
even well before The Bell Curve was published, that certainly
was not the case for the middle-class Chicago neighborhood
of Hyde Park from which Barack and Michelle Obama most
recently hail, and where they sent their two daughters to
a private elementary school at a combined tuition cost of
nearly $40,000 a year (a total above the annual income of
about half of all families in Chicago, and at least 40 percent
of families in the United States).

It is Obama's comfortable immersion in this arrogant,
self-congratulatory, and bourgeois-minded milieu that is
responsible for the few "blunders" he made during the 2008

presidential campaign. In comparison to other Democratic and Republican primary candidates, Obama was cautious and disciplined during the campaign. He was determined not to let carelessness scotch his ambitions. That's why his slips were revealing.

There were his widely publicized remarks at a fund-raiser in April 2008, for example, where he was speaking to a small group of supporters at a home in San Francisco's exclusive Pacific Heights neighborhood. The Democratic candidate was so at ease in that company that he let down his guard. His class prejudices poured out for all to hear.

Working people in the small Pennsylvania towns where Obama had just been campaigning, he said, and in "a lot of small towns in the Midwest," have been seeing job opportunities decline for a long time. "They fell throughout the Clinton administration, and the Bush administration, and each successive administration has said that somehow these communities are going to regenerate, and they have not. And it's not surprising, then, they get bitter, they cling to guns or religion or antipathy to people who aren't like them or anti-immigrant sentiment or anti-trade sentiment as a way to explain their frustrations."

Working people, you see, may be "bitter," intolerant gun-huggers, bible-thumpers, and jingoists—but that's "not surprising," since we're so insular, beaten down, and demoralized! (By the way, isn't it hard to imagine a more insular "small town" than sections of San Francisco? Or Manhattan's Upper West Side? Or Obama's own Hyde Park in Chicago?)

A bourgeois perversion of working-class gains

The fact that growing numbers in this "cognitive elite" social layer are African American today is something that would have been impossible thirty years ago. That testifies to the expansion of the Black middle class and the evolution of social attitudes we've already discussed. What by the latter

half of the 1960s came to be known as affirmative action—
that is, not simply the concept of equal justice under bourgeois law, fought for and more broadly codified through the
mass civil rights struggles, but explicit and transparent *quotas* in hiring, college admissions, and promotions—is what
broke down barriers that had long blocked large numbers of
African Americans from achieving such social status. And it
was the urban rebellions by proletarians who are Black during those same years—in Harlem, Watts, Chicago, Newark,
Detroit, and smaller cities all over the country—and the rise
of Black nationalist consciousness and organizations during
that same period, that convinced the U.S. rulers that they
had better concede something in addition to formal equality.
At least for a time, they had to accept the need for quotas.

Today the privileged layers the new president is part of
are proud of being color-blind in a way that is new to bourgeois society in the United States. The glue holding them
together is not color but social class—or, to be more accurate, their entrenchment in *a certain section* of a social
class. Whatever their racial or national background or sex,
virtually none of them perceive affirmative action as it has
evolved today as a threat to *their* status, and it's not uncom-
mon for some of those who are Black, Latino, or female to
note that, in their own individual cases, *they* got where *they*
are without need of quotas.

Affirmative action in the misshapen forms increasingly
implemented by the capitalist rulers has more and more been
incorporated into advancement of the meritocracy to the degree the bourgeoisie deems it necessary to the maintenance
and reproduction of stable bourgeois social relations. Given
this supraclass character, the main function of affirmative
action as it has come to be applied by the bourgeoisie in the
United States is to reinforce illusions in imperialist democracy. It is used to further divide African Americans and other
nationally oppressed layers along class lines, and to deepen

divisions within the working class as a whole.

While unconditionally opposing the rollback of any gains workers have registered in reversing racist and antiwoman patterns of hiring, promotions, firings, or college admissions, communists and other vanguard workers give no political support to the way in which the bourgeoisie has more and more often implemented what *they* call affirmative action over the past two decades. The ground taken by the working class in victories such as the *Weber* decision in 1979[21] is

---

21. In June 1979 the Supreme Court upheld a contract negotiated by the United Steelworkers of America with Kaiser Aluminum. In order to upgrade employment for those targeted by longstanding discrimination, the contract had established a quota that one-half of the places in a new job-training program would be reserved for Blacks and women. The court rejected claims by attorneys for Brian Weber, a worker at Kaiser's plant in Gramercy, Louisiana, that he had been illegally excluded from the training program because he was white. Prior to that, while 39 percent of the workers at the Gramercy plant were African American, only 5 of 273 skilled jobs at the plant had been held by Black workers, and none by women. At the time, socialist workers and others actively campaigned across the country and throughout the labor movement with the Pathfinder pamphlet *The Weber Case: New Threat to Affirmative Action; How Labor, Blacks, and Women Can Fight for Equal Rights and Jobs for All.* It cost 75¢. See also Jack Barnes, *The Changing Face of U.S. Politics* (Pathfinder, 1981, 1994, 2004), especially pp. 338–41 and 401–3 [2008 printing].

A decade later, however, the Supreme Court began handing down decisions that increasingly restricted—in the words of a January 1989 decision (*City of Richmond v. Croson*)—"the use of an unyielding racial quota." Following another such Supreme Court decision in 1995 (*Adarand Constructors, Inc. v. Peña*), the Clinton administration issued a memorandum aimed at further exacerbating divisions among working people by calling for the elimination of any program that creates "a quota," "preferences for unqualified individuals," or "reverse discrimination"—three longtime battle cries of opponents of the *Weber* decision and other prior victories. A 2003 Supreme Court decision (*Grutter v. Bollinger*), while conceding the University of Michigan Law School could continue to take discretionary measures to maintain "a diverse student body," ruled at the same time that "universities can-

On the pamphlet:

The Weber Case

New threat to affirmative action

Andy Rose

How labor, Blacks, and women can fight for equal rights and jobs for all

"**What came to be known as affirmative action—explicit and transparent quotas in hiring, college admissions, and promotions—helped break down barriers that had long blocked African Americans from achieving equal treatment,**" says Barnes. "**If the class struggle does not advance, however, what the working class wrested through victories such as the _Weber_ decision is perverted into programs that provide a golden key for some to enter an increasingly exclusive club further up the income rungs of U.S. society.**"

Top, strikers picket Newport News, Virginia, shipyard, February 1979. Successful battle there for Steelworkers union recognition registered strengthening of working class and labor movement in South and nationwide as a result of Black rights victories. Inset, pamphlet socialist workers campaigned with in response to effort initiated by Kaiser Aluminum employee Brian Weber to reverse affirmative action provision in union contract that set job-training quotas for Blacks and women. Many unions defended these measures, and in June 1979 Supreme Court rejected Weber's "reverse discrimination" claims.

like other gains by the toilers. If the class struggle does not advance, those gains will be perverted by the very workings of capitalist social relations themselves, as they become programs that provide a golden key for some to enter an exclusive club further up the income rungs of U.S. society.

With unemployment sharply rising today, and with the jobless rate for workers who are Black more than 75 percent higher than for workers who are white, the victories the working class has won through decades of struggle against racial divisions—divisions that are part and parcel of the workings of capitalism, and are consciously fostered by the bosses to pit us against each other and weaken the labor movement— are increasingly threatened. So long as capitalist relations exist, the fight for *quotas* in hiring, promotions, and school admissions—that is, openly stated numerical targets or separate lists for those facing discrimination based on their race or sex—will continue to be an indispensable element in forging class solidarity along the road toward the revolutionary fight by the working class to take state power, hold it, and aid those the world over fighting to do likewise.[22]

---

not establish quotas for members of certain racial or ethnic groups or put them on separate admissions tracks."

22. In the opening decades of the twentieth century, Bolshevik leader V.I. Lenin, responding to the increasingly Russian chauvinist policies of a rising privileged social caste in the government and party apparatus of the young Soviet workers and peasants republic, explained the proletarian character of measures to overcome the legacy of national oppression in a workers state. In a December 1922 letter to the upcoming Communist Party congress, Lenin wrote that internationalism "on the part of the oppressors or 'great' nations, as they are called (though they are great only in their violence, only great as bullies), must consist not only in the observance of the formal equality of nations but even in an inequality, through which the oppressor nation, the great nation, would compensate for the inequality which obtains in real life. Anybody who does not understand this has not grasped the real proletarian attitude to the national question; he is still essentially

Contempt for workers who are Black

What is so instructive about Barack Obama's class identification—and those of his milieu, regardless of race or sex—is not just, or even primarily, a patronizing view of workers who are white. When it comes to workers who are Black, Obama's attitudes, if anything, are even more contemptuous.

Take, for example, his remarks on Father's Day in June 2008 at Chicago's Apostolic Church of God, which has an overwhelmingly African American congregation. Much of the news coverage of that church service focused on the Democratic candidate's remarks about absent fathers, but he said a lot more than that. He scolded members of the congregation not to "just sit in the house and watch 'SportsCenter'. . . . [R]eplace the video game or the remote control with a book once in a while." (In February 2008, again speaking to a largely African American audience, he lectured those in attendance about feeding their children "cold Popeyes" for breakfast—unlike him and Michelle, we presume.)

"Don't get carried away with that eighth-grade graduation," Obama said at the Chicago church. "You're *supposed* to graduate from eighth grade." (It's less harmful to workers and farmers than getting carried away with a Yale or a Harvard law degree, but that's another question.)

And then he scornfully added, "We need fathers to recognize that responsibility doesn't just end at conception. That doesn't make you a father. What makes you a man is not the ability to have a child. Any fool can have a child. That doesn't make you a father. It's the courage to raise a child that makes you a father."

---

petty bourgeois in his point of view and is, therefore, sure to descend to the bourgeois point of view." From "Letter to the Party Congress" in *Lenin's Final Fight* (Pathfinder, 1995), p. 220 [2009 printing]. Also in V.I. Lenin, *Collected Works*, vol. 36, p. 608.

Too many fathers, Obama said, "have abandoned their responsibilities, acting like boys instead of men. And the foundations of our families are weaker because of it," he added. "You and I know how true this is in the African American community."

It was creepy. *It was all aimed at the voters of "white America."* Obama was holding individual Black family members primarily accountable for the quality of the education, nutrition, and health care their children receive. "If fathers are doing their part,. . ." he said, "then our government should meet them halfway." Halfway! And only "if."[23]

Workers' conditions decline . . . and converge

While the bourgeois-minded social layer the forty-fourth president of the United States is part of has seen its income rise sharply since the 1960s, there has been an even starker deterioration over that same period in the living and working conditions of a growing majority of the proletariat of all skin colors.

The hypocritical and fraudulent character of Obama's Fathers' Day concerns last year about "the foundations of our

---

23. This same patronizing, class-biased message of "personal responsibility" was central to Obama's remarks to the annual NAACP convention in New York in July 2009, six months after his inauguration. Just because "you're African American," and "the odds of growing up amid crime and gangs are higher," and "you live in a poor neighborhood," Obama said, "that's not a reason to get bad grades, that's not a reason to cut class, that's not a reason to give up on your education and drop out of school. . . . No excuses. No excuses."

Addressing himself to parents who are Black, Obama continued: "You can't just contract out parenting. For our kids to excel, we have to accept our responsibility to help them learn. That means putting away the Xbox, putting our kids to bed at a reasonable hour. . . . [O]ur kids can't all aspire to be LeBron or Lil Wayne. I want them aspiring to be scientists and engineers, doctors and teachers, not just ballers and rappers."

families" getting "weaker" became even clearer a few weeks later, when he took part in a televised presidential forum in southern California at the Saddleback Church of Rev. Rick Warren. When Warren asked him about "the most significant position you held ten years ago that you no longer hold today," Obama immediately pointed to his support today for the abolition of Aid to Families with Dependent Children (AFDC) by the Clinton administration and Congress in 1996. Obama said that he "was much more concerned ten years ago when President Clinton initially signed the bill that this could have disastrous results." But today, in August 2008, he said, he was "absolutely convinced" that Clinton's "welfare reform" had to remain "a centerpiece of any social policy."

What have been the results of this liberal "centerpiece," even prior to the long contraction in the rate of economic growth and working-class incomes—the depression—that began in 2007? Since the destruction of "welfare as we know it," as Clinton callously described his target, the number of people receiving cash assistance—now administered by state governments under AFDC's successor, Temporary Assistance for Needy Families (TANF)—has dropped to a more than forty-year low. Far from having productive jobs at good wages, however, those pushed off AFDC who were lucky enough to find work of any kind—only about half by 2005, according to a recent study[24]—were forced into low-paying, nonunion jobs with little or no health, pension, or other benefits.

By 2005 the 50 percent of former AFDC recipients who are Black and unemployed had fallen more than 30 percent

---

24. See "Welfare Reform in the Mid-2000s: How African American and Hispanic Families in Three Cities Are Faring" by Andrew Cherlin et al, in Douglas Massey and Robert J. Sampson, *The Moynihan Report Revisited: Lessons and Reflections after Four Decades*, special issue of *The Annals of the American Academy of Political and Social Science* (January 2009).

further below the official federal government poverty line than they had been in 1999—and, once again, this was well before today's deepening capitalist crisis. What's more, whereas cash payments to women eligible for AFDC increased during the 1974–75, 1981–82, and 1990–91 recessions, as of the end of 2008 cash benefits had been *reduced* in eight of the twelve states where unemployment had increased the most during the opening months of the current sharp contraction. The government's official jobless rate for Black women over twenty years of age—which we know is way below the actual level of unemployment—has shot up from 7.8 percent to 10.5 percent just over the twelve months since early 2008.

Whether it's the gutting of AFDC, cuts in pension and health-care funding, the reduction of already woefully inadequate child-care and preschool programs, or assaults on other aspects of workers' social wage, the blows rain down hardest on *women* in the working class, and heaviest of all on women workers of the Black or other oppressed nationalities. It didn't take the new Democratic administration more than a week after the January 20, 2009, inauguration to signal that such assaults would continue. As a result of the adoption of the reactionary Hyde Amendment in 1976, abortion since that time remains the one medical procedure for which women enrolled in Medicaid—today some 12 percent of all women of reproductive age—are denied federal funding. Just days after taking office, Obama succeeded in killing a provision in the so-called congressional stimulus plan that would have expanded access to financial support for birth control to women whose income, though low, is nonetheless too high to make them eligible for Medicaid.[25]

---

25. Speaking at the May 17, 2009, commencement at the University of Notre Dame in South Bend, Indiana, Obama called for finding "common ground" with opponents of a woman's right to abortion. Deciding to have this medical procedure, he said, is "a heart-wrenching decision

The gap in economic and social conditions between workers who are white and those who are Black *has* narrowed since the 1960s. But not because times have gotten better for most African Americans. The reason is that wages and living standards *have declined* for a growing majority of workers of all skin colors.

While the rate of births to unwed teenagers has risen sharply among both whites and African Americans since the 1960s, for example, the gap between young women who are Black and those who are white has dropped from a twelve-fold difference to about two to one today.[26]

A comparable driving down of the conditions facing all working people, with African Americans hit the hardest, is registered in the colossal increase in the size of the U.S. prison population over the past three decades. As of 2005

---

for any woman," with "both moral and spiritual dimensions." Aiming his remarks at opponents of a woman's right to choose abortion, the president said, "let us work together to reduce the number of women seeking abortion."

Only two weeks later a fascist-minded militant, a hater of women's rights, walked into the Reformation Lutheran Church in Wichita, Kansas, and murdered Dr. George Tiller. Tiller was the operator and physician at a clinic in Wichita that performed abortions, and one of only a handful of doctors in the United States who perform late-term abortions. Obama responded to the killing with nothing more than a two-sentence statement, saying, "However profound our differences as Americans over difficult issues such as abortion"—once again, abortion is not a woman's right, but "a difficult issue"—"they cannot be resolved by heinous acts of violence."

26. The same trend can be seen in the rising percentage of children born outside marriage. While the percentage of African American children born to unwed mothers has increased from 24 percent in 1965 to 72 percent in 2007, the proportion shot up from 6 percent to 28 percent for white children over that same period. The percentage of Latino children born to unwed mothers increased from 37 percent in 1990 to 51 percent in 2007.

more than 700 U.S. residents out of every 100,000 were in prison or jail in this country. With only 5 percent of the world's population, the United States holds nearly 25 percent of all prisoners on earth—more than 2.2 million people! The highest incarceration rate of any country in the world—yes, *any* country! And if you sum up all those behind bars, on parole, or on probation, the total comes to more than 7 million people—more than 3 percent of the adult U.S. population.

The largest increase has been among African Americans. Some 577,000 Blacks were in prison or jail in 2005, a 58 percent increase just since 1990. Black men are eight times more likely than white men to be behind bars. Altogether some 14 percent of Black men in their twenties were in jail or prison at some point in 2004. The numbers soar when you add in those on parole, probation, or doing "community service."

At the same time, in the years since 1980 there has also been a threefold increase in the imprisonment rate of white men in their twenties. Three times greater.

Fettering working people with debt

Working people in the United States, especially those with the lowest incomes, are also being hit hard by the disastrous consequences of the rulers' drive over the past quarter century to float their rate of profit on a sea of debt, in which *we* are left to drown. With real wages slowly declining throughout this period, it became more and more difficult for workers to cover the cost of basic necessities without relying on credit. This has reached the point in recent years where growing numbers of us have little or nothing left at the end of the month to pay off interest and principal on loans. We simply can't pay the bills.

How did this situation come about? Since the late 1960s the capitalists have confronted pressure on their average profit rate, which has gradually been trending down. The first post-1930s worldwide recession occurred in 1974–75. In face of this more than three-decade-long slowdown in capital accumulation, the rulers have held back expenditures for the expansion of productive capacity and large-scale employment of labor. In order to counter this stagnation, the political servants of the propertied rulers in the White House and Congress—Democrats and Republican alike—together with the Federal Reserve Board, have expanded the use of credit on a massive scale. They have done so not only by increasing the amount of funds on loan to previously unheard-of levels, but also by spreading the use of credit deep into the working class, including those with the lowest incomes. As the old Tennessee Ernie Ford song goes, many workers over the past century and more have "owed our souls to the company store," but never before in history has such debt spread its entangling roots so *widely* throughout the working class as in recent years.[27] Nor so extensively throughout layers of toilers in the semicolonial world.

Since the mid-1980s, Washington has not only flushed trillions of dollars into the banks but throughout the imperialist financial system has encouraged a degree of leverage that would make Las Vegas blush. The U.S. rulers have intervened continually in world markets to keep interest rates at historically low levels.[28] In combination, these measures

---

27. See "The Clintons' Antilabor Legacy: Roots of the 2008 World Financial Crisis" in *New International* no. 14, as well as *Capitalism's World Disorder* by Jack Barnes, "Capitalism's Long Hot Winter Has Begun" in *New International* no. 12 (2005), and "What the 1987 Stock Market Crash Foretold" in *New International* no. 10 (1994).

28. Keeping lending cheap in the United States has not been achieved, and could not have been, simply by the Federal Reserve board setting low interests rates on its own loans to U.S. banks, on banks' overnight loans to each other, etc. The U.S. rulers also actively intervened in world markets to keep interest rates low by holding down global gold prices (even as they denied doing so); promoted deals with the bour-

have kept banks in the United States awash with funds they needed to lend in order to boost their profit rates above those of competitors worldwide. The result has been a cascade of bank-driven "debt crises." Among the earliest targets of the banks were working farmers in the United States and the governments of oppressed nations across the Americas, Africa, and Asia—who were increasingly pushed toward default, and, in the case of farmers, into foreclosure and the loss of the land they tilled.

This simultaneous goading and luring of more and more layers of working people into ever-deeper indebtedness— credit card debt, student loans, auto "financing," mortgages and "home equity loans"—sharply accelerated through the 1990s and opening years of the twenty-first century. Total consumer debt, by government figures, has increased by nearly 400 percent since 1985. Credit card debt has nearly doubled over the last decade alone, and what the banks and other financial institutions call "delinquencies" have jumped by more than a third just since 2006, with nearly 12 percent of credit card loans more than ninety days past due in early 2009. What's more, these high-interest pieces of plastic are *aggressively* pushed on working people: 5 billion solicitations were mailed in the United States in 2001 alone, roughly 50 for each household. And they aren't mailed to the bourgeoisie!

Student loan debt, which has become impossible to shake off, even through bankruptcy (it lasts beyond the grave), has more than doubled since 1995. In 2007 nearly two-thirds of college graduates left school shouldering debt—and on top

---

geois Stalinist regime in Beijing to keep buying enormous quantities of U.S. Treasury bonds; and took advantage of U.S. imperialism's obscene degree of "seigniorage"—that is, its ability because the dollar is accepted as "the world's reserve currency" simply *to print money* to pay off U.S. debts to capitalists and governments the world over.

of that, some 15 percent of parents of college graduates (according to 2004 figures) had also taken out loans. In 2007 the average debt load of graduating students who had borrowed to finance their schooling was more than $22,000. Moreover, that average prettifies the situation of millions of students who graduate even more deeply in debt—some 10 percent owing more than $33,000 in 2004—not to mention those who go on to medical, law, or other postgraduate studies.

Meanwhile, college administrations—at state universities, as well as private ones—not only keep cranking up the cost of tuition, room, and board (a true "bubble"). More and more of them have also been found to be in bed—for a payoff—with "student loan finance companies" raking in extortionate interest payments. This line of work has a name that college officials take umbrage at being called.

Remember those TV commercials for auto loans only a year or so ago? "No job? No problem! Bad credit? No problem! Alimony payments? No problem!" Well, defaults on auto loans increased by 25 percent in 2008, and more and more working people are losing cars to the repo man each month. *Problem!*

The list could go on, and this doesn't even include the massive debt incurred by small businesses, corporations, and the government. Over the past quarter century, total debt in the United States—private and public—has risen by more than $45 trillion dollars, while the U.S. gross domestic product has grown by less than $11 trillion.

A large percentage of the federal government debt—a share that has spiked sharply since the White House and Congress launched their bloody assaults against the peoples of Afghanistan and Iraq earlier in this decade—goes to pay for Washington's wars. This includes not only increasing annual outlays on military spending but mounting payments of interest and principal to the wealthiest bondholders on the national debt from past wars.

The propertied families of the United States have not had much success over the past sixty years in maintaining popular support for their wars to continue the domination, exploitation, and oppression of the world's peoples. The wars against the people of Korea and Vietnam were unpopular. The rulers failed to win sustained patriotic backing for the Gulf War of 1990–91, the bombardment and intervention in Yugoslavia throughout the 1990s, or the more recent assaults on Iraq, Afghanistan (except immediately after 9/11), and now the border regions of Pakistan. In the absence of any broad outpouring of nationalistic fervor for such wars, the rulers face growing problems in rationalizing—under the banner of "patriotic sacrifice"—the inevitably inflationary consequences of massive military spending.

For example, in the 1960s as broad popular opposition to the Vietnam War increased, including among GIs at the front, Democratic president Lyndon Johnson sought to throw a smokescreen over the inflationary toll that rising military expenditures were inevitably going to take on workers' living standards. In order to do so, and to maintain the "Great Society" fiction of painlessly financing "guns" *and* "butter," Johnson took a number of steps *to appear* to reduce the size of the federal budget. In one of the biggest of the sleights of hand, the Democratic administration took the debt of the Federal National Mortgage Association—Fannie Mae—off the government balance sheet in 1968. Simply declared no longer to be a federal agency, Fannie Mae was dubbed "a government sponsored enterprise" (GSE), owned and operated by private shareholders. Two years later, in 1970, a second such GSE was launched, the Federal Home Loan Mortgage Corporation, or Freddie Mac—also off the federal balance sheet.

From the 1980s on, Fannie Mae and Freddie Mac were, in turn, among the capitalists' favored institutions for hobbling working people with an even wider variety of credit shackles—house mortgages, and then "home equity loans." This drive by the rulers to make us think and act like "homeowners" with a stake in the capitalist system accelerated to a dizzying degree in recent decades. In the process, Fannie's and Freddie's share of residential mortgage debt in the United States rocketed from 7 percent in 1980 to nearly 50 percent at the opening of the 2007 housing crisis; together they issued some 75 percent of so-called mortgaged-backed securities.[29]

Both the Clinton and the Bush administrations, for example, unrelentingly pushed workers to go into debt to buy houses and apartments, with a special eye to working people who are Black or Latino. Clinton mandated Fannie Mae and Freddie Mac to step up their trafficking in what are today called "subprime" loans, targeting working people, particularly Blacks. Bush—who set a goal of expanding "minority homeownership," especially by Mexican-Americans, by at least 5.5 million before 2010—told a gathering of commercial home builders in Ohio in 2004 that, "To build an ownership society, we'll help even more Americans to buy homes. Some families are more than able to pay a mortgage but don't have the savings to put money down."

That same year, then Federal Reserve Board chairman

---

29. The beginning of the surge in the percentage of working people, of whatever skin color, "owning" rather than renting the roofs over their heads came during the capitalist expansion following World War II. Living in terror of a return of prewar depression conditions and a resurgence of workers' struggles, the rulers adopted the GI Bill—not only to help finance college enrollment for veterans who would otherwise be jobless, but to offer them mortgage subsidies to spur housing construction. More than 20 percent of all single-family houses built during the two decades following the war were financed in part by GI Bill loans. Since the 1950s, the percentage gap between whites and Blacks has slowly but steadily continued to narrow, with some 48 percent of Black households "owning" houses in 2008 and some 75 percent of white households.

Alan Greenspan, in a February speech to the Credit Union National Association, gave a thumbs up to such high-risk loans. "[M]any homeowners might have saved tens of thousands of dollars had they held adjustable-rate mortgages rather than fixed-rate mortgages during the past decade," Greenspan said, adding that "American consumers might benefit if lenders provided greater mortgage product alternatives to the traditional fixed-rate mortgage."

Banks, "home finance companies," and other mortgage-origination sharks proved themselves more than happy to take advantage of the sales opportunity, while the big banks and financial intermediaries packaged the debt and confidently carried it on their books as leveraged "assets." Over the past decade or so they've lured many working people to manacle ourselves and our families with "low-down-payment" (or even "no-down-payment") loans, "adjustable rate" financing, and other forms of high-risk debt servitude. They've solicited and facilitated, in large numbers, what they cynically came to call "liars' loans" (that is, the lender and the borrower exchange mutual lies and winks when filling out mortgage applications, with the debtors eventually getting crushed while the creditors make off like the bandits they are).

"We believe that low-income borrowers"—a code word for workers—"are going to be our leading customers going into the 21st century," an executive for Norwest Mortgage (now merged with Wells Fargo) cynically and baldly told the press in 1998.

During the Clinton administration, between 1993 and 1997 alone, there was a substantial jump in the number of Blacks taking on debt in order to buy—or, the biggest lie of all, to "invest" in—houses and apartments, and the pace quickened until the availability of credit seized up beginning in 2007. As a result, there has been a sharp increase in real estate foreclosures over the past few years, tripling just since 2006 to a rate of 1.8 percent of mortgages nationwide by the end of 2008. Workers—especially those with the smallest houses, built with the cheapest materials—have been the hardest hit, once again with working people who are Black or Latino sustaining disproportionately heavy blows.

Meanwhile, the Obama administration is doing nothing to assist working people in face of this expanding social crisis, other than proposing yet another plan "encouraging" banks to "voluntarily" renegotiate the terms of mortgages inevitably gone sour. The result will be that banks stretch out their income stream from interest and principal payments a year or so longer, before *then* foreclosing on these workers—who face soaring unemployment and declining real wages—and repossessing their houses.[30]

What broader political advantage do the U.S. rulers and the two dominant wings of the party of capital, the Democrats and Republicans, reap by supporting the bankers (their bosses) in encouraging and accelerating real estate "ownership" by workers? They understand that under capitalism, owning a house also has a conservatizing impact on working people and the oppressed. It fosters the illusion that we too are "property holders."

As Greenspan candidly wrote in 2007 in defense of his earlier encouragement of "adjustable rate" loans: "I was aware that the loosening of mortgage credit terms for subprime borrowers increased financial risk, and that subsidized home ownership initiatives distort market outcomes. But I believed then, as now, that the benefits of broadened home ownership are worth the risk [*for the rulers!*—JB]. Protection of property rights, so critical to a market economy, requires a

---

30. A May 2009 report by Fitch, a major Wall Street "ratings" agency, found, as a "conservative projection," that within a year after "renegotiating" the principal and interests on their loans, between 65 percent and 75 percent of holders of subprime mortgages will once again have fallen behind sixty days or more on their payments.

critical mass of owners to sustain political support."[31]

Owning a house ties workers down with onerous mortgage payments and endless expenditures of time and money for physical upkeep and repairs. It subverts our habits of class solidarity by elevating relations and problems we share in common with "fellow owners," fellow "property-holding taxpayers," over those with fellow workers.

It makes us less footloose. It makes us less *free,* as Engels insisted—more tied to the land the "real estate" rests on. In his 1873 booklet on *The Housing Question,* Engels explained that a title to real property (sentimentally called "home" ownership by its bourgeois proponents who, with consummate cynicism, add a maudlin touch to all their nomenclature) is "a fetter" for workers in capitalist society. "Give them their own houses, chain them once again to the soil, and break their power of resistance" during "a big strike or a general industrial crisis," Engels wrote.[32]

We are already witnessing such modern-day steps backward toward greater bondage. As of March 2008, fewer people in the United States had moved over the past year than any time since 1962, when the population was 40 percent smaller!

Social conquests of Black rights struggle

One of the most important conquests of the mass, proletarian-led struggle for Black rights in the 1950s and 1960s was the substantial *extension* of workers' social wage that had been won as a by-product of working-class battles that built the industrial unions in the 1930s. As a direct

31. Alan Greenspan, *The Age of Turbulence: Adventures in a New World* (New York: Penguin, 2007), p. 233.

32. Frederick Engels, "The Housing Question," in *MECW,* vol. 23, p. 344.

result of the movement that brought down Jim Crow and the urban uprisings that turned the country and the confidence of the ruling class upside down, Medicare and Medicaid were won in 1965. And in 1972—thirty-five years after the original Social Security legislation—the Supplemental Security Income (SSI) program for the blind, disabled, and elderly was established.

The Social Security Act of 1935 had included small retirement supplements for many workers, federally mandated unemployment insurance and workers compensation, and aid for dependent children (paid to eligible mothers). It's important to remember that this legislation had been crafted by the Roosevelt administration to serve the needs of capital by *limiting* concessions as much as possible. For example, not only were retirement benefits financed in part by a payroll tax on workers (a regressive, anti-working-class measure), but the minimal sums paid out were meant only as a minor supplement to whatever workers were able to put aside for old age (usually nothing) or get from their adult sons and daughters.

What's more, since average life expectancy in 1935 was below sixty-two, and just below sixty for men, the anticipated government payout on pension benefits beginning at age sixty-five would be small—in fact, in close to a majority of cases, nary a penny!

Social Security payments were not intended to defend and strengthen the working class. They returned to workers no more than a token of the wealth produced by our social labor. Social Security was aimed at bolstering the responsibility of the petty-bourgeois family for meeting the needs of the young, the elderly, the disabled, and the ill, including reinforcing the social norm that the place of working-class women with dependent children was in the home. (I say working-class women, because the bourgeois family has always hired or retained a phalanx of wet nurses, nannies, tutors, and even dog-walkers—in the latter case, the comical twenty-first century surrogate for the old bourgeois stable staff.)

All sanctimonious prattle by the capitalist rulers and their spokespersons about "defending the working-class family" serves only to obfuscate bourgeois social relations in order to absolve the propertied ruling families and their government institutions of *social* responsibility for food and clothing, education, health care, housing, transportation, and more. It is the banner under which these responsibilities are pressed on individual workers—that is, primarily on women.

It is these capitalist property relations that are the root of so much individual and "family" misery today. Only when they are uprooted through revolutionary action by the working classes ourselves, only when economic compulsion—the wages system, the "cash nexus"—ceases to be the foundation of all social interaction, will new human relations eventually emerge. We cannot even begin to imagine what those relations will be, but the one thing we *can* be sure of is that they will have little in common with the petty-bourgeois family of today, much less the propertied family of the capitalist class.[33]

33. Contrary to the self-interested claims of capitalist ideologues, there is no such thing as the "working-class family." The word *family* is derived from the Latin *familia*, meaning the totality of household slaves that are the property of one man. From the origins of class society, the primary function of the family has been to preserve the accumulated wealth and private property of the ruling class—whether cattle, slaves, and estates, or capital in land, mines, mills, and factories—and assure its orderly transfer from generation to generation.

Today's counterpart of this institution among the propertyless working masses (also, and confusingly, known in everyday speech as a "family") is descended from the petty-bourgeois family of the peasantry—a productive unit in which every man, woman, and child of all generations labored under the father's domination to provide the necessities of life. The survival of individual members of this produc-

Working people have a vital stake not only in defending
the social wage we've fought for and won, but above all in
building a mass social and political movement of the working class *to extend these conquests as universal rights*—not
means-tested charity—*for all.* Through our labor, the working class, in this country and worldwide, produces more than
enough wealth to provide education, health care, housing, and
retirement to every human being on earth, for a lifetime.

---

tion unit depended on the mutual contributions of all.

With the rise of industrial capitalism, a hereditary proletariat was
born through the forcible dispossession of the peasantry from the
land. Members of the previously productive peasant family—children
and women first of all—were now forced to sell their labor power individually on the market to a capitalist employer, with all the brutality and suffering that produced. In the process, the petty-bourgeois
family was ripped asunder. In *The Condition of the Working Class
in England,* published in 1845, the young Frederick Engels, with great
eloquence and compassion, described the horrendous consequences of
this dispossession and proletarianization as it occurred there, and then
across Western Europe.

The working class everywhere organized and fought to curb the degree of that exploitation, demanding a shorter workday, curtailment
of child labor, higher wages, and legislation to regulate factory conditions. Meanwhile, armies of bourgeois and petty-bourgeois reformers
set out to reimpose on the toilers as individuals, and on women first
and foremost, the responsibility for reproducing and maintaining the
working class, including those too young, too old, or too sick to sell
their labor power. The concrete complexities of this historical transition from precapitalist to capitalist property and social relations have
differed from one part of the world to another. But the modern form
of the petty-bourgeois family is today as universally recognizable to
the factory worker in Shanghai as it is to his or her fellow worker in
Manchester, Atlanta, Cairo, Johannesburg, or Mexico City.

For a further discussion of the emergence of the family in class soci-
ety, see "Socialist Revolution and the Struggle for Women's Liberation"
by Mary-Alice Waters, resolution adopted by the Socialist Workers
Party national convention (August 1979), in Mary-Alice Waters (ed.),
Communist Continuity and the Fight for Women's Liberation, Part I
(Pathfinder, 1992).

None of these questions are new ones for class-conscious workers. In the founding document of the modern revolutionary working-class movement, the Communist Manifesto, Karl Marx and Frederick Engels recognized the "bourgeois claptrap about the family and education, about the hallowed co-relation of parent and child," [34] for what it really is. It is the rationalization for rejecting government responsibility for the social needs of the working classes. It is the ideological excuse by the capitalist class for imposing those obligations on the individual families of workers. It is a pretext to keep women the second sex.

Every move toward a "family-centered" social policy, instead of an independent proletarian course to advance the historic interests of working people, including the right of every woman to reproductive freedom . . .

Every step by "talented" youth from the working class toward "a career" as a ladder up (and *out* of their class) . . .

Every move toward state-funded and "faith-based" charity (and the new administration, with the election campaign behind them, is following in Bush's footsteps on the latter), instead of government-guaranteed education, health care, and pensions as *the universal social rights of the working class* . . .

Every move toward tightening the trap of mortgage debt slavery (that is, "home ownership"), as opposed to a revolutionary social movement of the toilers that demands nationalization of the land and the housing stock as we fight for pleasant, spacious, and affordable accommodations for all . . .

Every such move weakens the working class and labor movement, as it strengthens the hand of the rulers, who

---

34. Karl Marx and Frederick Engels, *The Communist Manifesto* (Pathfinder, 1970, 1987, 2008), p. 53 [2009 printing]. Also in *MECW*, vol. 6, p. 502.

seek to blame sections of our class and other scapegoats for the accelerating ills of the world capitalist order.

Every such move strikes a blow to what working people, including Blacks, women, and the foreign born, have fought for and conquered from the Civil War and Radical Reconstruction on—through the mass social movement that built the industrial unions, and the Black-led struggles of the 1950s, 1960s, and early 1970s that drove a stake through the heart of Jim Crow and fundamentally transformed social relations in the United States.

PART III

What the Bolshevik Revolution Taught Us

Everything New and Progressive Came from the Revolution of 1917

by James P. Cannon
1959

The Bolshevik Revolution of October 1917 in Russia laid a new foundation the world over for efforts to build revolutionary proletarian parties. Under the example of that revolution, a layer of class-struggle-minded workers began to recognize that, among other things, an uncompromising fight by them against national oppression is essential to the struggle to conquer state power from the capitalist and landlord exploiters. Led by V.I. Lenin, the Bolsheviks not only carried out this internationalist course inside the former tsarist empire's prison house of nations but also insisted, when the Communist International was launched in 1919, that the fight against national oppression be placed at the center of its strategy.

The "entire policy of the Communist International" in the fight against national oppression "must be based primarily upon uniting the proletarians and toiling masses of all nations and countries in common revolutionary struggle to overthrow the landowners and the bourgeoisie," Lenin explained in the "Theses on the National and Colonial Questions" drafted by him for the Second Congress of the Communist International in 1920. "Only such a unification will guarantee victory over capitalism, without which it is impossible to abolish national oppression and inequality."

An intransigent fight "against the most deeply rooted petty-bourgeois, nationalist prejudices (which are expressed in all possible forms, such as racism, national chauvinism, and anti-Semitism)," Lenin said, "must be given all the more priority as the question becomes more pressing of transforming the dictatorship of the proletariat from a national framework (that is, a dictatorship that exists only in one country and is incapable of carrying out an independent international policy) into an international one (that is, a dictatorship of the proletariat in at least several advanced countries, capable of exercising a decisive influence on all of world politics)."

For that reason, Lenin emphasized, "all Communist parties must directly support the revolutionary movement among the nations that are dependent and do not have equal rights (for example Ireland, the Negroes in America,[1] and so forth), and in the colonies. . . . Recognizing internationalism in word only, while diluting it in deed with petty-bourgeois nationalism and pacifism in all propaganda, agitation, and practical work, is a common practice not only among the centrist parties of the Second International but also among those that have left

---

1. In Lenin's January 1917 article "Statistics and Sociology," he wrote that Blacks in the United States "should be classed as an oppressed nation, for the equality won in the Civil War of 1861–65 and guaranteed by the Constitution of the republic was in many respects increasingly curtailed in the chief Negro areas (the South) in connection with the transition from the progressive, pre-monopoly capitalism of 1860–70 to the reactionary, monopoly capitalism (imperialism) of the new era, which in America was especially sharply etched out by the Spanish-American imperialist war of 1898 (i.e., a war between two robbers over the division of the booty)." V.I. Lenin, *Collected Works*, vol. 23, pp. 275–76.

that International, and often even among parties that now call themselves Communist."[2]

The young Communist movement in the United States, most of whose cadres had broken from the Socialist Party in 1919 to affiliate with the Communist International, did not initially pursue Lenin's course. Demands by Blacks "for economic, political, and social equality were viewed by the communists as just another form of reformism," Farrell Dobbs notes in *Revolutionary Continuity: Birth of the Communist Movement (1918–1922)*. Many cadres "failed to perceive the connection between revolutionary proletarian objectives and the aims and struggles of the oppressed nationalities [and were unable] to shape a course that both solidarized the communists with the democratic aspirations of these superexploited masses and imparted revolutionary political content to their struggles. No special effort was made to recruit militants among the Afro-American and other oppressed nationalities to the communist movement."[3]

James P. Cannon, who was part of the founding leadership of the communist movement in the United States and a direct participant in these early experiences, recounted lessons from them in *The First Ten Years of American Communism: Report of a Participant* (Pathfinder, 1973). Major excerpts from Cannon's account are printed below.

. . . American communists in the early twenties, like all other radical organizations of that and earlier times, had nothing

---

2. The original draft of the "Theses on the National and Colonial Questions" was written by Lenin. It is printed in *Workers of the World and Oppressed Peoples, Unite! Proceedings and Documents of the Second Congress (1920)* (Pathfinder, 1991), pp. 313–19 [2004 printing]. See also V.I. Lenin, *Collected Works*, vol. 31, pp. 144–51.

3. Farrell Dobbs, *Revolutionary Continuity: Birth of the Communist Movement (1918–1922)* (Pathfinder, 1983), p. 123 [2009 printing].

to start with on the Negro question but an inadequate *theory*, a false or indifferent *attitude* and the adherence of a few individual Negroes of radical or revolutionary bent.[4]

The earlier socialist movement, out of which the Communist Party was formed, never recognized any need for a special program on the Negro question. It was considered purely and simply an economic problem, part of the struggle between the workers and the capitalists; nothing could be done about the special problems of discrimination and inequality this side of socialism.

The best of the earlier socialists were represented by [Eugene V.] Debs, who was friendly to all races and purely free from prejudice. But the limitedness of the great agita-

---

4. Some early African American cadres of the Communist Party had been among the very few Black members of the Socialist Party. Others had been members of the African Blood Brotherhood (ABB), founded in 1919 in Harlem by Cyril Briggs, an immigrant from the Caribbean island of Nevis. The Brotherhood called for full equality and voting rights for Blacks in the South, the right of self-defense against Ku Klux Klan violence, and organization of Blacks into the trade unions. The ABB solidarized with Soviet Russia; condemned outrages by European colonial powers in Africa; championed the Irish struggle against British rule; and spoke out against anti-Semitism and Washington's racist exclusion of Chinese and Japanese immigrants. The ABB built branches in New York, by far its largest, as well as in Chicago; Omaha, Nebraska; Tulsa, Oklahoma; West Virginia coal mining areas; and elsewhere.

Two CP members who were Black, both also members of the African Blood Brotherhood, attended the Fourth Congress of the Communist International in Moscow in 1922. Otto Huiswoud was a delegate from the CP and ABB, and poet Claude McKay an invited guest. Huiswoud was asked by Comintern leaders to chair the Negro Commission and reported to delegates on its "Theses on the Negro Question," which were adopted November 30. McKay stayed on in Moscow for six months following the congress. Leon Trotsky's reply to questions by McKay about the place of the fight against Black oppression in the world proletarian struggle was published in the Soviet press and is available in *The First Five Years of the Communist International*, vol. 2 (Pathfinder, 1953, 1972).

tor's view on this far from simple problem was expressed in his statement: "We have nothing special to offer the Negro, and we cannot make separate appeals to all the races. The Socialist Party is the party of the whole working class, regardless of color—the whole working class of the whole world." (Ray Ginger: *The Bending Cross*.) That was considered a very advanced position at the time, but it made no provision for active support of the Negro's special claim for a little equality here and now, or in the foreseeable future, on the road to socialism.[5]

And even Debs, with his general formula that missed the main point—the burning issue of ever-present discrimination against the Negroes every way they turned—was far superior in this regard, as in all others, to Victor Berger [a Socialist Party leader in Milwaukee, Wisconsin], who was an outspoken white supremacist. Here is a summary pronouncement from a [1902] Berger editorial in his Milwaukee paper, the *Social Democratic Herald*: "There can be no doubt that the Negroes and mulattoes constitute a lower race." That was "Milwaukee socialism" on the Negro question, as expounded by its ignorant and impudent leader-boss. A harried and hounded Negro couldn't mix that very well with his Milwaukee beer, even if he had a nickel and could find a white man's saloon where he could drink a glass of beer—back of the bar.

Berger's undisguised chauvinism was never the official position of the party. There were other socialists, like William English Walling who was an advocate of equal rights for the Negroes, and one of the founders of the National Association for the Advancement of Colored People in 1909. But such individuals were a small minority among the so-

---

5. Ray Ginger, *The Bending Cross: A Biography of Eugene Victor Debs* (New Brunswick: Rutgers University Press, 1949). See also "On Race Prejudice," in *Eugene V. Debs Speaks* (Pathfinder, 1970).

cialists and radicals before the First World War and the Russian Revolution.

The inadequacy of traditional socialist policy on the Negro question is amply documented by the historians of the movement, Ira Kipnis and David Shannon.[6] The general and prevailing attitude of the Socialist Party toward Negroes is summed up by Shannon as follows:

"They were not important in the party, the party made no special effort to attract Negro members, and the party was generally disinterested in, if not actually hostile to, the effort of Negroes to improve their position in American capitalist society." And further: "The party held that the sole salvation of the Negro was the same as the sole salvation of the white: 'Socialism.'"

In the meantime, nothing could be done about the Negro question as such, and the less said about it the better. Sweep it under the rug.

Such was the traditional position inherited by the early Communist Party from the preceding socialist movement out of which it had come. The policy and practice of the trade union movement was even worse. The IWW barred nobody from membership because of "race, color or creed." But the predominant AFL unions, with only a few exceptions, were lily-white job trusts. They also had nothing special to offer the Negroes; nothing at all, in fact.

*

The difference—and it was a *profound* difference—between the Communist Party of the twenties and its socialist and radical ancestors, was signified by its break with this tradition. The American communists in the early days, un-

6. Ira Kipnis, *The American Socialist Movement, 1897–1912* (New York: Columbia University Press, 1952). David Shannon, *The Socialist Party of America: A History* (New York: Macmillan, 1955).

der the influence and pressure of the Russians in the Comintern, were slowly and painfully learning to change their *attitude*; to assimilate the new theory of the Negro question as a *special* question of doubly exploited second-class citizens, requiring a program of special demands as part of the overall program—and to start doing something about it.

The true importance of this profound change, in all its dimensions, cannot be adequately measured by the results in the twenties. The first ten years have to be considered chiefly as the preliminary period of reconsideration and discussion, and change of attitude and policy on the Negro question—in preparation for future activity in this field.

The effects of this change and preparation in the twenties, brought about by the Russian intervention, were to manifest themselves explosively in the next decade.

*

Everything new and progressive on the Negro question came from Moscow, after the revolution of 1917, and as a result of the revolution—not only for the American communists who responded directly, but for all others concerned with the question.

By themselves, the American communists never thought of anything new or different from the traditional position of American radicalism on the Negro question. That, as the above quotations from Kipnis's and Shannon's histories show, was pretty weak in theory and still weaker in practice. The simplistic formula that the Negro problem was merely economic, a part of the capital-labor problem, never struck fire among the Negroes—who knew better even if they didn't say so; they had to live with brutal discrimination every day and every hour.

There was nothing subtle or concealed about this discrimination. Everybody knew that the Negro was getting the worst of it at every turn, but hardly anybody cared about it or wanted to do anything to try to moderate or change it. The 90 percent white majority of American society, including its working-class sector, North as well as South, was saturated with prejudice against the Negro; and the socialist movement reflected this prejudice to a considerable extent— even though, in deference to the ideal of human brotherhood, the socialist attitude was muted and took the form of evasion. The old theory of American radicalism turned out in practice to be a formula for inaction on the Negro front, and—incidentally—a convenient shield for the dormant racial prejudices of the white radicals themselves.

The Russian intervention changed all that, and changed it drastically, and for the better. Even before the First World War and the Russian Revolution, Lenin and the Bolsheviks were distinguished from all other tendencies in the international socialist and labor movement by their concern with the problems of oppressed nations and national minorities, and affirmative support of their struggles for freedom, independence, and the right of self-determination. The Bolsheviks gave this support to all "people without equal rights" sincerely and earnestly, but there was nothing "philanthropic" about it. They also recognized the great revolutionary potential in the situation of oppressed peoples and nations, and saw them as important allies of the international working class in the revolutionary struggle against capitalism.

After November 1917 this new doctrine—with special emphasis on the Negroes—began to be transmitted to the American communist movement with the authority of the Russian Revolution behind it. The Russians in the Comintern started on the American communists with the harsh, insistent demand that they shake off their own unspoken prejudices, pay attention to the special problems and grievances of the American Negroes, go to work among them, and champion their cause, including among whites.

It took time for the Americans, raised in a different tradition, to assimilate the new Leninist doctrine. But the Russians followed up year after year, piling up the arguments and increasing the pressure on the American communists until they finally learned and changed, and went to work in earnest. And the change in the attitude of the American communists, gradually effected in the twenties, was to exert a profound influence *in far wider circles* in the later years.

✳

The Communist Party's break with the traditional position of American radicalism on the Negro question coincided with profound changes which had been taking place among the Negroes themselves. The large-scale migration from the agricultural regions of the South to the industrial centers of the North was greatly accelerated during the First World War, and continued in the succeeding years.[7] This brought some improvement in their conditions of life over what they had known in the Deep South, but not enough to compensate for the disappointment of being herded into ghettos and still subjected to discrimination on every side.

The Negro movement, such as it was at the time, patriotically supported the First World War "to make the world safe for democracy"; and 400,000 Negroes served in the armed forces. They came home looking for a little democratic payoff for themselves, but couldn't find much anywhere. Their new spirit of self-assertion was answered by a mounting score of lynchings and a string of "race riots" across the country, North as well as South.[8]

---

7. Ninety percent of U.S. Blacks lived in the South in 1910. By 1930, 79 percent of Blacks lived in the South, the big majority of them still in rural areas and small towns. As of 2002, some 55 percent of Blacks lived in the South, with less than 13 percent of them located in rural areas.

8. In 1919, with millions of demobilized soldiers vying for hard-to-come-by jobs, there were racist riots against African Americans in Chicago

All this taken together—the hopes and the disappointments, the new spirit of self-assertion and the savage reprisals—contributed to the emergence of a new Negro movement in the making. Breaking sharply with the Booker T. Washington tradition of accommodation[9] to a position of inferiority in a white man's world, a new generation of Negroes began to press their demand for equality. . . .

---

and some twenty-four other U.S. cities, from Omaha, Nebraska, to Knoxville, Tennessee, from Washington, D.C., to Bogalusa, Louisiana. There was a sharp rise in lynchings throughout the South. Two years later, from May 31 to June 1, 1921, racist mobs in Tulsa, Oklahoma, rioted against African Americans, demolishing the thirty-five-square block Black community, destroying more than 1,200 houses, and killing an estimated one hundred to three hundred people. Heavily outnumbered, Blacks—many of them World War I veterans—organized to defend themselves as best they could.

9. Booker T. Washington (1856–1915) opposed any mass struggle for Black rights, counterposing to it the perspective of accommodation with Jim Crow while working for vocational training and self-improvement.

The National Question
and the Road to the
Proletarian Dictatorship
in the United States

Discussions with Leon Trotsky
February 1933 and April 1939

I. Prinkipo, Turkey

In February 1933 the leadership of the Communist League of America—forerunner of the Socialist Workers Party—asked Arne Swabeck, the CLA's national secretary at the time, to visit Leon Trotsky to discuss and help advance the party's work. Key among the political questions Swabeck was asked to raise with Trotsky was the CLA's orientation to and activity in struggles for Black rights and the party's efforts to win workers who were Black.

At the time the Bolshevik leader was living in forced exile in Prinkipo, Turkey. In March 1923 V.I. Lenin had suffered a massive stroke that debilitated him until his death in January 1924. Over the next several years, Trotsky defended Lenin's proletarian course against the increasingly counterrevolutionary policies—both inside the Soviet Communist Party and in the Communist International—of a growing privileged, petty-bourgeois social layer in the state, trade union, and party apparatuses; Joseph Stalin was their dominant spokesperson.

In 1928 the Stalin leadership forced Trotsky into exile in Soviet Central Asia and in 1929 deported him from the Soviet Union. Trotsky had been expelled from the Communist Party of the Soviet Union in November 1927.

During these same years, in Communist parties around the world, supporters of Stalin's policies similarly expelled leaders and cadres organizing to advance Lenin's internationalist course. In the United States James P. Cannon, Swabeck, and others, having been driven out of the CP in October 1928, produced the first issue of the *Militant* newspaper in November and the following spring founded the Communist League of America.

Swabeck traveled to Turkey to meet with Trotsky in 1933 after participating as the CLA's delegate in an international conference in Paris of organizations committed to building the international communist movement on the foundations laid by the October Revolution and the Comintern under Lenin's leadership. Also present for the discussions in Prinkipo was Pierre Frank, one of Trotsky's secretaries. Below is a transcript of the discussion translated from German by Swabeck and originally published for the Communist League of America in an April 1933 party bulletin.

The Negro Question in America

February 28, 1933

ARNE SWABECK: Within the American [Communist] League we have no noticeable differences of an important character on this question, nor have we yet formulated a program. I present therefore only the views which we have developed in general.

How must we view the position of the American Negro: As a national minority or as a racial minority? This is of the greatest importance for our program.

The Stalinists maintain as their main slogan the one of self-determination for the Negroes and demand in connection therewith a separate state and state rights for the Negroes in the Black Belt.[10] The practical application of the latter demand has revealed much opportunism.

On the other hand, I acknowledge that in the practical work

---

10. In 1928 the Stalin-led Communist International lurched into an ultraleft jag on this and other questions, accompanied by factional attacks and physical assaults on political opponents. This leftist course continued for almost eight years. The Comintern in 1928 imposed on the Communist Party in the United States the slogan "self-determination for the Black Belt." The CP said that Blacks—in portions of the U.S. South where they constituted a majority or near majority—were an oppressed nation in that region and had the right to self-determination, including a separate state. The CP advocated a "Negro Soviet Republic in the South." A poster for the Communist Party's 1932 presidential ticket called for "Equal rights for Negroes everywhere! Self determination for the Black Belt." And a widely circulated CP pamphlet by James S. Allen the same year explained: "The Black Belt, which runs through 11 Southern states, includes not only the 195 counties with over 50% Negroes, but also the 202 counties with from 35 to 50% Negroes. These 397 counties form a continuous area in which the Negroes are over 50% of the total population."

The Communist Party's Black Belt "theory," in fact, was a caricature of Bolshevism's longstanding support for the right of self-determination of oppressed nations and nationalities, including separation if the majority of an oppressed people so chose. Far from being a demand based on the aspirations of Blacks in any region of the country, the Stalinists' Black Belt slogan was bureaucratically imposed from Moscow, with no origin or basis in the class struggle in the United States, or in the development of political consciousness among workers, first and foremost workers who were Black.

"In Russia, the Bolsheviks always fought for self-determination of national minorities, including the right of separation," explained Leon Trotsky in 1933. "Those American workers who say: 'The Negroes should separate if they so desire, and we will defend them against our American police'—those are revolutionists. I have confidence in them."

U.S. Communist Party's 1932 presidential ticket campaigned for a separate "Negro Soviet Republic" in parts of South where Blacks were majority or near majority, shown in map. The demand, "Self Determination for the Black Belt," did not grow out of struggles by Blacks anywhere in U.S., or development of political consciousness in working class. It was imposed on CP by Stalin-led Communist International and was a caricature of Bolshevism's support for national rights.

amongst the Negroes, despite the numerous mistakes, the [Stalinist Communist] party[11] can also record some achievements. For example in the southern textile strikes, where to a large extent the color lines were broken down.[12]

Weisbord, I understand, is in agreement with the slogan of self-determination and separate state rights. He maintains that is the application of the theory of the permanent revolution for America.[13]

We proceed from the actual situation: There are approximately thirteen million Negroes in America; the majority are in the southern states (Black Belt). In the northern states

---

11. The Communist League of America at this time still functioned as an expelled faction of the Communist Party, with the orientation of politically combating the Stalinist course of the CP leadership and seeking to reform the party and Communist International as revolutionary organizations. In January 1933, only a few weeks prior to Swabeck's visit to Trotsky, Adolf Hitler, head of the fascist National Socialist German Workers Party, had become chancellor of Germany. Due to the ultraleft and factional course imposed on the German Communist Party by the Stalinist misleadership in Moscow, the Nazis had been able to score this major triumph without united working-class resistance in the years leading up to the 1933 elections and in the months that followed. Neither within the German CP nor among the leadership of any other affiliate of the Comintern were substantial voices raised in opposition to the cover-up of the responsibility borne by the Stalinist leadership for this disastrous defeat for the world proletariat. Soon after Hitler's triumph, Trotsky, the CLA leadership, and their cothinkers around the world concluded that the Comintern and its parties could no longer be restored to a revolutionary course and set out to build a new international communist movement and parties.

12. Between 1929 and 1932, some 18,000 textile workers throughout the South carried out a number of strikes. These battles were important preparation for a national textile strike in 1934.

13. For a discussion of the place of Trotsky's theory of permanent revolution in the strategy and activity of the revolutionary workers movement over the past century, see *Their Trotsky and Ours* by Jack Barnes (Pathfinder, 2002).

the Negroes are concentrated in the industrial communities as industrial workers; in the South they are mainly farmers and sharecroppers.[14]

LEON TROTSKY: Do they rent from the state or from private owners?

SWABECK: From private owners, from white farmers and plantation owners; some Negroes own the land they till.

The Negro population of the North is kept on a lower level [than the white population]—economically, socially, and culturally; in the South, [they are kept] under oppressive Jim Crow conditions. They are barred from many important trade unions. During and since the war the migration from the South has increased; perhaps about four to five million Negroes now live in the North. The northern Negro population is overwhelmingly proletarian, but also in the South proletarianization is progressing.

Today none of the southern states has a Negro majority.[15] This lends emphasis to the heavy migration to the North. We put the question thus: Are the Negroes, in a political sense, a national minority or a racial minority?

The Negroes have become fully assimilated, Americanized, and their life in America has overbalanced the traditions of the past, modified and changed them. We cannot consider the Negroes a national minority in the sense of having their own

---

14. In the 1930s Blacks accounted for some 9 percent of iron and steel-workers in the United States, and in Alabama nearly 70 percent. Almost 10 percent of coal miners in the United States were African American, as were some 17 percent of workers in slaughterhouses and packinghouses (not counting skilled butcher positions, which remained a white job-trust).

15. Mississippi did have a narrow majority Black population at the time of the 1930 census (50.2 percent). Among the other eleven states of the old Confederacy, the only one with a population more than 40 percent Black in 1930 was South Carolina (45 percent). By 1940, according to the U.S. census, 49.3 percent of Mississippi's population was Black.

separate language. They have no special national customs, or special national culture or religion; nor have they any special national minority interests. It is impossible to speak of them as a national minority in this sense. It is therefore our opinion that the American Negroes are a racial minority whose position and interests are subordinated to the class relations of the country and dependent upon them.

To us the Negroes represent an important factor in the class struggle, almost a decisive factor. They are an important section of the proletariat. There is also a Negro petty bourgeoisie in America, but not as powerful or as influential or playing the role of the petty bourgeoisie and bourgeoisie among the nationally oppressed peoples (colonial).

The Stalinist slogan "self-determination" is in the main based upon an estimate of the American Negroes as a national minority, to be won over as allies. To us the question occurs: Do we want to win the Negroes as allies on such a basis, and who do we want to win, the Negro proletariat or the Negro petty bourgeoisie? To us it appears that we will with this slogan win mainly the petty bourgeoisie, and we cannot have much interest in winning them as allies on such a basis.[16]

---

16. Swabeck overstates the CLA leadership's homogeneity on this question. The draft platform presented to the CLA's founding conference in Chicago in May 1929, while condemning the CP's call for a "Negro Soviet Republic in the South," stated: "The Negro question is also a national question, and the Party must raise the slogan of the right of self-determination for the Negroes." At the conference itself, however, differences were expressed on this question. Cannon wrote in his article on the conference for the June 1 issue of the *Militant*, "Following a discussion of the disputed section of the platform on the slogan of the right of self-determination for the Negroes, it was decided to defer final action until more exhaustive material on the subject can be assembled and made available for discussion in the group." At the time of Swabeck's discussion with Trotsky four years later, the issue remained unresolved.

We recognize that the poor farmers and sharecroppers are the closest allies of the proletariat, but it is our opinion that they can be won as such mainly on the basis of the class struggle. Compromise on this principled question would put the petty-bourgeois allies ahead of the proletariat and the poor farmers as well. We recognize the existence of definite stages of development, which require specific slogans. But the Stalinist slogan appears to us to lead directly to the "democratic dictatorship of the proletariat and peasantry."[17] The unity of the workers, black and white, we must prepare proceeding from a class basis, but in that it is necessary to also recognize the racial issues and in addition to the class slogans also advance the racial slogans.

It is our opinion that in this respect the main slogan should be "social, political, and economic equality for the Negroes," as well as the slogans which flow therefrom. This slogan is naturally quite different from the Stalinist slogan of self-determination for a national minority. The [Communist] party leaders maintain that the Negro workers and farmers can be won only on the basis of this slogan. To begin with, it was advanced for the Negroes throughout the country, but today [it is put forward] only for [Negroes in] the southern states. It is our opinion that we can win the Negro workers

---

17. The revolutionary democratic dictatorship of the proletariat and peasantry was the formula used by Lenin and the Bolsheviks in the years leading up to the October 1917 Russian Revolution to provide, in Lenin's words, "a Marxist definition of the class content of a victorious revolution" in Russia. It points to the revolutionary worker-peasant alliance that was decisive in registering that victory and that formed the class foundation of the dictatorship of the proletariat in the Soviet Republic following the triumph. In the mid-1920s and 1930s, the Stalinists gutted the formula of its revolutionary class content to justify their support for certain bourgeois forces and leaderships in China and elsewhere in the colonial world. See *Their Trotsky and Ours* by Jack Barnes, especially pp. 78–79, 91–92, 109–12, and 127 [2008 printing].

only on a class basis, advancing also the racial slogans for the necessary intermediary stages of development. In this manner we believe also the poor Negro farmers can best be won as direct allies.

In the main, the problem of slogans in regard to the Negro question is the problem of a practical program. How will the Negroes be won over? We believe primarily with racial slogans: Equality with whites and the slogans which flow from this.

TROTSKY: The point of view of the American comrades appears to me not fully convincing. The right of self-determination is a democratic demand. Our American comrades counterpose the liberal demand [equality with whites] to this democratic demand. This liberal demand is, moreover, complicated. I understand what political equality means [a democratic demand]. But what is the meaning of economic and social equality within capitalist society? Does that mean a demand to public opinion that all should enjoy the equal protection of the laws? But that is political equality. The slogan "political, economic, and social equality" sounds ambiguous and is thus false.

The Negroes are a race and not a nation. [Nonetheless] nations grow out of racial material under definite conditions. The Negroes in Africa are not yet a nation, but they are in the process of forming a nation. The American Negroes are on a higher cultural level. But since they are under the [racist] pressure of the Americans, they become interested in the development of the Negroes in Africa. The American Negro will develop leaders for Africa, that one can say with certainty, and that in turn will influence the development of political consciousness in America.

We of course do not obligate the Negroes to become a nation; whether they are is a question of their consciousness, that is, what they desire and what they strive for. We say: If the Negroes want that then we must fight against imperialism to the last drop of blood, so that they gain the right, wherever and however they please, to separate a piece of land for themselves. The fact that they are today not a majority in any state does not matter. It is not a question of the authority of the states but of the Negroes. That there are and will be whites in areas that are overwhelmingly Negro is not the question, and we do not need to break our heads over the possibility that sometime the whites will be suppressed by the Negroes. In any case the suppression of the Negroes pushes them toward a political and national unity.

That the slogan "self-determination" will win over the petty bourgeois more than the workers—that argument holds good also for the slogan of "equality." It is clear that those Negro elements who play more of a public role (businessmen, intellectuals, lawyers, etc.) are more active and react more actively against inequality. It is possible to say that the liberal demand as well as the democratic one in the first instance will attract the petty bourgeois and only later the workers.

If the situation were such that in America common actions took place involving white and black workers, that class fraternization already was a fact, then perhaps our comrades' arguments would have a basis (I do not say that it would be correct); then perhaps we would divide the black workers from the white if we began to raise the slogan "self-determination."

But today the white workers in relation to the Negroes are the oppressors, scoundrels, who persecute the black and the yellow, hold them in contempt, and lynch them. If the Negro workers unite with their own petty bourgeois, that is because they are not yet sufficiently developed to defend their elementary rights. To the workers in the southern states the liberal demand for equal rights would undoubtedly mean progress, but the demand for self-determination, even greater progress. However, with the slogan "equal rights" they can be misled more easily ("according to the law you have this equality").

When we are so far [along the road of mass class struggle] that the Negroes say "we want autonomy," they then take a position hostile toward American imperialism. At that stage the workers will already be much more determined than the petty bourgeoisie. The workers will then see that the petty bourgeoisie is incapable of struggle and gets nowhere, but they will also recognize simultaneously that the white Communist workers fight for their demands and that will push them, the Negro proletarians, toward communism.

Weisbord is correct in a certain sense that the self-determination of the Negroes belongs to the question of the permanent revolution in America. The Negroes will, through their awakening, through their demand for autonomy, and through the democratic mobilization of their forces, be pushed on toward a class basis. The petty bourgeoisie will take up the demand for equal rights and for self-determination but will prove absolutely incapable in the struggle; the Negro proletariat will march over the petty bourgeoisie in the direction toward the proletarian revolution. That is perhaps for them the most important road. I can therefore see no reason why we should not advance the demand for self-determination.

I am not sure if the Negroes in the South do not speak their own Negro language. Now, at a time when they are being lynched just because of being Negroes they naturally fear to speak their Negro language; but when they are set free their Negro language will come alive again. I would advise the American comrades to study this question very seriously, including the language in the southern states.

For all these reasons I would in this question rather lean toward the standpoint of the [Stalinist Communist] party; of course, with the observation that I have never studied this question and that I proceed here from general considerations.

I base myself only upon the arguments brought forward by the American comrades. I find them insufficient and consider them a certain concession to the point of view of American chauvinism, which seems to me to be dangerous.

What can we lose in this question when we go further with our demands than the Negroes themselves do at present? We do not compel them to separate from the state, but they have the full right to self-determination when they so desire and we will support and defend them with all the means at our disposal in the winning of this right, the same as we defend all oppressed peoples.

SWABECK: I admit that you have advanced powerful arguments, but I am not yet entirely convinced. The existence of a special Negro language in the southern states is possible, but in general all American Negroes speak English. They are fully assimilated. Their religion is the American Baptist and the language in their churches is likewise English.

Economic equality we do not at all understand in the sense of the law. In the North (as of course also in the southern states), the wages for Negroes are always lower than for white workers and mostly their hours are longer; that is, so to say, accepted as natural. In addition the Negroes are allotted the most disagreeable work. It is because of these conditions that we demand economic equality for the Negro workers.

We do not contest the right of the Negroes to self-determination. That is not the issue of our disagreement with the Stalinists. But we contest the correctness of the slogan of self-determination as a means to win the Negro masses. The impulse of the Negro population is first of all in the direction toward equality in a social, political, and economic sense.

At present the party [the Stalinist CP] advances the slogan for self-determination only for the southern states. Of course, one can hardly expect that the Negroes from the northern industries should want to return to the South, and there are no indications of such a desire. On the contrary. Their unformulated demand is for social, political, and economic equality based upon the conditions under which they live. That is also the case in the South. It is because of this that we believe this to be the important racial slogan.

We do not look upon the Negroes as being under national oppression in the same sense as the oppressed colonial peoples. It is our opinion that the slogan of the Stalinists tends to lead the Negroes away from the class basis and more in the direction of the racial basis. That is the main reason for our being opposed to it. We are of the belief that the racial slogan in the sense as presented by us leads directly toward the class basis.

PIERRE FRANK: Are there in America special Negro movements?

SWABECK: Yes, several. First we had the Garvey movement, based upon the aim of migration to Africa.[18] It had a large following but busted up as a swindle. Now there is not much left of it. Its slogan was the creation of a Negro republic in Africa. Other Negro movements in the main rest upon a foundation of social and political equality demands as, for example, the League [National Association] for the Advancement of Colored People. This is a large racial movement.

TROTSKY: I also believe that the demand for equal rights should remain, and I do not speak *against* this demand. It is progressive to the extent that it has not yet been realized. Comrade Swabeck's explanation in regard to the question of economic equality is very important.

But that alone does not decide the question of the Negroes' fate as such, the question of the nation, etc. According to the arguments of the American comrades, one could say for example that Belgium too has no rights as a nation.

18. See glossary as well as footnote 30 in Part I, p. 73.

The Belgians are Catholics and a large section of them speak French. What if France wanted to annex them with such an argument? Also the Swiss people, through their historical connections, feel themselves to be one nation despite different languages and religions.

An abstract criterion is not decisive in this question; far more decisive is the historical consciousness of a group, their feelings, their impulses. But that too is not determined accidentally but rather by the situation and all the attendant circumstances. The question of religion has absolutely nothing to do with this question of nationhood. The Baptism of the Negro is something entirely different from Rockefeller's Baptism.[19] These are two different religions.

The political argument rejecting the demand for self-determination is doctrinairism. That is what we always heard in Russia in regard to the question of self-determination. The Russian experience has shown us that the groups which live a peasant existence retain peculiarities—their customs, their language, etc.—and given the opportunity these characteristics develop.

The Negroes have not yet awakened, and they are not yet united with the white workers. Ninety-nine point nine percent of the American workers are chauvinists; in relation to the Negroes they are hangmen as they are also toward the Chinese, etc. It is necessary to make them [the white workers] understand that the American state is not their state and that they do not have to be the guardians of this state. Those American workers who say: "The Negroes should separate if they so desire, and we will defend them

---

19. Oil baron John D. Rockefeller (1839–1937) was a well-known member of and financial contributor to the Northern Baptist Convention and its related mission societies and institutions. The largest associations of predominantly African American Baptist churches trace their origins to the National Baptist Convention founded in 1895.

against our American police"—those are revolutionists. I have confidence in them.

The argument that the slogan for self-determination leads away from the class point of view is an adaptation to the ideology of the white workers. The Negro can be developed to a class point of view only when the white worker is educated. On the whole the question of the colonial people is in the first instance a question of the education of the metropolitan worker.

The American worker is indescribably reactionary. This can be seen now in the fact that he has not yet even been won to the idea of social insurance. Because of this the American Communists are obligated to advance reform demands.

If the Negroes do not at present demand self-determination, it is of course for the same reason that the white workers do not yet advance the slogan of the dictatorship of the proletariat. The Negroes have not yet got it into their heads that they dare to carve out a piece of the great and mighty States for themselves. But the white workers must meet the Negroes halfway and say to them: "If you want to separate you will have our support." The Czech workers as well came to Communism only through disillusionment with their own state.

I believe that because of the unprecedented political and theoretical backwardness and the unprecedented economic progressiveness in America, the awakening of the working class will proceed quite rapidly. The old ideological covering will burst, all questions will emerge at once, and since the country is so economically mature the adaptation of the political and theoretical to the economic level will be achieved very rapidly. It is then possible that the Negroes will become the most advanced section. We have already a similar example in Russia. The Russians were the European Negroes. It is very possible that the Negroes will proceed through self-determination to the proletarian dictatorship in

Leon Trotsky (upper left) in Prinkipo, Turkey, April 1933, with (clockwise) Communist League of America leader Arne Swabeck and Trotsky's secretaries Pierre Frank, Rudolf Klement, Jean van Heijenoort.

Responding to Swabeck's remarks on CLA's orientation to Black rights struggles in U.S., Trotsky said: "It is very possible that the Negroes will proceed through self-determination to the proletarian dictatorship in a couple of giant strides, ahead of the great bloc of white workers. They will then be the vanguard. I am absolutely sure they will in any case fight better than the white workers. That, however, can happen only if the communist party carries on an uncompromising struggle not against the Negroes' supposed national prepossessions but against the colossal prejudices of white workers and makes no concession to them whatever."

a couple of gigantic strides, ahead of the great bloc of white workers. They will then be the vanguard.

I am absolutely sure that they will in any case fight better than the white workers. That, however, can happen only provided the communist party carries on an uncompromising, merciless struggle not against the supposed national prepossessions of the Negroes but against the colossal prejudices of the white workers and makes no concession to them whatever.

SWABECK: It is then your opinion that the slogan for self-determination will be a means to set the Negroes into motion against American imperialism?

TROTSKY: Naturally, by carving their own state out of mighty America, and doing that with the support of the white workers, the Negroes' self-confidence will develop enormously.

The reformists and the revisionists have written a great deal to the effect that capitalism is carrying on the work of civilization in Africa,[20] and if the peoples of Africa are left to

---

20. A reference to the class-collaborationist, Social Democratic leaderships of the Socialist International and its affiliated parties around the world. Lenin and the Bolsheviks had broken with the Socialist (Second) International in 1914, when the majority of its leaders supported "their own" bourgeois governments in the interimperialist First World War. Prior to that break, at the 1907 congress of the Socialist International in Stuttgart, Germany, the Bolsheviks led the opposition to a resolution submitted by the colonial commission stating, as paraphrased by Lenin, "that the Congress did not in principle condemn all colonial policy, for under socialism colonial policy could play a civilising role." That reactionary resolution, supported by the majority of delegates from the Social Democratic Party of Germany—the largest organization in the International—was defeated only by a slim majority of 128 to 110 with 10 abstentions. For an account of the debate, including Lenin's article on it, see "The Stuttgart Congress of 1907" in *Lenin's Struggle for a Revolutionary International: Documents (1907–1916)* (Pathfinder, 1984), pp. 27–87 [2002 printing].

themselves they will be all the more exploited by business-men, etc., much more than now where they at least have a certain measure of legal protection.

To a certain extent this argument can be correct. But in this case also it is foremost a question of the European workers: Without their liberation [from imperialist prejudices and support for the capitalist state], real colonial liberation is not possible. If the white worker performs the role of the oppressor he cannot liberate himself, much less the colonial peoples. The right of self-determination of the colonial peoples can in certain periods lead to different results; in the final instance, however, it will lead to the struggle against imperialism and to the liberation of the colonial peoples.

Before the war the Austrian Social Democracy (particularly Renner) also posed the question of the national minorities abstractly. They argued likewise that the slogan for self-determination would only lead the workers away from a class point of view, and that economically the minority state could not exist independently. Was this way of putting the question correct or false? It was abstract. The Austrian Social Democrats said that the national minorities were not nations. What do we see today? The separated pieces [of the old Austro-Hungarian empire] exist [as states]—bad to be sure, but they exist.

In Russia the Bolsheviks always fought for the self-determination of the national minorities, including the right of complete separation. And yet, after having achieved self-determination these groups remained with the Soviet Union. If the Austrian Social Democracy had carried out a correct policy regarding this question earlier, they would have said to the national minority groups: "You have the full right to self-determination, we have no interest whatever in keeping you in the hands of the Habsburg monarchy"—it would then have been possible after the revolution to cre-

"The policy of the Communist International in the fight against national oppression is aimed at uniting the proletarians and toiling masses of all nations in revolutionary struggle to overthrow the landowners and the bourgeoisie. Only such unity will guarantee victory over capitalism, without which it is impossible to abolish national oppression."

V.I. LENIN, 1920

Members of 134th Militia Battalion in Cuba celebrate victory over U.S.-organized invasion at Bay of Pigs/Playa Girón, April 1961. The Cuban Revolution, says Barnes, "not only opened the road to socialist revolution in the Americas. It marked a renewal in action of the proletarian internationalist course first pointed to by Marx and Engels more than a century earlier and carried out in life by workers and peasants in Russia in 1917 under the leadership of Lenin and the Bolshevik Party."

What Trotsky was explaining to us in 1933 and 1939 was not Black nationalism, but what winning the dictatorship of the proletariat opens up in the fight by Blacks and other working people against discrimination and oppression.

JACK BARNES, 2006

Facing page, top, the new Soviet workers and peasants republic recognized right to self-determination of oppressed nations within old tsarist empire. First Congress of Peoples of the East, in Baku, Soviet Azerbaijan, September 1920. Convened by Communist International, some 2,000 delegates representing workers and peasants of more than two dozen peoples of Asia discussed fight against imperialist domination, national oppression, and capitalist exploitation.

"Even before the First World War and Russian Revolution," James P. Cannon reminds us, "Lenin and the Bolsheviks were distinguished from others in the international socialist and labor movement by their concern with the problems of oppressed nations and national minorities." **Facing page, bottom,** workers install electrical transmission poles in Russian countryside, 1925. **This page, top,** literacy class in Soviet Caucasus, 1920s. **Above,** women rail workers in Russia hold on-the-job training class, December 1923.

Left, U.S. Socialist Party leader Eugene V. Debs with rail workers. "The best of the earlier socialists were represented by Debs," Cannon wrote. "But the limits of the great agitator's view were expressed in his statement: 'We have nothing special to offer the Negro and can't make separate appeals to all races. The SP is the party of the whole working class, regardless of color.' That was considered a very advanced position at the time."

Facing page, top, U.S. Communist Party delegation to Fourth Congress of Communist International, Moscow, November 1922, included Otto Huiswoud, front row, on left; Arne Swabeck in chair, far left; James P. Cannon, standing at back, fourth from left. "Everything new and progressive on the Negro question came from Moscow, after the Bolshevik revolution of 1917, and as a result of that revolution," wrote Cannon.

This page, top, Huiswoud (left) and fellow CP member Claude McKay at Fourth Congress—both also members of African Blood Brotherhood, many of whose leaders joined CP in early 1920s. "Theses on Negro Question" adopted by delegates was presented by Huiswoud.

Above, organizing meeting in Chicago of CP-led American Negro Labor Congress, launched in 1925 to fight racist discrimination and for right of Blacks to join unions.

"The young Communist Party's proletarian break with all previous positions held by American radicals on the Negro question coincided with large-scale migration of Negroes from agricultural regions of the South to industrial centers in the North, which was accelerated by World War I and continued in the 1920s."

JAMES P. CANNON, 1959

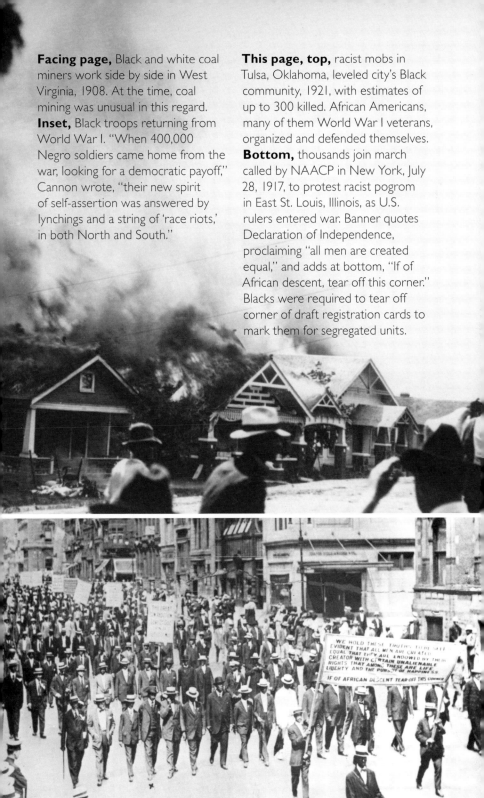

Facing page, Black and white coal miners work side by side in West Virginia, 1908. At the time, coal mining was unusual in this regard. **Inset,** Black troops returning from World War I. "When 400,000 Negro soldiers came home from the war, looking for a democratic payoff," Cannon wrote, "their new spirit of self-assertion was answered by lynchings and a string of 'race riots,' in both North and South."

This page, top, racist mobs in Tulsa, Oklahoma, leveled city's Black community, 1921, with estimates of up to 300 killed. African Americans, many of them World War I veterans, organized and defended themselves. **Bottom,** thousands join march called by NAACP in New York, July 28, 1917, to protest racist pogrom in East St. Louis, Illinois, as U.S. rulers entered war. Banner quotes Declaration of Independence, proclaiming "all men are created equal," and adds at bottom, "If of African descent, tear off this corner." Blacks were required to tear off corner of draft registration cards to mark them for segregated units.

In 1933 Trotsky observed that "common actions and class fraternization involving white and Black workers" do not occur in the U.S. This fact of the class struggle since the defeat of Reconstruction had only slowly begun to change in the course of struggles by farmers and workers after World War I.

JACK BARNES, 2006

ALL APPLICATIONS for MEMBERSHIP CAN BE MADE in the FOLLOWING PLACES
GRZIE MOŻNA SIE ZAPISAC DO UNII
COLUMBIA HALL   MICKIEOZ HALL   McDERMOTTS HALL   LOCAL 651
PULAWSKI HALL   LOCAL 212   HEADQUARTERS
                                                        4800 STATE ST.
COME IN NOW WHILE THE ADMISSION FEE IS SMALL. PAY UP YOUR DUES
WEAR A CAMPAIGN BUTTON SO AS WE WILL KNOW WHO IS UNION & WHO IS NOT.

Top, Chicago packinghouse workers, including Blacks and Polish immigrants, join union rally during organizing drive, 1919. With millions of GIs back from war, vying for hard-to-come-by jobs, anti-Black riots in Chicago later that year (and in some 24 other U.S. cities) led to defeat of this and other unionization efforts.

Bottom, Cotton workers strike for wage increase and union recognition near Corcoran, in California's Central Valley, 1933. The 1,800 strikers, a majority Mexican, included dispossessed farmers, Black and white, from Oklahoma, Arkansas, and Texas.

ate a great Danube federation.[21]

The dialectic of development shows that where tight centralism existed, the state went to pieces, and where complete self-determination was enacted, a real state emerged and remained united.

The Negro question is of enormous importance for America. The League must undertake a serious discussion of this question, perhaps in an internal bulletin.

II. Coyoacán, Mexico

In an April 1939 letter to Socialist Workers Party national secretary James P. Cannon, Leon Trotsky reported that he had recently had several discussions "with Comrade [C.L.R.] James," and that, "the two most important were on the Negro question." James was a Trinidadian-born writer who had joined the international communist movement in Britain in 1935. He had been living in the United States since late 1938 and collaborating with the SWP leadership to advance its work fighting the oppression of Blacks.

The discussions were held in Coyoacán, a suburb of Mexico City, where Trotsky had been living since January 1937. Due to pressure from the world Stalinist murder machine, fascist advances, campaigns by counterrevolutionary Russian exiles, and positions taken by the imperialist "democracies," the Bolshevik leader by then could no longer find asylum anywhere in Europe. In late 1936 the government of Lázaro Cárdenas

---

21. The Habsburgs were the ruling dynasty of the Austro-Hungarian Empire overthrown in the revolutionary upsurge of November 1918. Due to the counterrevolutionary course of the Social Democratic parties in Austria and other parts of the former empire, and the inexperience of the young Communist parties, the working class was unable to conquer power in any of these countries and lay the foundation to go forward to a Danube federation of soviet socialist republics.

opened Mexico's doors to Trotsky.

Also participating in the April 1939 discussions with Trotsky was Charles Curtiss, a member of the Communist League of America at its founding in 1929. At the time of the discussions, Curtiss was serving in Mexico as a representative of the Fourth International, the world organization the SWP helped found in 1938, and he remained a leading cadre of the party into the early 1950s. Sol Lankin, an SWP member serving as a guard in Trotsky's household, also joined the meetings.

In preparation for the discussion, James had written several pages of "preliminary notes," which Trotsky and others refer to in the transcripts published below. Trotsky expresses particularly strong disagreement with James's assertion that winning self-determination for Blacks in the United States would be reactionary.

"Self-determination for the American Negroes is (1) economically reactionary, (2) politically false because no Negroes (except C.P. stooges) want it," James wrote. "For Negroes it is merely an inverted segregation. . . . The Negro must be won for Socialism. There is no other way out for him in America or elsewhere. But he must be won on the basis of his own experience and his own activity. There is no other way for him to learn, nor for that matter, for any other group of toilers!

"*If he wanted self-determination*, then however reactionary it might be in every other respect, it would be the business of the revolutionary party to raise that slogan," James said. "If after the revolution, he insisted on carrying out that slogan and forming his own Negro state, the revolutionary party would have to stand by its promises and (similarly to its treatment of large masses of the peasantry) patiently trust to economic development and education to achieve an integration. But the Negro, fortunately for Socialism, does not want self-determination."[22]

---

22. James's "preliminary notes" were printed in June 1939 in a Socialist Workers Party bulletin.

The discussions with Trotsky took place in English. The transcripts, described by the stenographer as "rough notes uncorrected by the participants," were printed in an SWP bulletin in June 1939 in preparation for the party's convention in New York City the following month. Delegates to the July convention adopted the resolution "The Right of Self-Determination and the Negro in the United States of America," whose line and content were substantially shaped by the views Trotsky expressed during the discussions.[23]

Self-Determination
for the American Negroes

April 4, 1939

LEON TROTSKY: Comrade James proposes that we discuss the Negro question in three parts, the first to be devoted to the programmatic question of self-determination for the Negroes.

C.L.R. JAMES: The basic proposals for the Negro question have already been distributed, and here it is only necessary to deal with the question of self-determination. No one denies the Negroes' right to self-determination. It is a question of whether we should advocate it.

In Africa and in the West Indies we advocate self-

---

23. *The Founding of the Socialist Workers Party: Minutes and Resolutions (1938–39)* (Pathfinder, 1982), pp. 466–70 [2001 printing].

determination because a large majority of the people want it. In Africa the great masses of the people look upon self-determination as a restoration of their independence. In the West Indies, where we have a population similar in origin to the Negroes in America, there has been developing a national sentiment. The Negroes are a majority. Already we hear ideas, among the more advanced, of a West Indian nation, and it is highly probable that, even let us suppose that the Negroes were offered full and free rights as citizens of the British Empire, they would probably oppose it and wish to be absolutely free and independent. Therefore, both in Africa and in the West Indies, the International African Service Bureau advocates self-determination.[24] It is progressive. It is a step in the right direction. We weaken the enemy. It puts the workers in a position to make great progress toward socialism.

In America the situation is different. The Negro desperately wants to be an American citizen. He says, "I have been here from the beginning; I did all the work here in the early days. Jews, Poles, Italians, Swedes, and others come here and have all the privileges. You say that some of the Germans are spies. I will never spy. I have nobody for whom to spy. And yet you exclude me from the army and from the rights of citizenship."

In Poland and Catalonia there is a tradition of language, literature, and history to add to the economic and political oppression and to help weld the population in its progressive demand for self-determination. In America it is not so.

---

24. The International African Service Bureau was a small propaganda organization based in Britain that sought to organize support and solidarity with colonial independence and labor struggles. C.L.R. James, who was active in the organization, sought to develop support and raise funds in the United States for the bureau and its journal, *International African Opinion*.

Let us look at certain historic events in the development of the Negro in America.

Garvey raised the slogan "Back to Africa," but the Negroes who followed him did not believe for the most part that they were really going back to Africa. We know that those in the West Indies who were following him had not the slightest intention of going back to Africa, but they were glad to follow a militant leadership. And there is the case of the black woman who was pushed by a white woman in a street car and said to her, "You wait until Marcus gets into power and all you people will be treated in the way you deserve." Obviously she was not thinking of Africa.

There was, however, this concentration on the Negroes' problems simply because the white workers in 1919 were not developed. There was no political organization of any power calling upon blacks and whites to unite. The Negroes were just back from the war—militant and having no offer of assistance, they naturally concentrated on their own particular affairs.

In addition, however, we should note that in Chicago, where a race riot took place, the riot was deliberately provoked by the employers. Some time before it actually broke out, the black and white meatpackers had struck and had paraded through the Negro quarter in Chicago with the black population cheering the whites in the same way that they cheered the blacks. For the capitalists this was a very dangerous thing and they set themselves to creating race friction. At one stage, motor cars with white people in them sped through the Negro quarter shooting at all whom they saw. The capitalist press played up the differences and thus set the stage and initiated the riots that took place for dividing the population and driving the Negro back upon himself.[25]

---

25. During the Chicago "race riot" of 1919, 38 people were killed and 537 injured; more than 60 percent of the killed and injured were Black.

During the period of the crisis [the depression of the 1930s] there was a rebirth of these nationalist movements. There was a movement toward the forty-ninth state, and the movement concentrated around Liberia was developing. These movements assumed fairly large proportions up to at least 1934.[26]

Then in 1936 came the organization of the CIO. John L. Lewis appointed a special Negro department.[27] The New Deal made gestures to the Negroes. Blacks and whites fought together in various struggles. These nationalist movements have tended to disappear as the Negro saw the opportunity to fight [together] with the organized workers and to gain something.

The danger of our advocating and injecting a policy of self-determination is that it is the surest way to divide and confuse the workers in the South. The white workers have centuries of prejudice to overcome, but at the present time many of them are working with the Negroes in the south-

---

Some 1,000 people, mostly African Americans, were left homeless. African Americans accounted for roughly 4 percent of the city's population at the time. In June 1917, at the outset of a drive to unionize packinghouse workers in Chicago, a leader of the Amalgamated Meat Cutters and Butcher Workmen union and Stockyards Labor Council, John Kikulski, declared that "Polish, Irish, Lithuanian, and in fact every race, color, creed, and nationality is to be included." In the wake of the 1919 riot, however, the organizing drive was defeated.

26. The National Movement for the Establishment of the Forty-Ninth State was started in Chicago in the mid-1930s by Oscar C. Brown, a lawyer and businessman. It advocated self-determination through establishment of a Negro state as part of the U.S., which at the time had forty-eight states. It received little support. Liberia was one of the proposed destinations of the "Back to Africa" movement supported by Garvey and others.

27. Congress of Industrial Organizations (CIO) and John L. Lewis. See glossary.

ern sharecroppers' union,[28] and with the rise of the struggle there is every possibility that they will be able to overcome their age-long prejudices.

But for us to propose that the Negro have this black state for himself is asking too much from the white workers, especially when the Negro himself is not making the same demand. The slogans of abolition of debts, confiscation of large properties, etc., are quite sufficient to lead them both to fight together and on the basis of economic struggle to make a united fight for the abolition of social discrimination.

I therefore propose concretely: (1) That we are for the right of self-determination. (2) If some demand should arise among the Negroes for the right of self-determination, we should support it. (3) We do not go out of our way to raise this slogan and place an unnecessary barrier between ourselves and socialism. (4) An investigation should be made into these movements—the one led by Garvey, the movement for the forty-ninth state, the movement centering around Liberia. Find out what groups of the population supported them and on this basis come to some opinion as to how far there is any demand among the Negroes for self-determination.

CHARLES CURTISS: It seems to me that the problem can be divided into a number of different phases:

On the question of self-determination, I think it is clear that while we are for self-determination, even to the point of independence, it does not necessarily mean that we favor independence. What we are in favor of is that in a certain case, in a certain locality, they have the right to decide for themselves whether or not they should be independent or what particular governmental arrangements they should

---

28. The Share Croppers Union, founded in Alabama in 1931, was led by forces in and around the Stalinist Communist Party. The Southern Tenant Farmers Union, established in 1934 in Arkansas, was led by members of the Socialist Party.

have with the majority of the country.

On the question of self-determination being necessarily reactionary—I believe that is a little far-fetched. Self-determination for various nations and groups is not opposed to a future socialist world. I think the question was handled in a polemic between Lenin and Pyatakov from the point of view of Russia—of self-determination for the various peoples of Russia while still building a united country.[29] There is not necessarily a contradiction between the two. The socialist society will not be built upon subjugated people, but by a free people. The reactionary or progressive character of self-determination is determined by whether or not it will advance the social revolution. That is the criterion.

As to the point which was made, that we should not advocate a thing if the masses do not want it, that is not correct. We do not advocate things just because the masses want them. The basic question of socialism would come under that category. In the United States only a small percentage of the people want socialism, but still we advocate it. They may want war, but we oppose it. The questions we have to solve are as follows: Will it help in the destruction of American imperialism? If such a movement arises, will the people want it as the situation develops?

I take it that these nationalist movements of which you [James] speak were carried on for years, and the struggle was carried on by a handful of people in each case, but in the moment of social crisis the masses rallied to such movements. The same can possibly happen in connection with self-determination of the Negroes.

---

29. Lenin's 1916 polemics against fellow Bolshevik Y.L. Pyatakov (P. Kievsky), who was opposed to the right of self-determination, are printed in Lenin's *Collected Works*, vol. 23, pp. 22–76, and in *Lenin's Struggle for a Revolutionary International: Documents (1907–1916)*, pp. 491–97.

It seems to me that the so-called Black Belt is a super-exploited section of the American economy. It has all the characteristics of a subjugated section of an empire. It has all the extreme poverty and political inequality. It has the same financial structure—Wall Street exploits the petty-bourgeois elements [who] in turn [exploit] the poor workers. It represents simply a field for investment and a source of profits. It has the characteristics of part of a colonial empire. It is also essentially a regional matter, for the whites have also been forced to react against finance capital.

It would also be interesting to study the possible future development of the Negro question. We saw that when the Negroes were brought to the South they stayed there for many decades. When the war came, many emigrated to the North and there formed a part of the proletariat. That tendency can no longer operate. Capitalism is no longer expanding as it was before. As a matter of fact, during the depression many of them went back to the farms. It is possible that instead of a tendency to emigrate, there will now be a tendency for the Negro to stay in the South.

And there are other factors: The question of the cotton-picking machine, which means that the workers will be thrown out of work by the thousands.

To get back to the question of self-determination. There is the possibility that in the midst of the social crisis the manifestation of radicalism takes a double phase: Along with the struggle for economic and social equality, there may be found the demand for the control of their own state. Even in Russia, when the Bolsheviks came to power, the Polish people were not satisfied that this would mean the end of oppression for them. They demanded the right to control their own destiny in their own way. Such a development is possible in the South.

The other questions are important, but I do not think they are basic—that a nation must have its own language, culture, and tradition. To a certain extent they have been developing a culture of their own. In any public library can be found books—fiction, anthologies, etc.—expressing a new racial feeling.

Now from the point of view of the United States, the withdrawal of the Black Belt means the weakening of American imperialism by the withdrawal of a big field of investment. That is a blow in favor of the American working class.

It seems to me that self-determination is not opposed to the struggle for social and political and economic equality. In the North such a struggle is immediate and the need is acute. In the North the slogan for economic and political equality is an agitational slogan—an immediate question. From the practical angle, no one suggests that we raise the slogan of self-determination as an agitational one, but as a programmatic one which may become agitational in the future.

There is another factor which might be called the psychological one. If the Negroes think that this is an attempt to segregate them, then it would be best to withhold the slogan until they are convinced that this is not the case.

TROTSKY: I do not quite understand whether Comrade James proposes to eliminate the slogan of self-determination for the Negroes from our program, or is it that we do not say that we are ready to do everything possible for the self-determination of the Negroes if they want it themselves?

It is a question for the party as a whole, if we eliminate it or not. We are ready to help them if they want it. As a party we can remain absolutely neutral on this [on whether or not to seek to form a separate state].

We cannot say it will be reactionary. It is *not* reactionary.

We cannot tell them to set up a state because that will weaken imperialism and so will be good for us, the white workers. That would be against internationalism itself.

We cannot say to them, "Stay here, even at the price of economic progress."

We can say, "It is for you to decide. If you wish to take a part of the country, it is all right, but we do not wish to make the decision for you."

I believe that the differences between the West Indies, Catalonia, Poland, and the situation of the Negroes in the States are not so decisive. Rosa Luxemburg was against self-determination for Poland.[30] She felt that it was reactionary and fantastic, as fantastic as demanding the right to fly. It shows that she did not possess the necessary historic imagination in this case. The landlords and representatives of the Polish ruling class were also opposed to self-determination, for their own reasons.

Comrade James used three verbs: "support," "advocate," and "inject" the idea of self-determination. I do not propose for the party to advocate, I do not propose to inject, but only to proclaim our obligation to support the struggle for self-determination if the Negroes themselves want it. It is not a question of our Negro comrades. It is a question of thirteen or fourteen million Negroes. The majority of them are very backward. They are not very clear as to what they wish now, and we must give them a credit for the future. They will decide then.

What you said about the Garvey movement is interesting—but it proves that we must be cautious and broad and not base ourselves upon the status quo. The black woman who said to the white woman, "Wait until Marcus is in power. We will know how to treat you then," was simply expressing her desire for her own state.

The American Negroes gathered under the banner of the "Back to Africa" movement because it seemed a possible fulfillment of their wish for their own home. They did not want actually to go to Africa. It was the expression of a mystic

---

30. Rosa Luxemburg's views on self-determination can be seen in her 1915 article, "The Crisis in the German Social Democracy," also known as the Junius Pamphlet, in *Rosa Luxemburg Speaks* (Pathfinder, 1970).

desire for a home in which they would be free of the domination of the whites, in which they themselves could control their own fate. That also was a wish for self-determination. It was once expressed by some in a religious form, and now it takes the form of a dream of an independent state. Here in the United States the whites are so powerful, so cruel, and so rich that the poor Negro sharecropper does not say, even to himself, that he will take a part of this country for himself. Garvey spoke in glowing terms, that it was beautiful and that [in Africa] all would be wonderful. Any psychoanalyst will say that the real content of this dream was to have their own home. It is not an argument in favor of injecting the idea. It is only an argument by which we can foresee the possibility of their giving their dream a more realistic form.

Under the condition that Japan invades the United States and the Negroes are called upon to fight—they may come to feel themselves threatened first from one side and then from the other, and finally awakened, may say, "We have nothing to do with either of you. We will have our own state."

But the black state could enter into a federation. If the American Negroes succeeded in creating their own state, I am sure that after a few years of the satisfaction and pride of independence, they would feel the need of entering into a federation. Even if Catalonia, which is a very industrialized and highly developed province, had realized its independence, it would have been just a step to federation.

The Jews in Germany and Austria wanted nothing more than to be the best German chauvinists. The most miserable of all was the Social Democrat Austerlitz, the editor of the *Arbeiter-Zeitung*. But now, with the turn of events, Hitler does not permit them to be German chauvinists. Now many of them have become Zionists and are Palestinian nationalists and anti-German. I saw a disgusting picture recently of a Jewish actor, arriving in America, bending down to kiss the soil of the United States. Then they will get a few blows from the fascist fists in the United States, and they will go to kiss the soil of Palestine.[31]

There is another alternative to the successful revolutionary one. It is possible that fascism will come to power with its racial delirium and oppression, and the reaction of the Negro will be toward racial independence. Fascism in the United States will be directed against the Jews and the Negroes, but against the Negroes particularly, and in a most terrible manner. A "privileged" condition will be created for the American white workers on the backs of the Negroes.

The Negroes have done everything possible to become an integral part of the United States, in a psychological as well as a political sense. We must foresee that their reaction will show its power during the revolution. They will enter with a great distrust of the whites. We must remain neutral in the matter and hold the door open for both possibilities and promise our full support if they wish to create their own independent state.

So far as I am informed, it seems to me that the CP's attitude of making an imperative slogan of it was false. It was a case of the whites saying to the Negroes, "You must create a ghetto for yourselves." It is tactless and false and can only serve to repel the Negroes. Their only interpretation can be that the whites want to be separated from them.

Our Negro comrades, of course, have the right to participate more intimately in such developments. Our Negro

---

31. In July 1940 Trotsky wrote that "the future development of military events may well transform Palestine into a bloody trap for several hundred thousand Jews. Never was it so clear as it is today that the salvation of the Jewish people is bound up inseparably with the overthrow of the capitalist system." See Leon Trotsky, *On the Jewish Question* (Pathfinder, 1970), p. 16 [2005 printing].

comrades can say, "The Fourth International says that if it is our wish to be independent, it will help us in every way possible, but that the choice is ours. However, I, as a Negro member of the Fourth International, hold a view that we must remain in the same state as the whites," and so on. He can participate in the formation of the political and racial ideology of the Negroes.

JAMES: I am very glad that we have had this discussion, because I agree with you entirely. It seems to be the idea in America that we should advocate it as the CP has done. You seem to think that there is a greater possibility of the Negroes wanting self-determination than I think is probable. But we have a 100 percent agreement on the idea which you have put forward that we should be neutral in the development.

TROTSKY: It is the word "reactionary" that bothered me.

JAMES: Let me quote from the document: "If he wanted self-determination, then however reactionary it might be in every other respect, it would be the business of the revolutionary party to raise that slogan." I consider the idea of separating as a step backward so far as a socialist society is concerned. If the white workers extend a hand to the Negro, he will not want self-determination.

TROTSKY: It is too abstract, because the realization of this slogan can be reached only as the thirteen or fourteen million Negroes feel that the domination by the whites is terminated. To fight for the possibility of realizing an independent state is a sign of great moral and political awakening. It would be a tremendous revolutionary step. This ascendancy would immediately have the best economic consequences.

CURTISS: I think that an analogy could be made in connection with collective farms and the distribution of large estates. One might consider the breaking up of large estates into small plots as reactionary, but it is not necessarily so.

This question is up to the peasants, whether they want to operate the estates collectively or individually. We advise the peasants, but we do not force them—it is up to them. Some would say that the breaking up of the large estates into small plots would be economically reactionary, but that is not so.

TROTSKY: This was also the position of Rosa Luxemburg. She maintained that self-determination would be as reactionary as the breaking up of the large estates.

CURTISS: The question of self-determination is also tied up with the question of land and must be looked upon not only in its political but also in its economic manifestations.

A Negro Organization

April 5 and April 11, 1939

During two subsequent discussions in Mexico, Trotsky, Curtiss, James, and others exchanged views on the proposal in James's "preliminary notes" that the Socialist Workers Party initiate a call for "the organization of a Negro movement" that would fight "for the Negro right to vote, against social and legal discrimination, against discrimination in schools (and universities), against repressive rents," and around other issues.

In April 1939, as these discussions on the SWP's involvement in the fight against the national oppression of Blacks were under way, Trotsky wrote to SWP national secretary James P. Cannon that the "party cannot postpone this extremely important question any longer."[32] The SWP leadership took Trotsky's proposals to heart, and his contributions to the discussions in Mexico had a rapid and direct impact on the party's political work.

As the Socialist Workers Party campaigned over the next two years to prepare working people for Washington's inevitable entry into the spreading imperialist world slaughter, the party paid special attention to activity among workers and youth who were Black. When the Roosevelt administration declared war in December 1941, the SWP—eighteen of whose cadres and leaders had been sentenced to federal prison terms for organizing opposition to the imperialist war—joined with other supporters of Black rights across the United States in protest actions to demand an end to Jim Crow segregation in the armed forces; a halt to racist discrimination in war industries; and adoption and enforcement of federal legislation against lynchings and other night-riding terror targeting Blacks.

Through the *Militant* and inexpensive pamphlets, the SWP campaigned against the racist victimization of soldiers and sailors; for unionization of workers who were Black; for the arrest and prosecution of participants in "race riots" such as those against Blacks in Detroit and against Mexicanos in Los Angeles (the so-called Zoot suit riots); and in solidarity with anti-colonial struggles across Africa, Asia, and the Caribbean.

So well-known did the *Militant* become as a champion of such struggles that the U.S. government cited the paper's "stimulation of race issues" as a rationalization for revoking its second-class mailing rights in March 1943. Among the pamphlets produced and distributed by the SWP during these years were: *Why Negroes Should Oppose the War* (1939); *Defend the Negro Sailors of the USS Philadelphia* (1940); *The Negro and*

---

32. "More on Our Work in the Communist Party" (April 10, 1939) in *Writings of Leon Trotsky (1938–39)* (Pathfinder, 1969, 1974), pp. 341–42 [2004 printing].

the U.S. Army (1941); *Negroes March on Washington* (1941); *The March on Washington: One Year After* (1942); *The Struggle for Negro Equality* (1943); *Negroes in the Postwar World* (1944); and *A Practical Program to Kill Jim Crow* (1945).[33]

Below is the record of the April 5 and April 11 discussions in Mexico.

TROTSKY: It is very important [to decide] whether it is advisable and whether it is possible to create such an organization on our own initiative. Our movement is familiar with such forms as the party, the trade union, the educational organization, the cooperative; but this is a new type of organization which does not coincide with the traditional forms. We must consider the question from all sides as to whether it is advisable or not and what the form of our participation in this organization should be.

If another party had organized such a mass movement, we would surely participate as a fraction, providing that [the

---

33. Much of the material from the *Militant* and pamphlets based on them during these years can be found in *Fighting Racism in World War II* (Pathfinder, 1980).

James himself, however, was not part of this work. By September 1939, just a few months after the discussions in Mexico, he had joined a faction in the party led by Max Shachtman and was on the way toward breaking with the SWP and its communist course. Under pressure from bourgeois public opinion at the opening of World War II in Europe, and as U.S. entry into the war became inevitable, Shachtman, James, and others turned their backs on the SWP's defense of the Soviet workers state against imperialist assault and the party's decision to get the big majority of its cadres into the industrial working class and unions. The Shachtmanites, including James, formally split with the party in April 1940. In 1947 James rejoined the SWP for a brief period and then broke once again in 1951—this time over the party's unconditional defense of Korean national liberation forces and the Democratic People's Republic of Korea during Washington's murderous 1950–53 war against the Korean people. He was deported from the United States in 1953 and lived mostly in the United Kingdom until his death in 1989.

movement] included workers, poor petty bourgeois, poor farmers, and so on. We would enter for the purpose of educating the best elements and winning them for our party.

But this is another thing. What is proposed here is that we take the initiative. Even without knowing the concrete situation in Negro circles in the United States, I believe we can admit that realistically no one but our party is capable of [initiating] such a movement. Of course, the movements guided by the improvisatorial Negro leaders, as we saw them in the past, more or less expressed the unwillingness or the incapacity, the perfidy of all the existing parties.

None of the [bourgeois] parties can now assume such a task, because they are either pro-Roosevelt imperialists or anti-Roosevelt imperialists. Such an organization of the oppressed Negroes signifies to them the weakening of "democracy" and of big business. This is also true of the Stalinists. Thus, the only party capable of beginning such an action is our own party.

But the question remains as to whether we can take upon ourselves the initiative of forming such an organization of Negroes as Negroes—not for the purpose of winning some elements to our party but for the purpose of doing systematic educational work in order to elevate them politically. What should be the form—what is the correct line of our party? That is our question.

CURTISS: As I have already said to Comrade James, the [Stalinist] Communist Party organized the American Negro Labor Congress and the League of Struggle for Negro Rights.[34]

---

34. The American Negro Labor Congress (ANLC) was created in 1925 and lasted until 1930, when, at a conference in St. Louis, its name was changed to the League of Struggle for Negro Rights (LSNR). The CP dissolved the LSNR in 1936, when it took the initiative in forming the National Negro Congress to support the course of the Roosevelt administration and its "New Deal."

Neither one had great success. Both were very poorly organized. I personally think that such an organization should be organized, but I think it should be done carefully and only after a study of all the factors involved and also of the causes of the breakdown of the two organizations mentioned. We must be sure of a mass base. To create a shadow of ourselves would serve only to discredit the idea and would benefit no one.

TROTSKY: Who were the leaders of these organizations?

CURTISS: Fort-Whiteman, Owen, Haywood, Ford, Patterson; Bob Minor was the leader of the CP's Negro work.[35]

TROTSKY: Who are the leaders now?

CURTISS: Most of them are in the CP, so far as I know. Some have dropped out of the movement.

OWEN:[36] Comrade James seems to have the idea that there is a good chance of building such an organization in the immediate future. I would like to have him elaborate.

JAMES: I think that it should be a success, because on my arrival in New York I met great numbers of Negroes and spoke to many Negro organizations. I brought forward the point of view of the Fourth International, particularly on the war question, and in every case there was great applause and a very enthusiastic reception of the ideas. Great numbers of these Negroes hated the Communist Party, agreed entirely with the program put forward by the International African Service Bureau, and were extremely interested in the journal *International African Opinion*.

Up to the last convention, 79 percent of the Negro membership of the CP in New York State, 1,579 people, had left

---

35. See glossary for names. "Owen" probably refers to Gordon Owens, one of the members of the African Blood Brotherhood who joined the Communist Party in the early 1920s.

36. Owen's identity is not known. It is not the Owen mentioned a few lines earlier as a veteran Black leader of the Communist Party.

the CP.[37] I met many of the representative ones, and they were now willing to form a Negro organization but did not wish to join the Fourth International. I had come to the conclusion that there was this possibility of a Negro organization before I left New York, but waited until I had gone through various towns in the States and got into contact with the Negro population there. And I found that the impressions that I had gathered in New York corresponded to those that I found on the tour.

In Boston, for instance, I went to a Barbados organization and there found about twenty or thirty people who had some sort of free society, but after having spoken to them for five or ten minutes they became very much interested in the political questions that I raised; and the chairman told me that if I wanted to come back to Boston he could arrange a Negro meeting for me at which we would have about seven hundred people. I do not think that it is too much to say that that was characteristic of the general attitude of the Negroes in the various places at which I had meetings.

TROTSKY: I have not formed an opinion about the question because I do not have enough information. What Comrade James tells us now is very important. It shows that we can have some elements for cooperation in this field, but at the same time this information limits the immediate perspective of the organization.

Who are those elements? The majority are Negro intellectuals, former Stalinist functionaries and sympathizers. We

---

37. This statement is misleading. Although James's figures on the number of Blacks who had left the CP in New York by early 1939 jibe with other estimates, this did not represent a net decline in the party's African American membership, either in New York State or nationally. The Communist Party was still recruiting more members than it lost, including Blacks, until at least the Stalin-Hitler Pact in late August 1939. Following World War II, the CP's membership declined at a sharply accelerating pace.

know that now large strata of the intellectuals are turning back to the Stalinists in every country. We have observed such people who were very sympathetic to us: Eastman, Solow, Hook, and others. They were very sympathetic to us insofar as they considered us an object to protect. They abandoned the Stalinists and looked for a new field of action, especially during the Moscow trials,[38] and so for the period they were our friends. Now since we have begun a vigorous campaign, they are hostile to us.

Many of them are returning to all sorts of vague things—humanism, etc. In France, Plisnier, the famous author, went back to God as well as to democracy. But when the white intellectuals went back to Roosevelt and democracy, the disappointed Negro intellectuals looked for a new field on the basis of the Negro question. Of course we must utilize them, but they are not a basis for a large mass movement. They can be used only when there is a clear program and good slogans.

The real question is whether or not it is possible to organize a mass movement. You know for such disappointed elements we created FIARI.[39] It is not only for artists; anyone may enter. It is something of a moral or political "resort" for the disappointed intellectuals. Of course, it can also be used at times to protect us in certain ways, [to raise] money,

---

38. In the 1930s Stalin's bloody elimination of those he viewed as threats to his power and to the privileges of the bureaucratic caste he represented culminated in three Moscow trials—1936, 1937, and 1938—where the defendants "confessed" participation in conspiracies with Nazi Germany, fascist Italy, and the Japanese throne to restore capitalism in the USSR. See *The Case of Leon Trotsky* (Pathfinder, 1937, 1968, 2008) and *Not Guilty* (Pathfinder, 1938, 2008).

39. FIARI was the International Federation of Independent Revolutionary Art, initiated in 1938. Its manifesto, "Towards a Free Revolutionary Art," signed by French writer André Breton and Mexican muralist Diego Rivera, was written by Breton in collaboration with Trotsky and is included in Trotsky, *Art and Revolution* (Pathfinder, 1970, 1972).

to influence petty-bourgeois public opinion, and so on. That is one thing; but you consider these Negro intellectuals for the directing of a mass movement.

Your project would create something like a pre-political school. What determines the necessity? Two fundamental facts: that the large masses of the Negroes are backward and oppressed and this oppression is so strong that they must feel it every moment; that they feel it as Negroes. We must find the possibility of giving this feeling a political-organizational expression. You may say that in Germany or in England we do not organize such semipolitical, semi–trade union, or semicultural organizations; we reply that we must adapt ourselves to the genuine Negro masses in the United States.

I will give you another example. We are terribly against the "French turn."[40] We abandoned our independence in order to penetrate into a centrist organization. You see that this Negro woman writes that they will not adhere to a Trotskyist organization. It is the result of the disappointments that they have had from the Stalinist organizations and also the propaganda of the Stalinists against us. They say, "We are already persecuted, just because we are Negroes. Now if we adhere to the Trotskyists, we will be even more oppressed."[41]

Why did we penetrate into the Socialist Party and into

---

40. For a few years between 1934 and 1937, Trotsky urged communists in France, Spain, and the United States to enter the left wing of Social Democratic organizations in those countries, for a brief period only, in order to influence workers and youth who could be won to a revolutionary proletarian party. The tactic was called the "French turn," since it was first carried out in France. By 1939 Trotsky disagreed with those who continued to advocate the tactic; the moment had passed.

41. It is not known what letter or statement Trotsky is referring to here, but the woman's point seems clear.

the PSOP?[42] If we were not the left wing, subject to the most severe blows, our powers of attraction would be ten or a hundred times greater; the people would come to us. But now we must penetrate into other organizations, keeping our heads on our shoulders and telling them that we are not as bad as they say.

There is a certain analogy with the Negroes. They were enslaved by the whites. They were liberated by the whites (so-called liberation). They were led and misled by the whites, and they did not have their own political independence. They were in need of a pre-political activity as Negroes.

Theoretically it seems to me absolutely clear that a special organization should be created for a special situation. The danger is only that it will become a game for the intellectuals. This organization can justify itself only by winning workers, sharecroppers, and so on. If it does not succeed, we will have to confess that it was a failure. If it does succeed, we will be very happy, because there will be a mass organization of Negroes. In that case I fully agree with Comrade James, except of course with some reservations on the question of self-determination, as was stated in our other discussion.

The task is not one of simply passing through the organization for a few weeks. It is a question of awakening the Negro masses. It does not exclude recruitment. I believe that success is quite possible; I am not sure. But it is clear for us all that our comrades in such an organization should be organized into a group. We should take the initiative. I believe it is necessary. This supposes the adaptation of our transitional program to the Negro problems in the States—a very carefully elaborated program with genuine civil rights, political rights, cultural

42. In 1938 supporters of the Fourth International in France, with Trotsky's support, entered the centrist Workers and Peasants Socialist Party (PSOP) in order to win its left wing to communist politics. The PSOP disintegrated when World War II began in late 1939.

interests, economic interests, and so on. It should be done.[43]

I believe that there are two strata: the intellectuals and the masses. I believe that it is among the intellectuals that you find this opposition to self-determination. Why? Because they keep themselves separated from the masses, always with the desire to take on the Anglo-Saxon culture and of becoming an integral part of the Anglo-Saxon life. The majority are opportunists and reformists. Many of them continue to imagine that by the improvement of the mentality, and so on, the discrimination will disappear. That is why they are against any kind of sharp slogan.

JAMES: They will maintain an intellectual interest because the Marxist analysis of Negro history and the problems of the day will give them an insight into the development of the Negroes which nothing else can. Also they are very much isolated from the white bourgeoisie, and the social discrimination makes them therefore less easily corrupted, [than], for example, the Negro intellectuals in the West Indies. Furthermore, they are a very small section of the Negro population and on the whole are far less dangerous than the corresponding section of the petty bourgeoisie in any other group or community. Also what has happened to the Jews in Germany has made the Negro intellectuals think twice. They will raise enough money to start the thing off. After that we do not have to bother [about them] in particular. Some, however, would maintain an intellectual interest and continue to give money.

❋

[*During the April 11 discussion, C.L.R. James presented a plan for a Negro organization of the type he proposed. In connection with such an effort, James wrote, while it was important*

---

43. In 1969 the Socialist Workers Party adopted and campaigned with such a program. See *The Transitional Program for Socialist Revolution* (Pathfinder, 1973, 1974, 1977), pp. 259–84 [2009 printing].

to present a "positive economic and political analysis show-
ing that socialism is the only way out and definitely treating the
theory on a high level," such explanations "should come from
the party. . . . This discussion on socialism should have no part
in the weekly agitational paper" of a Black organization.

["While we cannot afford to have confusion on this question
in the leadership," James said, "we cannot begin by placing
an abstract question like socialism before Negro workers." His
comments elicited the following exchange.]

CURTISS: About opening the discussion of socialism in the bulletin [the proposed theoretical journal], but excluding it, at least for a time, from the weekly paper [of the proposed Black organization]: it seems to me that this is dangerous. This is falling into the idea that socialism is for intellectuals and the elite, but that the people on the bottom should be interested only in the common, day-to-day things. The method should be different in both places, but I think that there should at least be a drive in the direction of socialism in the weekly paper not only from the point of view of daily matters but also in what we call abstract discussion.

It is a contradiction—the mass paper would have to take a clear position on the war question, but not on socialism. It is impossible to do the first without the second. It is a form of economism that the workers should interest themselves in the everyday affairs, but not in the theories of socialism.[44]

JAMES: I see the difficulties and the contradiction, but there is something else that I cannot quite see—if we want to build a mass movement we cannot plunge into a discussion of socialism, because I think that it would cause more

---

44. Economism was a trend in the Russian workers movement at the turn of the twentieth century that viewed the working-class struggle primarily as an economic one developing spontaneously around "bread-and-butter" issues. Lenin's works include a number of polemics with economism, most notably *What Is to Be Done?*

confusion than it would gain support.

The Negro is not interested in socialism. He can be brought to socialism on the basis of his concrete experiences. Otherwise we would have to form a Negro socialist organization. I think we must put forth a minimal, concrete program. I agree that we should not put socialism too far in the future, but I am trying to avoid lengthy discussions on Marxism, the Second International, the Third International, etc.

SOL LANKIN: Would this organization throw its doors open to all classes of Negroes?

JAMES: Yes, on the basis of its program. The bourgeois Negro can come in to help, but only on the basis of the organization's program.

LANKIN: I cannot see how the Negro bourgeoisie can help the Negro proletariat fight for its economic advancement.

JAMES: In our own movement some of us are petty bourgeois. If a bourgeois Negro is excluded from a university because of his color, this organization will probably mobilize the masses to fight for the rights of the bourgeois Negro student. Help for the organization will be mobilized on the basis of its program, and we will not be able to exclude any Negro from it if he is willing to fight for that program.

TROTSKY: I believe that the first question is the attitude of the Socialist Workers Party toward the Negroes. It is very disquieting to find that until now the party has done almost nothing in this field. It has not published a book, a pamphlet, leaflets, nor even any articles in the *New International*. Two comrades who compiled a book on the question, a serious work, remained isolated. That book is not published, nor are even quotations from it published. It is not a good sign. It is a bad sign.[45]

---

45. A "Special Negro Number" of *New International*, the SWP's theoretical magazine, was published December 1939.

The manuscript referred to by Trotsky, "The Negro in the U.S.," by Barney Mayes and William Bennett, was never published. Following

The characteristic thing about the American workers' parties, trade union organizations, and so on, was their aristocratic character. It is the basis of opportunism. The skilled workers who feel set in capitalist society help the bourgeois class to hold the Negroes and the unskilled workers down to a very low scale. Our party is not safe from degeneration if it remains a place for intellectuals, semi-intellectuals, skilled workers, and Jewish workers who build a very close milieu which is almost isolated from the genuine masses. Under these conditions our party cannot develop—it will degenerate.

We must have this great danger before our eyes. Many times I have proposed that every member of the party, especially the intellectuals and semi-intellectuals, who, during a period of say six months, cannot each win a worker-member for the party should be demoted to the position of sympathizer. We can say the same in [relation to] the Negro question.

The old organizations, beginning with the AFL, are the organizations of the workers' aristocracy. Our party is a part of the same milieu, not of the basic exploited masses of whom the Negroes are the most exploited. The fact that our party until now has not turned to the Negro question is a very disquieting symptom. If the workers' aristocracy is the basis of opportunism, one of the sources of adaptation to capitalist society, then the most oppressed and discriminated are the most dynamic milieu of the working class.

We must say to the conscious elements of the Negroes that they are convoked by the historic development to become a vanguard of the working class. What serves as the brake on the higher strata? It is the privileges, the comforts that hinder them from becoming revolutionists. It does not exist for the Negroes.

the 1939 discussions, however, the SWP wrote and campaigned energetically on the fight against Black oppression, as described in the introductory note to this chapter.

At Trotsky's urging, the SWP stepped up activity in fight for Black rights heading into, during, and after World War II. In line with its proletarian course, party campaigned in support of Black-led March on Washington Movement's demands to end segregation in jobs, education, and public facilities, including war industries and armed forces, and for passage of federal anti-lynching laws. Using *Militant* and inexpensive pamphlets, SWP campaigned against racist victimization of soldiers and sailors; for unionization of workers who are Black; for prosecution of those involved in "race riots" against Blacks in Detroit and Mexicanos in Los Angeles; in solidarity with anticolonial struggles in Africa, Asia, and Caribbean. The *Militant* became so well known as champion of such struggles that government attacks against it began in November 1942. Citing "stimulation of race issues" as a rationalization, Washington revoked the paper's second-class mailing rights in March 1943. Government action against *Militant* was strongly backed by Stalinist Communist Party.

NOVEMBER 19, 1938

NOVEMBER 28, 1942

AUGUST 18, 1945

Father COUGHLIN Fascist Demagogue
5¢ by Joseph Hansen

1939

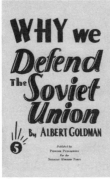

WHY we Defend The Soviet Union
By ALBERT GOLDMAN
Published by
Pioneer Publishers
For the
Socialist Workers Party

1940

DEFEND The NEGRO SAILORS the U.S.S. Philadelphia by Albert Parker 2¢

1940

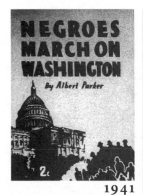

NEGROES MARCH ON WASHINGTON By Albert Parker 2¢

1941

TODAY'S FIGHT Against The Bosses
1c
Expropriate the War Industries!

1941

The Negro and the U.S. Army

1941

THE STRUGGLE FOR NEGRO EQUALITY
By John Saunders and Albert Parker
With an Introduction by Charles Jackson
PIONEER PUBLISHERS   10c

1943

NEGROES in the POST-WAR WORLD by ALBERT PARKER
PIONEER PUBLISHERS 5¢

1944

A Practical Program to KILL JIM CROW
UNITE!
by Charles Jackson   25
PIONEER PUBLISHERS

1945

What can transform a certain stratum, make it more capable of courage and sacrifice? It is concentrated in the Negroes. If it happens that we in the SWP are not able to find the road to this stratum, then we are not worthy at all. The permanent revolution and all the rest would be only a lie.

In the States we now have various contests. Competition to see who will sell the most papers, and so on. That is very good. But we must also establish a more serious competition— the recruiting of workers and especially of Negro workers. To a certain degree that is independent of the creation of the special Negro organization.

I believe the party should utilize the sojourn of Comrade James in the States (the tour was necessary to acquaint him with conditions) for the next six months, for behind-the-scenes organizational and political work in order to avoid attracting too much attention from the authorities. A six months' program can be elaborated for the Negro question, so that if James should be obliged to return to Great Britain, for personal reasons or through the pressure of the police, after a half year's work we have a base for the Negro movement and we have a serious nucleus of Negroes and whites working together on this plan.

It is a question of the vitality of the party. It is an important question. It is a question of whether the party is to be transformed into a sect or if it is capable of finding its way to the most oppressed part of the working class.

[*Later Trotsky returned to James's statement that "We cannot begin by placing an abstract question like socialism before Negro workers."*]

TROTSKY: I do not believe that we can begin with the exclusion of socialism from the organization. You propose a very large, somewhat heterogeneous organization, which will also accept religious people. That would signify that if a Negro worker, or farmer, or merchant, makes a speech in the organization to the effect that the only salvation for the Negroes is in the church, we will be too tolerant to expel him and at the same time so wise that we will let him speak in favor of religion, but we will not speak in favor of socialism. If we understand the character of this milieu, we will adapt the presentation of our ideas to it. We will be cautious; but to tie our hands in advance—to say that we will not introduce the question of socialism because it is an abstract matter—that is not possible. It is one thing to present a general socialist program; and another thing to be very attentive to the concrete questions of Negro life and to [counterpose] socialism to capitalism in these questions. It is one thing to accept a heterogeneous group and to work in it, and another to be absorbed by it.

JAMES: I quite agree with what you say. What I am afraid of is the putting forth of an abstract socialism. You will recall that I said that the leading group must clearly understand what it is doing and where it is going. But the socialist education of the masses should arise from the day-to-day questions. I am only anxious to prevent the thing's developing into an endless discussion. The discussion should be free and thorough in the theoretical organ.

In regard to the question of socialism in the agitational organ, it is my view that the organization should definitely establish itself as doing the day-to-day work of the Negroes, in such a way that the masses of Negroes can take part in it, before involving itself in discussions about socialism. While it is clear that an individual can raise whatever points he wishes and point out his solution of the Negro problems, yet the question is whether those who are guiding the organization as a whole should begin by speaking in the name of socialism. I think not. It is important to remember that those who take the initiative should have some common agreement as to the fundamentals of politics today, otherwise there will be great trouble as the organization develops. But although these, as individuals, are entitled to put forward their particular point of view in the general discussion, yet the issue is whether they should speak as a body as socialists from the very beginning, and my personal view is no.

TROTSKY: In the theoretical organ you can have theoretical discussion, and in the mass organ you can have a mass political discussion. You say that [the masses of Negroes] are contaminated by the capitalist propaganda. Say to them, "You don't believe in socialism. But you will see that in the fighting, the members of the Fourth International will not only be with you, but possibly the most militant." I would even go so far as to have every one of our speakers end his speech by saying, "My name is the Fourth International!" They will come to see that we are the fighters, while the person who preaches religion in the hall, in the critical moment, will go to the church instead of to the battlefield.

[*Trotsky then briefly commented on a number of concrete action proposals to advance Black rights. One was the position of the proposed Negro organization on the coming interimperialist world war.*]

TROTSKY: Yes, it is the most important and the most difficult question. The program may be very modest, but at the same time it must leave to everyone his freedom of expression in his speeches, and so on; the program must not be the limitation of our activity, but only our common obligation. Everyone must have the right to go further, but everyone is obliged to defend the minimum. We will see how this minimum will be crystallized as we go along in the opening steps.

[*On the proposal "to organize a campaign in some industry in behalf of the Negroes."*]

TROTSKY: That is important. It will bring a conflict with some white workers who will not want it. It is a shift from the most aristocratic workers' elements to the lowest elements. We attracted to ourselves some of the higher strata of the intellectuals when they felt that we needed protection: Dewey, La Follette, etc. Now that we are undertaking seri-

SWP leader Farrell Dobbs with Trotsky in Coyoacán, Mexico, January 1940.

During discussions in Coyoacán the previous year with SWP cadres on struggle for Black freedom, Trotsky emphasized that the party "is not safe from degeneration if it remains a place for intellectuals, semi-intellectuals, skilled workers. . . . Many times I have proposed that every party member, especially intellectuals, who cannot win a worker-member to the party over a six-month period should be demoted to sympathizer, and the same in relation to winning Negro members. It is a question of the vitality of the party—of whether the party is transformed into a sect or is able to find its way to the most oppressed part of the working class."

ous work, they are leaving us. I believe that we will lose two or three more strata [as we] go more deeply into the masses. This will be the touchstone.

[*On a campaign to address the crisis of housing and high rents facing Blacks.*]

TROTSKY: It is absolutely necessary.

CURTISS: It also works in very well with our transitional demands.

[*On a campaign of sit-ins by Blacks at segregated restaurants demanding to be served.*]

TROTSKY: Yes, and give it an even more militant character. There could be a picket line outside to attract attention and explain something of what is going on.

[*On a campaign aimed at winning support among domestic servants.*]

TROTSKY: Yes, I believe it is very important; but I believe that there is the *a priori* consideration that many of these Negroes are servants for rich people and are demoralized and have been transformed into moral lackeys. But there are others, a larger stratum, and the question is to win those who are not so privileged.

[*On how the proposed organization can advance working-class political independence from the imperialist Democratic and Republican parties.*]

TROTSKY: How many Negroes are there in Congress? One.[46] There are 440 members in the House of Representatives and 96 in the Senate. Then if the Negroes have almost 10 percent of the population, they are entitled to 50 members, but they have only one. It is a clear picture of political inequality. We can often [propose] a Negro candidate [in opposition] to a white candidate. This Negro organization can always say, "We want a Negro who knows our prob-

---

46. At the time, there was a single member of either house of Congress who was Black, Representative Arthur W. Mitchell from Illinois.

lems." It can have important consequences. . . .

It is a question of [our stance toward the candidate of] another organization for which we are not responsible, just as they are not responsible for us. If this organization puts up a certain candidate, and we find as a party that we must put up our own candidate in opposition, we have the full right to do so. If we are weak and cannot get the organization to choose a revolutionist, and they choose a Negro Democrat, we might even withdraw our candidate with a concrete declaration that we abstain from fighting, not the Democrat, but the Negro. We consider that the Negro's candidacy as opposed to the white's candidacy, even if both are of the same party, is an important factor in the struggle of the Negroes for their equality; and in this case we can critically support them. I believe that it can be done in certain instances.[47]

---

47. Trotsky was not proposing support for candidates of the Democratic or Republican parties. He was suggesting that under certain conditions the SWP might give critical support to the candidate of an independent Negro organization running *against* the candidates of the Democratic and Republican parties, even though the candidate nominated by the Negro organization might be a Democrat.

During the rise in the proletarian-led mass struggle for Black rights during the 1950s and 1960s, the Socialist Workers Party supported independent Black political campaigns on several occasions, including the 1958 campaign of Joseph King in Chicago (see Part IV, p. 321); the 1964 Freedom Now Party campaign in Michigan of Rev. Albert Cleage for governor (as well as other FNP candidates); the 1966 Lowndes County Freedom Organization (LCFO) campaign for local office in Alabama; and the 1965 campaign by Carl Stokes for mayor of Cleveland. In some cases, the candidates themselves were registered Democrats, but the campaigns were run independent of and against Democratic and Republican party candidates. (See *Independent Black Political Action 1954–78* [Pathfinder, 1982].) When Cleage, LCFO leader John Hulett, and Stokes later ran as Democratic Party candidates, the SWP did not support those campaigns. The SWP ran Syd Stapleton as its candidate for mayor in Cleveland in the 1969 race in which Stokes was reelected, this time on the Democratic Party ticket.

To Whom Belongs
the Decisive Word

by Leon Trotsky
June 1932

The task of communists emphasized by Leon Trotsky in the last of the three discussions in Mexico in 1939—the building of parties that are proletarian in composition, not just in program and strategy—was central to the revolutionary continuity he was organizing his co-thinkers in the Socialist Workers Party and worldwide to put into practice.

Trotsky had summarized this course much earlier in a June 13, 1932, letter urging the leadership of the world communist movement to actively work to recruit a group of Black workers in Johannesburg, South Africa, who had asked to join.

The Johannesburg comrades may not as yet have had the opportunity to acquaint themselves more closely with the views of the Left Opposition on all the most important questions. But this cannot be an obstacle to our working together with them as closely as possible at this very moment, and helping them in a comradely way to come into the orbit of our program and our tactics.

When ten intellectuals, whether in Paris, Berlin, or New York, who have already been members of various organizations, address themselves to us with a request to be taken into our midst, I would offer the following advice: put them through a series of tests on all the programmatic questions; wet them in the rain, dry them in the sun, and then after a new and careful examination accept maybe one or two.

The case is radically altered when ten workers connected with the masses turn to us. The difference in our attitude to a petty-bourgeois group and to the proletarian group does not require any explanation. But if a proletarian group functions in an area where there are workers of different races and, in spite of this, remains composed solely of workers of a privileged nationality, then I am inclined to view them with suspicion. Are we not dealing perhaps with the labor aristocracy? Isn't the group infected with slaveholding prejudices, active or passive?

It is an entirely different matter when we are approached by a group of Negro workers. Here I am prepared to take it for granted in advance that we shall achieve agreement with them, even if such an agreement is not yet evident, because the Negro workers, by virtue of their whole position, do not and cannot strive to degrade anybody, oppress anybody, or deprive anybody of his rights. They do not seek privileges and cannot rise to the top except on the road of the international revolution.

We can and we must find a way to the consciousness of the Negro workers, the Chinese workers, the Indian workers, and all the oppressed in the human ocean of the colored races to whom belongs the decisive word in the development of mankind.

PART IV

Ending the
Dictatorship of Capital,
Ending Racism

Black Liberation and the Dictatorship of the Proletariat

by Jack Barnes
January–March 2006

The following is based on reports presented to international leadership conferences organized by the Socialist Workers Party in January and March 2006. Participating in the leadership meetings, along with members of the SWP National Committee, were representatives of Communist Leagues in several countries, members of the national leadership of the Young Socialists, and leaders selected by SWP branches, the local units responsible for organizing the party's political work in cities across the United States.

Last week, when a Cuban American supporter of the revolution in Cuba who lives in South Florida first saw *Our History Is Still Being Written*, she asked why we had singled out three Chinese-Cuban generals to interview. "And why call them Chinese-Cubans?" Cubans of Chinese descent, she added, consider themselves Cuban, not Chinese-Cuban. For blacks it's the same. "They think of themselves as Cubans, not African-Cubans."[1]

She went on to say, however, that when she started reading the book, she liked it a lot and became convinced how politically useful it is both in the United States and Cuba. Her response to the book itself seemed to contradict her first reaction to the title, as well as the political prejudices that underlay that reaction. Good!

That reader was expressing a view widely held in Cuba. It reflects a particular, and unusual, political insularity in the broad revolutionary cadre there, a slowness in recognizing the social and political legacy among blacks—and the impact on capitalist society as a whole—of the historical consequences *worldwide* of the African slave trade, chattel slavery, lynch-mob violence, and anti-black racism and discrimination.

At the same time, there is also an enduring legacy of black-led *resistance* to this oppression and exploitation— in the United States, in Cuba, and in other parts of the Americas where, under the slave owners' lash, fields were tilled and products were manufactured by labor in a black skin. There is a history of slave revolts, efforts to press abolitionist movements onto a more militant course, and alliances with other toilers in the fight for land and in labor battles. Blacks have fought as soldiers in the U.S. Civil War (some 10 percent of the ranks of the Union army by the time of the victory in 1865); provided leadership during Radical Reconstruction in the states of the defeated Confederacy; engaged in organizing efforts of sharecroppers, tenant farmers, and industrial workers in the 1920s

---

1. At the time this report was given in January 2006, Pathfinder Press had just released, in English and Spanish, *Our History Is Still Being Written: The Story of Three Chinese-Cuban Generals in the Cuban Revolution*, by Armando Choy, Gustavo Chui, and Moisés Sío Wong. The book is edited by Mary-Alice Waters.

and 1930s; and led mass political struggles for Black rights during and after World War II, which reached new levels of radicalism within the ranks of the U.S. armed forces during the Vietnam War.

Here in the United States, the vanguard place of workers who are African American in the broad class struggle is a product of this record of political leadership in plebeian and proletarian struggles, combined with the greater working-class composition of the Black nationality in comparison to other sections of the population.

A legacy of resistance has shaped the class struggle in Cuba over the past century and a half, as well. The three wars for independence from Spain between 1868 and 1898 were integrally combined with the struggle to abolish slavery, peonage, and other forms of indentured servitude. Combatants who were black, as well as thousands of Chinese toilers, participated in Cuba's independence army and acquitted themselves at every level, both rank-and-file soldiers and officers up to Lieutenant Colonel José Bu and General Antonio Maceo. From the 1953 Moncada rebellion and 1956–58 revolutionary war until today, the movement led by Fidel Castro has acted decisively against racist actions and bigotry, in word and deed. And black Cubans have been surpassed by none in their support and sacrifice in advancing the socialist revolution.

None of that, however, erases the fact that there *are* millions of very dark-skinned Cubans of African descent, and that they continue to confront the social and political consequences of past discrimination. Close to half a century after the victory of the Cuban Revolution, this legacy is still registered in housing and employment patterns, composition of the prison population, and other social markers.

While the concrete history of Chinese-Cubans is different from that of black Cubans, some of the same political considerations apply. Among Cubans with Chinese forebears, there continues to be a social awareness of their roots that is very much alive. And there continues to be pride in those roots and in their rich cultural heritage. In fact, the proposal for the interviews that eventually became the book *Our History Is Still Being Written* came not from us but from Gustavo Chui.

Our understanding of where the Cuban Revolution came from, and where it's going, is enriched by Chui's description of his youth. It's enriched by his explanation of the complexities of the "Chinese consciousness" that he, as the son of a father who was Chinese and a mother who was black, was surrounded with as he grew up—including the anti-black racism that existed among many of Chinese origin in Cuba. Our understanding of the contradictory dynamics of the Cuban Revolution is enriched by Chui's story of how he was won to the revolutionary struggle in the 1950s. The same is true for the accounts by Armando Choy and Moisés Sío Wong. Each of them from a Chinese-Cuban family of shopkeepers, but at the same time each from a slightly different social stratum.

Throughout the book, working people can see how each of these young Cubans, in the course of revolutionary combat, discovered what he and others like him are really capable of—how they discovered their own worth. Working people can see the communist conclusions Chui, Choy, and Sío Wong were led to by their experiences in the clandestine struggle and revolutionary war, as well as in the building of a new Cuba.

What does the victory of the Cuban Revolution open up for all those who are victims of long-standing discrimination institutionalized under capitalism? For oppressed nations and nationalities? For women, the oppressed and majority sex? What does any socialist revolution open up for the oppressed and exploited? Above all, it opens the possibility of *using* the state power of the dictatorship of the proletariat, which is far and away the most powerful instrument fighting toilers can ever wield, to advance the battle to eradicate racism, national oppression, women's second-class status.

These forms of oppression, which are maintained and perpetuated as part of the daily reproduction of capitalist social relations worldwide, are carried over and reshaped from modes of production that dominated earlier periods in the history of class society. While they warp and come into conflict with the "most efficient" workings of the laws of capitalism, the bourgeoisie finds ways to incorporate them, and then politically *use* them, to deepen divisions among working people and reap the profits of superexploitation. Far from being quickly eradicated by the revolutionary seizure of state power by the working class, the consequences of all these degrading social relations inherited from class-divided society are more persistent and long-lasting than had generally been anticipated by earlier generations of socialist and of revolutionary proletarian militants.

What the conquest of workers power does is make available to a mass vanguard of the proletariat the most effective political weapon in history—one we can use to battle all forms of oppression and lay the basis to establish human solidarity on new, communist foundations. *That's* the challenge and the promise of the dictatorship of the proletariat: *Win* it, then *wield* it—to *finish* the job. And acting to help advance revolutionary struggle worldwide is *the way* to finish the job.

If the young founding leaders of the modern communist movement, Karl Marx and Frederick Engels, recognized that classes, the bourgeois and petty-bourgeois family, religion, and the state could not be abolished but would *wither away* as socialism is developed, how could it be otherwise for the historic forms of oppression—reflecting the deepest prejudices—carried over from class society?

What's most important, the withering away is not a *passive* process. These legacies of class-divided society don't just "wither"; their foundations have to be *withered*. There's nothing automatic about it. Like everything else in human history, the disappearance and replacement of these institutions is the product of practical social activity, of the struggles of the revolutionary toiling masses in countryside and city—their mobilization, leadership, and transformation. It is a product of the extension of the socialist revolution worldwide. The pace and thoroughness of this struggle determines not only whether the proletarian dictatorship advances, but whether or not inevitable pauses and retreats lead to its weakening and corrosion, to its becoming vulnerable over time to corruptions from within, and ultimately to defeat and destruction.

There are no guarantees beforehand. When the dictatorship of the propertied classes is overturned, however, and power is conquered by the toilers, the relationship of forces is qualitatively transformed to the advantage of all those fighting to eradicate capitalist exploitation and oppression root and branch.

If vanguard workers in the United States who are Black cannot be won to recognizing that the proletarian dictatorship is the most powerful instrument to open up the final and lasting battle for Black freedom, then how can communists expect them to fight heart and soul to make a socialist revolution in this country?

And why *should* they?

Yes, they will fight as part of the working class to free the toiling majority of humanity from capitalist exploitation. But they and their allies don't expect to find ongoing racial discrimination at the end of the road! Otherwise they'd be living and fighting in denial of who they are. And socialism—a society without discrimination, a society of freely associated producers—would be a hopeless goal.

The same is true for women and all oppressed layers, who are at the same time allies of the working class.

Trotsky's 1933 discussion with American communists

Given his experience side by side with Lenin from 1917 on, as a leader of the Bolshevik Party, the Soviet Union, and the Communist International, Leon Trotsky could not have thought other than this way about racist discrimination and the fight against it. These were his political assumptions in 1933 during discussions with Arne Swabeck, a leader of the Communist League of America, a forerunner of the Socialist Workers Party, who visited Trotsky after he had been expelled from the Soviet Union by the regime of Joseph Stalin. Trotsky was living in forced exile in Turkey at the time.

The transcript of that 1933 discussion, along with other material, has been available for many years in a small book with the title *Leon Trotsky on Black Nationalism and Self-Determination*. But much about how that book was prepared and edited—beginning with its title—hinders rather than helps the reader listen to and understand what Trotsky was saying. Title notwithstanding, it is *not* a book about Black nationalism. In fact, Trotsky never mentions Black nationalism a single time, either in the 1933 discussion or in the later 1939 exchange with party members also included in the book.

Trotsky discusses the Black struggle in the United States. He talks about the place and weight of workers who are Black in forging the vanguard of the working class along the line of march to conquering the dictatorship of the proletariat. He points to their proven fighting abilities. He assesses prospects for the organization of independent Black movements and proposes concrete actions to advance the battle against racism and national oppression. He demands that revolutionists support the right of Blacks to national self-determination. That's what the discussions with Trotsky are about. High among our editorial priorities is introducing and publishing these discussions in a new book in a manner that does justice to their content.[2]

It was Trotsky, basing himself on the political conquests of the Communist International, who first explained to us scientifically that it was awakening Black working people to their self-worth, not to their oppression, that would open new prospects for revolutionary struggle in the United States.

In response to questions the party leadership had asked Swabeck to discuss with Trotsky in 1933, the Bolshevik leader explained:

> The Negroes will, through their awakening, through their demand for autonomy, and through the democratic mobilization of their forces, be pushed on toward a class basis. The petty bourgeoisie will take up the demand for equal rights and for self-determination but will prove absolutely incapable in the struggle; the Negro proletariat will march over the petty bourgeoisie in the direction toward the proletarian revolution.

The meaning comes through loud and clear, even translated into English from the German-language notes taken by Arne, whose first language was Danish!

Twice in this country in the twentieth century, we've seen in practice how the Black proletariat had to "march over the petty bourgeoisie"—white and Black, including the trade union officialdom, with all their limitations and hesitations—in order to advance the struggle against Jim Crow segregation and other institutions of racist discrimination.

The first time was during the political radicalization that developed under the impact of the Bolshevik Revolution and

---

2. The book you are holding is that book. See Part III.

the spreading capitalist crisis in the decades following World War I. Struggles by exploited farmers and other working people in the 1920s laid the foundation for the labor battles and social movement of the 1930s centered on building mass CIO industrial unions. Workers regardless of skin color more and more fought shoulder to shoulder for union rights and other social goals. These interconnected working-class struggles gave such momentum to the fight to bring down Jim Crow that the impetus outlasted the broad retreat of the labor movement during and after World War II.

As for the second time, some of the people in this room lived through the Black rights battles of the 1950s, 1960s, and early 1970s and took an active part in them.

At its high point, Radical Reconstruction in major parts of the former slaveholding South was a plebeian, and if anything more socially advanced forerunner of these proletarian battles of the twentieth century. And the culmination of this history of marching "over the petty bourgeoisie in the direction toward the proletarian revolution" still lies ahead, of course. That's when the bourgeoisie will understand why the twenty-first century will be millennial for the working class.

Trotsky's starting point in the discussions with Swabeck was the fact that racist oppression and anti-Black prejudice in the United States were the largest obstacle to revolutionary unity of the working class. As a result of such oppression, Trotsky pointed out, few "common actions [take] place involving white and Black workers," there is no "class fraternization." "The American worker is indescribably reactionary," Trotsky said. "This can be seen now in the fact that he has not yet even been won to the idea of social insurance." And, Trotsky added, "The Negroes have not yet awakened, and they are not yet united with the white workers. Ninety-nine point nine percent of the American workers are chauvinists; in relation to the Negroes they are hangmen as they are also toward the Chinese, etc. It is necessary to make them [white workers] understand that the American state is not their state and that they do not have to be the guardians of this state."

Those conditions, of course, have changed substantially since 1933 as a result of class battles. They began shifting in the mid-1930s as a product of the labor struggles that built the CIO, growing opposition to fascism and the spreading imperialist world war, and motion toward a labor party independent of the Democrats and Republicans. These changes accelerated in the 1950s with the conquests of the mass civil rights movement and Black liberation struggles, which had their roots in the massive urbanization, migration to the North, and shifts in the composition of the industrial workforce that began prior to World War II. As a consequence of these struggles, and as a component of them, workers in the United States *did* fight for an important form of social insurance: Social Security. And as a result of the labor battles of the 1930s and civil rights struggles of the 1950s and '60s, they came to see an expanded version of that Social Security, including Medicare, Medicaid, and related programs, as *rights*.

With the rise of industrial unions, more and more workers who are Black, white, Asian, and Latino—native-born and immigrant—today *do* work alongside each other in many workplaces, often doing the same jobs. They *do* engage in common actions and class fraternization. But the fight to combat multiple forms of segregation and racism, and to overcome national divisions in the working class—through mutual solidarity and uncompromising struggles using any means necessary—remains the single biggest task in forging the proletarian vanguard in this country.

Trotsky, in his exchange of views with Swabeck, went on to point out that during a major rise of revolutionary struggle and proletarian class consciousness in the United States, it is then possible that the Negroes will become the most advanced section. . . . It is very possible that the Negroes will proceed through self-determination to the proletarian dictatorship in a couple of gigantic strides, ahead of the great bloc of white workers. They will then be the vanguard. I am absolutely sure that they will in any case fight better than the white workers.

But this can only happen, Trotsky emphasized, "provided the communist party carries on an uncompromising, merciless struggle not against the supposed national prepossessions of the Negroes but against the colossal prejudices of the white workers"—prejudices brought into the working class by the bourgeoisie and the imperialist masters, through their petty-bourgeois agents—"and makes no concession to them whatsoever."

This is what Trotsky had learned from Lenin, the central leader of the Bolshevik Party and Communist International, and from his own long revolutionary experience in the tsarist prison house of nations. Trotsky had deepened this understanding through his discussions with delegates from the United States to the first four congresses of the Communist International from 1919 through 1922. And this is what he worked with the Socialist Workers Party leadership and the rest of the world communist movement, from 1929 until his death, to apply in practice.

Struggle for a proletarian party

In April 1939, a little more than six years after his discussions with Swabeck, Trotsky took part in another exchange on the struggle for Black liberation and proletarian revolution in the United States. The discussions were held in Coyoacán, near Mexico City, where Trotsky was then living in exile. And this time they were not initiated by the central leadership of the Socialist Workers Party, but by C.L.R. James, a Trinidadian-born writer who had joined our world movement in Britain in 1935. James was in his mid-thirties at the time.[3]

Trotsky initially took an active interest in collaborating with this new Afro-Caribbean recruit. In a May 1938 letter to James P. Cannon, Trotsky noted that James had written a book (*World Revolution*) a year earlier criticizing Trotsky "very sharply from an organizational point of view." The ultraleft political line of the book, Trotsky said, was undoubtedly "a theoretical justification of [James's] own policy toward the Independent Labour Party" in the United Kingdom, one of several centrist organizations in Europe that James adapted to politically.[4]

Trotsky nonetheless urged Cannon to involve James in the work of the world movement and to seek to convince him "that his criticisms are not considered by any one of us an item of hostility or an obstacle to friendly collaboration in the future."[5] Toward the end of 1938 James visited the United States to live and travel for a period of time, and the SWP leadership collaborated with him to advance the party's work in defense of Black rights. In early 1939 James wrote to Trotsky proposing the discussions in Mexico.

---

3. Transcripts of the three discussions can be found in Part III of this book, pp. 257–91.

4. These centrist organizations included the Independent Labour Party (ILP) in Britain, the Workers Party of Marxist Unification (POUM) in Spain, the Socialist Workers and Peasants Party (PSOP) in France, and others. Between 1932 and 1939 they clustered together under the umbrella "The London Bureau." Zigzagging between Stalinism and Social Democracy, these organizations contributed to the bloody defeat of the revolution in Spain, added to the disorientation of the workers movement in France, and created substantial obstacles to efforts led by Trotsky to rebuild the world communist movement across Europe and beyond.

5. "On C.L.R. James" in *Writings of Leon Trotsky (1937–38)* (Pathfinder, 1976), pp. 385–86 [2009 printing].

At the time, the Socialist Workers Party had made relatively little progress since the discussion between Trotsky and Swabeck in involving itself in political work among workers and farmers who were Black. In preparing for the discussion with James, Trotsky wrote Cannon that the "party cannot postpone this extremely important question any longer."[6]

As with the discussions six years earlier, Trotsky's exchange with James opened on the question of the right to national self-determination for Blacks in the United States. Trotsky was taken aback by James's assertion—a position held by no one in the central leadership of the SWP—that self-determination for Blacks in the United States was "economically reactionary" and "politically false." Trotsky responded sharply and strongly: "We cannot say [self-determination] will be reactionary. It is *not* reactionary. . . . [W]e can say, 'It is for you [African Americans] to decide. If you wish to take a part of the country, it is all right, but we do not wish to make the decision for you.'"

First and foremost, however, the 1939 discussions with James put a spotlight on the working-class program *and* composition that is the bedrock of any revolutionary party capable of organizing and leading a victorious battle by the toilers to establish the dictatorship of the proletariat in the United States—or in any other capitalist country. The discussions took the form of an exchange on James's proposal that the Socialist Workers Party take the initiative to launch and help lead an independent Black organization of militant action. Acknowledging he was not familiar with "the concrete situation in Negro circles in the United States," Trotsky nevertheless took the proposal seriously and orga-

---

6. "More on Our Work in the Communist Party" (April 10, 1939), in *Writings of Leon Trotsky (1938–39)* (Pathfinder, 1969, 1974), pp. 341–42 [2004 printing].

nized two sessions with James, together with cadres of the SWP, to consider it.

"If another party had organized such a mass movement, we would surely participate as a fraction, providing that [the movement] included workers, poor petty bourgeois, poor farmers, and so on," Trotsky said. "We would enter for the purpose of educating the best elements and winning them for our party. But this is another thing. What is proposed here is that we take the initiative," said Trotsky.

Trotsky steered clear of tactical judgments about the SWP's work in the class struggle in the United States. But his political criteria for assessing this proposal were the opposite of James's. Trotsky focused on the *class orientation* of such an organization: Would our cadres seek to build it among workers and rural toilers who were Black? Would we fight within it for a revolutionary program to advance the struggle for power in the United States?

James pointed to some examples of individuals and currents that might be brought into such an organization. The information James provided "shows that we can have some elements for cooperation in this field," Trotsky said. At the same time, he noted, it "limits the immediate perspective of the organization." How and why did it limit those perspectives? Because, Trotsky said, it's necessary to ask the question: "Who are these elements?" And he answered: "The majority are Negro intellectuals, former Stalinist functionaries and sympathizers."

Trotsky noted that white intellectuals who earlier in the 1930s had been briefly attracted to communism had largely gone "back to Roosevelt and democracy"—imperialist democracy, that is. But "the disappointed Negro intellectuals looked for a new field on the basis of the Negro question," Trotsky continued. Yes, communist workers can and should seek to collaborate with them on defense campaigns, to raise money for common goals, and so on. "That is one thing," he told James, "but you consider these Negro intellectuals for the directing of a mass movement." And that was neither possible nor, above all, desirable.

Trotsky pointed to the danger that such an organization "will become a game for the intellectuals," whom, he added, "keep themselves separated from the masses, always with the desire to take on the Anglo-Saxon culture and of becoming an integral part of the Anglo-Saxon life"—that is, their desire to become integrated into the professional and middle classes of capitalist society, of "white" America.[7] An independent Black organization, Trotsky said, "can justify itself only by winning workers, sharecroppers, and so on."

These exchanges with James on our movement's proletarian orientation had a substantial impact on the two SWP members present for the discussions in Mexico: Charles Curtiss, a cadre of the party since the founding of the Communist League of America in 1929, and Sol Lankin, also a founding CLA member and at the time a guard in Trotsky's household. "Would this organization throw its doors open to all classes of Negroes?" Lankin asked James.

Yes, said James. "The bourgeois Negro can come in to help, but only on the basis of the organization's program." That didn't satisfy Lankin, however. "I cannot see how the Negro bourgeoisie can help the Negro proletariat fight for its economic advancement," Lankin added.

So James tried another tack. "In our own movement some

---

7. Except for a tiny handful of individuals, that desire was a vain hope in the Jim Crow America of the 1930s—the Jim Crow *America*, not just the Jim Crow *South*. As a by-product of the victorious Black rights struggles of the 1950s and 1960s, however, a layer of the African American population in the United States has today taken great strides toward achieving that aspiration. See "The Cosmopolitan 'Meritocracy' and the Changing Class Structure of the Black Nationality" in Part II of this book.—JB

of us are petty bourgeois," he replied to Lankin. That was James's attitude to the class composition of the party! It was a political approach that flew in the face of the systematic campaign being carried out by the majority of the SWP leadership and cadres at the time to proletarianize the party from top to bottom. This effort was being made at Trotsky's urgent insistence.

As delegates to the party's convention had decided some fifteen months earlier, "We will not succeed in rooting the party in the working class, much less to defend the revolutionary proletarian principles of the party from being undermined, unless the party is an overwhelmingly proletarian party, composed in its decisive majority of workers in the factories, mines, and mills." The January 1938 convention decided that such a "complete reorientation of our party, from the membership up to the leadership and back again, is absolutely imperative and unpostponable."[8]

Following up in response to James's comments, Trotsky underlined the life-or-death character of the proletarian orientation that guided the SWP, and its inseparable relationship with deepening the party's work among African Americans. "Our party is not safe from degeneration if it remains a place for intellectuals, semi-intellectuals, skilled workers," Trotsky emphasized. ". . . Many times I have proposed that every member of the party, especially the intellectuals and semi-intellectuals, who, during a period of say six months, cannot each win a worker-member for the party should be demoted to the position of sympathizer. We can say the same in [relation to] the Negro question."

Returning to points that had been central to his discus-

---

8. See "The Political Situation and the Tasks of the Party," and "The Trade Union Movement and the Socialist Workers Party," in *The Founding of the Socialist Workers Party* (Pathfinder, 1982), pp. 145, 162 [2001 printing].

sions with SWP leader Arne Swabeck several years earlier, Trotsky added:

> We must say to the conscious elements of the Negroes that they are convoked by the historic development to become a vanguard of the working class. What serves as the brake on the higher strata? It is the privileges, the comforts that hinder them from becoming revolutionists. It does not exist for the Negroes.
>
> What can transform a certain stratum, make it more capable of courage and sacrifice? It is concentrated in the Negroes. If it happens that we in the SWP are not able to find the road to this stratum, then we are not worthy at all. . . .
>
> It is a question of the vitality of the party. It is an important question. It is a question of whether the party is to be transformed into a sect or if it is capable of finding its way to the most oppressed part of the working class.

Malcolm X's political evolution

It was this communist continuity, our proletarian orientation, that gave our movement the confidence in the early 1960s to recognize the revolutionary significance of the political development of Malcolm X while he was still a leader of the Nation of Islam. We made no assumptions about when, if ever, he would leave the Nation. We imposed no preconceived limitations on his evolution—no limitations on his convergence with the line of march of the proletariat to the conquest of state power.

In January 1965, when another leader of the Young Socialist Alliance and I conducted an interview with Malcolm for the *Young Socialist* magazine, we asked him: "How do you define Black nationalism, with which you have been identified?"

Malcolm replied by telling us about the discussion he

had had during his trip to Africa in the spring of 1964 with the Algerian ambassador to Ghana. When Malcolm told the ambassador "that my political, social, and economic philosophy was Black nationalism," the Algerian revolutionary had asked where that left him. Because, as Malcolm explained, the ambassador "to all appearances . . . was a white man." That experience, Malcolm said, "showed me where I was alienating people who were true revolutionaries dedicated to overturning the systems of exploitation that exists on this earth by any means necessary."

As a result, Malcolm told us, "I had to do a lot of thinking and reappraising of my definition of Black nationalism. Can we sum up the solution to the problems confronting our people as Black nationalism? And if you notice, I haven't been using the expression for several months."

Well, in fact, we *hadn't* noticed. We had been acting as if we assumed, at least on this point, Malcolm could not transcend his initial positions.

The *Young Socialist* interview was a real back and forth, a genuine exchange. It wasn't an interview where we asked certain questions because we already knew the answers. We asked questions because, to the best of our ability and objectivity, they were the right ones to ask. The answers to those questions, and to our follow-up questions, added very substantially to our knowledge, and to the knowledge of others who read the interview. Whatever we hadn't been noticing, we weren't afraid of the conclusions. And Malcolm had not asked to see a single question beforehand, nor had he put any restrictions on the length of the interview, nor placed any subject out of bounds. (At the time, I had every reason to think it would be the first of a number of interviews with him.)

Malcolm wrapped up this particular exchange by acknowledging: "But I still would be hard pressed to give a specific definition of the overall philosophy which I think is necessary for the liberation of the Black people in this country."

Later in the interview, I asked Malcolm his "opinion of the worldwide struggle now going on between capitalism and socialism." And he responded, among other things, that "it's only a matter of time in my opinion before [capitalism] will collapse completely."

In the article "Two Interviews," published in the *Militant* in February 1966 on the first anniversary of Malcolm's assassination, I described Malcolm's reaction when I took him the edited interview to review prior to publication in the *YS*. When Malcolm got to his answer to that question on capitalism and socialism, his face opened with a wide smile and he told me: "This is the farthest I've ever gone. They will go wild over this." I asked Malcolm if he wanted to tone down the answer, and, as I wrote in the 1966 article, "without hesitation, he answered no."[9]

During this second visit, Malcolm also told me about the young revolutionaries he had met in Africa and Europe in the course of his recent trips there. He said he would give me a list so we could send them copies of the issue of the *Young Socialist* that included the interview. I mentioned to Malcolm that I might be going to Algeria later that year heading up the Young Socialist Alliance delegation to the World Festival of Youth and Students, scheduled for Algiers in late July and early August. Unlike previous such festivals organized by the world Stalinist movement, this one for the first time was being held not in Eastern or Central Europe or in the USSR, but right in the midst of an ongoing revolution. The YSA was looking forward to it, anticipating a broader geographical and political composition and greater anti-imperialist intransigence. I told Malcolm we might be able to meet some of his young contacts there, and he said

---

9. *Malcolm X Talks to Young People* (Pathfinder, 1991, 2002), pp. 127, 137 [2008 printing].

that would be a good experience, since "they have a hard time believing that revolutionaries exist in the United States." (How many times have we heard the exact same thing from Cuban revolutionists and others?) Malcolm said he would find time to prepare the list, and we agreed that I'd pick it up from him after the *Young Socialist* had been printed.

Malcolm was enthusiastic about the prospect of the young people he had met receiving copies of the *Young Socialist* containing the interview and meeting leaders of the Young Socialist Alliance. He looked forward to young revolutionaries working together, sharing material, and learning from each other. He was convinced that for *all* involved it would broaden our scope, as he used to say.

As it turned out, Malcolm was assassinated a few weeks after our second meeting, just as the *YS* was coming off the press. There would be no further interviews. And then, in June 1965, the workers and peasants government in Algeria led by Ahmed Ben Bella was overthrown. Our delegation to the world youth festival was heading down the Italian peninsula to get a ship to Algiers—we had gotten as far as Rome—when the coup occurred and the festival was canceled. So we were not able to follow through on this particular pledge to Malcolm.

In a more important sense, however, we did fulfill that pledge and continue to do so. We keep Malcolm's words in print, as well as the words of other revolutionaries the world over. We keep producing the *Militant*, a newspaper Malcolm considered such an important source not only of accurate information but of revolutionary political analysis for fighters. And have now begun its Spanish-language edition, *El Militante*. We keep reaching out with these materials to collaborate with revolutionary-minded working people and youth both in this country and around the world—from the Americas, to Africa, to the Pacific and Asia, to Europe; from Venezuela and China, to France, Iran, and Equatorial Guinea.

That kind of political work among revolutionaries never ends, even when we run up against unanticipated obstacles. We simply find other ways to accomplish it.

Since the day Malcolm was killed in February 1965, nobody can prove where he would have gone next politically. But those in my generation and others in the Socialist Workers Party leadership were convinced by Malcolm's course that he was moving toward becoming a communist. Politically he was converging with the Cuban Revolution, with the popular revolutionary government in Algeria led by Ahmed Ben Bella (and with the course of the SWP), that is, with the historic line of march of the working class toward power worldwide.

We just assumed Malcolm was dead serious when he said he no longer thought his political views could be summarized and described as "Black nationalism." The days were long gone when anybody could put words in Malcolm's mouth. Less than two months prior to his death, he told a radio interviewer that before he had broken with the Nation of Islam in early 1964, he'd often said things that weren't his views but those of Nation leader Elijah Muhammad. "They weren't my statements, they were his statements, and I was repeating them." But now, Malcolm said, "the parrot has jumped out of the cage."[10]

What Malcolm had to say about Black nationalism in the *Young Socialist* interview was part of our political convergence, since nobody can become a communist and at the same time remain a nationalist in your "overall philosophy." You can be a communist and at the same time champion and lead a struggle for national liberation, a struggle against national oppression. That's for sure. In fact, you *must* or else

---

10. "Our People Identify with Africa" (interview with Bernice Bass, December 27, 1964) in *Malcolm X: The Last Speeches* (Pathfinder, 1989), p. 99 [2008 printing].

you can't be a communist. But you can't remain a nationalist politically if you are to organize a movement to advance the working class and its allies, of all nations, along the line of march toward the dictatorship of the proletariat.

Why? Because nationalism—and here we're talking about the nationalism of the oppressed—is *not* the generalization of the line of march of a class toward power. There is no predetermined class direction, let alone class dictatorship, in the logic of its evolution. It has no stable program. A program has a concrete practical trajectory that represents the historic interests of a social class. There are no classless programs.

But Black nationalism has no political trajectory that advances the interests of working people whatever their skin color. Black nationalism is an ideology. It is the ideology of an oppressed nationality at certain stages of its political awakening, a nationality that in the United States is substantially proletarian in composition. To the degree Black nationalism has a class character, however, it can only be bourgeois. That's not an epithet; it's a scientific description. Trade union consciousness, too, is bourgeois; it seeks to increase the share of newly produced value going to the working class *within* the capitalist system, the wages system. At the same time, the age of bourgeois revolutions has been put behind us by the historic consolidation of finance capital, of imperialism.

Communism, however, is *not* an ideology, in the sense Marx and Engels used that word. As the pioneers of the modern revolutionary workers movement taught us at its origins nearly 160 years ago, "communism is not a doctrine but a *movement*"[11]—a movement of those who—on the field of practical activity, on the field of class combat—are "the most advanced and resolute section" of the working class. That's

---

11. Frederick Engels, "The Communists and Karl Heinzen," in Marx and Engels, *Collected Works* [hereafter *MECW*] vol. 6, p. 303.

what the Communist Manifesto, the founding document of our movement, explains. Communists consciously "point out and bring to the front the common interests of the entire proletariat, independently of all nationality." We "always and everywhere represent the interests of the movement as a whole." From the standpoint of program and theory, communists have "the advantage of clearly understanding the line of march, the conditions, and the ultimate general results of the proletarian movement."[12]

This was the direction the majority of central leaders of the SWP in the mid-1960s had come to believe Malcolm X was headed, as demonstrated by his words and deeds. We were convinced that this political evolution had been making him more effective, not less effective as a leader of the fight for Black liberation. (Even though his immediate audience would continue to narrow in the United States; neither Malcolm nor anyone else can evade the effects of shifts in the relationship of class forces.) Knowing what we knew about Malcolm, and knowing what we know about Marxism, why would a communist draw any other conclusion?

Why would any revolutionary-minded—and revolutionary-stomached—worker, farmer, or young person who looked to Malcolm for leadership stop listening to him because Malcolm had come to a broader and richer understanding of the capitalist roots of exploitation and racist oppression? Why would they lose interest in what he had to say because the economic, social, and political answers he presented were more concrete, more directly tied to the historic line of march of working people the world over? Or because he wanted to work together politically with young people, regardless of race or sex (or creed of forebears), attracted not only to

---

12. Marx and Engels, *Communist Manifesto* (Pathfinder, 1970, 1987, 2008), p. 47 [2009 printing]. See also "Manifesto of the Communist Party," in *MECW*, vol. 6, p. 497.

his own example but to the Young Socialist Alliance? Why would they stop listening to Malcolm because he wanted to pull down obstacles separating him from "true revolutionaries dedicated to overturning the system of exploitation that exists on this earth by any means necessary"?

Black liberation and proletarian dictatorship

All this leads to the proposal that we give priority to producing a book on the Black struggle and the march toward the proletarian dictatorship, with an up-to-date political introduction. A book that pulls together: (1) the discussions with Trotsky and our communist continuity going back to the founding of the Communist International, the continuity Trotsky was drawing on; (2) sections of a few party talks, reports, and resolutions since the SWP's turn to the industrial working class and unions in the late 1970s that deal with this continuity in something more than a conjunctural way; and (3) an accurate appreciation of the example and leadership of Malcolm X, which was so important to the preparation of the generations of our party cadre, starting with those who joined at the beginning of the sixties, who led the turn to industry.[13]

First and foremost, of course, such a book will be the

---

13. In February 1978 the Socialist Workers Party National Committee voted to immediately organize to get a large majority of the party membership and leadership into industry and the industrial unions. Following a quarter-century-long political retreat of the working class and labor movement during the post–World War II capitalist expansion and years of witch-hunting and reaction, opportunities were growing to once again advance the proletarian orientation of the party by building fractions of revolutionists engaged in communist political work in the industrial working class and unions. For the political record of the opening years of this turn to industry, see Jack Barnes, *The Changing Face of U.S. Politics: Working-Class Politics and the Trade Unions* (Pathfinder, 1981, 1994, 2002).

record of the programmatic and strategic conclusions communists have drawn from decades of practical activity in the class struggle in the United States, including in the fight for Black rights. Even limiting ourselves to the past sixty-five years, this activity includes:

• our campaign during World War II for *federal government* action against lynchings and against racist discrimination in war production industries and the armed forces;

• our participation in the Black rights movement of the 1950s and 1960s, including the movement in response to the lynching of Emmett Till in 1955, the Montgomery bus boycott in 1955–56, the Freedom Rides to desegregate interstate buses and bus terminals, the lunch-counter sit-ins in the early 1960s, the "kissing case" and support for self-defense efforts in Monroe, North Carolina, in face of racist night riders,[14] support for the Deacons for Defense in Louisiana and Mississippi and the Lowndes County Freedom Organization in Alabama, and other struggles and mobilizations of those years;

• the enthusiastic welcome we gave to the heightened pride and confidence among Blacks born of these mass proletarian struggles;

• our support for any authentic steps toward independent Black political action, even if initial ones, from the Joseph King campaign in Chicago in the 1950s,[15] to the Freedom

---

14. See "Robert F. Williams, the Cuban Revolution, and Self-Defense against Racist Violence" in Part II.

15. The 1958 campaign of Joseph King, a leader in Chicago's Black community, was organized jointly by the SWP; the Washington Park Forum, a predominantly Black organization influenced by the Communist Party; and others. "The unions should help build a party to fight for the emancipation of the human race," King said at the time. "The capitalists can't do that." The campaign helped win some Communist Party supporters away from the CP's support to capitalist politicians in the Democratic Party.

Now Party in the 1960s, to the National Black Independent Political Party in the 1980s;

• our participation in and leadership contributions to the Boston and Louisville busing and school desegregation struggles in the 1970s;

• our support for and leadership of various struggles by women who are Black for liberation from sexist prejudice and oppression;

• our political response over the past few decades to the Grenada revolution and Maurice Bishop, to Thomas Sankara and the revolutionary movement he led in Burkina Faso, to the African National Congress–led struggle against apartheid in South Africa;

• our understanding, in word and deed, of the importance of the fight against racism, and for affirmative-action quotas for Blacks and women, in forging the working-class unity necessary to advance the transformation of the unions into revolutionary instruments of class struggle;

• our involvement in innumerable defense cases over nearly a century, fights against police brutality, and other local and national struggles such as our successful battle to win release of government files kept secret by the FBI, CIA, and other intelligence and cop agencies, including records documenting the methods used to frame up and murder Black leaders such as Fred Hampton in Chicago and his fellow fighters around the country in the Black Panther Party and other Black organizations in the 1960s and 1970s;[16]

---

16. In 1986 the Socialist Workers Party and Young Socialist Alliance won a victory in their thirteen-year-long political fight against spying and harassment by the FBI and other government agencies and officials. That fight, organized around a lawsuit against these cop agencies, ended in a federal court ruling in favor of the SWP and YSA. That campaign encouraged initiatives by other targets of local, state, and federal police agencies across the United States. See *FBI on Trial: The Victory in the Socialist Workers Party Suit against Government Spying* (1988),

- our initiative to publish *From the Escambray to the Congo: In the Whirlwind of the Cuban Revolution* by Víctor Dreke, and our success in organizing a powerful speaking tour in 2002 by that Cuban revolutionary leader from Boston and New York to Atlanta and Miami;
- the leadership time and effort we've recently put into participation in the Equatorial Guinea book fair and related events, and the regional gatherings and campus meetings following up on that trip; and much more.[17]

We need such a book today because of what's happening in politics and the class struggle. We need it to educate our own cadres and reach out to the same working people and youth we're selling *Militant* subscriptions to.

How much we need it was called to our attention recently by a couple of letters Mary-Alice [Waters] received from one of the five imprisoned Cuban revolutionaries—René González.[18] René wrote that he had recently been given a

---

and *Cointelpro: The FBI's Secret War on Political Freedom* (1975, 1988), both published by Pathfinder.

17. See Mary-Alice Waters and Martín Koppel, *Capitalism and the Transformation of Africa: Reports from Equatorial Guinea* (Pathfinder, 2009).

18. In September 1998 the FBI announced ten arrests, saying that it had discovered a "Cuban spy network" in Florida. In June 2001, five defendants—Gerardo Hernández, Ramón Labañino, Antonio Guerrero, Fernando González, and René González—were each convicted of "conspiracy to act as an unregistered foreign agent." Guerrero, Hernández, and Labañino were also convicted of "conspiracy to commit espionage," and Hernández of "conspiracy to commit murder." Sentences ranged from fifteen years to a double life term plus fifteen years. These five framed-up revolutionaries—each of whom has been named "Hero of the Republic of Cuba"—had accepted assignments to take up residence in Florida in order to keep the Cuban government informed about counterrevolutionary groups in the United States planning terrorist attacks against Cuba. The case of the five has generated a broad international campaign de-

book that another inmate had praised to the skies as "anti-imperialist." When René read it, however, he said he "discovered it was a litany of anti-Semitism, racism, demagoguery, chauvinism and individualism. It certainly had some anti-corporate and isolationist rhetoric, but it came from some sort of fascist, narrow nationalism." So René asked: "What are the roots and development of that way of thinking? Is it related to the outcome of the Civil War? Any ties to the KKK? What about the religious right? Why that grudge against a corporate establishment that, in the end, serves them well? Do they have anything to do with the white supremacist militias?"

These are important political questions, ones the communist movement has had experience addressing in class combat as well as in words over the past century. We've written about them extensively—from reports and resolutions distributed by the Communist International in its early years; to articles by Trotsky on fascism and how to fight it; to writings on American fascism by Jim [Cannon], Farrell [Dobbs], and Joe [Hansen] that are available in several Education for Socialists publications; to books from recent decades such as *The Changing Face of U.S. Politics* and *Capitalism's World Disorder*, as well as various issues of *New International*.

The matters raised by René are wide-ranging politically, and they pose the need to understand the origins and concrete history of Black oppression in the United States and the social weight of the Black population—its disproportionately large proletarian composition, its political record in mass social struggles by toilers in city and countryside across the United States, and thus its vanguard place in the historic battles of the working class. With that

---

nouncing the harsh conditions of their imprisonment and demanding their release.

René González—one of five Cuban revolutionaries framed up and imprisoned in U.S. since 1998—read a book a fellow inmate recommended as "anti-imperialist." It turned out to be "a litany of anti-Semitism, racism, demagoguery, chauvinism and individualism," González wrote, an expression of "some sort of fascist, narrow nationalism." What are "the roots and development of that way of thinking?" González asked. "Is it related to the outcome of the Civil War? Any ties to the KKK?" González's questions, Barnes says, spurred SWP leaders to prepare this book.

Arrested in 1998, González and four other Cuban revolutionaries were convicted in 2001, some on charges of conspiracy to commit espionage and murder, and given draconian sentences for their actions to keep Cuban government informed of U.S.-based counterrevolutionary groups planning murderous attacks inside Cuba. Above, González, Antonio Guerrero, Ramón Labañino, Fernando González. Below, Gerardo Hernández, given double life sentence, is shown on internationalist combat mission in Angola (in back, right). Between 1975 and 1991, more than 300,000 Cuban volunteers helped defend Angola against invasions by South African apartheid regime.

in mind, Mary-Alice, in her reply to René, recommended that a good starting point would be the writings by Marx and Engels on the U.S. Civil War and its aftermath, adding that she would send him a copy of *Marx and Engels on the United States*.[19]

"You will find their writings on the Civil War especially helpful in thinking about the questions you raise in your letter to me," Mary-Alice wrote. "Marx and Engels followed the unfolding of the second bourgeois revolution in the U.S. with keen attention and insight. What they explain about the delayed development of a hereditary proletariat in the U.S. (as compared to Europe) due to the existence of slavery, the defeat of the post–Civil War Radical Reconstruction, and the availability of free land (and refusal to distribute much of it to the freed slaves) remains decisive to understanding the U.S. class struggle up to today."

It was that exchange of correspondence that spurred Mary-Alice to propose that we act now to prepare this book on the party's record in the fight for Black emancipation. Currently we have nothing similar on this central question of U.S. and world politics that revolutionary-minded workers can read, study, and *use* as a political weapon in campaigning and mass work.

The more we work together with other revolutionaries, including Cuban comrades; the more we not only fight shoulder to shoulder alongside them, but share lessons from the hard-fought battles of our class the world over—the more we learn from each other politically. René and others of the Cuban Five appreciate not just the books they

---

19. The selection *Marx and Engels on the United States* (Moscow: Progress Publishers, 1979) is no longer in print. Pathfinder will soon release *The Second American Revolution: Marx and Engels on the U.S. Civil War*.

receive. Like ourselves, they look forward to the exchange of ideas and views.

II [20]

I want to come back to the discussion we're having here on the Black struggle. It's useful to take a look at the preliminary draft "Where We Stand: Young Socialists Platform" that party leaders in the Young Socialists have made available to participants in this meeting. The opening sentence in the section of that draft on "Vanguard role of Black nationality" provides a useful concrete example of a central point we need to clarify here. That section opens with these words: "Blacks in the United States are an oppressed nationality."

But that's not the place for communists to begin. It doesn't help us understand the weight, the history, and the place in the United States of workers who are Black in relation to the working-class vanguard and its advance along a political line of march toward the dictatorship of the proletariat.

Vanguard place of toilers who are Black

Don't start with Blacks as an oppressed nationality. Start with the historical record of the vanguard place and weight of workers who are Black—a place and weight disproportionate to their percentage among the toilers in this country—in broad, proletarian-led social and political struggles in the United States.

This goes back to the closing years of the U.S. Civil War and especially to the postwar battle for a radical reconstruction, in which Black toilers provided leadership in substantial parts of the South both to freed slaves and to exploited

---

20. The following is from Barnes's preliminary summary of discussion at the January 2006 SWP leadership conference.

farmers and workers who were white. It continued in the late nineteenth and early twentieth centuries in the labor battles that built the United Mine Workers—at a time when most unions were not only organized along craft lines but either excluded Blacks or segregated them in separate locals. Sharecroppers, tenant farmers, and other rural toilers, both Black and white, waged struggles in the 1920s and through the Great Depression.

Workers who were Black were in the front ranks of key battles that built the CIO industrial unions in the 1930s. They were in the vanguard of working people during World War II who refused to subordinate or postpone struggles for justice in the name of "the patriotic war effort"—fighting discrimination in the war industries, protesting Jim Crow conditions in the armed forces, and demanding (unsuccessfully) that the Roosevelt administration and Democratic-dominated Congress pass federal legislation outlawing racist lynchings.[21] They were in the forefront of those who opposed that imperialist war. And many of us at this meeting know firsthand the lasting social and political impact on the working class and labor movement today of the mass civil rights movement and rise of the Black liberation struggle from the mid-1950s through the early 1970s.

We're not speculating about the future. We're pointing to a historical record. It's a matter of fact. It's a mind-boggling record, it seems to me. It bowls you over when you hear it. The same cannot be said of the big majority of oppressed nations or nationalities in general in other parts of the world. But this *is* the political record of the largely proletarian Black nationality in the United States. This *is* its specific political character since the defeat of chattel slavery, the effort to extend the victory in the Civil War throughout the South,

---

21. See *Fighting Racism in World War II* (Pathfinder, 1980).

and the beginning of the expansion of a modern hereditary proletariat in the United States.

It is this dynamic that Trotsky, already more than seven decades ago, was pointing to when he said it is possible "that the Negroes will become the most advanced section" of the working class, and "will proceed through self-determination to the proletarian dictatorship in a couple of gigantic strides, ahead of the great bloc of white workers." It was for that reason that he was "absolutely sure that they will in any case fight better than the white workers" on the whole. And it was that same record of struggle that eleven years earlier had led the Communist International to also point out—in its resolution on "The Negro Question" adopted by the 1922 Fourth Congress—that "the history of the Negro in America fits him for an important role in the liberation struggle of the entire African race."[22]

Two views of Malcolm X

Two divergent views of Malcolm's political evolution and its significance—if only slightly diverging at the beginning— coexisted in the Socialist Workers Party for almost two decades after his assassination. The difference was not over our movement's recognition of the importance of the rise of nationalism among Blacks in the United States as a product of the struggles and conquests of the 1960s and 1970s. As I said in a tribute to Malcolm X at the March 1965 memorial meeting organized by the Militant Labor Forum, the SWP and YSA led the way in teaching "the revolutionary youth of this country to tell the difference between the national-

---

22. The resolution, drafted in English, was printed in the January 5, 1923, issue of *International Press Correspondence*, published by the Communist International. A version apparently retranslated into English from German appears in Jane Degras (ed.), *The Communist International (1919–1943): Documents* (London: Frank Cass, 1971).

ism of the oppressed and the nationalism of the oppressor, to teach them to differentiate the forces of liberation from the forces of the exploiters; to teach them to hear the voices of the revolution regardless of the tones they take."[23] We were well known in the 1960s and 1970s for our political battles on these questions with opponents, including the Communist Party, which at least well into the 1970s dismissed Black nationalism as a "capitulation to racism," or "racism in reverse."

Party leaders from my generation, however, as well as Farrell [Dobbs], Joe [Hansen], and many others, believed that Malcolm had thought out, knew exactly what he was saying, and *meant it* when he said in the *Young Socialist* interview that he was "reappraising [his] definition of Black nationalism," that he truthfully no longer believed "we [can] sum up the solution to the problems confronting our people as Black nationalism," and that he hadn't been "using the expression for several months" because he didn't want to erect barriers to collaboration with other revolutionaries "dedicated to overturning the system of exploitation that exists on this earth." Just as Malcolm had thought out, knew exactly what he was doing, and *meant it* when he proposed giving the Young Socialist Alliance a list of names and addresses of young people he had met in Africa and Europe and assumed we would use the names appropriately. And meant it when he told us he wanted these youth to read the *Young Socialist* itself, not just the issue with his interview.

George Breitman, however, disagreed. Breitman, who was a member of the SWP National Committee at the time, deserves credit for the work he did in editing many of Malcolm's speeches for publication, with care and integrity. But he had become committed to insisting that Malcolm X was

---

23. See "He Spoke the Truth to Our Generation of Revolutionists: In Tribute to Malcolm X" in Part I, p. 43.

a Black nationalist until the day he was gunned down. And that Malcolm, had he lived, would have remained a Black nationalist for as far into the future as it made any sense to think about. In fact, Breitman devoted an entire chapter of the book *The Last Year of Malcolm X: The Evolution of a Revolutionary* to a more-or-less open polemic with what Malcolm had said in the *YS* interview.

The Last Year of Malcolm X is a useful book, clearly written and easy to read. It documents quite a bit about Malcolm's political development during that last year. But the chapter I'm referring to, entitled "Separatism and Black Nationalism," is dedicated to establishing that Malcolm could not have *meant* what he *said*.[24] After quoting in full Malcolm's answer to the question about Black nationalism in the *YS* interview, Breitman wrote:

> It was not until after the publication of the *Young Socialist* interview a few days after Malcolm's death that anyone looked back to see when Malcolm had stopped calling himself a Black nationalist. It was at the end of May, right after his first trip abroad in 1964. On his return from that trip, Malcolm spent the whole month of June organizing the OAAU [Organization of Afro-American Unity] in New York. When he had formed the Muslim Mosque, Inc., in March [1964], he had said it was Black nationalist. He did not say this about the OAAU at its first meeting on June 28, 1964. Nor did the "Statement of Basic Aims and Objectives of the Organization of Afro-American Unity," which he made public at that meeting, make any reference whatever to Black nationalism. . . . Early in 1965, Malcolm announced that the OAAU was

---

24. "Separatism and Black Nationalism" in George Breitman, *The Last Year of Malcolm X: The Evolution of a Revolutionary* (Pathfinder, 1967), pp. 64–82 [2008 printing].

preparing a new program. . . . But the "Basic Unity Program" did not call the OAAU Black nationalist; it never even mentioned the expression.

None of these facts helped settle the question for Breitman, however. He continued:

> Is it correct to still speak of Malcolm as a Black nationalist when we know that he had stopped calling himself that and was questioning the adequacy of Black nationalism as "the solution to the problems confronting our people"? The answer is yes, if we continue to use the definition of Black nationalism attempted earlier in this chapter.[25]

Breitman insisted that "Malcolm became a Black nationalist while he was in prison in the late 1940s—it was the starting point for all his thinking, the source of his strength and dynamism. And he remained a Black nationalist to his last hour, however uncertain he became about what to call himself or the program that he was trying to formulate."

Breitman continued, saying "light can be shed on Malcolm's reappraisal" if we understand that Malcolm was moving beyond what "can be called pure-and-simple" Black

---

25. Earlier in the chapter, Breitman had written that Black nationalism "can be seen as approximately the following: It is the tendency for Black people in the United States to unite as a group, as a people, into a movement of their own to fight for freedom, justice and equality. Animated by the desire of an oppressed minority to decide its own destiny, this tendency holds that Black people must control their own movement and the political, economic and social institutions of the Black community. Its characteristic attributes include racial pride, group consciousness, hatred of white supremacy, a striving for independence from white control, and identification with Black and other non-white oppressed groups in other parts of the world."

nationalism. "The pure-and-simple Black nationalist," Breitman said, "is concerned exclusively or primarily with the internal problems of the Negro community, with organizing it, with helping it to gain control of the community's politics, economy, etc. He is not concerned, or is less concerned, with the problems of the total American society, or with the nature of the larger society within which the Negro community exists."

That's hardly a dialectical picture of how capitalism functions in the United States! The workings of the capitalist system produce not only commodities but above all, in doing so, continually reproduce the social relations on which the wealth and power of the ruling families depend, including anti-Black racism and other forms of oppression and exploitation. Neither today nor ever in U.S. history has there been a self-enclosed, self-sufficient "Negro community" that "exists" within "the larger society." There were no self-contained Black peasant communities in the wilderness of North America. Nor is there any such "white community." We're talking about class relations and their inextricably interconnected racial and national divisions, not nested Russian dolls.

Breitman continued that Malcolm "has no theory or program for changing that [total American] society; for him that is the white man's problem."[26]

---

26. Breitman's conclusion that, right up until his assassination, Malcolm considered the revolutionary transformation of society in the United States (and the world) to be "the white man's problem" is impossible to reconcile with a review of what Malcolm himself said—on repeated occasions, and before different audiences—during the final months of his life. Take, for example, just the following statements quoted in "Malcolm X: Revolutionary Leader of the Working Class" in Part I of this book: "I for one will join in with anyone, I don't care what color you are, as long as you want to change this miserable condition that exists on this earth." (Oxford University, December 3, 1964). "I was alienat-

Breitman was evidently so concerned about how readers would respond to what Malcolm actually said about Black nationalism in the discussion with the YSA leaders that the editor's note to the *YS* interview administered a pre-emptive inoculation when it was reprinted in *By Any Means Necessary*. Here's what Breitman had to say there about Malcolm's answer: "It showed that Malcolm had been grappling with the problem of Black nationalism—not in the sense of rejecting it, but of reappraising it, in order to discover how it fitted into his overall philosophy and strategy."[27]

It's almost as if, to paraphrase Malcolm, the parrot couldn't be allowed to jump too far out of the Black nationalist cage.

According to Breitman, as a result of Malcolm's travels to Africa and the Mideast later in 1964, as well as other experiences, he "moved beyond pure-and-simple Black nationalism—toward Black nationalism plus." And then Breitman posed the obvious question: "Plus what?" Over the next few paragraphs, he attempts an answer to that question through a series of successive abstract, supraclass approximations:

---

ing people who were true revolutionaries dedicated to overturning the systems of exploitation that exists on this earth by any means necessary." (*Young Socialist* interview, January 18, 1965.) We are heading toward "a showdown between the economic systems that exist on this earth. . . . I believe that there will ultimately be a clash between the oppressed and those that do the oppressing. I believe that there will be a clash between those who want freedom, justice, and equality for everyone and those who want to continue the systems of exploitation. I believe that there will be that kind of clash, but I don't think that it will be based upon the color of the skin, as Elijah Muhammad had taught it."(Interview by Pierre Berton, January 19, 1965) "We are today seeing a global rebellion of the oppressed against the oppressor, the exploited against the exploiter." (Barnard College, February 18, 1965)—JB

27. Malcolm X, *By Any Means Necessary* (Pathfinder, 1970, 1992), p. 189 [2008 printing].

Black nationalism "plus radicalism." Black nationalism "plus fundamental social change." Black nationalism "plus the transformation of the whole society." And he concluded:

> Malcolm still was looking for the name, but he was becoming Black nationalist plus revolutionary. . . . What he was questioning about Black nationalism was not its essence but its pure-and-simple form. He was questioning this because it "was alienating people who were true revolutionaries"—in this case, white revolutionaries. A pure-and-simple Black nationalist wouldn't care what effect he had on whites, revolutionary or otherwise. Malcolm cared because he intended to work with white revolutionaries; he knew their collaboration was needed if society was to be transformed.
>
> Malcolm was beginning to think about the need to replace capitalism with socialism if racism was to be eliminated. He was not sure if it could be done, and he was not sure how it could be done, but he was beginning to believe that that was the road to be traveled.
>
> His uncertainty about the right name to call himself arose from the fact that he was doing something new in the United States—he was on the way to a synthesis of Black nationalism and socialism that would be fitting for the American scene and acceptable to the masses in the Black ghetto.

It's important to notice one thing before going any further. By the time of the *Young Socialist* interview, Malcolm had not only stopped using the term "Black nationalism." He also talked a lot less about "white revolutionaries." Malcolm said that the Algerian ambassador he had met in Ghana was a revolutionary, a "true revolutionary." That was the bottom line. And the fact that this revolutionary happened not to be black helped Malcolm come to the conclusion that the term

Black nationalism was inadequate and that he would no longer use it to describe his own views. Nor did Malcolm speak
of the Socialist Workers Party or Young Socialist Alliance as
"white revolutionaries," nor of young people he had met in
Africa and Europe as "black revolutionaries," "Arab revolutionaries," or "white revolutionaries." He just spoke of them
as revolutionaries—and if they offered their lives fighting
for the revolution, he called them *true revolutionaries*.

Malcolm X wasn't "on the way to a synthesis of Black nationalism and socialism that would be fitting for the American scene and acceptable to the masses in the Black ghetto."
By the way, Breitman never claimed that was the goal of
the Socialist Workers Party. But why not, if a "synthesis of
Black nationalism and socialism" would be "fitting for the
American scene"? Did Breitman think proletarian revolutionaries who were Black made an error in joining the Socialist Workers Party? If not, why block off the possibility
of that same political evolution for others?

Why not just stick to the facts, at least to Malcolm's own
words?

Malcolm had become a *revolutionary* long before these
final months of his life. He had long been an uncompromising opponent of imperialism. He had already achieved "a
synthesis" of Black nationalism with all that for a number
of years. What he was "on the way to" in late 1964 and early
1965, however, was something more dialectical, inclusive,
internationalist, and socialist.

Malcolm had become a champion of the socialist revolution in Cuba and of its proletarian internationalist leadership.
He hailed the revolutionary government in Algeria headed by
Ahmed Ben Bella and other leaders, who openly proclaimed
their socialist course and convictions. Malcolm promoted the
Militant newspaper and was deepening his political collaboration with the Socialist Workers Party and Young Socialist Alliance, two communist organizations. In fact, the great bulk of

Don't start with Blacks as an oppressed nationality. Start with the last century and a half, with the vanguard place and weight of workers who are Black in broad, proletarian-led social and political struggles in the United States. From the Civil War to today, the historical record is mind-boggling. It bowls you over when you hear it.

JACK BARNES, 2006

Above, some 20,000 jobless World War I veterans camped near U.S. Capitol in Washington, D.C., from May to July 1932 demanding federal "Soldiers' Bonus" be paid. "Bonus March," among first mass actions by working people during Great Depression, ended with military assault, killing two workers and wounding many. **Right,** soldiers at U.S. base at Con Thien, Vietnam, December 1968. "Mass struggles for Black rights reached new levels of radicalism during the Vietnam War," Barnes says.

BLACK POWER
IS
NUMBER ONE

Twice in the twentieth century we've seen in practice what Trotsky explained would happen, that the Black proletariat would simply "march over the petty bourgeoisie"—white as well as Black, including the trade union officialdom—in order to advance the struggle against racist discrimination.

JACK BARNES, 2006

"Sharecroppers, tenant farmers, and other rural toilers, both Black and white, waged struggles in the 1920s and through the Great Depression," says Barnes. **Top,** members of Southern Tenant Farmers Union meet in St. Francis, Arkansas, 1937.

"Workers who were Black were in front ranks of battles that built the industrial unions in the 1930s," says Barnes. **Above,** strike by tobacco factory workers in 1936 in Harlem, New York.

Montgomery bus boycott's central organizer wasn't Martin Luther King but E.D. Nixon, "a savvy, longtime union militant and NAACP leader," notes Barnes. "Nixon did believe in being prepared for self-defense. Young workers and veterans were central to his efforts." **Top,** Nixon (center) at packed tribute to him in New York hosted by Militant Labor Forum on boycott's 10th anniversary, December 1965. Anniversary organizers in Montgomery hadn't invited Nixon. Beside him are Farrell Dobbs, Socialist Workers Party national secretary, and Arlette Nixon, boycott activist and E.D. Nixon's wife. Dobbs helped organize 1956 effort to supply vehicles for community shuttle service during boycott and drove station wagon to Montgomery.

Above, 1968 strike by sanitation workers in Memphis, Tennessee, became catalyst of final stage of struggle consolidating defeat of Jim Crow.

Skills learned in factory work and in union struggles before and during World War II increased confidence among workers who were Black. So did experiences in the armed forces, including in segregated units. That leavening made possible the rise of the proletarian-led struggle for Black rights in the 1950s and 1960s.

JACK BARNES, 1987

Workers who are Black, says Barnes, "were in the vanguard of working people during World War II who refused to postpone struggles for justice in the name of 'the patriotic war effort.'" **Above,** 1942 rally in New York called by March on Washington movement demands end to discrimination in war industries and armed forces and denounces legal lynching of framed-up Virginia sharecropper Odell Waller.

Facing page, top, loading ammunition at Port Chicago naval depot, California, during World War II. In October 1944, 50 Navy enlisted men who were Black were court-martialed for "mutiny" for refusal to return to jobs after explosion in which 320 sailors and others were killed. Enlistees were given 15 years plus dishonorable discharge, later reduced to 17 months and demotion. NAACP and *Militant* newsweekly campaigned to overturn convictions.

Post–World War II Black struggle in U.S., says Barnes, "was part of a wave of revolutionary victories against imperialist domination and capitalist exploitation" in Asia, Africa, the Mideast, the Caribbean, and Latin America. **Right,** November 1945 *Militant* hails battle by Indonesian toilers against U.S.- and British-backed efforts to reimpose Dutch colonial rule. **Inset,** *Militant* ad for December 1945 Socialist Workers Party meeting demanding withdrawal of Allied imperialist troops from Indonesia, China, Vietnam.

The core of the activists defending the Cuban Revolution were young people who had cut their political eyeteeth as participants in civil rights battles. We placed the struggle for Black rights within the world class struggle. For us it became totally intertwined with the stakes in defending the Cuban Revolution. JACK BARNES, 2001

New York, November 26, 1960, picket line of more than 500 called by Fair Play for Cuba Committee outside United Nations building to protest moves by U.S. Navy fleet in Caribbean.

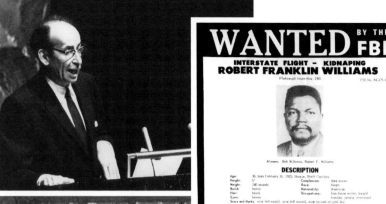

Above, Robert F. Williams, leader of Monroe, North Carolina, NAACP (at head of table), in Cuba during July 1960 Fair Play for Cuba Committee tour. Eight African Americans, including Williams and writer LeRoi Jones (now Amiri Baraka, seated to left of Williams) were among thirty signers of April 1960 *New York Times* ad launching committee **(facing page)**.

Top right, FBI "Wanted" poster for Williams, who was framed on kidnapping charges in 1961 and driven into exile for organizing self-defense of Black community in Monroe against Ku Klux Klan nightriders.

Top left, Cuban foreign minister Raúl Roa speaking at UN after defeat of U.S.-organized invasion at Bay of Pigs, April 1961. Roa read message Robert F. Williams asked him to convey to Washington: "Now that the United States has proclaimed military support for people willing to rebel against oppression, oppressed Negroes in the South urgently request tanks, artillery, bombs, money, use of American air fields and white mercenaries to crush racist tyrants who have betrayed the American Revolution and Civil War."

The lynch-mob terror of organized white-supremacist night riders came closer to fascist violence on a broad scale, and over an extended period, than anything else ever seen in this country.   JACK BARNES, 2001

Organizers of lynch mobs, says Barnes, often took photos and produced "actual postcards of these outrages," distributing them widely "to legitimatize lynching as a 'family activity.'" **Above,** lynching of 32-year-old tenant farmer Rubin Stacy, Fort Lauderdale, Florida, July 19, 1935.

Facing page, center, John Boyd, president of National Black Farmers Association, speaking at April 2009 rally in Washington, D.C., against discriminatory farm lending by U.S. Agriculture Department. Mule at forefront recalls continuity of fights today with struggles for land reform by freed slaves during Reconstruction—"40 acres and a mule!" was the battle cry.
Current struggles by farmers who are Black, says Barnes, are "often a link in battles that go back more than a century."

Top, Cuban revolutionary leader Víctor Dreke (right) visiting farm of Willie Head (left) in Georgia during 2002 U.S. speaking tour of Dreke and Cuban doctor Ana Morales (center). Head has been active in fight of Black farmers to stay on land. During fact-finding trip to Cuba in February 2000, Head and five other farmers learned how Cuban Revolution guarantees no farmer is foreclosed on or forced to sell land to bank or better-off farmer.

Above, right, 50,000 march in Columbia, South Carolina, January 17, 2000, to demand removal of Confederate battle flag from state capitol. That flag, says Barnes, "is a banner under which assaults against African Americans, immigrants, Jews, abortion clinics, gays, and other targets of reaction *are* and *will* be launched until the capitalist roots of that Dixie rag are ripped from the ground by toilers and replaced by the dictatorship of the proletariat."

The gap in social conditions between workers who are white and those who are Black has narrowed since the 1960s. But not because times have gotten better for most African Americans. It is because conditions are declining for the majority of workers of all skin colors.

JACK BARNES, 2009

Above, workers line up for jobs in New York, June 2008. "With unemployment sharply rising," says Barnes, "and joblessness for workers who are Black at the highest levels, victories won by the working class against racial divisions fostered by the bosses are increasingly threatened."

Conditions in today's overpacked prisons, says Barnes, remain like those against which 1,300 inmates rebelled in 1972 at New York State's Attica prison "using the only means left to them to bring to the world's attention the horrors of America's penitentiaries." **Facing page, center,** Attica prison yard after assault by state police. Despite cover-up by cops and politicians, official state commission later found police responsible for deaths of all 29 prisoners and 10 hostages slaughtered during retaking of prison, some after surrendering.

Right, Clinton signs law ending Aid to Families with Dependent Children (AFDC), August 1996. "Since the destruction of what Clinton callously described as 'welfare as we know it,'" says Barnes, "the number of working people receiving cash assistance has dropped to a more than forty-year low."

A New Beginning
Welfare to Work

Rulers pushed workers to go into debt to buy houses, says Barnes, aiming "to subvert class solidarity by elevating relations among 'fellow property holders' over those with 'fellow workers.'" **Right,** mural commissioned for 2002 White House Conference on Minority Homeownership was titled "Stepping into the American Dream"—one that has become "American nightmare" for millions.

The 2008 election of Barack Obama is not "a Black thing." It's a product of the explosive growth of a new stratum of bourgeois-minded professionals and middle-class individuals *of all colors and hues*—foundation- and university-centered, largely unconnected to production of social wealth, and alien to the conditions of life of working people of any racial or national background.

JACK BARNES, 2009

Right, June 2009 *BusinessWeek* cover story on Ursula Burns, Xerox's new CEO. "As recently as 1988 there had never been a single chief executive officer of a major U.S. corporation who was Black—*not one, not ever,*" says Barnes. "Today there are more than twenty."

Facing page, center, candidate Obama giving widely covered talk, Father's Day, June 2008, at Chicago's Apostolic Church of God, with large African American congregation. Echoing class prejudice of privileged layers of all skin colors, he held Black family members responsible for their children's poor education and care. Scolding "absent fathers," he added, "Any fool can have a child."

Facing page, right. The "meritocracy," says Barnes, "is in large part what Richard Herrnstein and Charles Murray modestly dub 'the cognitive elite' in their 1994 book *The Bell Curve: Intelligence and Class Structure in American Life.* They seek to provide a 'scientific' rationalization for the rapidly rising income and class privileges of the middle-class social stratum they describe."

"Affirmative action in the misshapen forms increasingly implemented by the capitalist rulers," says Barnes, "is used to reinforce illusions in imperialist democracy, further divide African Americans along class lines, and deepen divisions among workers." **Top,** cartoon on website of parents' association at U.S. Naval Academy highlights "diversity" of class of 2013, in which 35% of plebes—the highest ever—are Hispanic, Asian, Black, or Native American. Capitalist rulers need officer corps whose face more closely mirrors working-class ranks of armed forces.

If vanguard workers in the U.S. who are Black cannot be won to recognizing the proletarian dictatorship as the most powerful instrument that can be wielded to win a final and lasting battle for Black freedom, why would they fight heart and soul to make a socialist revolution? And why *should* they?   JACK BARNES, 2006

"Win the battle against discrimination!" declares March 26, 1959, issue of *Revolución*, newspaper of July 26 Movement. Four days before, speaking to a million Cubans, prime minister Fidel Castro announced—and new revolutionary government began enforcing—laws barring job bias against Blacks and ending segregation at schools, beaches, parks, and elsewhere.

Right, Cubans of all skin colors in early 1960s swim at what before had been all-white beach club of Havana's wealthy families.

Facing page, top, Petrograd, July 1920, V.I. Lenin speaks at opening of second congress of Communist International, which adopted resolution drafted by Lenin on fight against national oppression. "There was nothing 'philanthropic' about" the Bolsheviks' support for national rights, wrote James P. Cannon. "They recognized the great revolutionary potential of oppressed peoples and nations as allies of the international working class in the revolutionary struggle against capitalism."

Above, December 1994, Chechen women confront Russian soldier near capital city of Grozny, which was devastated during Moscow's 1994 and 1999 invasions.

"In Russia the Bolsheviks fought for self-determination of national minorities, including the right of separation," Leon Trotsky said in 1933 discussion with U.S. communist leader. Reversal of this course by Stalinist privileged caste lives on in Moscow's brutal assaults against former Soviet republics such as Georgia and Chechnya.

Malcolm X was an intransigent opponent of the Democratic and Republican parties, an opponent of the two-party system that has tied working people to capitalist politics for more than a century. JACK BARNES, 1987

Above, Farrell Dobbs, Socialist Workers Party candidate for president of U.S. in 1948, campaigns in Detroit working-class neighborhood. "Labor must break all ties with the capitalist parties," said party's platform.

Clifton DeBerry was first African American nominated for president of United States by any party, running in 1964 on Socialist Workers Party ticket with Ed Shaw for vice-president. **Right,** DeBerry (third from left) marches in December 1964 picket line outside UN in New York demanding, "Hands Off Congo!"

Rev. King Wins Place on Ballot Despite Challenge by Democrats

CHICAGO, Aug. 30 — The United Socialist Campaign to elect Rev. Joseph P. King to Congress from the Second District won a resounding victory yesterday when the Board of Election Commissioners upheld his right to a place on the ballot.

In a desperate attempt to keep King off the ballot, the machine of incumbent Democratic Congressman Barratt O'Hara had earlier instigated two challenges of King's nominating petition as being permeated with "fraud." Unable to substantiate this crude charge at the official hearings, the challengers tried to whip up a red-baiting atmosphere. But Rev. King's case was so strong that, despite its two-to-one domination by Democrats, the election board had no choice but to rule in favor of the socialist candidate. His campaign committee had filed

to look at King's nominating petition, and that, as a matter of fact, he had examined only 150 sheets out of the total 508.

He asserted that in his opinion "200 to 225 names" were "couplets" or, in a few cases, "triplets," where apparently the names of a husband and wife, or the names of three persons in the same household, had been entered by one person.

No effort was made by the O'Hara forces to bring to the hearing, voluntarily or by subpoena, those voters whose signatures they were contesting. Even if these charges of the hired expert could be proved to be true in the small number of cases alleged — at most it was claimed that 100 husbands or wives signed for one another — it would in no way justify the wild charge of "forgery and fraud" which the O'Hara machine spread in

witch-hunting, demanded that Howard Mayhew, Chicago Chairman of the Socialist Workers Party, who was in the audience, be put on the stand.

Mayhew was sworn, gave his name and address. Dowd then asked if he was a sponsor and backer of King's candidacy. Mayhew responded with an emphatic yes. Dowd then demanded if he was a member of the Socialist Workers Party and a communist. The attorneys for Rev. King objected to this line of questioning as immaterial and irrelevant. The objection was upheld and the SWP organizer was excused from further interrogation.

DIDN'T SPECIFY

Illinois election law requires that any objection brought against a candidate's petitions "shall state fully the nature of the objections to the nominating papers." The objection to

In 1950s and '60s SWP supported several independent election campaigns by Blacks, including 1958 candidacy of Joseph King for U.S. Congress in Chicago and 1964 Freedom Now Party candidates in Michigan.

Inset, coverage in September 1958 *Militant* of King campaign in Chicago. **Above right,** Malcolm X at Detroit airport, February 15, 1965, with Milton Henry, Freedom Now Party candidate for Congress in 1964 running against Democrat John Conyers and Republican Robert Blackwell.

In 1980s SWP members "participated in and campaigned to build the National Black Independent Political Party (NBIPP) and other organizations seeking to advance Black rights along proletarian lines," Barnes explains. **Above left,** NBIPP supporters join April 20, 1985, March on Washington against U.S. military intervention in Central America and Caribbean.

In the imperialist epoch, revolutionary leadership of the highest political capacity, courage, and integrity converges with communism. What comes out of that is not a "synthesis" of nationalism and socialism, but a proletarian movement richer in variety, experience, cultural breadth, social understanding, and combat capacity.

JACK BARNES, 2006

"If Malcolm X is to be compared with any international figure, the most striking parallel is with Fidel Castro," said Barnes, speaking at 1965 memorial tribute. **Above,** Malcolm X and Castro, September 1960, at Hotel Theresa, Harlem, New York, where Malcolm and thousands of neighborhood residents welcomed Cuban delegation to UN General Assembly.

"I love a revolutionary," Malcolm told Harlem audience on December 13, 1964, before reading solidarity message from Cuban leader Che Guevara. **Right,** Guevara speaking to UN General Assembly two days earlier.

Top, Maurice Bishop, central leader of 1979–83 Grenada Revolution, talks with nurses during revolution. Bishop came to working-class politics under impact of Black rights movement in U.S. and Caribbean, including example of Malcolm X, and came to Marxism from example of Cuban Revolution.

Above, Thomas Sankara, leader of 1983–87 revolution in Burkina Faso, West Africa, in October 1985. "We are heirs of all the world's revolutions," Sankara told UN General Assembly in 1984—the American Revolution, the French Revolution, and "the great October Revolution that brought victory to the proletariat and realized the Paris Commune's dreams of justice."

Combating the diverse expressions and legacy of racism and segregation, and overcoming divisions based on skin color and national origins, remains the single biggest task before the working class in forging the proletarian vanguard in this country. JACK BARNES, 2006

Signs read: "WE ARE all are equal", "GRANT AMNESTY", "HONK for HUMAN RIGHTS"

Above, Waterloo, Iowa, May 2008, working people demand release of 400 workers at Agriprocessors packinghouse in nearby Postville, swept up in federal police raid against immigrants. **Right,** Charleston, South Carolina, January 2000, longshore workers defend themselves against cop assault on picket line protesting bosses' union-busting.

Battles like these, Barnes says, remind us we organize and fight in "a different world today, and with a different working class—one that's larger, substantially more immigrant, with a weightier component that is Black."

the "true revolutionaries" Malcolm admired and worked with were communists: in Cuba, in Algeria, those he sometimes called the "MLFers"[28]—the YSA and SWP. Those are facts.

What is so essential in understanding Malcolm X is that we can see the fact—not the hope, not the faith, the *fact*—that, in the imperialist epoch, revolutionary leadership on the highest level of political capacity, courage, and integrity converges *with* communism, not simply *toward* the communist movement. That truth has even greater weight today as billions around the world, in city and countryside, from China to Nigeria to Brazil, are being hurled into the modern class struggle by the violent expansion of world capitalism. From seeing in life how that process unfolds, we draw confidence in the prospects for world revolution, in the development of a genuinely worldwide proletarian revolutionary leadership.

What comes out of such a convergence is not a "synthesis" of nationalism and socialism (much less nationalism "plus revolutionary"), not a synthesis of an ideology and the line of march of a class. What comes out of it is a movement of the proletariat and its fighting allies. What comes out of it is a proletarian movement that not only strengthens its own political continuity but transforms the channels through which that continuity flows. A proletarian movement that becomes more inclusive, richer in its variety, experience, cultural breadth, social understanding, political intelligence and savvy, and—above all—combat capacity. One capable of leading the toilers in conquering the dictatorship of the proletariat and *using* it to put an end to national oppression and all the other consequences of centuries of class society.

---

28. In informal conversation with members of the Socialist Workers Party and Young Socialist Alliance, Malcolm X sometimes called us "MLFers," since he had met many of us for the first time at the Militant Labor Forum in New York, where he spoke three times in 1964 and early 1965.—JB

Malcolm and the communist movement

The *Militant* was the paper of record for Malcolm's speeches, including during the final period when he was still in the Nation of Islam. (*Muhammad Speaks* had ceased printing them.) Our movement and our press were known for having recognized the revolutionary political logic of Malcolm X's course in early 1963. Already at that time, Malcolm would sometimes demonstratively buy the *Militant* on his way into a meeting where he was speaking.

I remember selling the *Militant* along with other party and YSA comrades from Chicago and Detroit at a meeting where Malcolm spoke in late 1963, together with Rev. Albert Cleage; Gloria Richardson, a militant Black rights leader from Cambridge, Maryland; and others. It was the concluding rally of the Grass Roots conference held at the King Solomon Baptist church in Detroit.[29] The meeting was overwhelmingly Black in composition, and most of us selling the paper were white. The situation was a little tense at the beginning. Then Malcolm came by. He saw the *Militant*, asked someone in his defense team to get him a copy, gave us a nod, and walked into the church. After that, the tensions relaxed and sales picked up quite a bit. And this was when Malcolm was still a public figure in the Nation of Islam.

Later, following Malcolm's break with the Nation, we began collaborating with members of his general staff—Reuben Francis, James Shabazz, and others. They knew the *Militant* was just about the only place anyone could get regular, reliable information about what Malcolm was saying and doing. And they said so. And not just to us.

Malcolm spoke at Militant Labor Forums three times between April 1964 and January 1965. Major excerpts from all three talks are reprinted in *Malcolm X Speaks*, published

---

29. "Message to the Grass Roots" opens *Malcolm X Speaks* (Pathfinder, 1965, 1989), the first selection of Malcolm's speeches ever published.

by Pathfinder just months after the assassination in 1965. And portions of the question-and-answer period from the first forum appear in *By Any Means Necessary*. This was unusual for Malcolm. Because although he had spoken to numerous campus audiences around the United States and elsewhere, including while he was still in the Nation, these three forums were the only times he had agreed to be on the platform at a meeting of a revolutionary political organization outside Harlem, "downtown," as Malcolm said. (He appeared with Progressive Labor Party leader Bill Epton once or twice at PL-sponsored meetings in Harlem.)

The first forum, "The Black Revolution," was in early April 1964, just before Malcolm's first trip to Africa and the Middle East. It was held at the Palm Gardens meeting hall on 52nd Street in Manhattan.

The second forum, "On the Harlem 'Hate Gang' Scare," was in late May, shortly after Malcolm's return from that trip. If you were able to go back and dig up a leaflet for that forum, which was held at our hall at 116 University Place, just south of Union Square, you wouldn't find Malcolm listed as a speaker; you'd find James Shabazz. But James called us at the last minute and said that Malcolm had requested to speak. James asked if we had any objection if Malcolm replaced him on the program. We didn't. In opening his talk there, Malcolm said he hadn't known about the forum until James told him about it that afternoon, "and I couldn't resist the opportunity to come."

Malcolm spoke at the third Militant Labor Forum, also held at Palm Gardens, in early January 1965, not long after returning from his most recent Africa trip and a couple weeks before the *YS* interview. "It's the third time that I've had the opportunity to be a guest of the Militant Labor Forum," he said. "I always feel that it is an honor and every time that they open the door for me to do so, I will be right here. The *Militant* newspaper is one of the best in New York

"Malcolm X," says Barnes, "put great store in meeting and collaborating with other revolutionaries, at home as well as around the world."

Malcolm spoke three times at Militant Labor Forums in New York City hosted by Socialist Workers Party and Young Socialist Alliance. Above, top and bottom, April 8 and May 29, 1964, forums. Inset, January 7, 1965, meeting was chaired by Clifton DeBerry, SWP candidate for president of U.S. in 1964.

"It's the third time I've had the opportunity to be a guest of the Militant Labor Forum," Malcolm said at opening of 1965 talk. "I always feel it is an honor and every time they open the door for me, I will be right here."

City. In fact, it is one of the best anywhere you go today," adding that he had seen copies in Paris and various parts of Africa. "I don't know how it gets there," he said. "But if you put the right things in it, what you put in will see that it gets around."

Malcolm even looked physically different as his political perspectives evolved over the last year before the assassination. He no longer needed the austere suits that were the badge of ministers in the Nation of Islam. His beard grew a little more full. His face softened. He wore clothing, still respectful and dignified, that he felt like wearing. He was stripping away everything that was gloss, everything that was revolutionary theater, anything that could be seen as selling wolf tickets. He was shucking off everything unnecessary to simply saying what needed to be said, working as hard as he could, and collaborating with revolutionaries, "true revolutionaries," in order "to change this miserable condition that exists on this earth," as he put it. You're living "at a time of revolution"—that was Malcolm's message to youth and working people over and over again in 1964 and 1965.

When you read Malcolm's talks and interviews from this period, you'll also find the evidence there to clear up numerous myths about him. First and foremost, by reading and studying Malcolm you'll understand the inaccuracy of those who argue that despite the value of the written record of his work, it pales in comparison to his spoken word—to his effectiveness as a public speaker. George Breitman, for example, certainly thought it was important to get Malcolm's speeches into print; he edited several selections of those talks.

But in his foreword to the first of those books, *Malcolm X Speaks*, here's what Breitman had to say: "Malcolm was primarily a speaker, not a writer. . . . The printed speeches do not convey adequately his remarkable qualities as a speaker, their effect on his audiences and the interplay between him and them. We would have preferred to publish a series of long-playing record albums presenting this material in his own voice, with its tones of indignation and anger, with its chuckles, and with the interruptions of applause and laughter from the audience. . . . Since we lack the resources and time to publish and distribute such recordings and since the cost would limit the number of people who could buy them, we are doing the next best thing."

But that was not true. We *wouldn't* have preferred to produce records—or today CDs—of Malcolm instead of the books. Yes, Malcolm was an unusually effective speaker. But our efforts over the past forty years to publish Malcolm X in his own words—efforts that have so far borne fruit in eight books, six in English and two in Spanish,[30] as well as two pamphlets—are hardly "the next best thing." Unlike the recordings, they are essential to making Malcolm's ideas and example accessible for study to new generations. And to those around the world (the great majority) whose first language is not English.

Nobody can seriously "study" a recording. It's much more difficult to go back to refresh your memory, or to look something up. This is important, since as Malcolm's political evolution seemed to accelerate more and more over the last months, the "wit and wisdom" aspect of his talks receded. What came to the fore instead, translatable into any language, were his efforts to think out and then explain the biggest political questions and challenges before revolutionary-minded working people and youth the world over. The written record of that work is and will remain the long-term test of Malcolm's political "relevance" to the future. That's where we find the *continuity*, the cumulative political conquests that

---

30. The two books in Spanish, *Habla Malcolm X* and *Malcolm X habla a la juventud*, have also been published in Cuba by the publishing houses Ciencias Sociales and Editora Abril.

advance program and strategy.

The same is true of other outstanding revolutionary leaders of our class—Karl Marx, V.I. Lenin, Leon Trotsky, James P. Cannon, Fidel Castro, Maurice Bishop, Thomas Sankara, to name just a few. Each of them worked hard as speakers to present revolutionary ideas to working people as clearly and effectively as possible. Some of them, as we know either from our own experience or published accounts, were powerful speakers. Where tapes are available, they're useful and fun to listen to—once or twice. But it is impossible to seriously study and absorb working-class program and strategy just by listening to a recording. You need to have them before you in black and white, on paper. Either the ideas stand up in print, in any language and without an audience, or they don't. *Malcolm's do!* And there's still plenty of wit, plenty of pure humanness.

There's another myth about Malcolm that can be exploded by a careful reading of what he *said* and what he *did*—both of which can be found in some detail in the books of Malcolm's speeches. That's the notion that while Malcolm was a great propagandist, a great explainer of what so many people wanted to say about themselves and what they are capable of accomplishing, that Malcolm was never an organizer—or, at least, he never had a chance to become an organizer. But just from his own words alone, you'll see that's not true. Malcolm was all of the above, but he was simultaneously a skilled revolutionary organizer. What was cut short was the possibility of his putting those skills to further and broader work. The enemies of the proletariat understood that fact better than "pro–Malcolm X radicals," both when he was alive and today.

During the final months of his life, Malcolm moved away from using religious phrases and stances, even religious examples, in political activity, too. He explained in the clearest language possible exactly what he was doing, what he was seeing, what he was coming to understand and to believe.

Malcolm was on the road to becoming a communist. Why would we conclude anything else? What evidence would propel us to do so? Why would we place limitations on Malcolm—on Malcolm of all people!—that we wouldn't place on anyone else? Why would we say he was moving toward a "synthesis" of Black nationalism and socialism? That's not what Malcolm *said*. And the evidence is to the contrary. That's not what he was *doing*.

Malcolm insisted he had stopped calling himself a Black nationalist because Black nationalism was inadequate to explain what experience had taught him needed to be done to transform the world, a world that had in many ways in the imperialist epoch become a "white world." But Malcolm knew that Black men and women were inextricably connected to *that* world, and stitched into it, by a million threads. The world was unimaginable without that interaction. Once you stopped hunkering down, there were no separate white and Black worlds in any way, whether in place or in time. Most importantly, there was—and remains—a single capitalist state that must be overthrown in each country.

While nobody won to communism remains a Black nationalist, at the same time you don't stop being Black! You don't stop having pride. You don't stop marveling at how much of the truth about Black people has been kept out of "histories." That had better be understood too! Nobody is going to trust a socialist who is Black who acts as if they've forgotten they're Black (as if being a communist somehow makes a person less Black). And with good reason. They may get along for a while in capitalist society and begin thinking they're not Black. But as Joel [Britton] once warned regarding illusions in the labor officialdom, "then there's the rude awakening." Every time there's a retreat in the class struggle, they'll be *reminded* they're Black. They'll be reminded by Caucasians who are convinced *they* are "white"—"God's color." And this will remain true not only between now and a victorious socialist revolution, but to a lesser degree during the initial transition period of the proletarian dictatorship, as well. So these are realities of class-divided society that a communist can neither forget nor deny, but instead integrates into a proletarian internationalist strategy of how our class can lead all the oppressed in fighting effectively to win.

Recognizing and embracing the world-class political leadership of revolutionists who are Black—whether an African American such as Malcolm X, or leaders such as Maurice Bishop and Thomas Sankara—doesn't lead militant workers and youth in the political direction of nationalism or Pan-Africanism. Otherwise, why would we put such leadership time and resources into keeping their words in print? Why would we give such high priority to getting those books and pamphlets into the hands of working people in the United States, Africa, Latin America, Asia—the world over—as part of our overall political arsenal?

We do so because reading and studying what Malcolm, Maurice Bishop, and Thomas Sankara had to say—each of them concretely and at different times—helps us and others better understand the necessity of revolutionary workers parties, of *proletarian* internationalism, and of a *world* communist movement. What leaders such as these have been saying and doing over decades converges with the activity of communists worldwide and helps set up the next stage of human history.

The race question, the color question is on the rise in many parts of the world. It's coming more to the fore in Latin America, in those countries where there was significant chattel slave labor in the eighteenth and nineteenth centuries. It's a weighty political question in Brazil, in Colombia, in Venezuela, in substantial parts of Central America and the Caribbean, and elsewhere. It converges with the struggles of the indigenous populations, that is, the populations of pre-Columbian origins. It strengthens prospects for revolution across the Americas. It strengthens possibilities for the development of revolutionary leadership in Africa in new ways. It enriches the challenges and opportunities to build revolutionary proletarian parties throughout much of Europe and the "Anglosphere."[31]

The history of the past century has taught us that in order to defend and extend the international revolutionary struggle for national liberation and socialism, the establishment and extension of the dictatorship of the proletariat, the working class must have a genuine *world* leadership. It needs a leadership today that is more multinational, that has a larger component that is Black than during the opening half of the twentieth century. It needs a leadership that includes women in numbers and in ways never before seen in the workers movement—and never before possible.

We're not utopians. We're not oblivious to limitations in history and to the stubborn consequences of class exploitation and oppression, of uneven development of capitalist social relations on a world scale. In fact, we understand that these contradictory legacies are the very channels—longer lasting than we want or hope—through which the modern class struggle flows. We know revolutions will conquer with communist leaderships short of a "perfect" social composition (whatever that is imagined to be), short of the kind of human solidarity and unity that can only begin to be forged once the toilers have conquered power.

But we also know that the revolutionary workers move-

---

31. The "Anglosphere" is a term used by some bourgeois commentators to refer to the United States, the United Kingdom, Canada, Australia, and New Zealand—what Marxists would call the imperialist countries where English is the main language—as well as to the common law, institutions, and social relations these "English-speaking peoples" are alleged to share.

ment cannot conquer without reflecting in our ranks and in our leaderships how far our class and its allies have come in history in carving out a vanguard of political equals. Without registering the gains of struggles by the oppressed and exploited.

Why would anyone simply assume today that all the "Lenins" of the twenty-first century will be Caucasian? That's a political question, not a moral question. It's a concrete and historical question. Even more important, when millions no longer care what "color" Lenin is, then the working class will be much, much closer to building the kind of revolutionary parties and world movement we need to fight effectively and win. (Anyway, the ultraright always knew that Lenin wasn't white. Even a passing glance at a photo of that "slant-eyed" commie settled that! I leave aside "the Jew" Trotsky, even less "white" in the eyes of rightists.)

Modern land and labor league

At the big public meeting here in New York two days ago, we encouraged participants to visit the exhibition on "Slavery in New York" at the New York Historical Society. Among many other things, the exhibit describes the New York Manumission Society founded in 1785. I noted that John Jay—president of the Continental Congress for several years during the American Revolution, and later governor of New York and Chief Justice of the United States—was a founder of the society and had included in its constitution the following words: "The benevolent Creator and Father of men [has] given to them all an equal right to Life, Liberty and Property."

I contrasted this favorably to Thomas Jefferson's decision, in drafting the Declaration of Independence a decade earlier, to alter those words—much used by bourgeois opponents of monarchical tyranny and feudal reaction at the time—and replace them with the more intangible phrase: "Life, Liberty and the Pursuit of Happiness." With the exception of the four children of Sally Hemings, none of the other slaves owned by Thomas Jefferson were freed by him, even in his will; 130 were sold at auction when he died. Possibly that puts into some perspective Jefferson's practical understanding of "life, liberty, and the pursuit of happiness."

The banner "Life, Liberty and Property" was much more in the interests of *all* working people. It was the dispossession of independent toiling producers by capital that left us with no other choice but to sell our labor power to an employer in order to survive and thus gave rise to our class, the hereditary proletariat. They took away our free use of tools. They drove us off the land, and out of independent crafts and trades. They deprived us of our own means of production. They took over the commons. And it was the brutal denial of *both* liberty and property—even the *right* to hold property, much less the opportunity to do so—that marked chattel slavery and many other forms of bonded labor. In the chapters of *Capital* on "So-Called Primitive Accumulation," Marx describes in some detail how, as a result of these combined processes, the capitalist mode of production came into the world "dripping from head to toe, from every pore, with blood and filth."[32]

Once we've established a workers and farmers government and expropriated the capitalist class, working people will be plenty competent to take care of our own "pursuit of happiness"—and we'll pursue a lot of it on the way. Contrary to the bourgeois misrepresentation of communists as utopian social engineers, proletarian revolutionists—like most other workers—firmly believe that many things in life are best left to the individual. The right to privacy is real. We think the state, including a workers state, should

---

32. Marx, *Capital*, vol. 1 (London: Pelican Books, 1976), p. 926.

keep its nose out of our "pursuit of happiness."

Neither the proletarian dictatorship, nor the communist society it is a bridge toward, has anything to do with some great collective barracks of humanity. That's not what communism is about. To the contrary, as the Communist Manifesto explains, "In place of the old bourgeois society, with its classes and class antagonisms, we shall have an association in which the free development of each is the condition for the free development of all."[33] We have little idea what it will be like, but it will be a lot better for working people.

Today, more than 130 years after Marx identified the class forces capable of making the third American revolution—a socialist revolution—that same alliance remains central to the task: free labor, free farmers exploited by capital, and the men and women who freed themselves from the defeated slavocracy. Those forces remain at the heart of building a modern land and labor league,[34] the revolutionary proletarian party that can do the job.

---

33. Marx and Engels, *Communist Manifesto*, p. 58. Also in *MECW*, vol. 6, p. 506.

34. The Land and Labour League was launched by a conference of workers in London, England, in October 1869. It was organized at the initiative of the leadership of the International Working Men's Association (IWMA, the "First International"), of which Karl Marx and Frederick Engels were central leaders. Writing to Engels about the founding of the new organization—which aimed to unite industrial workers in the cities with farm laborers and other rural working people in England, Ireland, Scotland, and Wales—Marx said that "here, the workers' party makes a clean break with the bourgeoisie" politically. Marx joined the Land and Labour League, and a number of its leaders were members of the IWMA General Council. By late 1870, however, bourgeois forces gained dominance in the league's leadership, putting the organization on a course away from the IWMA and from its own founding declaration "that nothing short of a transformation of the existing social and political arrangements [can] avail, and that such a transformation [can] only be effected by the toiling millions themselves."

Amid the powerful nationwide strikes sparked by rail workers in 1877, Marx wrote to Engels:

> This first eruption against the oligarchy of associated capital which has arisen since the Civil War will of course be put down, but it could quite well form the starting point for the establishment of a serious labour party in the United States. . . .
>
> The policy of the new President [of withdrawing Union troops backing Radical Reconstruction governments across the South] will turn the Negroes into allies of the workers, and the large expropriations of land (especially fertile land) in favour of railway, mining, etc., companies will convert the peasants of the West, who are already very disenchanted, into allies of the workers.[35]

As I explained in the 1984 SWP convention report, "The Fight for a Workers and Farmers Government in the United States":

> But this was not to be. The economic and political reserves of the rising U.S. industrial bourgeoisie were far from exhausted, and thus the class-collaborationist illusions among working people still had deep taproots. The class-struggle leadership of the working class and its revolutionary core were still too small in numbers and inexperienced in class combat. Over the next half century the United States would become the world's mightiest imperialist power, and the U.S. labor officialdom would become Uncle Sam's handmaiden.
>
> Moreover, the defeat of Radical Reconstruction dealt a devastating blow to Blacks and other U.S. working people.

---

35. Marx to Engels, July 25, 1877, in *Marx and Engels on the United States*, p. 272. Also in *MECW*, vol. 45, p. 251.

The U.S. working class became more deeply divided by the national oppression of Blacks that was institutionalized in the South on new foundations in the bloody aftermath of 1877. U.S. labor's first giant step toward the formation of major industrial unions did not come for another six decades, and the formation of a labor party, anticipated by Marx 108 years ago, remains an unfulfilled task of our class to this day.

Nonetheless, Marx could not have been more correct about the alliance of social forces that would have to be at the center of a successful revolution in the United States—the working class, toilers who are Black, and exploited farmers.[36]

That remains the prognosis for the American revolution, for the conquest of power and establishment of the dictatorship of the proletariat in the United States, to this day.

III [37]

During one of the breaks, a comrade from Iceland brought to my attention a section from *The Changing Face of U.S. Politics* called "Proletarian and Petty-Bourgeois Nationalism."[38] He asked if I could address it in the summary, in light of what we've been discussing here in relation to the Black struggle, Black nationalism, and the weight of workers who are Black in the fight for the proletarian dictatorship.

---

36. See "Radical Reconstruction: Its Conquests and the Consequences of Its Defeat" in Part II of this book.

37. From the summary of the discussion at the January 2006 meeting.

38. Jack Barnes, *The Changing Face of U.S. Politics: Working-Class Politics and the Unions*, pp. 327–28 [2008 printing].

The section is from a report I gave to a National Committee meeting in April 1979, almost thirty years ago. It deals with the party's turn to get the overwhelming majority of our members and leadership into industrial jobs and unions, and the shifts in politics and the working class that made these steps both necessary and possible. The turn to industry, I said, put the party "in a good position today to clarify our understanding of Black nationalism." There was no reason, I noted, "to revise our view that nationalist consciousness deepens among Blacks as the class struggle deepens."

I pointed to some pitfalls in the ways comrades sometimes attempt to distinguish various political currents in the Black struggle—drawing an inaccurate distinction between "cultural" and "political" nationalism, for example. Closer to being accurate, but still wide of the mark, we sometimes used expressions like "consistent and inconsistent nationalism." Malcolm X was "consistent in fighting for the interests of the Black masses," I pointed out. "That pushed him toward anti-imperialism, toward the class struggle, and toward a bloc with revolutionary socialists. That wasn't a fluke; it was the logic of the consistent pride, self-confidence, and self-assertiveness of an oppressed, overwhelmingly proletarian nationality."

That statement still seems correct to me, as far as it goes, and, above all, we can be proud we *acted* on it. But it's not yet a complete class explanation.

"The Black population is not homogeneous," I noted in the 1979 report. "And the pressures on it originate from different classes. It has petty-bourgeois layers, including many at the head of Black organizations. Black nationalism can be an expression of proletarian consciousness, or it can be petty-bourgeois.

"What is consistent Black nationalism? Proletarian nationalism.

"What is inconsistent Black nationalism? Petty-bourgeois nationalism."

This passage is not as accurate or precise as what we've been discussing at this meeting of the National Committee and what we've been saying for some time. But both the passage from *Changing Face* and what we're discussing here are consistent with how revolutionists have conducted ourselves politically in the class struggle for half a century and more.

Consistent Black nationalism does *not* lead to socialism, however. That's not true. As Sam [Manuel] pointed out in the discussion, who's to say that Louis Farrakhan is not a "consistent Black nationalist"? Or that Elijah Muhammad was not a "consistent Black nationalist"? What criteria would you use? (Once you use *class* criteria, you're no longer talking about nationalism.)

One thing's for sure, from Malcolm's own account, the political views he had come to by late 1964 were not the product of "consistent Black nationalism." In fact, to come to those views, Malcolm said he had to pull back from considering himself a Black nationalist in order to open himself up to true revolutionaries around the world who could have never been nor become Black nationalists of any kind, consistent or not. It was necessary in order to open himself up to *their* experiences, trajectories, and futures. Because revolutionaries the world over had to fight together in a disciplined manner to overturn the social system that breeds exploitation and oppression.

Even more important, there is no such thing as "proletarian nationalism." The only consciousness that is *proletarian* is *class consciousness*, leading to the liberation of the working class and its allies from exploitation and oppression by capital through the fight for the dictatorship of the proletariat. Yes, the proletarian struggle takes place country by country, against particular national ruling classes and the dictatorship of capital carried out by their states. At the same time, however, it is part of the *worldwide* battle for socialism waged by an *international* class, the working class.

That is the material basis of proletarian internationalism, which is inseparable from communism.

Nationalism to communism: a class break

What we were attempting to explain in the 1979 report, as a political guide to *what to do*, was not accomplished by referring to proletarian nationalism versus petty-bourgeois nationalism. We were trying to account for the conflicting *political conduct* of various individuals and currents that call themselves Black nationalists, or had done so at one time. In whose class interests do they fight? Do they seek to advance the interests of the big working-class majority of the oppressed Black nationality? Are their deeds, how they live their lives, their political trajectory consistent with those goals? Are they uncompromisingly internationalist?

When Malcolm left the Nation of Islam in early 1964, it wasn't just a moral break over Elijah Muhammad's hypocritical conduct toward women in the organization—although that was much more important to Malcolm and his deep commitment to integrity than it's usually credited with being, or than we recognized at the time. Malcolm's departure from the Nation wasn't even just a *political* break. Yes, both the moral and political dimensions were important to Malcolm's decision, as he told the *Young Socialist*. "I felt the movement was dragging its feet in many areas," he said in the interview. "It didn't involve itself in the civil or civic or political struggles our people were confronted by. All it did was stress the importance of moral reformation—don't drink, don't smoke, don't permit fornication and adultery. When I found that the hierarchy itself wasn't practicing what it preached, it was clear that this part of its program was bankrupt."

But Malcolm also made a *class* break. While he would not have called it that at the time, Malcolm over the next eleven months deepened his political orientation to the working class, toward the revolutionary proletarian movement on a world scale. He did not fear to go where the political logic of uncompromising struggle against oppression and exploitation took him, regardless of earlier notions and beliefs. Regardless of where in the world he found himself. Regardless of whether it led him across color lines. Regardless of whether it led him across religious lines. (Neither the leadership of Algeria's National Liberation Front nor of the revolutionary Cuban government pretended to be guided by religion. Quite demonstratively the opposite. And Malcolm knew this well.)

And regardless of widespread political prejudice—that is, red-baiting—against those he increasingly recognized as allies, as fellow revolutionists. (That did not include the Stalinists, social democrats, or centrists.)

Malcolm passed all these tests. And it was this class political trajectory that led him to the conclusion to stop using the term Black nationalism to describe his revolutionary course. It was this that led him to insist that any such political course—what at this stage he called an "overall philosophy"—needed to be one that not only centrally incorporated race and its reflection in politics in the imperialist world, but went beyond that toward collaboration with other revolutionaries *to overthrow* that worldwide system. And *that task*, to say the least, was not just "the white man's problem."

During that last year of his life, Malcolm had as yet no precise explanation for the *Militant*'s revolutionary caliber, for its trustworthiness and integrity in printing his speeches, for its accurate coverage of developments in U.S. and world politics that could be found nowhere else. For its fearlessness. He had as yet no precise explanation for the Socialist Workers Party and Young Socialist Alliance, some of whose cadres and leaders he had come to know, to respect, and to trust. These were organizations the majority of whose members were white, but with whom he could work as fellow revolutionists and as political equals—whether with a brother like Clifton DeBerry,[39] or with numerous others of us who weren't "brothers" in that sense.

Malcolm had no final or complete explanation for any of this. But he sure was curious. Why did he come to the Militant Labor Forum the first time in April 1964? Why did he come to speak at a public meeting "downtown," as he put it—something he had never done before in New York? I think he was curious. *Politically* curious. He wanted to meet the organizers and see the audience. What kind of people were they? What kind of organizations? How would they act? How would they respond to him? How would they organize the meeting? How would they chair it? How would they report it in the *Militant*?

And how would they organize *to defend* it? From the day Malcolm held the press conference in March 1964 announcing his break with the Nation of Islam, if not before, he knew full well that individuals in and around the Nation's leadership were planning his assassination, and that cop agencies at every level kept themselves informed of these efforts and sought to exploit them to the rulers' advantage. We knew it too, and acted accordingly in organizing to ensure the security of Malcolm and everyone participating in each one of the three Militant Labor Forums at which he spoke. Malcolm made sure his own bodyguards cooperated fully in that effort. But the central responsibility and decisions were ours. Seldom have party leaders felt the enormity of such a

---

39. Clifton DeBerry (1923–2006) had long been a union militant and Black rights fighter. He had been a Communist Party member before being recruited to the Socialist Workers Party by Farrell Dobbs in Chicago in 1953. DeBerry was a leader of the SWP and its candidate for president of the United States in 1964—the first African American to be nominated by any party as its presidential candidate.

responsibility more than we did at those three meetings. What Malcolm was interested in finding out about the SWP and YSA were not small questions. And pursuing the answers drew him to work with these revolutionaries in more and more uncharted waters.

What Malcolm discovered, combined with what he already knew about the *Militant,* was enough for him to take the initiative to ask to come back and speak after returning from his first Africa trip in 1964. Malcolm hadn't been invited. But "Brother James [Shabazz] told me about it," Malcolm said, and he asked to speak. What Malcolm discovered was enough for him to accept an invitation to speak again at a forum in January 1965. Enough to grant an interview to the *Young Socialist* magazine. Enough to propose giving YSA leaders a list of his young contacts in Africa and Europe to write to and collaborate with. Enough to give serious consideration to a YSA-organized campus speaking tour later in 1965. Enough to demonstratively place a stack of *Militants* for sale each week in the OAAU headquarters. And to ask Clifton DeBerry to be one of those giving a political leadership class, in Clifton's case a class on Marxism, to cadres of the OAAU.

As Malcolm advanced politically following the break with the Nation, he began moving away from ideology—that is, away from false consciousness, which was the only "program" possible in an organization such as the Nation. He began rejecting the Nation's "program" piece by piece. He began looking toward developing a program for liberation that could win, in the world as it exists—not a Black world or a white world, but a dialectically interconnected imperialist world, with strong and brutal states, with the armed power they wielded.

To understand where Malcolm was heading, however, don't turn to the OAAU's "Statement of Basic Aims and Objectives" from June 1964, or even to its "Basic Unity

Program," which was to be announced at the meeting in Harlem where he was assassinated in February 1965. Malcolm's developing program was the generalization of how he acted, and what he had to say in his speeches—speeches Pathfinder Press never allows to go out of print, and that anyone can read and study. Nothing esoteric. No "inside information" was necessary. What you saw, what you heard—and what you can now read in more languages— was the real deal.

The program was still very much a work in progress when Malcolm was killed. It was still more tactics than strategy. It was open to different interpretations. It didn't yet provide those who looked to Malcolm with a coherent world outlook or a regular political rhythm of disciplined activity, of things to do to advance those perspectives. As Malcolm said in the *YS* interview just a few weeks before the assassination: "I still would be hard pressed to give a specific definition of the overall philosophy"—the program, the strategy, the revolutionary practice—"which I think is necessary for the liberation of the Black people in this country."

What was key for Malcolm in the months before his assassination were the practical things. They were the footsteps that could actually be seen in the profane world. They were the footsteps reflecting what he called an "overall philosophy"—*a practical course.* What he was doing. What he was clarifying and explaining. What he was demonstrating by deeds—by where he went, by the cautions he rejected about what "not to do."

As I noted earlier, Malcolm had explained during the *Young Socialists* interview in January 1965 that while he was a leader of the Nation of Islam he had become increasingly frustrated that the organization "didn't involve itself in the civic or civil or political struggles our people were confronted by." More than once while still a leader of the Nation, Malcolm had bridled against this abstentionism.

In 1962, for example, he organized mounting protests in Los Angeles in response to a murderous police assault against several Nation members, until Elijah Muhammad put the kibosh on his course.[40] And in New York City Malcolm led protests by hundreds of Muslims in early 1963 after two members of the Nation were arrested on disorderly conduct charges while selling *Muhammad Speaks* and later convicted, one serving a sixty-day sentence. But Malcolm didn't go into the streets only when Nation of Islam members were assaulted or jailed. While Elijah Muhammad disapproved of such actions, at least they revolved around the Nation.

By the early 1960s, Malcolm on a number of occasions had joined with forces outside the Nation in broader protests by Blacks and other working people. In July 1962 he spoke at a rally in support of a hard-fought strike by New York City health care workers to organize two hospitals. Malcolm publicly praised Local 1199 president Leon Davis, a Jew, for serving thirty days in jail because he rejected a court order to halt the strike. And the following July Malcolm marched in a picket line called by CORE, the Urban League, and the Bedford-Stuyvesant Ministerial Conference to protest hiring discrimination at a construction site in Brooklyn.

None of this was the kind of thing any other Nation of Islam leader did, or was *supposed* to do.

As early as March 1964, on the very day he announced his break with the Nation, Malcolm had told the *New York Times*, "I am prepared to cooperate in local civil rights actions in the South and elsewhere and shall do so because every campaign for specific objectives can only heighten the political consciousness of the Negroes and intensify their

---

40. See Part I, pp. 91–92.

identification against white society. . . ." Saying that Elijah Muhammad had blocked him and other Muslims from participating in civil rights struggles in the South, Malcolm added, "I am going to join in the fight wherever Negroes ask for my help, and I suspect my activities will be on a greater and more intensive scale than in the past."[41]

Shedding this political abstentionism was easier said than done, however. Almost all the members of the OAAU had a similar training to Malcolm's own in the Nation of Islam but much less political experience, confidence, and fewer capacities. It was a small organization. And *political* discipline was a new challenge.

Malcolm wired Martin Luther King in June 1964 offering to send OAAU militants to help defend demonstrators in St. Augustine, Florida, against racist assaults. But the OAAU didn't then organize any of its members to go to Florida to join in the protests and, even if largely in one-on-one discussions, present their own views on self-defense and the road to Black freedom.

Malcolm spoke to young Black rights activists in Selma, Alabama, in February 1965, going there at the last-minute insistence of students whom he had addressed at a campus

---

41. M.S. Handler, "Malcolm X Splits with Muhammad," *New York Times*, March 9, 1964. Even in December 1963, soon after he had been silenced by Elijah Muhammad, Malcolm had told journalist Louis Lomax that most members of the Nation did not share Muhammad's "gift of divine patience with the devil. The younger Black Muslims want to see some action." (Cited in *The Last Year of Malcolm X: Evolution of a Revolutionary*, p. 27.) And in the *Autobiography*, Malcolm wrote that while he was in the Nation, "I felt that, wherever black people committed themselves, in the Little Rocks and the Birminghams and other places, militantly disciplined Muslims should also be there—for all the world to see, and respect, and discuss. It could be heard increasingly in the Negro communities: 'Those Muslims *talk* tough, but they never *do* anything, unless somebody bothers Muslims.'" (*Autobiography* [Penguin edition], p. 397.)

meeting in nearby Tuskegee the day before. Malcolm told the youth in Selma that he was "100 percent for the effort being put forth by the Black folks here . . . to gain the vote." And none of the young people there doubted that. Yet once again the OAAU had not organized its members or others to participate in the marches and protests in Selma.

These abstentionist pressures were not something unique to Malcolm or to the OAAU, of course. To the contrary, overcoming resistance to reaching out to work for common goals with other forces is the art of proletarian politics; it is the most important practical test confronting *any* small revolutionary organization. This is especially the case during periods when a revolutionary course strikes a chord only among small numbers of vanguard working people. When objective political conditions foster what SWP leader Farrell Dobbs once described as a "semisectarian existence," sections of the leadership and membership can become comfortable with relative isolation, organizing even public forums and social activities to guarantee they will become internal gatherings of members and organized periphery at which nonmembers feel like outsiders.

Malcolm recognized this problem of abstentionism. He discussed it publicly on several occasions. Just a week prior to his assassination, for example, he told participants in an OAAU rally in Harlem that while he had been in the Nation, "most of the action that Muslims got involved in was action that I was involved in myself. Where it happened in the country, where there was an action, it was action that I was involved in, because I believed in action."

During the discussion period at that same meeting, someone in the audience asked Malcolm, "Don't you think the organization should have some direct demonstrations, for instance, on discrimination in housing?" Malcolm replied: "I'm for anything you're for as long as it's going to get some results. . . . As long as it's intelligent, as long as it's disciplined, as long as it's aimed in the right direction, I'm for it."[42]

And when, during the *Young Socialist* interview, we asked him about "the activity of white and Black students who went to the South last summer and attempted to register Black people to vote," and about the three young civil rights workers who had been murdered in Mississippi while taking part in that effort, Malcolm spoke positively of the campaign. He added, "but I think they should be permitted to use whatever means at their disposal to defend themselves from the attacks of the Klan, the White Citizens' Council, and other groups."

Malcolm was determined to organize and train the kind of politically disciplined cadre that would make it possible to begin addressing these challenges in action. And to learn in the process—the only way any of us can.

※

Malcolm *did* follow the logic of his revolutionary convictions and discoveries. He didn't flinch when that trajectory meant dashing preconceived notions he had held much of his adult life. As his anti-imperialist, anticapitalist, and internationalist convictions deepened, he had to confront the fact that humanity is not majority Black. And he didn't play cute tricks. He wasn't a demagogue. He didn't simply say, well, humanity is majority nonwhite, as if that solved the contradiction.

Malcolm also faced up to what must have seemed another substantial obstacle: the fact that most revolutionaries in the twentieth century are neither Islamic nor religious in any way. Malcolm didn't move sideways to avoid these hurdles; he leaped right over them. The important thing about the Algerian he had met, Malcolm told us, was that

---

42. "There's a Worldwide Revolution Going On," in *February 1965: The Final Speeches*, p. 139 [2008 printing].

he was "extremely militant" and he was a revolutionary, "a true revolutionary"—demonstrated in the only way possible, revolutionary combat.

That's how Malcolm worked with "the *Militant* people," with the "MLFers," as James and Reuben would say when they came down to 116 University Place to talk. That's how Malcolm worked with members of an organization that was majority Caucasian in racial composition, 100 percent nonbelievers, and communists to boot. Because we were revolutionaries. Because of what we said, what we did, and how we did it—consistently, over time, uncompromisingly. Because of how he sized up individuals he met abroad who were not only acquainted with the *Militant* but also found it useful in their work (including as the only source of accurate news and analysis about Malcolm and the political goals he was working to advance).

In short, *because of where we were going politically.* That's where Malcolm wanted to go too. It was a *political* convergence.

A revolutionary course toward the fight for state power was not much of a leap for Malcolm at that stage—not with the Cuban, Algerian, and other examples for him to study.

If we can understand this, then we're armed to organize and to act on what we know about the historical record of political combat by workers who are Black. We're prepared to recognize that what Trotsky was explaining to SWP leaders in 1933 and 1939 was not Black nationalism, but what the dictatorship of the proletariat opens up for Blacks and other oppressed layers among the broad forces that dare "to storm the heavens," as Marx said. We're equipped to recognize that the increasing involvement of workers who are Black among the most capable, militant, and fearless fighters for revolutionary class-struggle objectives opens up *the possibility* of conquering the proletarian dictatorship in the United States. We can understand why we are right that the

Black question—that Black militancy, Black pride, Black dignity, Black creativity—will come to the fore any time there is a major upsurge in the class struggle, and any time the proletariat advances.

And we will understand why those who deeply aspire to wipe every hated, bloody form of racist oppression and superexploitation off the face of the earth—as much as, if not more so, than anyone—are those who want the dictatorship of the proletariat as a powerful weapon in their hands.

IV [43]

A few final points from our discussions the last several days are important and deserve comment.

First, we have to separate out the Black liberation struggle in the United States from battles against racist bigotry in general and for immigrant rights. And this includes struggles to advance the rights and conditions of immigrants from Haiti, from the English-speaking Caribbean, and from Africa. There are many points of intersection, of course, and, when they combine, the power and solidarity of these interrelated battles reverberate internationally. But the Black struggle in the United States is more than simply one instance, even the politically weightiest instance, of a worldwide struggle against the legacy of African chattel slavery and racist oppression of those with black skin.

James [Harris] took issue during the discussion with remarks by Maggie [Trowe] that SWP branches often don't pay sufficient political attention to sales and political work in the Black community. James said that at least with regard to sales of our press, he didn't think that was accurate. If

---

43. From Barnes's summary remarks to the March 2006 Socialist Workers Party leadership conference.

you looked at the *Militant* subscription base in most areas, James said, you'd find a disproportionately high percentage of subscribers who are Black given their percentage in the population.

That might be true, but it doesn't address the political question that Maggie was posing, at least as I understood it. Let's take Miami, for example. You can drive around the area where the Socialist Workers Party campaign hall is located, and where a number of comrades live, and think you've ended up in Port-au-Prince. There are lots of black faces. There are countless manifestations of the consequences of racism, super-exploitation, and discrimination against immigrants. But we can do lots of sales and political work there without ever getting anywhere close to Liberty City, Overtown, or other parts of the Black community in Miami. That was Maggie's point, I believe. Where do we concentrate our sales and sub-bing in Miami? And I'm sure the relevance of that point is not limited to Florida.[44]

More than a fight against racism

The Black question in the United States is not rooted simply in skin color or African origins. Haitian Americans and African Americans don't share a common political history, a common record of vanguard struggle in this country. As we discussed yesterday, Blacks in the United States can trace their heredity back ten to fifteen generations in North America—through chattel slavery, the Civil War against the slavocracy, the rise and fall of Radical Reconstruction,

---

44. During discussion at a later National Committee meeting in May 2006, James Harris said that he had been stunned when he returned to Los Angeles in March and actually checked the figures on the number of subscriptions sold to Blacks during the winter campaign. He concluded that Maggie Trowe's remarks had been much more accurate than his rejoinder.

resistance to Jim Crow oppression and terror, battles against near peonage and for the right to continue farming the land, massive urban and northern migration, unionization battles and other proletarian-led social struggles, the Black rights movement, the formation of armed self-defense units, organization inside the armed forces during the Vietnam War, and other vanguard—exemplary—political and social fights. That can't be said, in the same way, of those from Haiti, or the English-speaking Caribbean, or Africa. And that fact has social and political implications for the vanguard of the working class, as well as practical consequences for our work.

In a political sense, the Black struggle in the United States is a different question from struggles by those of more recent immigration. For a lesson in how different, read the front page of the paper this morning. The article, headlined "Plight Deepens for Black Men, Studies Warn," reports, among other things, that 72 percent of male high school "dropouts" in their twenties who are Black are jobless (compared to 34 percent of "dropouts" who are white), and that 60 percent of male "dropouts" who are Black have spent time in prison by their mid-thirties. Those figures come from several recent studies, and there's every reason to believe they are at least roughly representative of the actual situation. These conditions affect the African American population in this country in ways that are substantially different from first- or second-generation immigrants, including those of African ancestry.

Yes, it's important—very important—that we carry out political work among Haitian workers in Miami, Washington, D.C., New York, Boston, and other areas where there are concentrations. Yes, we want to attract Africans living in the United States to the communist movement, and we have an added political tool—above and beyond our overall Marxist political arsenal—in our books and pamphlets by

Thomas Sankara, as well as by Nelson Mandela.[45]

But it's possible to do all these things and not touch the question of advancing our participation in the struggles of workers and youth who are African Americans. *To do that* takes political consciousness. It takes habits of discipline, political objectivity, and revolutionary centralism. And it takes an understanding of the strategic and programmatic questions we've been discussing at the last two National Committee meetings.

A number of comrades have commented at both these meetings that workers who are Black respond with interest not just to *Militant* headlines and articles on the fight against anti-Black racism, but to those on union questions, defense of political rights, immigration, women's liberation, the U.S. war against Iraq, the Cuban Revolution, the class struggle in Venezuela, and so on. If that weren't true, then nothing we're saying would make sense politically. But it is true, and for all the reasons we've been discussing about the historical record of struggle by workers who are Black.

A U.S. question and a world question

As comrades from Canada have pointed out in the discussion, the situation there is different. A much larger percentage of the population that is black are relatively recent immigrants.[46]

---

45. Among the titles that can be found on Pathfinder's web site (www .pathfinderpress.com), as well as in the ads at the end of this book, are *Thomas Sankara Speaks, Women's Liberation and the African Freedom Struggle* by Thomas Sankara, *Nelson Mandela Speaks, How Far We Slaves Have Come!* by Nelson Mandela and Fidel Castro, and *Capitalism and the Transformation of Africa: Reports from Equatorial Guinea* by Mary-Alice Waters and Martín Koppel.

46. According to 2001 Canadian government figures, of the more than 660,000 blacks in Canada, 10 percent had parents who were both born in Canada.

Throughout the entire history of the Communist League and its predecessors in Canada, comrades have been involved in resistance to anti-black racism, cop brutality, and other struggles. They increasingly keep running into militant workers who are black—on and off the job, in Toronto, Montreal, Vancouver, and elsewhere. Over the past couple of years, as comrades have described here, they've sold books and subscriptions and developed relations with a layer of workers from Sudan who were leaders and cadres of the strike by packinghouse workers in Brooks, Alberta, organized by the United Food and Commercial Workers.

The question we've been discussing, however, is very specific.

Politically, the Black question in Canada is an extension of the Black question in the United States. That's true, above all, because the Black struggle in this country since the 1950s has had such a powerful political impact on those of African ancestry (and other targets of racism) everywhere in the world. That's true from Canada, to the Caribbean and Latin America (the Black Power movement of the late 1960s and early 1970s was a powerful expression of black pride that politically transformed the Caribbean), to Western Europe, to Africa itself. The impact in many ways has been even more direct in Canada due to the geographical and cultural closeness of the two countries.

I remember when I was in the Chicago branch in the early 1960s we'd often go over to Detroit on regional trips. In the course of comrades' week-to-week activity there, they always knew workers and students who were Black from Windsor and elsewhere in Ontario. People involved in Black rights activity and other political work went back and forth across the border all the time, and still do. Many Blacks in Canada were deeply influenced politically by Malcolm X and by political developments in the U.S. class struggle. All that continues to be the case.

The Black question in Canada is an American question for another reason too—its origins. After losing the war in the first American revolution, the British army organized an amazing military and social feat. Earlier in the conflict they had promised emancipation to any slave or indentured worker in the thirteen colonies who took up arms against the rebel colonists. And thousands did. (The rebels did *not* promise emancipation.)[47] In 1783, after their defeat, the British forces evacuated more than 3,000 Blacks from the port of New York and resettled them in Nova Scotia. That was the first substantial Black population in Canada, and many of their descendents remain there today. More than 13,000 Blacks live in Halifax and—unlike in the rest of Canada—more than 90 percent are native-born. Other descendents emigrated from Nova Scotia to elsewhere in Canada or abroad.

In face of anti-Black racism, of course, all those of African origin in Canada—whether born in Halifax or Windsor; or in Kingston, Jamaica; Port-au-Prince, Haiti; Accra, Ghana; or Dakar, Senegal; whether their main European language is English or French or Spanish—come to recognize that they are simply Blacks in the eyes of bigots. The same is true of immigrants of African origin in the United Kingdom and continental Europe, as well as in parts of Latin America and the Caribbean.

---

47. In November 1775, Lord Dunmore—a leader of British military forces based in Virginia—issued a proclamation granting freedom to all indentured servants or Black slaves held by supporters of independence "that are able and willing to bear Arms" and join "His Majesty's Troops." Not until more than three years later in early 1779—as British troops swept across Georgia and South Carolina—did the rebels' Continental Congress urge the governments of those two states to raise an army of Black slaves who would be freed and their former owners compensated. General George Washington, himself a slave owner, refused to approve this proposal. And it was flatly and indignantly rejected by both the Georgia and South Carolina state governments.

Nationality is a social and political question, a historical question, not a biological one. In Sudan, Sudanese may consider themselves Arab or African, Muslim or Christian. Some give priority to a tribal identification, while others consider themselves first and foremost Sudanese. In North America or Europe, however, regardless of their pigmentation, they are simply considered Black. This is not a science of the rainbow. It's the class reality of social and political life under the imperialist world order.

That's important. The fight against Black oppression, as the Communist International recognized more than eighty years ago, is a world question. But the common history of struggle that marks the Black nationality in the United States gives it a unique weight and place in the revolutionary fight for the dictatorship of the proletariat in this country, and—because of the power of U.S. imperialism—in the worldwide struggle for socialism as well.

Forged in victories, not defeats

During the discussion, a comrade used a shorthand formulation that I've heard before: that the Black nationality in the United States "was forged by the defeat of Radical Reconstruction."

That's not accurate.

If Radical Reconstruction *had not been defeated,* of course, and if the fight for "forty acres and a mule" *had succeeded,* then it wasn't foreordained that the freed slaves would have emerged as an *oppressed* nationality by the late 1800s. That's true. They would have been part of a vast, fighting proletarian social movement of workers, free farmers, and former slaves.

But what forged the Black nationality in the United States was not what Farrell had accurately called "the worst setback" in the history of the U.S. working class! The Black nationality was forged not by a defeat but by the capacities, the vanguard class-struggle activity, and the social and political consciousness of the emancipated slaves. It was forged as they *used* their freedom to transform themselves from slaves into vanguard workers and farmers, into makers of history, into those who *act*.

The smashing of Radical Reconstruction was a bloody counterrevolution carried out by armed rightist gangs such as the Ku Klux Klan, Knights of the White Camelia, and others. Following adoption of the Reconstruction Acts of 1867, federal troops were stationed throughout the South in order, among other things, to enforce the citizenship and voting rights of freed slaves under the Fourteenth and Fifteenth Amendments.[48] By the mid-1870s these federal forces initially began being ordered not to intervene to defend elected Reconstruction state governments, and by 1877 the troops were withdrawn altogether.

That defeat not only closed the door to any further radical, popular, plebeian extension of the American bourgeois revolution deepened by the Civil War and the elimination of slavery; it threw the gears into reverse for nearly a century.

Don't forget, we have always recognized the Civil War, together with Radical Reconstruction, as the Second American Revolution. By the closing years of the 1800s, however, it was already too late in the United States for any additional successful advances of the bourgeois revolution. With the growth of capitalist monopolization and the rising dominance of finance capital during the three decades following the Civil War, the United States emerged as an imperialist power by the end of the century. What is called in the United States the Spanish-American War was the world's first imperialist war. From that point forward, further advances in the struggle for Black rights—despite repeated defaults

---

48. See discussion of Thirteenth, Fourteenth, and Fifteenth Amendments in Part II, p. 160.

and betrayals by the class-collaborationist officialdom of the unions and misleaders of social democratic and Stalinist organizations—have been inextricably bound up with the line of march of the working class toward the conquest of power and establishment of the proletarian dictatorship.

Record of accomplishments

Coming out of the Civil War, toilers who were Black fought to stop the reimposition of slavery-like contract gangs in the fields across the South. They fought for land. They waged battles during Radical Reconstruction for schools, for suffrage, for cheap credit and agricultural extension services, and other needs of the toilers as a whole. They organized armed resistance to violent rightist assaults on the Reconstruction state governments.

The capitalist rulers try to hide the history of Radical Reconstruction, just as they try to hide the history of labor battles in this country. In school most of us were taught little more about Reconstruction than tales of the scandalous "scalawags" from the South and notorious "carpetbaggers" from the North. They want to hide the truth because it explodes every racist and anti-working-class notion about what Blacks can accomplish, about the potential of fighting alliances between toilers who are Black and white, and much more. That falsification only began to be undone on a broad scale by the rise of a mass proletarian movement led by Blacks.[49]

---

49. In fact in 1955, just as the mass Black rights struggles were getting under way in Montgomery, Alabama, a little book entitled *The Strange Career of Jim Crow* was published, written by a historian born in the South named C. Vann Woodward (New York: Oxford University Press, 1955, 2002). That book ended up being adopted by many civil rights militants and used by them to prove that social relations in the South after the Civil War had not always been as they became under Jim Crow segregation.

W.E.B. Du Bois's *Black Reconstruction 1860–1880* (New York: The

Radical Reconstruction also marked the high point of the fight to recognize Asian immigrants—especially the large numbers of Chinese laborers brought here to build the transcontinental railroad—as human beings, worthy of the same rights to citizenship and property as those whose skin was black, white, or any other shade in the spectrum. Political equality for Asian workers too was set back for nearly a century by the defeats of 1877. (The publication of *Our History Is Still Being Written* should remind us of how the U.S. rulers also hide the true story of the accomplishments and oppression of immigrant Chinese labor in this country, as they have falsified history with regard to Native Americans and Mexicanos for many decades, too.)

Small farmers and wageworkers who were white became involved in the struggles that marked Radical Reconstruction as well. The social conquests of the most advanced Reconstruction regimes, as in South Carolina, were extremely popular among toilers, whatever their skin color. Many working farmers and wageworkers in the mountains and elsewhere throughout the South had never supported slavery. They resisted the Confederacy during the Civil War, including sometimes by refusing conscription and payment of special taxes. After the war, they recognized they had never *had* local governments like many that arose during Reconstruction. They had never *had* governments that provided free public education, that helped them obtain low-interest loans, that set up agricultural schools and sent itinerant farming consultants into rural areas. All this was very popular.

Free Press, 1935, 1998) offers a rich and detailed description of what actually unfolded across the South during those years, despite its "third period" Stalinist exaggerations, such as depicting some Reconstruction governments as the dictatorship of the proletariat. If you construe Du Bois's phrase "Black Reconstruction" to mean "disproportionately Black-led Reconstruction," then the title of the book points to the vanguard place of African American toilers in this process.—JB

After the defeat of Radical Reconstruction, Blacks waged countless skirmishes—during the 1880s and 1890s, and on into the twentieth century—against the imposition of Jim Crow segregation and racist terror across the South. They fought to hold onto their land, and continue to do so. And they have been in the vanguard of all the proletarian-led social and political struggles of the twentieth century that we've pointed to.

This *record of struggle* is what initially forged the Black nationality. It was the product of a positive political conquest, not a great historic defeat. The Black nationality was carved out of these *accomplishments*, not out of its own *oppression*. It was a registration of consciousness of political *worth*.

We have to recognize both pieces of what happened. We need to understand the defeat of Radical Reconstruction, which laid the basis for the bloody imposition of Jim Crow terror and segregation. That was when the oppressed character of the Black nationality was settled, something that will not be undone short of a successful proletarian revolution. But we must also see the struggles before, during, and since Radical Reconstruction that forged a nationality that has produced generation after generation of vanguard militants in the weightiest, the most plebeian, social and political struggles in this country.

We need to be clear when we talk about the forging of the Black nationality. Because what toilers in this country, Black and white, laid the historic foundations for during the Civil War and Radical Reconstruction, the Second American Revolution, is one of the great pledges of what mass proletarian and popular movements can achieve when working people establish governments that truly act in the interests of the exploited and the oppressed.

Glossary

African National Congress (ANC) – Founded 1912. Led struggle against apartheid regime in South Africa. Banned 1960–90. In 1994 won South Africa's first election based on universal suffrage, with ANC leader Nelson Mandela elected president.

Austerlitz, Friedrich (1862–1931) – Class-collaborationist leader of Austrian Social Democracy; editor of its daily *Arbeiter Zeitung*.

Babu, Abdulrahman Mohamed (1924–1996) – Leader of anticolonial struggle in African country of Zanzibar. Served as foreign minister after independence from Britain in 1964. Following union with Tanganyika, held posts in Tanzanian government until 1972. Sentenced to death on treason charges 1975; released 1978 after international campaign.

Ben Bella, Ahmed (1918–) – Leader of National Liberation Front (FLN) that led 8-year struggle for Algeria's independence from France. President of workers and peasants government that came to power in 1962. Collaborated with Cuban leadership to advance anti-imperialist struggles in Africa and Latin America. Overthrown in June 1965 coup led by Houari Boumedienne.

Berger, Victor (1860–1929) – Leader of right wing of U.S. Socialist Party from Milwaukee; promoted anti-immigrant and anti-Black views. Socialist Party member of Congress 1910–12, 1922–28.

Bishop, Maurice (1944–1983) – Central leader of New Jewel Movement of Grenada that overthrew U.S.-backed dictatorship of Eric Gairy in March 1979. Prime minister of workers and farmers government. Murdered in October 1983 counterrevolutionary coup by Stalinist forces loyal to Deputy Prime Minister Bernard Coard.

Breitman, George (1916–1986) – Author *The Last Year of Malcolm X: Evolution of a Revolutionary*; editor of several books of Malcolm X's speeches. Joined communist movement 1935; member Socialist Workers Party National Committee 1939–81. Split from SWP 1983.

Cannon, James P. (1890–1974) – A founding leader of U.S. Communist Party 1919; expelled 1928 for supporting political fight led by Leon Trotsky in Communist International to continue implementing Lenin's proletarian internationalist course. First editor of *Militant*; founding leader of Communist League of America 1929. Socialist Workers Party national secretary 1938–53; national chairman 1953–74.

Carter, James (1924–) – Democratic Party president of U.S. 1977–81.

Castro, Fidel (1926–) – Central leader of Cuban revolutionary struggle from 1952; founder and central leader of July 26 Revolutionary Movement; commander in chief Rebel Army 1956–58. Prime minister revolutionary government 1959–76; president Council of State and Council of Ministers 1976–2008, commander in chief Revolutionary Armed Forces 1959–2008. First secretary Communist Party of Cuba from founding in 1965.

Chiang Kai-shek (1887–1975) – Leader of bourgeois Nationalist Party (Kuomintang) in China from 1925. After bloody crushing of second Chinese Revolution of 1925–27, headed dictatorship overthrown by third Chinese Revolution in 1949. Fled to Taiwan and established U.S.-backed counterrevolutionary regime there.

Choy, Armando (1934–) – Brigadier general Revolutionary Armed Forces (FAR). Fought in Cuban revolutionary war. Currently delegate of Ministry of Transportation to Maritime Port Operations and president of Working Group for Cleanup, Preservation, and Development of Havana Bay. Coauthor *Our History Is Still Being Written: The Story of Three Chinese-Cuban Generals in the Cuban Revolution*.

Chui, Gustavo (1938–) – Brigadier general Revolutionary Armed Forces. Fought in Cuban revolutionary war. Currently part of national leadership of Association of Combatants of the Cuban Revolution. President of Havana Chung Wah Society, umbrella organization of Chinese societies in Cuba. Coauthor *Our History Is Still Being Written: The Story of Three Chinese-Cuban Generals in the Cuban Revolution.*

CIO (Congress of Industrial Organizations) – Founded 1935 as Committee for Industrial Organization within craft-union-based American Federation of Labor, at initiative of United Mineworkers of America president John L. Lewis. Suspended from AFL 1936, expelled 1938. Drives to organize previously nonunion steel, auto, rubber, and other industries spurred proletarian-led social movement in mid-1930s. Merged with AFL 1955.

Cleage, Albert (Jaramogi Abebe Agyeman) (1911–2000) – Organizer Black nationalist Grass Roots conference, Detroit, November 1963, at which Malcolm X gave last talk as Nation of Islam leader. Founding leader with Milton Henry and others of Freedom Now Party, an independent Black party; FNP candidate for Michigan governor 1964. Later returned to Democratic Party. Christian minister.

Coard, Bernard (1944–) – Deputy prime minister Grenada, 1979–83. Led Stalinist secret faction in New Jewel Movement that overthrew workers and farmers government and assassinated Maurice Bishop and other revolutionaries. Arrested after 1983 U.S. invasion. Convicted of Bishop's murder 1986; death sentence commuted 1991. Released September 2009.

CORE (Congress of Racial Equality) – Black rights organization founded 1942. In 1960s initiated Freedom Rides to desegregate interstate bus and other public transportation in South; led other civil rights actions across U.S.

Cox, Courtland (1941–) – A leader of Student Nonviolent Coordinating Committee (SNCC) in mid-1960s; later head of minority business development in Commerce Department in Clinton administration.

Curtiss, Charles (1908–1993) – Early member of Communist League of America. Worked with Trotsky in Mexico as representative of Fourth International secretariat 1938–39. Left Socialist Workers Party 1951.

Deacons for Defense – Organized self-defense for Black communities and civil rights militants, primarily in Louisiana and Mississippi, from 1964 to 1968

DeBerry, Clifton (1923–2006) – A longtime leader of Socialist Workers Party, union militant, and Black rights fighter. Member of Communist Party before joining Socialist Workers Party 1953. SWP candidate for U.S. president 1964, first African American nominated for that office by any political party.

Debs, Eugene V. (1855–1926) – Five-time presidential candidate of Socialist Party and spokesperson for party's left wing prior to 1917 Russian Revolution. Campaigned against first imperialist world war and in solidarity with Bolshevik revolution. For opposition to war, convicted in 1918 of violating federal Espionage Act; served 2 years and 8 months of 10-year prison sentence. Remained in SP following 1919 founding of Communist Party.

Dobbs, Farrell (1907–1983) – Socialist Workers Party national secretary 1953–72. Joined Communist League of America 1934. A central leader of 1934 Minneapolis Teamsters strikes; general organizer in late 1930s of Teamsters' 11-state over-the-road campaign that organized tens of thousands of drivers and other workers across Upper Midwest. Served 12 months in federal prison 1944–45 after 1941 conviction on frame-up conspiracy charges under federal Smith "Gag" Act for organizing working-class opposition to Washington's aims in World War II. Four-time SWP candidate for president of U.S. Author of 4-volume series on Teamster struggles and 2-volume *Revolutionary Continuity: Marxist Leadership in the U.S.*

Dreke, Víctor (1937–) – Rebel Army combatant in Cuba's 1956–58 revolutionary war. Commanded Cuban units in Escambray mountains 1962–65, cleaning out U.S.-backed counterrevolutionary forces. Second in command under Che Guevara of Cuban volunteer column in Congo, 1965. Led Cuban internationalists aiding national liberation forces in Guinea-Bissau

1966–68. Has held major responsibilities for Cuba's relations with countries of Africa for four decades.

Du Bois, W.E.B. (1868–1963) – Leader in struggle for Black rights in U.S.; a founder of NAACP in 1909. Author *Black Reconstruction, The Souls of Black Folk,* other works.

Eastman, Max (1883–1969) – Supporter of Russian Revolution and translator of works by Trotsky in 1930s. By late '30s renounced socialism; became anticommunist and an editor of *Reader's Digest.*

Eisenhower, Dwight (1890–1969) – Republican president of U.S. 1953–61.

Epton, Bill (1932–2002) – Chairman of Harlem branch of Maoist Progressive Labor Party in 1960s.

Farmer, James (1920–1999) – A founding leader of Congress of Racial Equality. After leaving CORE in late 1960s, was assistant secretary of health, education and welfare in Nixon administration.

Farrakhan, Louis (1933–) – Joined Nation of Islam 1955; leader of Boston Temple. Helped lead campaign demonizing Malcolm X. Since 1978 split in Nation, main leader of group still using name.

Ford, James W. (1893–1957) – Communist Party vice-presidential candidate 1932, 1936, 1940.

Fort-Whiteman, Lovett (1894–1939) – Early member of Communist Party and national organizer, American Negro Labor Congress. Assigned to work in Soviet Union 1933; arrested 1937 during Stalin purges; died in labor camp in Siberia.

Fourier, Charles (1772–1837) – French utopian socialist.

Francis, Reuben – Leading member of Organization of Afro-American Unity; chief bodyguard of Malcolm X.

Freedom Now Party (FNP) – Independent Black political party founded August 1963. Based primarily in Michigan, fielded 39 candidates there in 1964 elections; ran campaigns in San Francisco, New York, New Haven. Disbanded soon after elections.

Frank, Pierre (1905–1984) – A founder of opposition in French Communist Party to Stalinist counterrevolution against Lenin's

course; secretary to Trotsky in Turkey 1932–33. Longtime
leader of Fourth International and its French section.

Gairy, Eric (1922–1997) – First prime minister of Grenada following independence from Britain 1974–79, establishing tyran-
nical regime. Overthrown 1979 by popular revolution led by
Maurice Bishop.

Garvey, Marcus (1887–1940) – Founded Universal Negro Improvement Association in 1914 in native Jamaica, advocating "back to
Africa" movement. Moved to New York 1916. Recruited thousands to UNIA in U.S. and Caribbean, with chapters in many
cities and towns. Imprisoned in U.S. 1925; deported 1927.

Goldwater, Barry (1909–1998) – Republican U.S. senator from Ari-
zona 1953–64, 1969–87. Party's presidential candidate 1964.

González, Fernando (1963–) – One of Cuban revolutionaries
known as Cuban Five. Internationalist combatant in Angola
1987–89; awarded combat medals. Volunteered in early 1990s
for assignment in U.S. monitoring activities of CIA-trained
Cuban counterrevolutionaries. Arrested by FBI 1998. Convicted in 2001 frame-up trial of being "unregistered foreign
agent" and other charges; sentenced to 19 years in prison. In
2008 federal appeals court ordered his sentence reduced.

González, René (1956–) – One of Cuban revolutionaries known as
Cuban Five. Born in Chicago, returned to Cuba with family
1961. Active in Union of Young Communists. Internationalist
combatant in Angola 1977–79; decorated for bravery. In 1990
accepted volunteer mission in U.S. monitoring counterrevolutionaries organizing attacks on Cuba. Arrested 1998; convicted
in 2001 frame-up trial of being "unregistered foreign agent"
and other charges. Sentenced to 19 years in prison, reduced
in December 2009 to 17 years and 9 months.

Greenberg, Jack (1924–) – Director-counsel of NAACP Legal Defense Fund, 1961–1984.

Guerrero, Antonio (1958–) – One of Cuban revolutionaries known
as Cuban Five. Born in Miami, went to school in Havana; active in Union of Young Communists. Graduated University
of Kiev as airport construction engineer; artist and poet. In
early 1990s volunteered to live in South Florida, monitoring

counterrevolutionary groups organizing attacks on Cuba. Arrested 1998; framed up and convicted 2001 of "espionage conspiracy" and other charges. Sentenced to life term plus 10 years, reduced in October 2009 to 21 years and 10 months.

Guevara, Ernesto Che (1928–1967) – Argentine-born leader of Cuban Revolution. Rebel Army commander during Cuba's 1956–58 revolutionary war. Held central responsibilities in revolutionary government, including minister of industry and president of National Bank. Led volunteer internationalist columns in Congo 1965, Bolivia 1966–67; wounded, captured, and murdered by Bolivian army in CIA-organized operation.

Haley, Alex (1921–1992) – Conducted and edited interviews that became *The Autobiography of Malcolm X*; author of *Roots*.

Halstead, Fred (1927–1988) – Socialist Workers Party leader and party's 1968 presidential candidate. Longtime writer for *Militant* and a leader of anti–Vietnam War movement in U.S. Author *Out Now! A Participant's Account of the Movement in the U.S. against the Vietnam War*.

Hamer, Fannie Lou (1917–1977) – Former sharecropper. Active in SNCC in Mississippi. Cofounded Mississippi Freedom Democratic Party 1964, challenging all-white state delegation to Democratic National Convention. Democrats seated all-white delegation.

Hansen, Joseph (1910–1979) – Joined Communist League of America 1934. Secretary to Leon Trotsky in Mexico 1937–40. A longtime central leader of Socialist Workers Party. Member SWP National Committee 1940–75. Editor of *Militant, International Socialist Review,* and *Intercontinental Press.* Author *Dynamics of the Cuban Revolution, The Leninist Strategy of Party Building: The Debate on Guerrilla Warfare in Latin America* and *Cosmetics, Fashions, and the Exploitation of Women.*

Harper's Weekly – New York-based magazine 1857–1916. Known for its woodcut drawings of U.S. Civil War and Reconstruction and cartoons by Thomas Nast pillorying Tammany Hall machine in New York.

Haywood, Harry (1898–1978) – Member of African Blood Brotherhood before joining Communist Party 1925. First national secretary of CP-led League of Struggle for Negro Rights 1930. Advocate of CP's call in late '20s and early '30s for separate "Negro soviet republic" in southern "black belt." Broke with CP 1958 and became Maoist.

Henry, Milton (Gaidi Obadele) (1919–2006) – Leader of Freedom Now Party in Detroit and FNP candidate for U.S. Congress 1964. Later a founding leader of Republic of New Afrika.

Henry, Richard (Imari Obadele) – Leader of Freedom Now Party in Detroit. Later a founding leader of Republic of New Afrika.

Hernández, Gerardo (1965–) – One of Cuban revolutionaries known as Cuban Five. Graduate of Higher Institute of International Relations in Havana. Internationalist combatant in Angola 1989–90; decorated for combat missions. In early 1990s volunteered to monitor counterrevolutionary groups in U.S. organizing attacks on Cuba. Arrested 1998; convicted 2001 on frame-up "murder conspiracy," "espionage conspiracy," and other charges. Sentenced to two life terms plus 15 years.

Hook, Sidney (1902–1989) – Taught philosophy at New York University. Sympathizer of communist movement in 1930s. Member of American Workers Party 1934. Vocal anticommunist by 1940s.

Hoover, J. Edgar (1895–1972) – Director of Federal Bureau of Investigation 1924–72.

Huiswoud, Otto (1893–1961) – Immigrant to U.S. from Dutch Guiana (today Suriname). Member of African Blood Brotherhood in Harlem; founding member of U.S. Communist Party 1919. Delegate to Fourth Comintern Congress 1922, where he chaired Commission on Negro Question. Barred from U.S. after World War II; moved to Netherlands.

Jay, John (1745–1829) – President of Continental Congress during American Revolution 1778–79; first chief justice of U.S. Supreme Court 1789–94.

Jefferson, Thomas (1743–1826) – Drafted U.S. Declaration of Independence 1776. President of U.S. 1801–09.

Johnson, Andrew (1808–1875) – Democratic U.S. senator from Tennessee 1857–62. Remained in Senate after secession and supported Union in Civil War. Elected vice president on National Union ticket with Lincoln 1864. President of U.S. 1865–69; actively opposed Radical Reconstruction.

Johnson, Lyndon (1908–1973) – Democratic president of U.S. 1963–69.

July 26 Revolutionary Movement – Founded June 1955 by Fidel Castro and other Moncada combatants, along with other forces, to advance revolutionary struggle to overturn U.S.-backed tyranny of Fulgencio Batista. After 1959 victory fused with other groups backing revolution, leading to founding of Cuban Communist Party 1965.

King, Coretta Scott (1927–2006) – Civil rights activist; wife of Martin Luther King.

King, Joseph P. (b. 1909) – President Washington Park Forum in Chicago's Black community and pastor International Church. Active in fight against Jim Crow since 1930s; led protests in Chicago against 1955 lynching of Emmett Till. Ran for Congress in 1958 against capitalist parties as candidate of United Socialist Election Campaign.

Labañino, Ramón (1963–) – One of Cuban revolutionaries known as Cuban Five. Jailed in U.S. since 1998. High school student leader in Cuba, joining Union of Young Communists. Officer in Interior Ministry. In early 1990s volunteered for mission to monitor counterrevolutionary groups in U.S. organizing attacks on Cuba. Convicted on "espionage conspiracy" frame-up and other charges. Sentenced to life in prison plus 18 years, reduced in December 2009 to 30 years.

Lankin, Sol (1910–1969) – Founding member of Communist League of America. Guard in Trotsky's home in Mexico 1939.

Lenin, V.I. (1870–1924) – Founder of Bolshevik Party. Central leader of 1917 October Revolution in Russia. Chair of Council of People's Commissars (Soviet government) 1917–24; member Executive Committee of Communist International 1919–24.

Lewis, John (1940–) – Chairman Student Nonviolent Coordinating Committee (SNCC) 1963–66. Democratic congressman from Georgia since 1986.

Lewis, John L. (1880–1969) – President United Mine Workers of America 1919–60; president CIO 1935–40.

Lincoln, Abraham (1809–1865) – Republican president of U.S. 1861–65; commander in chief of Union Army in Civil War. Assassinated in plot by Confederate supporters.

Lumumba, Patrice (1925–1961) – Leader of Congo's fight for independence from Belgium. First Congolese prime minister June 1960; overthrown September 1960 in imperialist-backed coup led by Joseph Mobutu. Murdered January 1961 with complicity of UN troops and support of U.S., Belgian, and other imperialist governments.

Luxemburg, Rosa (1871–1919) – Polish-born leader of revolutionary wing of German Social Democratic Party. Jailed 1915 for opposing World War I. Founder of German Communist Party; murdered by army officers at instigation of Social Democratic government.

Maceo, Antonio (1845–1896) – Military leader in Cuba's 19th century independence war against Spain. Black Cuban, popularly known as Bronze Titan. Refused to lay down arms in 1878 in action known as Baraguá Protest. Killed in battle.

Mandela, Nelson (1918–) – Leader of African National Congress of South Africa. Imprisoned by apartheid regime 1962–90; released amid advancing revolutionary struggle. Elected president of South Africa in first post-apartheid election 1994, serving until 1999.

McKay, Claude (1889–1948) – Jamaican-born writer and immigrant to U.S. Supporter of Russian Revolution and member of Communist Party in early 1920s. Attended Fourth Comintern Congress 1922. Lived in Europe for decade before returning to U.S. in early 1930s and breaking with communism.

Militant, The – Published since 1928, based in New York. Identified on masthead as "A socialist newsweekly published in the interests of working people." Broadly reflects positions of Socialist Workers Party.

Minor, Robert (1884–1952) – Radical cartoonist and anarchist before World War I; joined CP 1920. Later became leading Stalinist functionary.

Moncada Rebellion – On July 26, 1953, some 160 revolutionaries under Fidel Castro's command launched insurrectionary attack on Moncada army barracks in Santiago de Cuba and garrison in Bayamo, opening revolutionary struggle against Fulgencio Batista dictatorship. After attack's failure, more than 50 captured revolutionaries were massacred. Castro and others were sentenced to up to 15 years; released May 1955 after mass defense campaign forced Batista regime to grant amnesty.

Muhammad, Elijah (1897–1975) – Leader of Nation of Islam from 1934 to his death.

NAACP (National Association for the Advancement of Colored People) – Civil rights organization founded in 1909 by W.E.B. Du Bois and others.

National Black Independent Political Party (NBIPP) – Founded November 1980 at Philadelphia convention of 1,500. Propagandized for political action by Blacks independent of Democratic and Republican parties and to "oppose racism, imperialism, sexual oppression, and capitalist exploitation," in words of charter. Ceased functioning in mid-1980s.

Nation of Islam – Formed in Detroit 1930 by Wallace Fard; led by Elijah Muhammad 1934–75. Grew rapidly in 1950s, with Malcolm X as best-known spokesman until his break in early 1964.

Parks, Gordon (1912–2006) – U.S. author, photographer, and film director; interviewed Malcolm X in February 1965.

Patterson, William (1891–1980) – Joined U.S. Communist Party in mid-1920s. Executive secretary of International Labor Defense and Civil Rights Congress, becoming CP leader as party consolidated Stalinist course in late 1920s and '30s.

Pyatakov, G.L. (P. Kievsky) (1890–1937) – Bolshevik leader who opposed right to self-determination of oppressed nations. After 1917 held leading posts in Soviet industry. Supporter of communist opposition led by Trotsky 1923–28; capitulated to Stalin but executed during Moscow trials.

Randolph, A. Philip (1899–1979) – Founding president Brotherhood of Sleeping Car Porters, 1925. President National Negro

Congress, 1936–40. Central leader of March on Washington movement during World War II. Active in civil rights movement in 1950s and '60s. Backed Democrat Lyndon Johnson in 1964 presidential election.

Renner, Karl (1870–1950) – Social Democratic chancellor of Austria 1918–20; president of national assembly 1930–33.

Richardson, Gloria (1922–) – Leader Nonviolent Action Committee, which organized street protests against segregation in Cambridge, Maryland 1962–64. Refused to urge nonviolence in face of racist thugs or call off protests despite National Guard occupation of Cambridge.

Roa, Raúl (1907–1982) – Cuba's foreign minister 1959–76. Known as "Chancellor of Dignity." Rebuilt and led diplomatic corps in revolution's early years. Member Communist Party Central Committee from 1965; vice president National Assembly at time of death.

Roosevelt, Franklin D. (1882–1945) – Democratic president of U.S. 1933–45. New Deal and War Deal policies in Great Depression sought to divert working-class militancy, maintain capitalist rule, and consolidate U.S. imperialism's world dominance.

Rustin, Bayard (1910–1987) – An organizer of August 1963 March on Washington civil rights action. Leader of pro-imperialist Social Democrats USA and AFL-CIO–backed A. Philip Randolph Institute.

Sandinista National Liberation Front (FSLN) – Founded 1961 by Carlos Fonseca to organize struggle against U.S.-backed Somoza dictatorship. Led workers and peasants government after 1979 revolution. In late 1980s leadership retreated from government's initial revolutionary proletarian course.

Sankara, Thomas (1949–1987) – Central leader of popular democratic revolution in Burkina Faso from 1983 until his assassination in counterrevolutionary coup led by Blaise Compaoré.

SCLC (Southern Christian Leadership Conference) – Founded 1957 to organize civil rights activity across South. Led by Martin Luther King until his death in 1968.

Shabazz, James (Abdullah H. Abdur-Razzaq) – Split from Nation of Islam along with Malcolm X, becoming his secretary.

A leader of Muslim Mosque Inc. and Organization of Afro-American Unity.

Shaw, Ed (1923–1995) – Joined Socialist Workers Party as merchant seaman 1944. Member SWP National Committee 1959–81. Midwest director Fair Play for Cuba Committee early 1960s. SWP candidate for vice president 1964.

Sío Wong, Moisés (1938–) – Fought in 1956–58 Cuban revolutionary war. Brigadier general in Revolutionary Armed Forces. President National Institute of State Reserves, 1986–2008. President Cuba-China Friendship Association. Coauthor *Our History Is Still Being Written: The Story of Three Chinese-Cuban Generals in the Cuban Revolution.*

SNCC (Student Nonviolent Coordinating Committee) – Formed April 1960 out of Woolworth sit-ins. Active in Black rights battles in early and mid-1960s.

Solow, Herbert (1903–1964) – Labor journalist in 1930s and sympathizer of Communist League of America. During 1934 Teamster strikes in Minneapolis assisted union in producing its newspaper, *The Organizer*. Renounced Marxism at opening of World War II.

Stalin, Joseph (1879–1953) – Leader of privileged bureaucratic layers in Soviet state, Communist Party, and Communist International that, from mid-1920s on, reversed Lenin's proletarian course. Organized 1936–38 frame-up trials and murder of most Bolshevik leaders of Lenin's time, including 1940 assassination of Trotsky.

Stoner, J.B. (1924–2005) – Segregationist and Ku Klux Klansman; leader of National States Rights Party. Convicted 1980 for conspiracy in 1958 bombing of Bethel Street Baptist Church in Birmingham, Alabama; served 3 1/2 years in prison.

Swabeck, Arne (1890–1986) – Founding leader of Communist Party 1919. Expelled for supporting political fight led by Trotsky in Communist International to continue Lenin's proletarian course. National secretary Communist League of America, early 1930s. Became Maoist and left Socialist Workers Party 1967.

Tambo, Oliver (1917–1993) – Founding member African National Congress Youth League with Mandela 1944. ANC acting president 1967–77; president-general 1977– 91; national chairman 1991–93.

Trotsky, Leon (1879–1940) – A central leader of October Revolution in Russia and of Bolshevik Party and Communist International in early years of Soviet republic. From mid-1920s principal leader of fight to continue Lenin's communist course against reversal by counterrevolutionary privileged caste headed by Stalin. Expelled from Soviet Union 1929. Assassinated in Mexico by Stalin's agents.

Union League – First formed in North during Civil War to mobilize support for victory over Confederacy. Under Radical Reconstruction, chapters were set up across South, often uniting freed slaves, poor whites, and other supporters of Reconstruction governments. Formed self-defense units; carried out political education; promoted building of schools; waged strikes for better wages and fair division of harvest for sharecroppers. Declined as racist terror mounted in mid-1870s and northern bourgeoisie withdrew Federal Army.

UNITA (National Union for the Total Independence of Angola) – Founded 1966 to fight Portuguese colonial rule; led by Jonas Savimbi. In 1975 joined with apartheid South Africa and Washington to try to topple newly independent Angolan government led by MPLA (Popular Movement for the Liberation of Angola). For next 25 years waged war killing hundreds of thousands. Signed ceasefire in 2000, after Savimbi's death.

Urban League – Founded 1910 as service agency to help Blacks migrating from South. In 1950s and '60s joined civil rights struggles in some parts of U.S.

Walling, William English (1877–1936) – Socialist Party author and journalist; a founder in 1909 of NAACP, one of several leaders who were white. Backed U.S. entry into World War I, breaking with SP over opposition to war by majority of SP leaders.

Weisbord, Albert (1900–1977) – Communist Party member and leader of Passaic, New Jersey, textile strike 1926; left CP 1930. Declared himself partisan of Trotsky but opposed Communist League of America and organized rival Communist League of Struggle.

White League – Organized across Louisiana in 1874 with goal of overturning Reconstruction government and restoring white supremacy. Violently broke up Republican campaign events, killed officeholders, and terrorized farmers and artisans who were Black.

Wilkins, Roy (1901–1981) – NAACP leader from 1931; executive secretary 1955–77.

Woodward, C. Vann (1908–1999) – University professor of U.S. history, including at Johns Hopkins 1946–1961, Yale 1961–1977. Author *The Strange Career of Jim Crow*, books on Reconstruction, and other topics.

Young, Andrew (1932–) – Southern Christian Leadership Conference staff 1961–70, executive director from 1964. Top aide to Martin Luther King. U.S. Congressman from Georgia 1973–77; U.S. ambassador to United Nations 1977–79; mayor of Atlanta 1982–89.

Young, Whitney (1921–1971) – Executive director Urban League 1961–71.

Note on Previous Publication

Part I

"He Spoke the Truth to Our Generation of Revolutionists: In Tribute to Malcolm X" and " 'Young Socialist' Interview" were first published in 1965 in the *Young Socialist* magazine and in the Young Socialist pamphlet *Malcolm X Talks to Young People*. They were later published in a second edition of the pamphlet (Pathfinder, 1969) and in the book of the same title (Pathfinder, 1991, 2002).

Part II

"Radical Reconstruction: Its Conquests and the Consequences of Its Defeat" is an excerpt from "The Fight for a Workers and Farmers Government in the United States" by Jack Barnes, in *New International* no. 4 (1985).

"Jim Crow, the Confederate Battle Flag, and the Fight for Land" is an excerpt from "Our Politics Start with the World" by Jack Barnes, in *New International* no. 13 (2005).

Part III

"Everything New and Progressive Came from the Revolution of 1917" is an excerpt from "The Russian Revolution and the American Negro Movement" in *The First Ten Years of American Communism: Report of a Participant* by James P. Cannon (Pathfinder, 1962, 1973).

"To Whom Belongs the Decisive Word" is an excerpt from a letter by Leon Trotsky first published in the *Militant* of July 2, 1932. The entire letter can be found under the title "Closer to the Proletarians of the 'Colored' Races!" in *Writings of Leon Trotsky (1932)* (Pathfinder, 1973).

Part IV

"Black Liberation and the Dictatorship of the Proletariat" first appeared in issue no. 14 of *New International* (2008), under the title, "Revolution, Internationalism, and Socialism: The Last Year of Malcolm X" by Jack Barnes.

Credits: Photos and Illustrations

Photo section after page 128

Watts: GETTY IMAGES • Malcolm in Brooklyn: BOB ADELMAN/MAGNUM • Malcolm in Los Angeles: GORDON PARKS • Malcolm and Elijah Mohammad: EVE ARNOLD/MAGNUM • South Africa: ELI WEINBERG • Gloria Richardson: FRED WARD/BLACK STAR • Burkina Faso: PAT WRIGHT/MILITANT • Morocco: GETTY IMAGES/FRANCO ORIGLIA • Burning bus: CORBIS • Lowndes County: MILITANT • Deacons for Defense: CORBIS • Antiwar protest: JOSEPH HANSEN/MILITANT • Tuskegee students: P.H. POLK/COURTESY OF TUSKEGEE UNIVERSITY • Cuban bus drivers: RAÚL CORRALES • Cuban rally: BOHEMIA • Angola: JUVENTUD REBELDE • New York "summit": AP/WIDE WORLD • Johnson and Weaver: DONALD STODERL/LBJ LIBRARY • Fort Jackson 8: LARRY SEIGLE/MILITANT

Photo section after page 176

Fording creek: SCHOMBURG CENTER/NEW YORK PUBLIC LIBRARY • Freedmen's Bureau: HARPER'S WEEKLY • 1868 campaign meeting: HARPER'S WEEKLY • Vicksburg school: HARPER'S WEEKLY • Baltimore march: COURTESY OF MARYLAND HISTORICAL SOCIETY

Photo section after page 256

Cuban militia: BOHEMIA • Baku congress: HUMBERT-DROZ ARCHIVES • Soviet literacy class: AGE FOTOSTOCK • U.S. delegates in Moscow: COURTESY ED SWABECK • Eugene Debs: EUGENE V. DEBS MUSEUM • Huiswoud and McKay: BEINECKE LIBRARY/YALE UNIVERSITY • Tulsa riot: BERYL FORD COLLECTION, TULSA CITY-COUNTY LIBRARY • NAACP march: SCHOMBURG CENTER/NEW YORK PUBLIC LIBRARY • Cotton strikers: SCHOMBURG CENTER/NEW YORK PUBLIC LIBRARY

Photo section after page 336

Bonus March: AP/WIDE WORLD • E.D. Nixon: ELI FINER/MILITANT • 1937

Index

Malcolm X

Malcolm X Talks to Young People

"The young generation of whites, Blacks, browns, whatever else there is—you're living at a time of revolution," Malcolm told youth in the United Kingdom in December 1964. "And I for one will join with anyone, I don't care what color you are, as long as you want to change this miserable condition that exists on this earth." Four talks and an interview given in Ghana, the United Kingdom, and the United States in the last months of Malcolm's life. $15. Also in Spanish and French.

Malcolm X Speaks

Speeches following the evolution of Malcolm's views in 1964–65 on racism, U.S. intervention in the Congo and Vietnam, capitalism, socialism, political action independent of the parties of the exploiters, and more. $20. Also in Spanish.

February 1965: The Final Speeches

"There will be a clash between those who want freedom, justice, and equality for everyone and those who want to continue the systems of exploitation. But I don't think it will be based upon the color of the skin," said Malcolm X in his last public talk—one of more than 20 speeches and interviews in this book. $19

in his own ──words

By Any Means Necessary

"In every country you go to, the degree of progress can never be separated from the woman," said Malcolm X returning from a trip to Africa in late 1964. "So I became convinced during my travels of the importance of giving freedom to the women, giving her education." Eleven speeches and interviews by the revolutionary leader from the last year of his political activity. $16

Malcolm X on Afro-American History

Recounts the hidden history of the labor of people of African origin and their achievements. $11

Two Speeches by Malcolm X

"It's impossible for a chicken to produce a duck egg. . . . The system in this country cannot produce freedom for an Afro-American." Speeches and interviews from the last year of Malcolm's life. $5

Also:

- **Malcolm X: The Last Speeches**, $17

- **Habla Malcolm X**. In Spanish. $19

Robert Parent

New York, November 1964

www.pathfinderpress.com

Is Socialist Revolution in the U.S. Possible?

A Necessary Debate
MARY-ALICE WATERS

In two talks, presented as part of a wide-ranging debate at the Venezuela International Book Fairs in 2007 and 2008, Waters explains why a socialist revolution in the United States is possible. Why revolutionary struggles by working people are inevitable, forced upon us by the crisis-driven assaults of the propertied classes. As solidarity grows among a fighting vanguard of working people, the outlines of coming class battles can already be seen. $7. Also in Spanish, French, and Swedish.

Cuba and the Coming American Revolution

JACK BARNES

The Cuban Revolution of 1959 had a worldwide political impact, including on working people and youth in the imperialist heartland. As the mass, proletarian-based struggle for Black rights was already advancing in the US, the social transformation fought for and won by the Cuban toilers set an example that socialist revolution is not only necessary—it can be made and defended.

This second edition, with a new foreword by Mary-Alice Waters, should be read alongside *Is Socialist Revolution in the U.S. Possible?* $10. Also in Spanish and French.

www.pathfinderpress.com

Class Struggle in

The First Ten Years of American Communism
James P. Cannon

A founding leader of the communist movement in the US tells the story of the early years of the effort to build a proletarian party emulating the Bolshevik leadership of the October 1917 revolution in Russia. Among other things, Cannon writes, "Everything new and progressive on the Negro question came from Moscow, after the Bolshevik revolution and as a result of it." $22

Teamster Rebellion
Farrell Dobbs

How Teamsters Local 574 in Minneapolis, during two 1934 strikes, defeated not only the trucking bosses but strikebreaking efforts of the city, state, and federal governments. The first of a four-volume participant's account of how strikes and organizing drives across the Midwest in the 1930s paved the way for industrial unions and a fighting working-class social movement. These battles showed what workers and their allied producers on the land can achieve when they have the leadership they deserve. Dobbs, a young worker at the time, was a central part of that class-struggle leadership. $19. Also in Spanish, French, and Swedish.

The Great Labor Uprising of 1877
Philip S. Foner

In 1877 a battle against wage cuts by West Virginia rail workers effectively shut down the US rail system and turned into the country's first nationwide general strike. Welcomed by Karl Marx as the "first eruption against the oligarchy of associated capital" since the US Civil War, the uprising coincided with the bourgeoisie's betrayal of Radical Reconstruction in the South and the first steps in the rise of US imperialism and its counterrevolutionary course worldwide. $23

the United States

Fighting Racism in World War II
From the pages of the Militant

A week-by-week account from 1939 to 1945 of struggles against racist discrimination and lynch-mob terror in face of patriotic appeals to postpone such resistance until after US "victory" in the second world imperialist war. These struggles—of a piece with rising anti-imperialist battles in Africa, Asia, and the Americas—helped lay the basis for the mass Black rights movement in postwar decades. $25

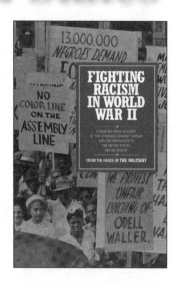

America's Revolutionary Heritage
George Novack

A materialist analysis of key chapters in the history of the class struggle in the United States, from the genocide against Native Americans to the first two American revolutions—the war for independence and the war that overturned the system of slavery—the rise of industrial capitalism, and the first wave of the fight for women's rights. $25

Out Now!
A Participant's Account of the Movement in the United States against the Vietnam War
Fred Halstead

A firsthand account of the fight to organize working people, GIs, and youth and help lead growing world opposition to the Vietnam War. Gaining momentum from the mass struggle for Black rights, along with unyielding revolutionary resistance by Vietnamese national liberation fighters, the antiwar movement helped force Washington to bring the troops home, altering the dynamic of the class struggle in the US. $35

Eugene V. Debs Speaks
Speeches by the US socialist and labor leader jailed for opposing Washington's imperialist aims in World War I. Debs speaks out on capitalism and socialism, against anti-immigrant chauvinism, on how anti-Black racism weakens labor, on Rockefeller's massacre of striking miners at Ludlow, Colorado, and more. $25

From the dictatorship of capital...

The Communist Manifesto

Karl Marx, Frederick Engels

Why is all recorded history "the history of class struggles"? Why is the capitalist state "but a committee for managing the common affairs of the whole bourgeoisie"? How does the fight for "the proletariat organized as the ruling class" open the only way forward for humanity? The answers to these questions, addressed in the founding document of the modern working-class movement in 1848, remain as vital today as they were at the time. $5. Also in Spanish, French, and Arabic.

The Civil War in France

Karl Marx

In 1871 insurgent working people in Paris rose up and established the first workers government in history, one crushed in blood 72 days later by troops of the French bourgeoisie. In his 20th anniversary introduction to Marx's contemporary account of the Paris Commune, Engels wrote that middle-class misleaders in the workers movement have "been filled with wholesome terror at the words: Dictatorship of the Proletariat. Well and good, gentlemen, do you want to know what this dictatorship looks like? Look at the Paris Commune." $5

State and Revolution

V.I. Lenin

"The relation of the socialist proletarian revolution to the state is acquiring not only practical political importance," wrote V.I. Lenin in the preface to this booklet, finished just months before the October 1917 Russian Revolution. It also addresses the "most urgent problem of the day: explaining to the masses what they will have to do to free themselves from capitalist tyranny." In *Essential Works of Lenin*. $12.95

...to the dictatorship of the proletariat

Their Trotsky and Ours
Jack Barnes

To lead the working class in a successful revolution, a mass proletarian party is needed whose cadres, well beforehand, have absorbed a world communist program, are proletarian in life and work, derive deep satisfaction from doing politics, and have forged a leadership with an acute sense of what to do next. This book is about building such a party. $16. Also in Spanish and French.

The History of the Russian Revolution
Leon Trotsky

A classic account of the social and political dynamics of the first socialist revolution, told by one of its central leaders. Trotsky describes how, under Lenin's guidance, the Bolshevik Party led the working class, peasantry, and oppressed nationalities to overturn the monarchist regime of the landlords and capitalists and bring to power a workers and peasants republic that set an example for toilers the world over. Unabridged, 3 vols. in one. $38. Also in Russian.

The Transitional Program for Socialist Revolution
Leon Trotsky

In this 1938 founding document drafted for the Socialist Workers Party in the US and the world movement it is part of, Bolshevik leader Leon Trotsky explains an interconnected program of slogans and demands that "lead to one and the same political conclusion: the workers need to break with all traditional parties of the bourgeoisie in order, jointly with the farmers, to establish their own power." $20

www.pathfinderpress.com

New International

A MAGAZINE OF MARXIST POLITICS AND THEORY

NEW INTERNATIONAL NO. 12

CAPITALISM'S LONG HOT WINTER HAS BEGUN

Jack Barnes

and "Their Transformation and Ours," Resolution of the Socialist Workers Party

Today's sharpening interimperialist conflicts are fueled both by the opening stages of what will be decades of economic, financial, and social convulsions and class battles, and by the most far-reaching shift in Washington's military policy and organization since the US buildup toward World War II. Class-struggle-minded working people must face this historic turning point for imperialism, and draw satisfaction from being "in their face" as we chart a revolutionary course to confront it. $16. Also in Spanish, French, and Swedish. *Capitalism's Long Hot Winter Has Begun* is available in Arabic.

NEW INTERNATIONAL NO. 14

REVOLUTION, INTERNATIONALISM, AND SOCIALISM: THE LAST YEAR OF MALCOLM X

Jack Barnes

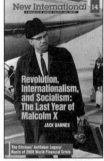

"To understand Malcolm's last year is to see how, in the imperialist epoch, revolutionary leadership of the highest political capacity, courage, and integrity converges with communism. That truth has even greater weight today as billions around the world, in city and countryside, from China to Brazil, are being hurled into the modern class struggle by the violent expansion of world capitalism."—Jack Barnes

Also in No. 14: "The Clintons' Antilabor Legacy: Roots of the 2008 World Financial Crisis"; "The Stewardship of Nature Also Falls to the Working Class"; and "Setting the Record Straight on Fascism and World War II." $14. Also in Spanish, French, and Swedish.

WWW.PATHFINDERPRESS.COM

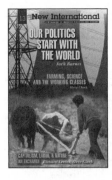

OUR POLITICS START WITH THE WORLD

Jack Barnes

The huge economic and cultural inequalities between imperialist and semicolonial countries, and among classes within almost every country, are produced, reproduced, and accentuated by the workings of capitalism. For vanguard workers to build parties able to lead a successful revolutionary struggle for power in our own countries, says Jack Barnes in the lead article, our activity must be guided by a strategy to close this gap.

Also in No. 13: "Farming, Science, and the Working Classes" *by Steve Clark.* $14. Also in Spanish, French, and Swedish.

U.S. IMPERIALISM HAS LOST THE COLD WAR

Jack Barnes

Contrary to imperialist expectations at the opening of the 1990s in the wake of the collapse of regimes across Eastern Europe and the USSR claiming to be communist, the workers and farmers there have not been crushed. The toilers remain an intractable obstacle to imperialism's advance, one the exploiters will have to confront in class battles and war. $16. Also in Spanish, French, Swedish, and Icelandic.

CHE GUEVARA, CUBA, AND THE ROAD TO SOCIALISM

Articles by Ernesto Che Guevara, Carlos Rafael Rodríguez, Carlos Tablada, Mary-Alice Waters, Steve Clark, Jack Barnes

Exchanges from the opening years of the Cuban Revolution and today on the political perspectives defended by Guevara as he helped lead working people to advance the transformation of economic and social relations in Cuba. $10. Also in Spanish.

THE COMING REVOLUTION IN SOUTH AFRICA

Jack Barnes

Writing a decade before the white supremacist regime fell, Barnes explores the social roots of apartheid in South African capitalism and tasks of urban and rural toilers in dismantling it, as they forge a communist leadership of the working class. $14. Also in Spanish and French.

The Cuban Revolution and

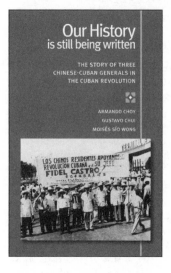

Our History Is Still Being Written
THE STORY OF THREE CHINESE-CUBAN GENERALS IN THE CUBAN REVOLUTION

In Cuba, the greatest measure against racial discrimination "was the revolution itself," says Gen. Moisés Sío Wong, "the triumph of a socialist revolution." Armando Choy, Gustavo Chui, and Sío Wong talk about the historic place of Chinese immigration to Cuba, as well as more than five decades of revolutionary action and internationalism, from Cuba to Angola and Venezuela today. Through their stories we see how millions of ordinary men and women changed the course of history, becoming different human beings in the process. $20. Also in Spanish and Chinese.

From the Escambray to the Congo
IN THE WHIRLWIND OF THE CUBAN REVOLUTION
Víctor Dreke

The author describes how easy it became after the Cuban Revolution to take down a rope segregating blacks from whites in the town square, yet how enormous was the battle to transform social relations underlying all the "ropes" inherited from capitalism and Yankee domination. Dreke, second in command of the internationalist column in the Congo led by Che Guevara in 1965, recounts the creative joy with which working people have defended their revolutionary course—from Cuba's Escambray mountains to Africa and beyond. $17. Also in Spanish.

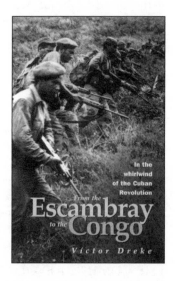

Renewal or Death
Fidel Castro

"To really establish total equality takes more than declaring it in law," Fidel Castro told delegates to the 1986 congress of the Cuban Communist Party, pointing to the revolution's enormous conquests in the fight against anti-black racism. "We can't leave it to chance to correct historical injustices," he said. "We have to straighten out what history has twisted." In *New International* no. 6. $16

World Politics

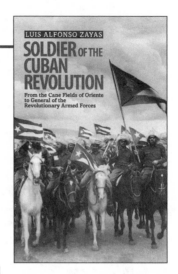

Soldier of the Cuban Revolution
FROM THE CANE FIELDS OF ORIENTE TO GENERAL OF THE REVOLUTIONARY ARMED FORCES
Luis Alfonso Zayas
The author recounts his experiences over five decades in the revolution. From a teenage combatant in the clandestine struggle and 1956–58 war that brought down the US-backed dictatorship, to serving three times as a leader of the Cuban volunteer forces that helped Angola defeat an invasion by the army of white-supremacist South Africa, Zayas tells how ordinary men and women in Cuba changed the course of history and, in the process, transformed themselves as well. $18. Also in Spanish.

Che Guevara Talks to Young People
The Argentine-born revolutionary leader challenges youth of Cuba and the world to study, to work, to become disciplined. To join the front lines of struggles, small and large. To politicize themselves and the work of their organizations. To become a different kind of human being as they strive with working people of all lands to transform the world. Eight talks from 1959 to 1964. $15. Also in Spanish.

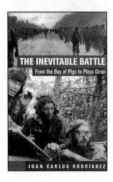

The Inevitable Battle
FROM THE BAY OF PIGS TO PLAYA GIRÓN
Juan Carlos Rodríguez
The US-led invasion of Cuba in April 1961 was defeated in 66 hours by militia battalions composed of worker and peasant volunteers, along with soldiers from the Cuban armed forces. Cuban historian Juan Carlos Rodríguez explains that the human material available to Washington could not match the courage and determination of a people fighting to defend what they had gained through the continent's first socialist revolution. $20. Also in Spanish.

www.pathfinderpress.com

The Bolsheviks and the Fight against National Oppression

Lenin's Final Fight

Speeches and Writings, 1922–23
V.I. LENIN

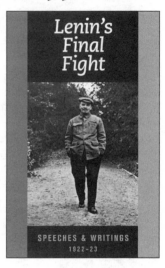

In the early 1920s Lenin waged his last political battle in the Communist Party leadership in the USSR to maintain the course that had enabled workers and peasants to overthrow the tsarist empire, carry out the first socialist revolution, and begin building a world communist movement. The issues posed in this fight—from the leadership's class composition, to the worker-peasant alliance and battle against national oppression—remain central to world politics today. $20. Also in Spanish.

Workers of the World and Oppressed Peoples, Unite!

Proceedings and Documents of the Second Congress of the Communist International, 1920

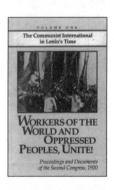

Offering a vivid portrait of social struggles in the era of the Bolshevik-led October Revolution, the reports, resolutions, and debates—among delegates from 37 countries—take up key questions of working-class strategy and program: the fight for national liberation, the revolutionary transformation of trade unions, the worker-farmer alliance, participation in bourgeois parliaments and elections, and the structure and tasks of Communist Parties. Two volumes. $65

Questions of National Policy and Proletarian Internationalism

V.I. LENIN

Why the fight of oppressed nations for self-determination is decisive in the worldwide proletarian struggle to take and hold power. Why workers and farmers in imperialist countries have a deep class interest in championing this right. $16

To See the Dawn

Baku, 1920—First Congress
of the Peoples of the East

How can peasants and workers in the colonial world throw off imperialist exploitation? How can they overcome national and religious divisions incited by their own ruling classes and fight for their common class interests? As the example of the October Revolution echoed around the world, these questions were addressed by 2,000 delegates to the 1920 Congress of the Peoples of the East. $24

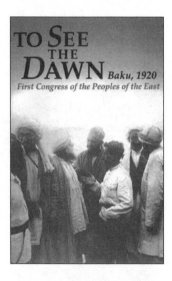

Lenin's Struggle for a Revolutionary International

Documents, 1907–1916; The Preparatory Years

In the years leading up to World War I, Lenin led the political battle within the leadership of the international workers movement for a revolutionary course to oppose imperialist war by organizing to lead the toilers in overthrowing the capitalist rulers. The articles and documents in this collection bring that debate alive. $38

The Revolution Betrayed

What Is the Soviet Union and Where Is It Going?
LEON TROTSKY

In 1917 workers and peasants of Russia were the motor force for one of the deepest revolutions in history. Yet within ten years a political counterrevolution by a privileged social layer whose chief spokesperson was Joseph Stalin was being consolidated. This classic study of the Soviet workers state and the degeneration of the revolution illuminates the roots of the disintegration of the Soviet bureaucracy and sharpening conflicts in and among the former republics of the USSR. $20. Also in Spanish.

www.pathfinderpress.com

EXPAND *Your Revolutionary Library*

The Working Class and the Transformation of Learning
The Fraud of Education Reform under Capitalism
JACK BARNES

"Until society is reorganized so that education is a human activity from the time we are very young until the time we die, there will be no education worthy of working, creating humanity." $3. Also in Spanish, French, Swedish, Icelandic, Farsi, and Greek.

Capitalism's World Disorder
Working-Class Politics at the Millennium
JACK BARNES

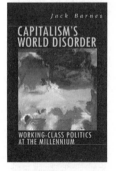

Social devastation and financial panic, coarsening of politics, cop brutality, imperialist aggression—all are products not of something gone wrong with capitalism but of its lawful workings. Yet the future can be changed by the united struggle of workers and farmers conscious of their capacity to wage revolutionary battles for state power and transform the world. $25. Also in Spanish and French.

Capitalism and the Transformation of Africa
Reports from Equatorial Guinea
MARY-ALICE WATERS, MARTÍN KOPPEL

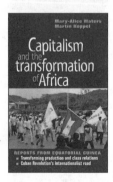

The transformation of production and class relations in a Central African country, as it is drawn deeper into the world market and both a capitalist class and modern proletariat are born. As Cuban volunteer medical brigades collaborate to transform social conditions there, the example of Cuba's socialist revolution comes alive. Woven together, the outlines of a future to be fought for today can be seen—a future in which Africa's toilers have more weight in world politics than ever before. $10. Also in Spanish.

www.pathfinderpress.com

Thomas Sankara Speaks
The Burkina Faso Revolution, 1983–87

Led by Sankara, the revolutionary government of Burkina Faso in West Africa set an electrifying example. Peasants, workers, women, and youth mobilized to carry out literacy and immunization drives; to sink wells, plant trees, build dams, erect housing; to combat women's oppression and transform exploitative relations on the land; to free themselves from the imperialist yoke and solidarize with others engaged in that fight internationally. $24. Also in French.

Maurice Bishop Speaks
*The Grenada Revolution
and Its Overthrow, 1979–83*

The triumph of the 1979 revolution in the Caribbean island of Grenada had "importance for all struggles around the world," said Maurice Bishop, its central leader. Invaluable lessons from that workers and farmers government, overturned in a Stalinist-led coup in 1983, can be found in this collection. $25

The Jewish Question
A Marxist Interpretation
ABRAM LEON

Traces the historical rationalizations of anti-Semitism to the fact that, in the centuries preceding the domination of industrial capitalism, Jews emerged as a "people-class" of merchants, moneylenders, and traders. Leon explains why the propertied rulers incite renewed Jew-hatred in the epoch of capitalism's decline. $22

Building a PROLETARIAN PARTY

The Changing Face of U.S. Politics
Working-Class Politics and the Trade Unions
JACK BARNES

Building the kind of party working people need to prepare for coming class battles through which they will revolutionize themselves, their unions, and all society. A handbook for those seeking the road toward effective action to overturn the exploitative system of capitalism and join in reconstructing the world on new, socialist foundations. $24. Also in Spanish, French, and Swedish.

The Struggle for a Proletarian Party
JAMES P. CANNON

"The workers of America have power enough to topple the structure of capitalism at home and to lift the whole world with them when they rise," Cannon asserts. On the eve of World War II, a founder of the communist movement in the US and leader of the Communist International in Lenin's time defends the program and party-building norms of Bolshevism. $22

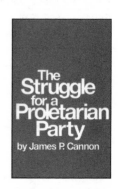

Revolutionary Continuity
Marxist Leadership in the U.S.
FARRELL DOBBS

How successive generations took part in struggles of the US labor movement, seeking to build a leadership capable of forging an alliance of workers and farmers and linking up with fellow toilers around the world.

Two volumes: *The Early Years: 1848–1917*, $20; *Birth of the Communist Movement: 1918–1922*, $19.

WOMEN'S LIBERATION & SOCIALISM

Cosmetics, Fashions, and the Exploitation of Women

JOSEPH HANSEN, EVELYN REED, AND MARY-ALICE WATERS

How big business plays on women's second-class status and social insecurities to market cosmetics and rake in profits. The introduction by Mary-Alice Waters explains how the entry of millions of women into the workforce during and after World War II irreversibly changed US society and laid the basis for a renewed rise of struggles for women's emancipation. $15

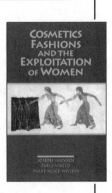

Feminism and the Marxist Movement

MARY-ALICE WATERS

Since the founding of the modern workers movement 150 years ago, Marxists have championed the struggle for women's rights and explained the economic roots in class society of women's oppression. $6

Problems of Women's Liberation

EVELYN REED

Six articles explore the social and economic roots of women's oppression from prehistoric society to modern capitalism and point the road forward to emancipation. $15

Communist Continuity and the Fight for Women's Liberation

Documents of the Socialist Workers Party 1971–86

How did the oppression of women begin? Who benefits? What social forces have the power to end women's second-class status? 3 volumes, edited with preface by Mary-Alice Waters. $30